POLITICAL SCIENCE ANNUAL

CO-EDITORS FOR THE
POLITICAL SCIENCE ANNUAL

JOHN H. KESSEL
WILLIAM C. MITCHELL
RAYMOND TANTER

POLITICAL SCIENCE
ANNUAL

An International Review

VOLUME FIVE—1974

EDITED BY

CORNELIUS P. COTTER

THE BOBBS-MERRILL COMPANY, INC.
INDIANAPOLIS AND NEW YORK

EDITOR'S PREFACE

This is the second of three volumes of the *Political Science Annual* to appear under the present editor and co-editors. The history and purposes of the *Annual* are reviewed at length in the prefaces to Volumes One (1966) and Four (1973). The appearance of Volume Three in 1972 inaugurated annual publication, which the editors hope will justify the last word in the title, and continuance of which will be justified by reader reception of the series.

Like Volume Four, the present volume is a joint enterprise involving co-editor participation in the selection of topics and authors, and in reading the critical examinations of the literature specially prepared for this volume by the authors. We wish here to express to the authors our gratitude for selfless motives, respect for deadlines, competent performance, and tolerance of criticism.

The editors have attempted to impart a certain internal coherence to each of the three volumes for which they are responsible. Thus the chapters in Volume Four fit under the common rubric of coalition theory. The table of contents in Volume Five reflects the theme of collective decision-making. Volume Six, to appear in 1975, will review work that shares the focus of individual decision-making.

Authors and editors have combined efforts to avoid redundancy between chapters; but a certain amount of duplication of subtopics (albeit, with differing emphases and slants) is inescapable in a volume such as this.

We repeat the invitation, extended to readers in Volume Four, to evaluate the purposes stated there, and the extent to which the present volume meets them. We also welcome suggestions about courses the *Annual* might follow in the future.

The editors wish again to acknowledge the help of Bobbs-Merrill in making it possible to plan ahead for three volumes of the *Annual*, thereby

putting it on an annual basis. Lynn McGuire and assistants at Bobbs-
Merrill have suggested many improvements and gently raised vexatious
questions during the course of copyediting. We wish also to thank Monica
C. Escher for careful checking of bibliography and assistance in putting
the manuscript in shape for copyediting.

CORNELIUS P. COTTER

Milwaukee, Wisconsin
April 1973

CONTENTS

The Contributors   xi

THEORIES OF COLLECTIVE CHOICE   1

Kenneth A. Shepsle

Choice-Theoretic Perspective   4
Rational Behavior   8
  Outcomes   11
  Actions   11
  The Relationship Between Actions and Outcomes   12
  Logical Structure of Preference and Choice   14
  Uncertainty   15
The Nature of Collective Choice   17
Arrow's Mathematical Politics   22
Arrow's Theorem and Its Consequences For
  Operating Democracies   35
A Positive Theory of Social Choice: Spatial Models   44
  Citizen Evaluations   50
  Citizen Participation   53
  The Preference Distribution of the Electorate   55
  Candidate Goals   57
  Equilibrium and Convergence   58
Institutional Complexities   65
Some Concluding Remarks   69
Appendix: Recent Advances in Choice Theory   70
Bibliography   77

THE IMPACTS OF PUBLIC POLICY   89

Kenneth M. Dolbeare

Definitions and Purposes in "Policy Impact" Studies   90
  Public Policy   90

Impact   93
The Purposes of Inquiry   95
Political Science and Policy Impact Research: An Overview   97
    What Happened?   97
        Intragovernmental impact   98
        Direct impact upon segments of the public   99
        Impact in a context of ongoing social processes   100
    How and Why Did It Happen This Way?   103
        Law and change   103
        Policy effects   105
    To What Extent Are Government Program Goals
    Being Achieved? How Might Things Be Done Better?   108
    Political scientists in the evaluative arena   108
        Evaluative research generally: some problems of
        concept and method   111
            Conceptual problems   112
            Methodological problems   115
    What Does This All Mean For General Theories
    and Explanations of Policies?   117
Problems and Prospects: A Critical Evaluation   118
Major Problems: A Summary   119
Possible Solutions   120
Prospects   122
Bibliography   124

ORGANIZATIONAL CONSTRAINTS AND PUBLIC BUREAUCRACY   131
Lawrence C. Pierce

Collective Choice and Organizational Constraints   133
Environmental Constraints   140
    Physical Constraints   141
    Resource Constraints   142
    Demand Constraints   144
    Legal Constraints   149
    Political Constraints   151
    Normative Constraints   153
Internal Constraints   154
    Programmed Decision-Making   156
    Process Decision-Making   158
        Occasion for search   160

Search strategies 161
Evaluating alternatives 162
Systems Decision-Making 163
Goals 164
Estimating consequences 165
Political Decision-Making 167
Summary 168
Agenda for Future Research 169
Bibliography 172

THE DECISION-MAKING CULTURE OF AMERICAN
PUBLIC EDUCATION 177

Harmon Zeigler, M. Kent Jennings, and G. Wayne Peak

Policy Levels 178
Policy Actors 179
Types of Decisions 179
Power and Exchange 180
The Market Place: Strategies of Influence 184
Recruitment 185
Linkage: The Environment and the Schools 190
The Board-Superintendent Exchange 198
Conclusions 213
Bibliography 220

THE PRESIDENCY, CONGRESS, AND NATIONAL
POLICY-MAKING 227

John F. Manley

Studies of the Presidency 228
Decision-Making in the Institutionalized Presidency 234
Power as Position 237
Planning, Programming, Budgeting 238
Presidents as Individuals 241
Congress and National Policy-Making 244
The Senate 248
Articulation and resolution of new policy issues 249
Incubation-plus: the functions of the Senate in the
policy process 254
The House of Representatives 256
The policy problem of the House 256

Political parties   258
Seniority   260
The committee system   261
Fenno's approach to comparative committee analysis   262
Conclusion: Toward Understanding National Policy-Making   264
Bibliography   267

THE CONTRIBUTORS

KENNETH M. DOLBEARE

Kenneth M. Dolbeare is Professor of Political Science at the University of Washington. He previously taught at the University of Wisconsin. His fields are American public policy and American political thought, and he has written several works in those areas.

M. KENT JENNINGS

M. Kent Jennings is Professor of Political Science and Program Director at the Institute for Social Research, University of Michigan. He has written extensively on political socialization, public opinion, elections and voting behavior, schools and political education, and state, local, and metropolitan government.

JOHN F. MANLEY

John F. Manley is Associate Professor of Political Science at Stanford University. He is the author of *The Politics of Finance* (1970) and his articles have appeared in the *American Political Science Review, Journal of Politics,* and the *Annals.*

G. WAYNE PEAK

G. Wayne Peak is a member of the faculty at Virginia Polytechnic Institute and State University. He has written on interest groups, the governing of schools, and the sociology of education.

LAWRENCE C. PIERCE

Lawrence C. Pierce is Associate Professor of Political Science at the University of Oregon and a member of the Center for the Advanced Study of Educational Administration. He has been a Fulbright lecturer and American Political Science Association State Legislative Services Fellow. His major research and writings have been in the areas of economic policy formation, educational finance, and legislative politics.

KENNETH A. SHEPSLE

Kenneth A. Shepsle is Associate Professor of Political Science at Washington University, St. Louis. He has co-authored a monograph on formal theories of ethnic conflict in plural societies and maintains a long-standing interest in mathematical theories of social phenomena. His recent research has focused on decision-theoretic models of campaigning and party competition, and on formal models of institutionalized processes in the U. S. Congress.

HARMON ZEIGLER

Harmon Zeigler is Professor of Political Science and Program Director, Center for the Advanced Study of Educational Administration, University of Oregon. He has written extensively on lobbying, the politics of education, and the electoral process.

POLITICAL SCIENCE ANNUAL

Theories of Collective Choice

KENNETH A. SHEPSLE*

This essay is concerned with the set of processes or activities varyingly called collective choice, collective action, social choice, public choice, or collective decision-making. The theories falling under one or another of these rubrics span several scholarly disciplines, vary in their coverage, their methodologies and their philosophical underpinnings, and, as a result, defy simple characterization. Despite the danger of appearing to oversimplify, it is useful, at the outset, to identify some of the features common to all of the theories examined in this essay.

The field of collective choice has been characterized by two of its earliest students, James Buchanan and Gordon Tullock (1962, p. 13), as the set of phenomena involving "the action of individuals when they choose to accomplish purposes collectively rather than individually." Moreover, for them "the government [or collectivity] is seen as nothing more than the set of processes, the machine, which allows such collective action to take place."

Several features of this characterization should be noted. First, the collectivity to which Buchanan and Tullock allude is quite general. In its broadest usage it is identical to the polity. Yet, certainly, individuals "choose to accomplish purposes collectively" through devices less inclusive than the polity. Since we shall want to accommodate decision-making in a variety of collective settings, we shall be content to retain a rather abstract notion of "collectivity," leaving particular identifications to the interests of the reader. At a minimum, a collectivity may consist of members of a family, tribe, or clan, a community of buyers and sellers of goods and services, a corporate board of directors or gathering of stockholders,

* It is always a pleasure to acknowledge the critical assistance of friends and colleagues. I therefore thank Professors Theodore C. Bergstrom, Peter C. Ordeshook, Robert P. Parks, Alvin Rabushka, Robert H. Salisbury, John D. Sprague, and Mr. Robert Becker. Their comments and criticisms strengthened both the argument of this essay and its exposition. National Science Foundation Grant GS-33053 provided the time to revise an earlier draft.

1

a committee or legislature, a jury or panel of judges, the staff of an administrative agency or interest group, a convention, or a set of electors. The theoretical domain of theories of collective choice, then, includes most of political science and economics, and certainly overlaps with large parts of sociology, management science, and jurisprudence.

The second feature of the Buchanan-Tullock definition worth noting is its individualistic basis. The basic unit of analysis in most theories of collective choice is the individual, not the collectivity. Collective action is that which emerges from the choices, actions, and behaviors of individuals in a social setting. These theories stand in stark contrast to organic theories which submerge the individual in a complex of system processes (although a resurgent interest in cybernetics is beginning to blur this distinction; see Simon, 1968).

Third, the definition provided by Buchanan and Tullock emphasizes the purposefulness of individual behavior. The behavior of the individual assumes social significance precisely because his purposes may clash (or coincide) with the purposes of others. Thus, theories of collective choice, to the extent that they explicate the consequences of patterns of purpose in conflict and harmony, provide a foundation for understanding social institutions.

But what connects purpose with behavior? After all, it is behavior that counts. While unexpressed intention may be of metaphysical interest, it is beyond the pale of a scientific enterprise that purports to account for empirical phenomena. The connecting link identified by Buchanan and Tullock, and shared by most other students of collective decision-making, is the choice paradigm. From this perspective many aspects of social reality are identified and explained by conceiving of them as the consequences of individual choices.

The intellectual roots of this paradigm and its attendant philosophical commitments can be traced to the political arithmeticians, market economists, and social philosophers of the seventeenth and eighteenth centuries; see Black (1958, part 2), Lazarsfeld (1961), and Stigler (1950) for historical background. In many respects, however, the choice paradigm is a twentieth-century product. Its utility as a framework for political analysis—the main evaluative task of this essay—is of even more recent vintage; see Ostrom and Ostrom (1971), Riker (1961), and Taylor (1971).

Let me, in concluding these introductory remarks, hazard a brief definition that incorporates the themes of the Buchanan-Tullock definition while explicitly extending them in several substantive directions. Theories of collective choice, as I conceive them, concern the implementation and conduct of decision-making processes by and/or for collections of individuals, and the enforcement and administration of the decisions that emerge from these processes. While various theories may alternately emphasize implementation (a theory of constitutions), conduct (a theory of institutions), or enforcement and administration (a theory of social control), most share the properties suggested above, namely a tendency to be general theories of collectivities; reliance on the individualist perspective and the assumption of purposeful behavior; and employment of some form of the choice paradigm to link purpose with behavior.

While the primary focus of this essay is on theories of political choice, it is useful at the outset to examine the structure of choice, rational behavior, and collective decision-making in some detail unencumbered by much substantive or normative baggage. These tasks are accomplished in the first three sections below and in the Appendix at the conclusion of this essay. The aim there is to provide a fairly complete exposition of rational individual choice and, having done so, to examine the impact of social setting on behavior.

At that point we cheat history a bit by picking up the tail end of an intellectual debate in welfare economics that culminated in Kenneth Arrow's classic *Social Choice and Individual Values*—what Samuelson (1967) called "Arrow's Mathematical Politics." We shall not be able to examine a number of issues in welfare economics related to political choice. On this score the reader is referred to Baumol's *Welfare Economics and the Theory of the State* (1965). We shall take time, however, to review Arrow's contribution, both as a normative model of political choice and as framework for a positive theory of politics. We shall also examine Arrow's theory of social choice as a theory of political constitutions. The guiding question in this analysis is: how should a self-governing community of reasonable individuals govern itself? The work of other scholars who address this question—most notably Sen, Rawls, and Buchanan and Tullock—is briefly examined at this point.

In our second pass at Arrow we bring positive aspects of his work to the forefront. Viewing his model and the modifications of it suggested by others as a theory of institutions, we seek to determine how rational men will respond to alternative decision-making arrangements. Together with more normative concerns, this theory, to the extent that it is found acceptable, may serve as the foundation for a science of institutional design (see Arrow, 1971).

We then turn to a series of models which have followed in the wake of

Arrow's monograph and have been inspired by one of Arrow's students, Anthony Downs. Spatial models of democratic collective choice, formidable mathematical structures that they are, are still in their infancy. However, growing pains and other problems notwithstanding, they represent and reflect the great strides that have taken place in the last decade in the development of formal political theory. Appended to my discussion of spatial models is a consideration of some complicating features that scholars are only beginning to examine and incorporate in their work.

I devote very little space in this essay to empirical studies of collective choice. There is an unfortunate paucity of empirical political research conducted in the collective choice framework. Although from time to time I shall refer to some of the studies that do exist, I regard the virtual absence of empirical concern as a major weakness in the collective choice literature.

Though this essay is broad-ranging, it is by no means comprehensive. Its prime focuses are the choice of decision-making rules in constitutional settings, and committee and electoral decision-making. I shall not deal with topics identified as "public policy analysis" since this requires, as any student of bureaucracy knows, a theory of implementation and administration. Unfortunately, we possess little formal understanding of decision-making in the nonvoting circumstances that prevail in bureaucracies. In addition, I briefly note in the concluding section two large bodies of literature—theories of coalition formation and theories of public goods—which are given only cursory treatment in the essay.

CHOICE-THEORETIC PERSPECTIVE

Most of the theories of politics examined here rely on the "deductive model of explanation." Premises, in this mode of explanation, are made explicit and consequences are deduced according to the strict rules of logic (and often mathematics). The premises are taken as characterizing the "real world," though they may abstract away nongermane features; the consequences deduced stand as *a priori* expectations about the phenomena in question.

The choice-theoretic perspective is a deductive framework that involves two sorts of commitments. The first is an ontological commitment to individualism, a perspective in which the individual is taken as the fundamental acting unit. Various social phenomena are characterized as aggregations or summations, often by complex rules of combination, of individual actions. "In the individualistic approach, the polity is examined as a social organization in a manner similar to that in which the economy has traditionally been analyzed. The political structure is conceived as something that *emerges* from the choice processes of individual participants" (Buchanan, 1966, p. 26). The polity is not conceived as an entity distinct from the individuals that comprise it.[1]

Although a commitment to individualism involves a rejection of organic theories, it does not require the banishment of theoretical statements about institutions, structures, or processes. It simply requires that they not be transformed into entities that exist apart from individual behavior and interaction. Thus social structure or political institutions may be incorporated, for example, as constraints on individual activities, or as elements which inform individual calculations and expectations.

Of course it is entirely possible that unadulterated individualism will not serve us well. To focus on individual activities is to effect an abstraction, and there is no guarantee that this sort of abstraction is useful in achieving the scientific goals of prediction and explanation. In this essay, I adopt Buchanan's balanced evaluation as my own:

> In the scientific house there are many mansions, and, in analyzing politics, there is surely room for alternative models. For some purposes, an organic model may be helpful; for others, a ruling-class or force theory of the state. And in many instances, a model that bypasses the individual and begins with the interplay of group interests may yield fully satisfactory predictions. At base, it is claimed only

[1] Although sociologists tend to be among the chief proponents of an organic view of society and polity (despite Marx's warning, cited in Sen, 1971, p. 1, that "what is to be avoided above all is the re-establishing of 'Society' as an abstraction vis-a-vis the individual"), often seeking "functions" that need to be performed and "structures" that perform them, some of their number come close to sharing Buchanan's individualist view. Homans, for example, observes:

> We social scientists talk as if "society" were the big thing. But an institution is functional for society only because it is functional for men. There is no functional prerequisite for the survival of a society except that the society provide sufficient rewards for its individual members to keep them contributing activities to its maintenance, and that it reward them not just as members of that society but as men. Even when we talk as if "society" provided the rewards, we always, ultimately, mean that men provide them. . . . If you look long enough for the secret of society you will find it in plain sight: the secret of society is that it was made by men, and there is nothing in society but what men put there (Homans, 1961, pp. 384–85).

For an excellent critique of organic theories by someone whose home is in the individualist camp, see Harsanyi (1969).

that the model which derives the whole political process from the decisions made by individual persons who are assumed to behave rationally, explains elements of politics that seem awkward in other models, by providing some "explanations" of reality that are not consistent with alternative theories (1966, p. 27).

The second theoretical commitment of the choice-theoretic perspective is the choice paradigm, itself—a paradigm in the sense of Kuhn (1970)—which finds its justification as a framework within which to do science. Whereas the individualist ontology focuses on the individual actor as the principal theoretical unit and characterizes social structure and process as that which *emerges* from the interactions of individuals, it does not specify mechanisms of "individual action." The choice paradigm fills this theoretical gap. In this view, individual behavior is *rational and goal-directed*. More specifically, the individual is assumed to possess preferences about alternative states of nature, to discern (subjective) likelihoods of events in nature, and to combine these two decisional components in an appropriate fashion in order to make choices about his behavior. The mechanism, then, of "individual action" is *choice*.

It is important to note that rationality entails no more than *consistent goal-seeking* in choice behavior. Several significant consequences emerge from this. First, it follows that *irrational* behavior is simply inconsistent or random behavior. That is, rationality does not depend upon the content of goals or the particular form that subjective estimates of event probabilities take. It simply requires that one act on these pieces of "information" in a consistent fashion.[2]

A second and related point is the open-ended nature of goals in the choice paradigm. Individuals may act on the basis of a narrow self-interest, on the basis of trust and altruism, or on any other basis. It is a mistaken impression to suppose that a choice-theoretic world is populated exclusively by *homo economicus* who is motivated by blind greed. In fact, it is precisely at the prechoice stage that social structures and processes may have impact on the criteria of individual choice. That social context

[2] While irrational behavior is random, it does not follow that all random behavior is irrational. One of the significant contributions of game theory is the theoretical concept of *mixed strategy*, a course of action in which the individual, *in the pursuit of his goals*, purposely behaves randomly. See Luce and Raiffa (1957, chap. 4) and von Neumann and Morgenstern (1964). In the context of electoral competition, one may observe candidates behaving ambiguously in their campaigning. This is another form of random, but purposeful, goal-seeking behavior (see Shepsle, 1971, 1972a, b). Finally, it may be noted that random behavior in a given context may betray, not confusion and inconsistency of goals, but the absence of goals or indifference.

may affect decision criteria, goals, information, and values is clearly stated by Sen:

> The society in which a person lives, the class to which he belongs, the relation that he has with the social and economic structure of the community, are relevant to a person's choice not merely because they affect the nature of his personal interests but also because they influence his value system including his notion of "due" concern for other members of society. The insular economic man pursuing his self-interest to the exclusion of all other considerations may represent an assumption that pervades much of traditional economics, but it is not a particularly useful model for understanding problems of social choice (1971, p. 6).

Finally, it should be clear that rationality in the context of the choice paradigm is divorced from the more normative connotations of an earlier usage of the term. Though choice-theoretic models may be put to normative use—as in parts of welfare economics—they are not normative models. Rather they are *positive* (conditionally normative) models that provide expectations (predictions) about individual choice and behavior. From the choice theorist's perspective, a given set of goals is judged as "good," not if it conforms to some prior normative standard, but rather if it provides expectations about behavior which account for observed regularities. The standard is scientific, not normative.

As a practical matter, the choice theorist comprehends individual action in at least two ways: by observing behavioral regularities and by postulating individual goals. Because each method is subject to error—observed regularities may be spurious and goals imputed to individuals may simply be wrong—the process of theory construction ordinarily moves back and forth between them, using the one as a partial check on the other. Riker and Ordeshook call these methods of *revealed preference* and *posited preference*, respectively, of which they write:

> Which approach, revealed or posited preference, one uses is largely determined by the particular problem that one is trying to solve. Indeed, all social science works back and forth between the two methods. In the study of the behavior in organizations, for example, one posits for individuals the goal officially adopted for the organization and discovers that some behavior is well-explained. In complicated decision problems of the sort now studied by methods of systems analysis like game theory or linear programming, the goal posited is, of course, the official goal, like making a profit, winning, etc. The analyst then says to the decision-maker, "If your goal is the official

one, then your best choice of alternative actions is. . . ." Turning game theory from a [conditionally] normative to a descriptive use, one posits that the decision-maker in fact has the official goal, and then looks to see how much behavior is described by that assumption. If, as is often the case in micro-economics but seldom the case in the study of non-profit organizations, it turns out that a large enough proportion of behavior is explained by this method to permit accurate predictions, then one can cease the description. That is, one has learned that the official goal is the operative goal. If not, however, one proceeds by means of revealed preference in which one assumes only that behavior follows logically from goals and asks what structure of goals could have produced these choices. Then one discovers other goals motivating behavior, even perhaps, private goals quite at odds with official ones. In either case, however, one has discovered goals (1972, chap. 2).

The hallmark of rational choice models is a focus on individual goals (whether by imputation or observation), logical consistency among goals, and the direct relationship between goals, choices, and behavior. Assumptions about goals, consistency, and choice behavior impose a logical structure and coherence on an otherwise complex maze of mass and motion: "[their] function is to serve as a filing system for organizing empirical material and facilitating our understanding of it" (Friedman, 1953, p. 76). Frequent appeal is made to the "as if" principle, for a rational choice model is a description of an artificial world—one in which "attendant circumstances" have been abstracted away:

> [P]eople behave *as if* they order their alternative courses of action and choose that which is most preferred. If a person does not actually make, or is not able to understand, the rationalistic calculations we impute to him, the rationality assumption may still satisfactorily account for his behavior by providing a parsimonious explanation from which predictions can be made (Brams, 1973, p. 6).

Having characterized the choice-theoretic perspective, we turn in the next section to the formal components of rational choice, namely, assumptions about preferences.

RATIONAL BEHAVIOR

Choice theory owes its most recent development to advancements in two mathematical traditions: relational logic (see Jeffrey, 1967 and Suppes, 1957) and set theory (see Halmos, 1960). For a long time, however, it had been used, in varying degrees of formality, to inform thinking about economic behavior. In these theories economic man was assumed to evaluate various states of nature (typically conceived in abstract form as consumption bundles or factor bundles and often referred to simply as *outcomes*), to assess the efficacy of the actions available to him in producing the different states of nature, to coordinate actions with evaluations, and to choose accordingly. Here, "to choose accordingly" means to apply some criterion in the "selection" of an action, for example, utility maximization or profit maximization.

Until the end of the nineteenth century, valuation of outcomes was conceived of in terms of a valuation function (utility function, revenue function, etc.), and the object of choice was to select an action that maximized this function. Although a number of battles were to be fought, especially in the welfare economic tradition (see Rothenberg, 1961), it was found that many theoretical results could be established by postulating something mathematically less demanding than a valuation *function*. And if Occam's Razor were not sufficient grounds for relaxing a *functional* representation of value, then the fact that for some interesting choice situations no mathematical function existed (Debreu, 1954) gave these grounds. The upshot of all this—the ordinal revolution—was a choice theory that depended only upon a *preference relation*. A numerical representation of preference or value was not required.[3]

With the notion of a preference relation we may begin to specify what is meant by rational or goal-seeking behavior. To accomplish this I characterize below the components of *one* theory of rational choice. After discussing each of the components in turn, I complicate things a bit in order to accommodate a wider range of phenomena. The version of rational choice presented below is one among many. Slight perturbation of the assumptions generates an entire family of rational choice concepts. The particular formulation I present is, I think, one of the tried and true versions. However, for more extensive discussion of alternative rational choice formulations, the reader should see Adams (1960), Edwards (1954,

[3] The ordinal revolution in economics has given some cause for hope for political science, where the search for metrics has been singularly unsuccessful. Indeed, as I show below, a great deal may be learned about political phenomena with only an ordinal concept of preference. However, we should not be too sanguine about the prospects for a very broad-based or enlightening ordinal theory of politics. Many tricky theoretical issues, both in political science and economics, seem to require a more fully cardinal notion of preference. Uncertainty, as we shall see, is one of the (many) culprits; distributional questions are another. For some thoughtful work on the possibility of introducing cardinal representations in choice theory, see Sen, 1971, chap. 8, 8*.

1961), Becker and McClintock (1967), and the forthcoming essay by Wade and Curry.[4]

The exposition of the elements of a theory of choice, below, is technical, but necessary for what is to follow. The accompanying interpretation should provide the untrained reader with a grasp of the notation. In the choice-theoretic view, rational individual behavior is identified by:

1. a set of outcomes or goals, $0 = \{ o_1, o_2, \ldots, o_n \}$.

2. a set of actions or behaviors available to the individual, $A = \{a_1, a_2, \ldots, a_m\}$.

3. a subjective causal view of the world which relates actions to outcomes for the individual. This is represented by a mathematical function, f, whose arguments are elements of the set A. Thus $f(a_1) = o_2$ means that outcome o_2 results when the individual chooses to behave according to a_1. We require that f be complete —that each element in A has an outcome in 0 associated with it.

4. a binary preference relation, R, defined on pairs of elements of 0, such that: (a) for any two elements in 0, say o_1 and o_2, it is the case that $o_1 \, R \, o_2$ (read: o_1 is "at least as preferred as" o_2), $o_2 \, R \, o_1$, or both; and
(b) for any three elements in 0, say o_1, o_2, and o_3, if $o_1 \, R \, o_2$ and $o_2 \, R \, o_3$ then $o_1 \, R \, o_3$.

Whenever it is necessary to refer to the preferences of a *particular* individual—say the kth legislator or the kth voter—I shall add a subscript to the preference relation, viz., R_k.

5. an imputed binary preference relation, R^*, defined on pairs of elements in A, such that $a_1 \, R^* \, a_2$ (read: action a_1 is imputed to be "at least as preferred as" action a_2) if and only if the outcome associated with a_1 (say o_1) is at least as preferred as the outcome associated with $a_2(o_2)$—that is, $a_1 \, R^* \, a_2$ if and only if $o_1 \, R \, o_2$.

6. a set of "most-preferred" elements in A, called the *maximal set*.

7. an element chosen from the maximal set.

---

[4] In addition, an excellent, readable, economic treatment is given in Walsh (1970). The advanced reader may also wish to consult Chipman (1960), Debreu (1959), Fishburn (1970a, b, c), Katzner (1970), and Krantz, Luce, Suppes, and Tversky (1971).

Having skimmed the strange epsilontics of this list, the reader may well take refuge in the sentiment of the economist John Maurice Clark that "an irrational passion for dispassionate rationality takes the joy out of life." Some brief explanation hopefully will clarify things.

OUTCOMES

Since theories of rational choice presume behavior to be goal-directed, it is only natural to begin with the set 0 of goals. Like any abstract mathematical set, it is simply a collection of objects. Although statement 4 limits this collection in particular ways, the collection of goals may vary widely in composition. Thus, 0 might contain all presidential contenders in a given election, or alternative revenue-sharing schemes, or possible occupational categories, or constitutional and institutional arrangements—that is, any collection of items for which it makes sense (from someone's point-of-view) to use the verb "to choose" or "to prefer." Throughout most of this essay it is assumed, as the notation indicates, that 0 is finite (i.e., n is a finite, positive integer), containing at least two elements (in the subsequent discussion of spatial models, n is allowed to be infinite). However, there is no reason, after making appropriate mathematical adjustments, why 0 cannot contain an infinity of elements. In fact, there are often very real advantages both in logical reasoning and in discourse to expand 0 (in natural ways) to an infinite set.

But where do outcomes or goals come from? Rational choice models are purposely vague on this matter. The idea is to provide a perfectly general calculus of choice, leaving to the sociologist and psychologist, as well as the theorist who applies the choice paradigm to a particular substantive question, the task of determining the origins of goals. In many instances, the origin of goals is irrelevant to scientific explanation. Rational choice models, then, "take goals and choices as given and focus exclusively on the logical implications that the satisfaction of goals has on an actor's choices and vice versa. This approach makes goals and choices the 'facts,' and we explain them by relating them in a structure that gives them logical coherence and intelligibility" (Brams, 1973, p. 7).

ACTIONS

Choice from the set A is the "variable" controlled by the individual. Individuals *evaluate* elements in 0, but they *choose* from among elements in A. Thus, A is often conceived of as a set of instruments. Choice from A, then, is instrumental behavior—and this is precisely what goal-seeking entails.[5]

The action set A, like the outcome set 0, is an abstract collection of elements; its content depends on the problem at hand. And like the outcome set, its specification may be wrought with ambiguities. However, in many instances, as is indicated below, the specification problems are not unsurmountable.

To complete our discussion of the components of choice theory, the "causal" mechanism relating actions to outcomes must be specified, after which some logical structure is added.

THE RELATIONSHIP BETWEEN ACTIONS AND OUTCOMES

Statement 3 posits the existence of a function f that maps actions to outcomes. It is, in effect, the individual's subjective model of causality. If it were the case that an individual believed his activities had no consequences for outcomes—if an individual felt completely inefficacious—then a choice calculus would be irrelevant, for behavior would then be random.[6]

Technically, the function f in 3 is overly restrictive. By insisting upon a *functional* (in the mathematical sense) relation between actions and outcomes, one requires that each action in A be unequivocally related to some unique outcome in 0. This feature is characteristic of decision models under *certainty*. However, it is frequently the case that individuals, by their own admission, have only sketchy and imperfect causal notions. Thus, as Arrow suggests, "there is no need to enlarge upon the importance of a realistic theory explaining how individuals choose among alternate

---

[5] A common criticism of this formulation rejects cool rationality and instrumental choice as explanations of behavior. Actions, it is argued, are not chosen solely on instrumental grounds, not exclusively with an eye toward the outcome set. One must consider as well the action in and of itself. Thus, people may vote, for example, not only because of their preferences for a particular candidate or public policy (outcomes), but also because of the private, noninstrumental benefits derived independent of the outcome, e.g., the fun and excitement of entering the voting booth and making a choice. C. P. Snow, in *The Masters* (1951, p. 328), gives literary force to this criticism. Riker and Ordeshook (1972, chap. 3) attempt to accommodate this criticism by building into the choice calculus both an instrumental "comparative evaluation of social consequences" and a less instrumental (vis-a-vis the set 0) "comparative evaluation of private consequences." They put this orientation to good use in a study of the calculus of voting (Riker and Ordeshook, 1968).

[6] In a tautological sense, random behavior is accounted for in a choice model; it is a betrayal of the absence of goals and/or inefficaciousness.

courses of action when the consequences of their actions are incompletely known to them. It is no exaggeration to say that every choice made by human beings would meet this description if attention were paid to the ultimate implications" (1951, p. 404). Accordingly, statement 3 may be relaxed in order to allow for contingencies of *risk* and *uncertainty*, a task taken up shortly.

It should be noted, since it does not receive enough emphasis in the literature on rational choice, that the subjective causal mechanism f is as much a part of the choice paradigm as preferences, goals, and actions. Critics of rational choice, who point to the effects of advertising, inter-personal persuasion, and education on the pursuit of goals, often identify these phenomena with the absence of individual goals, or at least with their malleability (see, for example, MacRae, 1971, for a discussion of this). Indeed, an entire tradition in psychology places prime emphasis on the affective need for cognitive consistency. Choice behavior, in this view, is nothing more than rationalizing behavior in which preferences are brought into balance with choices, after the fact, and are not related to choices in an instrumental sense (see Shapiro, 1969, for a review of this argument in the context of voting choice). However, instead of debating essentially metaphysical questions—do people really have preferences?— it might be of more use to examine these phenomena in terms of their effects on the individual's model of causality. For example, a Clairol advertisement, in this view, does not alter preferences, but may lead one to believe that buying Clairol and dyeing one's hair blonde leads to more fun! Goldberg argues along these lines for the case of education and its effect on political choice. In his analysis he assumes that

> effective rationality, i.e., the accuracy of one's expected value calcu-
> lations, increases as a function of education. Education is assumed to
> lower information costs, e.g., by improving one's ability to read and
> comprehend such information sources as *The New York Times,* and
> thus to improve the accuracy of one's estimates of relevant proba-
> bilities. Education is also assumed to act upon innate intelligence
> so as to develop it toward its full potential. Thus, errors in the per-
> formance of calculations ought to be reduced. *In brief, education is
> assumed to facilitate accurate perceptions of means-ends relation-
> ships and to facilitate appreciation of the import of such relation-
> ships for one's own goals* [emphasis added] (1969, p. 6).

Thus, the choice paradigm accommodates advertising and education, despite their frequently bizarre effects, without forsaking the notion of preference.

LOGICAL STRUCTURE OF PREFERENCE AND CHOICE

The heart of the rational choice model is the preference concept, its logical structure, and the logical structure it imposes on actions and choice. These themes are symbolically stated in statements 4-7 above. Statement 4 postulates an individual preference relation, R, defined on his set of goals, 0. Part (a) of this statement requires comparability. It requires, for any arbitrary pair of outcomes, say (o_1, o_2), that the individual say either that the first component is at least as preferred as the second, the second component is at least as preferred as the first, or both (since o_1 and o_2 are arbitrary, they may, in fact, be identical; thus the trivial comparison is allowed as well). If he asserts both o_1 R o_2 and o_2 R o_1, he is said to be *indifferent* between the outcomes. On the other hand, if he asserts o_1 R o_2, but not o_2 R o_1, he is said to *strictly prefer* o_1 to o_2. Statement 4(a), then, is a completeness axiom.

Statement 4(b) requires a modicum of consistency in preferences. It demands that the preference comparisons be consistent with a unique *ordering* of the elements of 0. That is, if it were the case that o_1 R o_2 and o_2 R o_3, but not o_1 R o_3 (a violation of 4(b)), there would be no unique ordering of the triad of outcomes—o_3 would simultaneously be first and last in the ordering. Statement 4(b)—*transitivity*—prevents this.[7]

If completeness and transitivity were employed solely as devices to organize the set 0, they would still be of interest in characterizing tastes, but would not be of much practical utility in characterizing *choice behavior*. However, the existence of a causal mechanism, f, relating actions to outcomes (statement 3), permits the imputation of a preference ordering to the set A, the choice set. And this is precisely the meaning of statement 5: if o_1 is preferred by Mr. k to o_2, and if a_1 results in o_1 and a_2 in o_2, then Mr. k ought to "prefer" a_1 to a_2. The binary relation, $R_k°$, is an artificial preference relation on A, derived from R_k and f. $R_k°$, in effect, orders the elements of A in terms of imputed preference.

The result is the maximal set of A. This set is the subset of A containing the "best" elements, as imputed by $R°$. This set often contains a single element—the best element. However, it is entirely possible for it to contain several elements. For example, if two distinct actions each result in the most-preferred outcome, then both are elements of the maximal

---

[7] See Becker and McClintock (1967) for commentary, and Schwartz (1972) for a critique of the "money pump" argument to which allusion is frequently made in this context.

set. At this point we are home free: rational choice is the selection of an action in the maximal set of A (statement 7).

Put simply, rational behavior requires individuals to order the set O in terms of preference, to impute an order on the set A consistent with the order on O via f, and to choose one of the maximal elements of A. Except for the complications due to uncertainty, which we turn to next, statements 1-7 serve as a complete characterization of the individuals who populate the collectivities that are our primary interest. "Attendant circumstances" are abstracted away and metaphysical issues and entities, which very often lead into theoretical cul-de-sacs, are avoided. The individual is conceived of in terms of his preference structure and his notions of causality. As Tullock observes, we do not "engage in elaborate speculation about the nature of man or the reasons for an individual's desire of some certain thing. We observe that different people want different things, and that the same person will want different things at different times" (1967, p. 1).

UNCERTAINTY

The major weakness in the characterization of rational choice above is the stipulation of a functional relation between actions and outcomes (statement 3). Uncertainty in the environment often precludes a direct and deterministic relation. Consider the Congressman with an eye toward an approaching election who must determine whether to vote Yea or Nay on an important piece of legislation (or, indeed, whether to vote at all). He undoubtedly has a partially articulated model of constituency response in his head, but it is fraught with uncertainty. First, he may be uncertain about constituency preferences. Second, he may be unsure of the manner in which (some of) his constituents will respond to this particular vote— will it be salient in their vote decision? Will it affect the collection of a campaign chest? etc. Third, he will be uncertain about the ability of his electoral opponent to bring this vote to the level of public debate in the constituency. (Fiorina, 1972, presents a decision-theoretic analysis which addresses precisely these issues.)

This example points to a difficulty in the above decision calculus when the causal relation between actions (a_1: vote Yea, a_2: vote Nay, a_0: abstain) and outcomes (various electoral consequences) is incompletely specified. If it is the case, and I believe a strong case can be made, that uncertainty pervades most instances of political choice, then statement 3 is simply too strong. It is possible, however, to salvage the characterization above with an appropriate generalization of 3. A more general formulation assumes that the individual's "causal model" links actions with outcomes in a probabilistic, rather than a deterministic, manner:

   (3′) Define a set $P = \{(p_1, p_2, \ldots, p_n)\}$, where the p_i are subjective probability numbers. A (more general) causal view of the world, f^*, is a function that maps elements of the action set to elements of P.

The elements of P are probability distributions over various outcomes in 0. The probabilistic causal model, f^*, reflects the fact that, in many circumstances, the individual decision maker is unsure of the consequences of his choices. It is as if he reasons to himself, "In choosing a_j I'm not confident of what's going to happen. My *belief* is that (for example) either o_1, o_2, or o_3 may occur. My subjective estimate of the likelihoods of these outcomes is $p_1{}^j$, $p_2{}^j$, and $p_3{}^j$, respectively. Thus, if I choose action a_j, I am in effect choosing the *lottery* ($p_1{}^j$ o_1, $p_2{}^j$ o_2, $p_3{}^j$ o_3)." That is, in general, actions are equated with lotteries and decision-making via f^* is equivalent to choosing among lottery tickets.[8] What is required, then, is a decision calculus that permits choice over alternative lotteries.

   It is easy to see that statement 3 is a special case of statement (3′)— that certainty is a degenerate form of uncertainty. If, for example, a_1 results in o_1 with certainty, then according to (3′) a_1 is equivalent to a lottery ticket in which $p_1{}^1 = 1$, $p_2{}^1 = p_3{}^1 = \ldots = p_n{}^1 = 0$, i.e., $(1,0,0\ldots,0)$.

   To choose in an environment of "risky choice," where (3′) is operative, a preference structure more detailed than that provided for in statement 4 is required. The R-relation on outcomes is no longer sufficient to generate an R^*-relation on actions. A simple example makes this point. Suppose Mr. k prefers o_1 to o_2 and o_2 to o_3. If action a_2 leads to o_2 with certainty, but if a_1 leads to o_1 with probability one-half and o_3 with probability one-half, then it is unclear whether k ought to choose a_1 or a_2. That is, the maximal set of actions is not well-defined.

   In order to determine whether o_2 for certain (the result of a_2) is better, according to Mr. k's values, than a fifty-fifty chance of o_1 or o_3 (the

---

[8] It is important to reiterate that uncertainty is reflected in actions equated to probability distributions over *outcomes*. This is to be contrasted with a device, known in game theory as a *mixed strategy*, in which strategic considerations dictate implementing random behavior. A mixed strategy is equivalent to a probability distribution over *actions*. Unless otherwise noted, I shall be concerned with the former.

result of a_1), a *metric* on preferences is required. The most commonly adopted procedure for "cardinalizing" preferences is that proposed by von Neumann and Morgenstern (1944, 1964, pp. 617–632).[9] This procedure allows the assignment of numbers, called *utilities*, to the elements of 0, which, in turn, permit calculations of mathematical expectation. Thus, in the case above, the utility of a_2 is simply the utility of its consequence— $u(o_2)$, whereas the utility of a_1 is the *expected* utility of its consequence— $1/2u(o_1) + 1/2u(o_3)$. The $u(o_i)$'s are the utility numbers assigned to elements of 0. Generally, the utility of an action is the expected utility of the lottery over outcomes it provides. Thus, for $a_j \equiv (p_1{}^j o_1, p_2{}^j o_2, \ldots, p_n{}^j o_n)$:

$$u(a_j) = p_1{}^j u(o_1) + p_2{}^j u(o_2) + \ldots + p_n{}^j u(o_n)$$

The maximal set of A is the subset of actions having the highest expected utility. Rational choice, as before, is the selection of one of the maximal elements. In the example above, a_2 is in the maximal set of A if $u(o_2) \geq 1/2 u(o_1) + 1/2 u(o_3)$; a_1 is in the maximal set if the inequality stands in the opposite direction; and both are maximal elements if both inequalities stand (in which case $u(a_1) = u(a_2)$).

With provision for uncertainty, the choice paradigm encompasses a wide variety of phenomena. Rational behavior, in this view, is *maximizing* behavior (for a delightful discourse on maximizing principles, see the Nobel Prize acceptance speech of Paul Samuelson, 1971). Goal seeking entails the rationalization of preferences and the assessment of event probabilities.[10] Each of these aspects is subjective: the former depends on personal tastes and values, the latter on private notions of causality and information.

THE NATURE OF COLLECTIVE CHOICE

I have devoted so much attention to individual choice because the choice theoretic perspective requires an understanding of individual choice behavior in order to comprehend aggregate phenomena. Yet there

[9] For variations on the axiom system of von Neumann and Morgenstern see Marschak (1950) and Luce and Raiffa (1957, chap. 2).

[10] In some more recent work, consistent goal seeking does not even require rationalized preferences (as exemplified by statements 4 and 5 above). Rather, it simply demands consistent *choice*, something much less restrictive than rational preferences. See Schwartz (1972) and the Appendix.

is more to collective choice than the choices of individuals, though the latter are central components. In addition we must consider what may be called "social context." This includes the rules which convert the choices (behaviors) of individual into aggregate outcomes, i.e., processes of social choice, and the effects of individuals on one another, i.e., strategic interaction.

Collective choice involves "selecting" one of the available elements of 0, thereby committing the resources and moral authority of the collectivity to the attainment of that outcome. Before this selection can take place, however, several constitutional issues must be resolved, namely:

1. Who shall participate in collective deliberations?
2. How shall these deliberations be constituted? and
3. What is the "appropriate" set of outcomes 0 over which to deliberate?

Although all three questions have concerned social philosophers for centuries, most of the recent formal literature on collective choice has focused on the second. Needless to say, rules of participation and procedures of agenda-building have normative import and cannot be separated from other aspects of collective choice. The politics of agenda-building has received recent, nonchoice-theoretic attention by Bachrach and Baratz (1962, 1963), Cobb and Elder (1972), and Schattschneider (1960), but has been virtually ignored in more formal treatments (although Badger [1972] has given it indirect attention). Similarly, rules of participation have received slight attention.[11]

A more general and ambitious examination of the normative aspects of collective choice is found in the work of Rawls (1972). The touchstone of his analysis is the just social institution or social process. An institution or process is just if it would be selected by individuals in "the original position"—a condition of complete uncertainty about individual psychic, social, and economic endowments. With the "original position" as the conceptual analogue of the "state of nature," Rawls provides a provocative foundation for the contract theory of the State.

With the exception of the work by Rawls, most theories of social choice

---

[11] Indirect attention to the question of participation is evident, but the general question has received scant consideration. On the effects of group size, see Niemi and Weisberg (1972). On the issue of compulsory participation, see Tingsten (1963). For a general systems-theoretic analysis of franchise extension, see Pzeworski (1971). It should also be noted that recent work by Plott (1968, 1971a, b, c, d) directly addresses both agenda-building and participation problems. For a brief discussion of Plott's general framework, consult the Appendix.

are concerned mainly with "appropriate" institutional arrangements for the selection of collective outcomes. Agenda and participation considerations are either begged or treated as exogenous phenomena. As a result, I focus primarily on the second question—the constitution of collective deliberations.

In some instances collective choice processes are conceived of simply as the collective interactions of choosing individuals under a system of rights. Economic exchange, which results in alterations in the distribution of goods, services, and factors of production through voluntaristic interaction in the "marketplace," is just such an instance. In these models the institutional terrain is rather sparse. That which we call the economy is an artificial construct, the result of a decentralized process involving a host of individual choices and a system of property rights.

Political choice, on the other hand, though it involves individual interaction and choice, ordinarily takes place under a more formalized set of rules. Political choice amounts to the *selection* of an element in 0, often in the form of an instruction to some supra-individual entity—the State, the group, the leaders—to do some such thing. Unless the particular element in 0 selected happens to be the status quo, in which case no alterations are required, there is no guarantee that a collective choice will be *enforced*. A theory of political collectivities, then, requires both a theory of choice and a theory of enforcement (see Riker and Ordeshook, 1972, chap. 1). A theory of collectivities that ignores either runs the very real risk of being a sterile exercise. Unfortunately, most work to date has concentrated on the former, often to the total exclusion of the latter. That being the case, the bulk of this essay focuses on choice.

We begin with a set of N individuals, $I = \{1, 2, \ldots, k, \ldots, N\}$ (with Mr. k the generic decision maker), a set of n outcomes, $0 = \{o_1, \ldots, o_n\}$, and the preference relations (orderings) of the N individuals over the n outcomes, $R = \{R_1, R_2, \ldots, R_k, \ldots, R_N\}$. A social choice is defined as the result of a collective selection process from 0, for any choice environment, by some transformation or aggregation of the set of individual R-orderings. Thus we may write a social choice process as a function or mapping that takes individual R-orderings as its arguments. This function embodies all those complex rules of combination to which I referred in the introduction to this essay.

Three features of this description should be underscored. First, the collection of individuals whose preferences are taken as arguments of the choice process has been introduced via the back door. Who they are and how they come to be the "appropriate" set of individuals are questions generally not addressed in positive theories of collective choice. That the identification of the set of participants is fundamental to descriptions and explanations of actual collective choices, however, is undeniable. Students of legislatures, for example, who limit their investigations to the behavior of individual legislators, discover the hard way that there are relevant nonlegislative actors who contribute to the determination of policy outputs.[12] Nonetheless, it is often suitable to regard "rules of participation" as exogenous without detracting from their significance.

The second point relates to the arguments of the choice process. They are individual *orderings*, and are important as much for what they preclude as for what they provide. An individual R-ordering is a binary preference relation whose only properties are completeness and transitivity. Thus, it is only these properties that may be exploited in a choice-theoretic conceptualization of a social process as defined above. No room is left to consider the *intensity* with which preferences are held, or the *salience* of a particular choice situation to the individual. To the extent that these additional features are significant in collective choice (and this student believes they are), the characterization above must be altered. However, for now we stick with the original formulation.

Third, when social choice is identified as a process of selection (see Plott, 1971b, c, d, 1972) "for any choice environment," two things are implied. First, to be well-defined, a choice process must yield a selection for any configuration of individual R-orderings. We will not have defined a very general collective choice process if, for some configurations of individual preferences, no collective choice materializes. Generality with regard to the collection of preference orderings would thus appear to be a minimal *a priori* demand of any selection process. However, as is shown in the next section, it is precisely on this point that a large family of choice processes founders. Second, for a given set of individual R-orderings defined on an outcome set 0, a further *a priori* demand is that the selection process be efficacious for subsets of 0, and that choices from subsets be mutually consistent in several ways (see Sen, 1971, pp. 16–20). That is, if it is discovered after a choice process has been implemented that some of the elements in 0 are infeasible or otherwise unavailable, e.g., a simultaneous reduction of inflation and unemployment, then that same choice process ought to be able to produce a selection from the feasible subset of 0. Moreover, if at different times different feasible sub-

---

[12] See, for example, Weidenbaum (1970), who demonstrates that a significant proportion of the federal budget passes through no annual authorization or appropriation process, so that no legislative committee reviews its contents.

sets are available, and if the individual R-orderings remain unchanged, then there ought to be a modicum of consistency among the collective choices. Sen (1971, p. 16) concentrates on two sorts of consistency. Suppose, for example, that $0 = \{o_1, o_2, o_3, o_4\}$ is the set of outcomes under consideration and that $0^* = \{o_1, o_2\}$ and $o^{**} = \{o_1, o_2, o_3\}$ are alternative feasible subsets of 0. Initially it may be the case that a collectivity believes it is choosing from 0^{**}. That is, it has been determined that o_4 is infeasible. In instituting its choice process (which, for now, is undefined), assume that o_2 is the chosen element. Now if the collectivity should learn that in fact it were choosing from 0^*—that o_3 was infeasible as well—this should make no difference. If o_2 is collectively preferred to o_1 in the presence of o_3, it should still be preferred to o_1 when o_3 is unavailable. Sen (1971, p. 16) calls this property a, which he formally states as follows:

> *Property a:* If $o_i \epsilon \ 0^*$ (and hence an element of 0^{**} [since 0^* is a subset of 0^{**}]), and if the social process chooses o_i from 0^{**}, then it must also choose o_i from 0^*.

Alternatively, suppose the collectivity believes it is choosing from 0^* and (perhaps because of indifference) chooses *both* o_1 and o_2. If it should later discover that it is, in fact, choosing from 0^{**}, and still chooses o_1, then it must choose o_2 as well. Again, the presence or absence of o_3 should not affect the "social preference" as between o_1 and o_2. Following Sen, we state:

> *Property β:* For $o_i, o_j \epsilon \ 0^*$, if both o_i and o_j are chosen by a social choice process from the set 0^*, and moreover if o_i is also chosen from 0^{**}, then it must be the case that o_j is chosen from 0^{**} as well.

"To give an example, property a states that if the world champion in some game is a Pakistani, then he must also be the champion in Pakistan, while property β states that if some Pakistani is a world champion, then *all* champions of Pakistan must be champions of the world" (Sen, 1971, p. 18). We shall see that while many social choice processes satisfy a, they often fail to satisfy β.

From the definition of a social choice process and the three features I discussed above, we may write a social choice as a set-valued mapping, say F, operating on a collection of R-orderings:

$$\text{social choice} = F(\{R_1, \dots, R_N\})$$

But what is the "dependent variable" in this equation? Will the *a priori* demands concerning the generality and consistency of social choices provide enough structure to specify the "dependent variable" completely? These are the issues which theorists of collective choice debate. Kenneth Arrow, in initiating the debates, provided the following solution to the "case of the undefined dependent variable": the dependent variable, the result of a social choice process, must itself be an R-ordering. Social choice, in this view, requires the construction of a *social preference relation*, R_S. We examine this solution next.

ARROW'S MATHEMATICAL POLITICS

Consider a faculty of a political science department composed of fifteen members. Their dean has permitted them to hire an additional member, and, as a result, they have carefully interviewed three candidates: Mr. X, Mr. Y, and Mr. Z. After due consideration (and probably some politicking!) each of the fifteen members arrives at an assessment of the candidates. This assessment takes the form of a preference ordering, the collection of which we write as $\{R_1, R_2, \ldots R_{15}\}$. One of the professors then raises the critical question; namely, how shall the collectivity arrive at a decision to hire one (and only one) of the candidates? A number of decision rules are available, some of which are listed below:

1. let the dean, whose preferences are R_0, decide;
2. choose Mr. X, independent of $R_1, \ldots, R_{15}$;
3. choose Mr. Y, independent of $R_1, \ldots, R_{15}$;
4. choose Mr. Z, independent of $R_1, \ldots, R_{15}$;
5. let Professor 1 choose, independent of the preferences of the other 14;

. . . .

19. let Professor 15 choose, independent of the preferences of the other 14;
20. choose that candidate who receives a simple majority of the votes when paired against all other candidates, each in turn;
21. choose that candidate who receives a special majority[13] of the votes when paired against all other candidates, each in turn;
22. choose that candidate who is unanimously preferred to each of his competitors;

---

[13] Since a simple majority requires 8 of 15 votes, there are six distinct special majority rules for which the critical proportions are, respectively, 9 of 15, 10 of 15, . . . , 14 of 15.

23. choose that candidate who receives a plurality of the votes in a single balloting.

Of course there are many other possibilities, some more perverse than others, but this list of "chairman's rules of social choice" (Riker and Ordeshook, 1972, chap. 4) will suffice for our purposes.

We have here a question of constitutional procedure: How shall (or perhaps how should) the collectivity select an outcome from the set 0 = {X, Y, Z}? Although there are several strands of theory on this and related questions, I focus here on the procedure followed by Kenneth Arrow (1963). After developing Arrow's argument, we may use it as a standard against which to evaluate the "chairman's rules" above.[14]

Arrow conceives of a theory of social choice as an analysis of *processes* which transform the preferences of the individuals in society into a schedule of social preferences. He calls a process of this kind a *social welfare function* (SWF) which he defines as

... a process or rule which, for each set of individual orderings R_1, ..., R_n for alternative social states [elements o 0], states a corresponding social ordering of alternative social states, R[i.e., what I have called R_S] (1963, p. 23).

He defends this formulation on several grounds. First, he maintains that it is "natural" that an SWF, which amalgamates a collection of individual R-orderings, should produce an ordering, R_S. One need not give R_S the same ontological status as any of the R_k's. That is, although an SWF produces a *social* preference ordering, one is not required to conjure up a supra-individual entity called SOCIETY to which this social preference ordering in some sense belongs.

Second, it has been maintained that a social *ordering* is required in order to make collective choices "in any choice environment."[15] For example, if our political science faculty above resolves its choice problem contrary to an SWF, by simply identifying a single element, say candidate X (that is, the choice process produces, not a social ordering over 0 = {X, Y, Z}, but simply selects an element from 0, *viz.*, X) and Mr. X de-

---

[14] Space limitations preclude extensive discussion of contributions by other scholars, most notably Buchanan and Tullock (1962), Rae (1968), Taylor (1969), Schofield (1972), Badger (1972), and Curtis (1972).

[15] Although I can find no direct statement to this effect in his writings, Arrow comes close to saying this explicitly at several points in a recent article: "The process of formation of welfare judgments is logically equivalent to a social decision process or *constitution*. Specifically, a constitution is a rule that associates to each possible set of individual orderings a social choice function, i.e., a rule for selecting a preferred action out of every possible environment" (p. 13); and, "Recall that a constitution is a rule

clines the offer, i.e. becomes infeasible, then the choice process fails in its task since it is unable to specify an element from the feasible set (in this case {Y, Z}). If, on the other hand, the choice process used by the political science faculty generates an ordering, say XYZ (read: X preferred to Y, Y preferred to Z, and X preferred to Z), and if it is determined that X is infeasible, then the choice process is still determinate: it dictates that an offer be made to Y.

The third justification offered by Arrow in support of the social preference ordering formulation falls under the rubric of *independence of path*. In Arrow's quasi-normative analysis, he is concerned that social choices depend solely on the preferences of individuals. There is no room in his analysis for the peculiar kinds of biases he might observe in real-world decision procedures, e.g., the positively advantaged position of the *status quo* under the Rules of the House of Representatives. A choice procedure which may be manipulated by clever parliamentary tactics, then, is unacceptable because it yields choices not solely dependent upon individual preferences; social choice, in this case, depends on parliamentary skill as well. Arrow claims that a choice process that generates a social ordering will preclude these corrupting influences and thus will guarantee ". . . the independence of the final choice from the path to it. Transitivity [a defining property of an ordering] will insure this independence; from any environment, there will be a chosen alternative, and, in the absence of a deadlock, no place for the historically given alternative to be chosen by default." (1963, p. 120)[16]

---

that assigns to any set of individual preference orderings a rule for making society's choices among alternative social actions in any possible environment. Thus, for a given set of individual orderings the result of the process is a particular social value system . . . ; that is, a rule for making selections out of all possible environments. . . . *In other words, social choice system has the same structure as that which we have already assumed for individual value systems"* (Arrow, 1967, p. 15, emphasis added).

[16] As far as it goes, this statement is correct. However, the implied *necessity* of an ordering to insure independence of path is false. Plott (1971d, p. 23) constructs a clever example which gives a process that produces choices independent of path, *but it is not a social ordering.*

It is a bit below the belt to present Arrow's defenses for his formulation in the text, while at the same time taking pot shots at those defenses in the marginal notes. However, this is, I believe, an accurate appraisal of one of the thrusts of social choice theory over the last decade, namely an attempt to explicate the logical structure of Arrow's arguments and then to attack its points of weakness. Yet the mere fact that Arrow's is the formulation that has served these last twenty years as the vehicle for the logical analysis of social choice problems secures for it a central place in the intellectual development of this kind of inquiry.

To summarize, then, a social choice process (or an SWF, as Arrow calls it) is a rule that transforms a collection of individual preference orderings $\{R_1, R_2, \ldots, R_N\}$ into a social preference ordering, R_S. Because it is an ordering, R_S must possess the following properties:

Axiom I: For any two elements o_i, $o_j \epsilon 0$, either $o_i R_S o_j$ or $o_j R_S o_i$ (or both).

Axiom II: For any triple of elements o_i, o_j, $o_k \epsilon 0$, if $o_i R_S o_j$ and $o_j R_S o_k$, then $o_i R_S o_k$.

The first axiom, *connectivity*, assures that the social choice process is decisive for any pair of outcomes, where decisiveness entails "uttering" either strict preference or indifference. It is a completeness axiom. The second axiom, *transitivity*, insures a certain sort of consistency in social preferences. These axioms, then, restrict the dependent variable in the equation $R_S = F(\{R_1, \ldots, R_N\})$ to orderings. However, there are to this point no restraints on the process itself. The function F may take any form so long as it produces an ordering in the end. For example, F may be the rule that states: randomly choose an $R_k \epsilon \{R_1, \ldots, R_N\}$ and take that as the social preference ordering, R_S. Or, to take a more bizarre case, F may be the rule that states: Give no weight to the elements $R_1, \ldots, R_N$ and instead simply order the elements of 0 in random fashion, taking that ordering as R_S. The twenty-three rules for the faculty-decision problem are still other examples.

Arrow provided a set of conditions or restraints on F, not only to exclude patently absurd possibilities, but also to impose standards or values to which all "reasonable men" would subscribe. Also he sought to exclude mechanisms or processes that were not fully general in their scope. Arrow's conditions have taken several forms since their original statement (1951, pp. 24–31). I paraphrase below a more recent statement of these conditions (1967, pp. 15–17):[17]

Condition I (Universal Domain): All logically possible individual R_k-orderings are admissable.

Condition II (Pareto Principle): For any o_i, $o_j \epsilon 0$, if o_i is preferred to o_j by all N individuals in the society, then R_S ranks o_i above o_j.

Condition III (Independence of Irrelevant Alternatives): Social

---

[17] A slightly different statement of the conditions, supplemented by extensive discussion, is found in Riker and Ordeshook (1972, chap. 4). Also see Luce and Raiffa (1957, pp. 333–340).

choice in any choice environment depends only on the individual orderings of *those outcomes in the given environment.*

Condition IV (*Nondictatorship*): There is no individual whose preferences determine R_S independent of the preferences of other citizens in the society.

These conditions, and their logical equivalents, have provided the battleground for a whole host of intellectual skirmishes, most of which I have chosen to avoid in this essay (for a thorough-going review see Rothenberg, 1961, chaps. 2, 6–8, 11–13). However, some brief comments are in order. The condition of universal domain requires that the social choice process F produce a social preference ordering for all possible social configurations. In the faculty personnel problem, for example, where each of the fifteen faculty members may adopt as his R_k any one of six strict preference orderings:

(1)	(2)	(3)	(4)	(5)	(6)
X	X	Y	Y	Z	Z
Y	Z	X	Z	X	Y
Z	Y	Z	X	Y	X

or any one of seven orderings which reflect some degree of indifference:

(7)	(8)	(9)	(10)	(11)	(12)	(13)
X–Y	X–Z	Y–Z	X	Y	Z	X–Y–Z
Z	Y	X	Y–Z	X–Z	X–Y	

there are 15^{13} (or approximately 2×10^{15}) different social configurations possible. Condition I requires that F be efficacious in producing an R_S regardless of which of this very large number of possible societies obtains.

Condition II, the Pareto Principle, insures two things. It guarantees, first of all, that the social preference ordering responds positively or nonperversely to changes in individual preferences.[18] Certainly this is a minimal normative commitment, and lies at the very heart of the individualistic framework. The second aspect of the Pareto Principle is *nonimposition.*[19] It requires that social choices be derived from the preferences of citizens and forbids that it be imposed by some external

---

[18] In fact, when this condition is disaggregated into its two components, the first component condition has been varyingly called the condition of nonperversity, positive responsiveness, or nonnegative responsiveness. See Arrow (1963, pp. 25–26, 96–100).

[19] Elsewhere Arrow calls it *citizen sovereignty* (1963, pp. 28–30).

standard. External standards generally require their interpreters, high priests, philosopher-kings, or great legislators, and this, as we shall see, is outlawed by Condition IV.

The independence-of-irrelevant-alternatives condition is by all measures the most controversial of Arrow's conditions. Put simply, this condition requires social choices to emerge from a *binary* choice process. It asserts that if a process F aggregates a set of individual preference orderings $\{R_1, \ldots, R_N\}$ with the result, as given in R_S, that $o_i\ R_S\ o_j$, and if an "irrelevant" alternative o_h is deleted from 0, or moves up or down in some individuals' R_k's, but without affecting the position of o_i vis-a-vis o_j in any R_k, then F should still yield the result $o_i\ R_S\ o_j$. The only *relevant* consideration in determining whether o_i is socially preferred to o_j (or vice versa) is how o_i stands in comparison to o_j in each individual's preference ordering. "To give an analogy, in an election involving Mr. A and Mr. B, the choice should depend on the voters' orderings of A vis-a-vis B, and not on how the voters rank Mr. A vis-a-vis Lincoln, or Lincoln vis-a-vis Lenin" (Sen, 1971, p. 37).

The loudest clamor over Condition III involves whether it prohibits a role for preference intensity in social choices, and if so, whether it ought to (see Hildreth, 1953). The "intensity problem" (see Kendall and Carey, 1968), of course, has historically been the unwanted stepchild of both welfare economics and democratic theory. No one seems to know what to do with intense minorities! I do not propose to deal with this issue or the lengthy debate about it here (see Riker and Ordeshook, 1972, chap. 4, and Riker, 1961). However, as Samuelson (1967) has observed, even if Condition III were relaxed, intensity considerations would nonetheless be proscribed in Arrow's formulation. Arrow formulates the analysis of social choice exclusively in terms of an SWF; and the definition of an SWF requires that R_k-orderings be the only arguments of the social choice process F. Part of the reason for Arrow's formulation of the problem in this manner is his concern with observable processes (also see Plott, 1971c). Whereas individual preference may be revealed in observable choice situations (and there may even be problems here), preference intensity is less amenable to observation. Though preference intensities may exist in people's minds, a social choice process should not rely on them if they are not observable (Rabushka and Shepsle, 1972, attempt to deal with some possible behavioral consequences of preference intensity). Thus intensity is barred at the definitional stage. In the next section we examine some of the consequences of this condition as it relates to alternative principles of collective decision-making.

The last of Arrow's conditions, *nondictatorship*, seems the least controversial. However, more recently a minor controversy has arisen over it (see Sen, 1970). It may be argued that Condition IV violates even the minimal properties of political liberalism and sanctions "nosiness." That is, it may be argued that some issues, e.g., whether I eat Cheerios or Wheaties in the morning, are so personal that the individual involved ought to be decisive in its resolution:

> A very weak form of asserting this condition of liberalism (condition L) is that each individual is entirely decisive in the social choice over at least one pair of alternatives. . . . A still weaker requirement than condition L is given by condition L*, which demands that at least two individuals should have their personal preferences reflected in social preference over one pair of alternatives each. This condition is extremely mild and may be called the condition of "minimal liberalism," since cutting down any further the number of individuals with such freedom (i.e., cutting it down to one individual) would permit even a complete dictatorship, which is not very liberal (Sen, 1971, p. 79).

Thus we may distinguish between "global" and "local" dictators, perhaps tolerating some form of the latter. However, as the title of a recent essay by Sen (1970)—"The Impossibility of a Paretian Liberal"—betrays, this leads to no good, for it may be shown that Conditions I and II are violated if condition L (L*) is admitted. For expanded discussion of the liberal's dilemma, the reader is referred to Sen's recent monograph (1971, chaps. 6–7).

There are two remaining items on the agenda. First, we must examine the general theoretical consequence of Arrow's model—the famous Impossibility Theorem; and second, we must trace out some of the practical implications of the Arrow formulation for operating polities. To motivate the discussion of each of these questions, it is useful to return to the faculty recruitment example which introduced this section. I proposed twenty-three decision rules for collectively choosing from the set of three candidates. It is possible now to examine whether they comply with Arrow's SWF (as defined by Axioms I and II) and conditions I–IV. It will be shown that none of them does.

Decision rule 1 affirms the identity of R_S and R_o, where the latter is the preference ordering of the dean. If we redefine the collectivity, thereby including the dean (who, in the original statement of the problem, is not a member), i.e. $\{R_o, R_1, \ldots, R_{15}\}$, then the dean is clearly a dictator, contrary to condition **IV**. On the other hand, if the dean is not a member of the collectivity, then the assertion that $R_S = R_o$ violates condition **II**: it is imposed by appeal to an external standard. In any event, then, rule 1 is unsatisfactory.

Rules 2-4 sanction the imposition of choice, independent of the individual R_k- orderings, thus violating condition **II**.[20] Rules 5-19, on the other hand, establish dictatorships, contrary to condition **IV**. We may thus reject them all.

To dispose of rule 20—the simple majority decision rule—one may appeal to the well-known *paradox of voting*.[21] Suppose the faculty members partition themselves into three preference groupings. The first subset, $\{R_1, R_2, \ldots, R_5\}$, has the preference ordering XYZ (read: X is preferred to Y, Y to Z, and X to Z); the second, $\{R_6, R_7, \ldots, R_{10}\}$, the ordering YZX; and the third, $\{R_{11}, \ldots, R_{15}\}$, the ordering ZXY. For the pair (X, Y), the first and third groups prefer X to Y, while the second prefers Y to X; the 10-5 vote yields X R_S Y. For the pair (Y, Z) the first two groups prefer Y to Z, while the third prefers Z to Y; again, the 10-5 vote indicates Y R_S Z. Now, if Axiom **II** is to be satisfied, X R_S Z must hold (since X R_S Y and Y R_S Z). However, to the contrary, the second and third groups prefer Z to X, indicating Z R_S X. Thus, for one configuration of preferences, admissible under condition **I**, Axiom **II** is violated. As a general rule, then, rule 20 is not an SWF that produces a social ordering.

Since the simple majority rule occupies a special place in democratic theory and is appealing to some because of its alleged welfare properties, scholars have taken considerable interest in the expected frequency of the voting paradox. I defer detailed comment on this topic to the next section.

Rule 21 is disposed of in either of two ways. First preference configuration can be constructed which generate a voting paradox (a violation of Axiom **II**) under a special majority voting rule. Our example above serves as well as an example of a voting paradox under a two-thirds rule as it

---

[20] Moreover, they do not comply with the definition of an SWF because they fail to provide a complete social ordering. However, even if we rewrote rules 2–4 as thirteen distinct rules specifying the choice of one of the thirteen possible orderings independent of individual preferences, condition II would still be violated.

[21] This puzzling phenomenon, initially discovered by the Marquis de Condorcet in the eighteenth century, has been passed down under a number of names: l'effet Condorcet, the cyclical majority problem, Arrow's paradox. For historical discussion see Black (1958, part II), Riker (1961), and Grofman (1969).

did for the simple majority rule case. Second, admissible preference configurations under rules of special majority often lead to an *incomplete* social preference relation (a violation of Axiom I). For example, with a two-thirds rule and a preference configuration consisting of nine professors with the ordering XYZ and six with the ordering ZYX, no decisions at all are forthcoming. That is, for no pair of alternatives does one element secure the necessary ten of fifteen votes.

A similar argument removes rule 22 from consideration. The unanimity rule (or Pareto rule) is often incomplete—in particular, in those instances where unanimity is absent. In fact, the only instances in which the Pareto rule does work are free of conflict—hardly a very "political" situation.[22]

Finally, a simple example will demonstrate the incompatibility of the plurality decision rule with Arrow's axioms and conditions. Suppose our faculty members again partition themselves into three preference groupings:

(7)	(5)	(3)
I	II	III
X	Y	Z
Y	Z	Y
Z	X	X

where the numbers in parentheses give the number of professors with the given preference orderings. Thus, X receives seven votes, Y five votes, and Z three votes, and R_S is XYZ. However, now suppose that, after additional evidence has been gathered, candidate Z drops to the bottom of everyone's ordering:

(7)	(5)	(3)
I	II	III
X	Y	Y
Y	X	X
Z	Z	Z

Notice that the position of X vis-a-vis Y has not changed in anyone's ordering. The configuration now is: XYZ (7), YXZ (8). The social ordering is YXZ and it is seen that the relative positions of X and Y have

---

[22] Sen (1971, pp. 28–30, 74–77), however, demonstrates that an *extended Pareto rule* does satisfy the Arrow conditions. An extended Pareto rule simply completes the unanimity rule with the instruction that if o_i is not unanimously preferred to o_j and o_j is not unanimously preferred to o_i, then they are declared socially indifferent.

changed in R_S because of a change in evaluation of an irrelevant alternative, contrary to condition III.[23]

In several fell swoops I have demonstrated that a rather considerable number of decision rules are inappropriate according to the standards set by Arrow. With the General Impossibility Theorem, which is now stated, Arrow showed that the effect is even more profound:

> *General Impossibility Theorem:* "There can be no constitution simultaneously satisfying the condition of Collective Rationality [Axioms I and II and Condition I], the Pareto Principle [Condition II], the Independence of Irrelevant Alternatives [Condition III], and Non-Dictatorship [Condition IV]" (Arrow, 1963, pp. 97–100; 1967, p. 18).[24]

That is, no social choice process can satisfy conditions I–IV and simultaneously insure an SWF. Alternatively put, the theorem asserts that any ethnically satisfactory social decision process may fail to be satisfactory on other grounds.

It is important to note the broad class inclusion of Arrow's theorem. It does not assert that for *some specific society*, i.e., some specific preference configuration, it is impossible to construct a decision rule consistent with Axioms I and II and Conditions II–IV. A trivial illustration is the instance in which all fifteen faculty members order the job candidates identically. The unanimity rule, *for this society*, generates an SWF consistent with conditions II–IV. What Arrow's theorem does assert is the impossibility of constructing a decision rule, consistent with conditions II–IV, that produces an SWF (Axioms I and II) *for any configuration of preferences* (condition I). And this is the relevant issue at the prior, constitutional stage, when preference configurations are unknown.

Arrow's result is profound, yet embarrassing, for it tells us that we

---

23 Technically, the plurality rule violates the notion of *rationality* rather than the Independence of Irrelevant Alternatives (IIA) condition. If choices under the plurality rule are rational, then they can be rationalized by a binary relation, R_S, where these choices are R_S-maximal. With the first preference configuration above, Mr. X is R_S-maximal, i.e., X R_S Y and X R_S Z. With the second preference configuration Z drops in each preference ordering. This should not affect the R_S-maximality of X, yet it does. In the latter configuration Y R_S X. The IIA condition, in the presence of a rationality condition, requires that the choice process be binary—precisely what is violated in this instance. There is a general confounding of rationality properties and the IIA condition on which I comment in the Appendix (for an example, see the incorrect statement of IIA in Hansson [1968b]). I thank Professor Richard McKelvey for raising this point.

24 For general proofs of this theorem see Arrow (1963, pp. 97–100), Luce and Raiffa (1957, pp. 339–340), and Riker and Ordeshook (1973, chap. 4).

cannot avoid a social decision rule that is either confused—intransitive or incomplete—or unjust. Much of the social-choice literature of the last two decades has attempted to minimize the damage of this admission. Reactions to Arrow's Impossibility theorem fall into four groups. The first is characterized by the following question: Is it possible, while still preserving Arrow's notion of consistent social choice, to require something less stringent than an SWF, which, at the same time, is an ethically satis-factory social choice process? This group of research reformulates the social choice problem in terms of *nonempty choice sets*, rather than SWF's.

The issue to which the second group of research is addressed revolves around the *likelihood* that "troublesome" preference configurations emerge in a society. As noted above, for specific preference configurations any of a number of social choice rules work smoothly in accord with Arrow's axioms and conditions. What is sought is an estimate of the probability that such "trouble-free" configurations arise. Or, to put it another way, what is the cost (in terms of occasional intransitivities in collective preferences) of adopting an ethically satisfactory decision rule. In the next section some investigations of the probability of the paradox of voting are examined.

Like the previous group, the third collection of research takes the Impossibility theorem at face value—a nasty fact of social life—and seeks to place some boundaries on its scope. And again like the second group, this research exploits the fact that, for some families of preference con-figurations, a smooth Arrowian choice process may be constituted. Its aim, however, is to determine the logical properties of trouble-free pref-erence configurations. That is, instead of seeking to determine, under varying probability assumptions, the likelihood that an Arrowian SWF emerges (the aim of the second group of research), it searches for the weakest logical restrictions on condition I (universal domain) that guar-antee the impossibility of a voting paradox or of an otherwise confused collective choice process. The restriction to receive the most interest and attention is Duncan Black's *single-peakedness* (1958, pp. 14–18). We examine it and other more general restrictions in the context of majority rule decision-making in the next section.

The final collection of research efforts has focused on the Independence of Irrelevant Alternatives condition. I have alluded to the controversy surrounding this condition (and avoided any detailed discussion of it) and shall not focus on it any further. In addition to the items cited earlier, the reader may consult Arrow (1963, pp. 109–120; 1967, pp. 18–20), Plott

(1971a, b, c, d), Pattanaik (1971, pp. 42–47), Murakami (1968, pp. 105–122 under the title "Farewell to Pairwise Comparison"), Rothenberg (1961, pp. 127–144), and Tullock (1967b, pp. 37–50).[25]

I conclude discussion of Arrow's mathematical politics with a few observations related to the first group of research mentioned above. The central theme of this research is the possible inappropriateness of the Arrow formulation of social choice processes. However, unlike most critiques of the Arrow formulation, which quarrel for the most part on the basis of normative issues, this research points to *logical* problems.

An SWF is a very special kind of social choice process, namely one that maps a collection of R_k-orderings to a social ordering, R_S. A social *ordering*, Arrow argued, is the appropriate "dependent variable" if the social choice process is to insure that "from any environment, there will be a chosen alternative" (1963, p. 120). Let us, following Sen, call a social choice process that produces a chosen alternative from any environment a *social decision function* (SDF). The relevant question, then, is: Are all SDF's also SWF's? The answer is no. As Sen (1971, lemma 1*1, p. 16) demonstrates, a binary relation that is complete and acyclic (acyclicity is logically weaker than, and hence is implied by, transitivity) is necessary and sufficient for a "nonempty choice set." Thus, SDF's exist which fail to satisfy Axiom II (transitivity), yet still generate choices as prescribed by Arrow. In fact, a "possibility theorem" for SDF's may be proven and contrasted with the "impossibility theorem" for SWF's.

The celebration of this important distinction between SDF's and SWF's did not last long, however (this discussion closely follows Sen, 1971, pp. 47–55). For one thing it may be shown that any SDF that satisfies Arrow's conditions I–IV and that yields a nonempty choice set "must represent an 'oligarchic' form of decision-making. There would be an identifiable and unique group of persons in the community such that if any one of them strictly prefers any x to any y, society must regard x to be at least as good as y; and if all members of the group strictly prefer x to y, then society must also prefer x to y" (Sen, 1971, p. 50). In some instances the result is not "evil" because the size of the oligarchy is sufficiently large (i.e., larger than a majority) and thus is normatively palatable. Nonetheless, it is also possible to have group dictators that are far less attractive. The irony of these observations is this: the SDF formu-

---

[25] There have, in addition, been a series of critics of Arrow's formulation in welfare economics. Rothenberg (1961) reviews many of their arguments. As well, see Graaf (1957) and Little (1950).

lation, whose strong suit in its critique of Arrow is its weaker logical form, leads to the conclusion that Arrow's conditions are too *weak*.

[T]he fact remains that the Arrow conditions must be recognized to be too weak rather than too demanding, as is usual to assume in the context of his 'impossibility' result. An SDF can pass all the tests of Arrow [conditions I–IV] and still look very unappetizing (Sen, 1971, p. 50).[26]

A second reason for not being too sanguine about the SDF approach to social choice is purely logical, involving the consistency of SDF's (as specified by properties a and β given in the section on The Nature of Collective Choice above). It may be demonstrated (see lemmas 1°m and 1°q in Sen, 1971, pp. 17, 19) that while all SDF's satisfy property a, only a special subset of SDF's satisfy property β. That subset (irony #2) happens to be the set of SWF's. That is, the only SDF's that are consistent in the sense of property β are Arrowian social choice processes; and these, as Arrow's theorem demonstrates, may violate one of the four conditions. Since it is on the issue of consistency that much of the social choice literature concentrates, I quote Sen at length on the subject:

> Various selection processes do not, in fact, satisfy property β. Two Australians may tie for the Australian championship in some game, neither being able to defeat the other, but it is perfectly possible for one of them to become the world champion alone, since he might be able to defeat all non-Australians, which the other Australian may not be able to do. Similarly, two poets or scientists could get the same national honors, with only one of them receiving some international honor such as the Nobel Prize, without this appearing as irrational in any significant sense.
>
> Whether social choice functions should be required to satisfy property β this remains a somewhat problematic issue. Given everything else, it would of course appear to be better that β be satisfied rather than that it be violated. But there *is* a real conflict involved here, and other things are not necessarily the same. We know that a

[26] Arrow's conditions are "too weak" in another sense as well. Sen has demonstrated that the extended Pareto rule (see note 22) satisfies all of Arrow's conditions. But the extended Pareto rule simply indicates that the social choice should come from among the Pareto optimal alternatives (that is, the elements of O that are not universally inferior to any other given alternative according to all individuals' preference orderings). However, in any society with a modicum of cultural diversity, this is bound to be a rather large set. Moreover, in most political choice contingencies the problem is not that of isolating the set of Pareto optimal alternatives, but rather that of *choosing a particular alternative from the Pareto set*. The extended Pareto rule provides absolutely no guidance on this question.

relation generating a choice function that satisfies property β must be an ordering (Lemma 1*q). Hence an SDF that generates preference relations yielding choice functions satisfying β must be an SWF. The Arrow impossibility theorem about SWFs will get readily transformed into an impossibility theorem about SDF's if property β is also imposed as a necessary condition of social choice. . . . Then at least one of the four conditions of Arrow must be suppressed for the sake of consistency. The real question is, therefore, not whether property β is a good thing, but whether it is a better thing than any of the other four conditions in the context of an SDF (Sen, 1971, p. 51).

The dilemma to which Sen alludes is not unique. In the logical analysis of social choice processes, there are many paradoxes, impossibility theorems, dilemmas, and conflicts. Analyses of social choice are complex exercises in mathematical logic. For this reason, we do not pursue this line of research here. Rather, we turn to the consequences of Arrow-type problems for the operation of actual social choice systems, and more particularly to its impact on majority-rule arrangements.[27]

ARROW'S THEOREM AND ITS CONSEQUENCES FOR OPERATING DEMOCRACIES

In our discussion of rule 20 above—the simple majority decision rule—it was shown that for some preference configurations no alternative can secure a majority against all its competitors. The contingency is disturbing because it assures that a majority will be frustrated. Recall the fifteen faculty members partitioned into three preference groupings of five each:

(5)	(5)	(5)
I	*II*	*III*
X	Y	Z
Y	Z	X
Z	X	Y

If X is chosen, then a majority (II, III) that prefers Z to X is frustrated; if Y is chosen, then the majority that prefers X to Y (I, III) is frustrated;

[27] After I had completed a draft of this section, a copy was made available to me of Michael Taylor's excellent review of theories of social choice to appear in *The Handbook of Political Science* (under the general editorship of Fred I. Greenstein and Nelson W. Polsby). Although there are slight differences in coverage in the two essays, and Taylor's seems to emphasize certain more technical aspects, a common perspective is evident. Noteworthy is the fact that both of our reviews rely heavily on the contributions of Sen. For more recent developments in choice theory not reviewed by Taylor, the reader may consult the Appendix to this essay and the literature cited there.

finally, if Z is chosen a majority composed of groups I and II, that prefers Y to Z, is frustrated. Thus, no matter what the choice, a majority is
dissatisfied.

One might first ask (and many have) how likely this contingency is.
The hope here is that if such occurrences are infrequent, all is not lost.
Most investigations of the probability of the paradox of voting suggest,
however, that all may well be lost. Under a variety of theoretical assumptions, it has been determined that the probability of majority frustrations
is an increasing function of both the number of choosers and the number
of choice alternatives, and is especially sensitive to the latter.[28] For example, with five or more alternatives and large electorates, the probability is
at least one quarter, and may be as large as .8, that a voters' paradox
arises.[29]

These *a priori* probability calculations are misleading, however, on at
least two counts, and it is difficult to determine how they ought to be
qualified. In order to generate an *a priori* probability of a voting paradox,
an assumption about the frequency with which various admissible individual orderings appear is needed. Typically, Laplace's Law of Insufficient Reason is invoked, from which it is assumed that all individual preference orderings are equally likely. From here, it is simply a matter of
combinatorials to generate the *a priori* probabilities that "troublesome"
preference configurations will arise. But, as Williamson and Sargent note
(1967), the equiprobable assumption all but denies the notion of society.
Sen (1971, p. 165) observes, in support of this point, that "individual preferences are determined not by turning a roulette wheel over all possible
alternatives, but by certain specific social, economic, political, and cultural forces. This may easily produce some patterns in the set of individual preferences." Williamson and Sargent show that if some preference
orderings are "slightly" more likely to be adopted than others (and
this, it seems to me, is but a minimal measure of the linkages between
individuals in the same culture or society), then the probability of a social
intransitivity is reduced substantially.[30] The point, here, is that one may

[28] See Black (1958), Campbell and Tullock (1965), DeMeyer and Plott (1970),
Garman and Kamien (1968), Gleser (1969), Klahr (1966), Niemi (1969, 1970),
Niemi and Weisberg (1968), Pomeranz and Weil (1968), Riker (1961, 1965), and
Williamson and Sargent (1967).

[29] For attempts to assess empirically the extent to which majorities will be frustrated,
see Bowen (1972), Niemi (1970), and Weisberg and Niemi (1972).

[30] Tullock's well-known belief that the General Impossibility Theorem is generally
irrelevant follows from similar considerations (1967a, b).

generate a *whole family* of *a priori* probability distributions for trouble-some and trouble-free preference configurations, each one depending upon a different probability assumption for the occurrences of individual preferences. While the equiprobability assumption is reasonable for an analysis of the normative aspects of constitution construction, it is of little help in assessing, empirically, the frequency with which we may expect troublesome configurations to occur. This is especially true in light of Williamson and Sargent's "sensitivity analysis."

A second objection to the calculation of *a priori* probabilities involves what Farquharson calls "sophisticated behavior" (1969; also see Kramer, 1973). Since social choices take place in a social context, there may be rational reasons for one to misrepresent his preferences. For example, in the configuration of preferences of faculty members given at the beginning of this section, members of the first group may misrepresent their preferences, voting for Y over X despite their preference for X over Y, thereby insuring that Y will be the chosen alternative (since Y can also secure a majority over Z). Although with this strategy they forego the possibility that X will be selected, they also preclude the choice of Z by the collectivity; and in some circumstances rational individuals will find this "compromise" appealing.

On the other hand, individuals, through misrepresentation of preferences, may purposely generate a voting paradox in order to secure an outcome that would not otherwise be forthcoming. This is an especially likely prospect when the order of pairwise voting is specified ahead of time, either by rules of procedure, e.g., the Rules of the House of Representatives, or by a (not necessarily disinterested) chairman. Riker (1965) presents two historical instances—the Senate vote on the Seventeenth Amendment and recent House votes on aid to education—in which this kind of sophisticated behavior appears evident (also see Riker, 1958). In each of these cases, identifiable groups seem to have voted contrary to their preferences at one stage of voting in order to secure a preferred outcome at the conclusion of the voting process. Of course, this strategy can be neutralized by sophisticated behavior on the part of others.[31]

---

[31] Farquharson (1969) proves, for all binary voting procedures, that an equilibrium outcome—one which no *individual* has any incentive to upset by behaving differently—is guaranteed by "hyper-sophisticated" behavior. However, his results are less conclusive regarding the possibility that a *group* of individuals may have incentives to coordinate behaviors in order to upset an alleged equilibrium outcome. An investigation of this possibility leads to the various concepts of the *core* in n-person game theory. On this, see Aumann (1967). For a generalization of Farquharson's result to n-dimensional outcome spaces, see Kramer (1973).

Ward (1965) provides a general strategy through which an individual (or group) may purposely generate a voting paradox that redounds to his (their) advantage. This may also involve misrepresentation of preferences, though it need not. Consider the following example. Suppose the fifteen faculty members, having interviewed Mr. X and Mr. Z, divide into two preference groupings:

(8)	(7)
I	II
X	Z
Z	X

A clever entrepreneur in the minority preference group, if he also is able to influence the order of voting, should scout around for a third candidate, Mr. Y, who splits group I:

(4)	(4)
Ia	Ib
Y	X
X	Z
Z	Y

while only mildly impressing group II:

(7)
II
Z
Y
X

In this instance Y defeats X (Ia, II) and Z defeats Y (Ib, II). Thus, if Z enters the voting at the last stage, he will win (see Black, 1958, for a general proof of this).

The net effect of strategic ploys, some of which I have presented, is to mitigate the intent of *a priori* probability calculations. Some of these ploys increase, and others decrease, the probability of "troublesome" preference configurations. Thus, in the absence of additional contextual information, *a priori* probability calculations are difficult to interpret.

An alternative line of inquiry, as I noted in the last section, exploits the fact (also exploited by the probability calculators) that some preference configurations are trouble-free. The question posed in this research is: What characteristic(s) of preference configurations *insure* an Ar-

rowian SWF? The essence of the Arrow theorem is that for *any* normatively satisfactory decision rule, i.e., one that satisfies conditions II–IV,
some preference configuration, admissable by condition I, exists that fails
to produce a social ordering when "operated on" by the rule. *No rule
whose domain is universal is both normatively satisfactory and an SWF.*
How, then, might the domain of a social choice rule be limited (thus
making condition I more restrictive) so as to exclude configurations that
fail to generate a social ordering? This is the question addressed by the
research to which we now turn.

Duncan Black (1948) asked this question even before Arrow's work
appeared. He had noticed that whenever a collection of individual preferences jointly share certain unimodal characteristics, a simple majority
decision rule is (in Arrow's later terminology) an SWF. This unimodal
property, *single peakedness,* was first characterized in geometric terms by
Black (1948; 1958, pp. 14–18), and later in logical form by Arrow (1963,
p. 77). Geometrically, single-peakedness is characterized with the aid of
a two-dimensional coordinate system. The abscissa gives *some* ordering
of the alternatives and the ordinate gives preference ranks. An individual
preference ordering may be mapped onto the coordinate system, where
each point represents an alternative and its rank position in the individual's ordering. Connecting these points gives a preference "curve." A
preference curve is single-peaked if, as the label suggests, it has a single-
peak and preference ranks decrease uniformly on either side of the peak:
"a single-peaked curve is one which changes its direction at most once,
from up to down" (Black, 1958, p. 7). It will always be possible to find
an arrangement of alternatives on the abscissa that furnishes a single-
peaked representation of an individual's preference ordering. A collection
of preference orderings—what I have been calling a preference configuration—is single-peaked if, under some arrangement of alternatives on the
abscissa, *all* individual preference curves are simultaneously single-
peaked. What Black noticed and proved as a theorem is that majority
rule, when its domain is restricted to single-peaked preference configurations and the number of voters is odd, is an SWF. As Sen (1971, p. 167)
puts it, "If the number of voters is odd, then irrespective of the total number involved and irrespective of the distribution of that total over the
spectrum, majority decisions will be transitive."

In the second edition of *Social Choice and Individual Values,* Arrow
generalizes Black's concept in two different ways. First, he shows that
single-peakedness need only apply to *triples* of alternatives. If every
triple of alternatives is single-peaked (and if the number of voters is odd),

then the method of majority rule is an SWF, satisfying conditions II–IV (Arrow, 1967, p. 78). Single peakedness for triples is logically weaker than single-peakedness for the entire set of alternatives. Second, Arrow's definition of single-peakedness, which we give below, permits a "plateau" in preference curves in some circumstances (for more general development along this line, see Dummett and Farquharson, 1961).

The essential feature of Arrow's definition of single-peakedness is a limited form of consensus. More specifically, Arrow's definition requires that, in each triple of alternatives, all choosers must agree on one alternative that is "not worst" in any of their preference orderings. They may, of course, have drastically different views on which element in the triple is "best." But so long as there is this limited sort of common evaluation for each triple of alternatives, and the number of choosers is odd, then an SWF will be produced by the method of majority rule. For example, if one of the faculty members in our continuing illustration has the preference ordering XYZ, then so long as the remaining fourteen professors have preference orderings in which Y is not worst:

X	Y	Y	Z	X–Y	Y–Z	Y
Y	X	Z	Y			
Z	Z	X	X	Z	X	X–Z,

or alternatively, in which X is not worst:

X	X	Z	Y	X–Y	X–Z	X
Y	Z	X	X			
Z	Y	Y	Z	Z	Y	Y–Z,

then the method of majority rule produces a social ordering, R_S.

The effect of the single-peakedness restriction is to identify a family of preference configurations for which the method of majority rule is an SWF. In an important sense, however, it requires too much since there are preference configurations that yield a social ordering under majority rule which are not single-peaked. Thus, though single-peakedness is *sufficient* for majority rule to be an SWF, it is not *necessary*. In fact, Vickrey (1960) has suggested a parallel restriction—single-cavedness—in which the limited consensus takes the form of each chooser agreeing that a particular alternative in each triple is "not best." Single-cavedness also assures that majority rule is an SWF, though it too is not necessary.

Sen (1966) has subsumed both varieties of limited consensus—single-peakedness ("not worst") and single-cavedness ("not best")—and added a third variety of consensus ("not medium") under the rubric of *value restriction*. Of this condition he says:

. . . the generalized condition of "value restriction" requires that all agree that some alternative is not best, or all agree that some alternative is not worst, or all agree that some alternative is not medium in anyone's ranking in the triple. If value restriction (hereafter, VR) holds for every triple, then majority rule will be transitive if the number of voters is odd. It is not necessary that the same subclass of VR holds for each triple. In some triple some alternative may be "not best," in another some alternative may be "not worst," in a third triple some alternative may be "not medium," and so on, and transitivity will still hold. In fact a further weakening of the condition is possible. While persons indifferent over all three alternatives in a triple violate value restriction, they really cause no serious problem for transitivity. So indifference over entire triples (i.e., "unconcerned" individuals) are permitted and all that is needed is that the number of "concerned" individuals be odd (1971, p. 168).

Sen's condition of value restriction also subsumes Ward's (1965) *condition of latin squarelessness*. This latter condition is the special case of value restriction in which only strict preference is permitted (i.e., expressions of indifference are not allowed).

There are other patterns of partial consensus or conflict, i.e. other restrictions on condition I, which assure that the method of majority rule is an SWF.[32] However, their statement would require a rather lengthy logical development, a digression that is inappropriate here. Suffice it to say that in a wide variety of contingencies the method of majority rule is an equitable (vis-a-vis conditions II–IV) and decisive (in the sense of an SWF or an SDF) choice procedure. Unfortunately, there are no estimates of the frequency with which these contingencies occur empirically.

In this discussion we have been dealing with a very special decision

---

[32] Moreover, if instead of concentrating on social choice processes that are SWF's we are concerned with processes that are *decisive* (i.e., yield nonempty choice sets) and are consistent in the sense of property α—what have come to be called *social decision functions* (SDF)—then a whole series of "possibility" theorems may be proved about majority rule and more general decision rules. Both Sen and Pattanaik investigate several different kinds of "majority rule," and Murakami and Pattanaik investigate a variety of multi-stage decision processes. Much of this research (through 1970) is summarized in Sen (1971, chaps. 10 and 10°) and Pattanaik (1971, chaps. 4, 5, 6, and 7). In addition the reader may consult Murakami (1968), Inada (1955, 1964, 1969, 1970), and Fishburn (1971a).

rule—the method of majority rule. However, it may be observed that many operating democracies rarely employ this device, even if institutional complexities (nominations, primaries, and other agenda-building devices) are ignored for the moment. I simply note in passing that other decision rules have been examined, though not with the rigor evident in the social choice literature reviewed above.[33]

Let me close this section with a few caveats. Investigations of the last decade have disclosed a number of rather general conditions sufficient to insure the transitivity of the simple majority decision rule. Each of these, in a sense, reflects a recognition of society and the interdependencies in tastes and preferences entailed in social interaction, those "certain specific social, economic, political, and cultural forces" to which Sen alluded (see above). One need not deny society, however, to observe that strategic behavior may mitigate some of the effects of social interdependence, thereby reducing what consensus (however minimal) might previously have existed. I cannot, therefore, be so sanguine as Tullock (1967b) in labelling Arrow's General Impossibility Theorem as "generally irrelevant." A simple example makes this point. Suppose the preferences of the fifteen faculty members for candidates X, Y and Z are:

(5)	(5)	(5)
I	*II*	*III*
X	Y	Z
Y	Z	Y
Z	X	X

As Figure 1 shows, this preference configuration is single-peaked. The resulting social preference ordering, determined by pairwise comparisons and majority rule, is YZX, with Z defeating X, and Y defeating both Z and X, by 10–5 votes. Suppose, however, that the members of group III misrepresent their preferences in the vote on (X, Y), voting for X, even though Y is more preferred by them. Since Z can defeat X, and Y can defeat Z, the result is social intransitivity—ZXYZ. Moreover, if group III is able to control the order of voting, under some rules of procedure (those that

---

[33] See Rae (1967) for an empirical study of election laws in common use in the Western democracies. For a logical analysis of various election and committee procedures, including proportional representation and rule by special majority, see Black (1958, chaps. 10–12). For an interesting debate on the plurality voting rule (in which the Independence of Irrelevant Alternatives condition and the notion of "sophisticated voting" are intimately involved) see the exchanges between Casstevens (1968, 1971) and Kramer (1968, 1971).

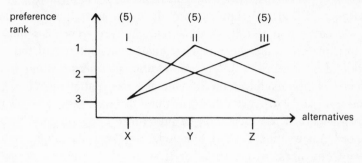

Figure 1

do not require "round robin" voting) Z may emerge as the social choice. Thus, despite single-peakedness, *expressed* social preferences may be subject to manipulation and, at any rate, may fail to be transitive. This is likely to be an especially severe problem in *committee* decision-making where small perturbations in expressed preferences will often have significant impact on collective outcomes (see Niemi and Weisberg, 1972a).

Misrepresentation of preferences is one aspect of a larger and more profound issue that has been subtly neglected in most general theories of social choice (however, see Majumdar, 1956). The motivating question of most social choice analyses is: what set of institutions and processes succeed in reflecting the preferences of individuals, fairly and equitably, in collective choices? Typically, however, the only "data" on individual preferences available to be processed by social institutions is *that which the individual chooses to reveal*, either in actual choices or in response to questions put to him. And revealed preferences may differ rather substantially from "actual" preferences. The divergence in revealed and actual preferences is especially pronounced when the objects of choice are public goods (see Olson, 1965 and Buchanan, 1968). In these instances it may be possible for an individual to consume large amounts of public goods, such as unpolluted air, without actually revealing a preference for them, thereby receiving a "cheap ride" if not a "free ride." A science of institutional design must tackle problems of revealed preference, and this appears to be a central unresolved difficulty of rational choice models.

The conditions that guarantee an SWF in majority rule provide important insights about the role of consensus, varyingly defined, in determining just and unconfused social preferences. A broader strategic overview is required, however, to get a handle on how decision rules actually operate. In this sense, the contributions of Farquharson (1969) and Kramer (1973) on "sophisticated" behavior are of especial importance. Moreover, a more fully cardinal notion of preference is required in order to explain certain phenomena regularly encountered in the actual operation of decision rules. In a word, additional *structure* is required.

A social choice model of recent vintage—the spatial model of party competition—adds structural detail in three distinct ways. First, it relies on a mathematical representation of preference more detailed than the binary ordering relation. Second, it includes topological assumptions about the set of outcomes. In particular, it is assumed that outcomes may be represented as points in an n-dimensional Euclidean space. Third, this class of models posits behavioral rules, thus distinguishing different sets of actors and making the underlying motivational basis for choice explicit. The central focus of the "broader strategic overview" of these models is the concept of equilibrium.

One final observation about these models should be made. They are models of *political* choice in which elements reflecting the "peculiarities" of political decision structures are consciously included. Thus, though they may lack the broad generality of models of social choice à la Arrow, they probably will better serve us as scientific models of political decision-making.

A POSITIVE THEORY OF SOCIAL CHOICE: SPATIAL MODELS

Spatial representations of social conflict and choice have been around for a long time. Axelrod (1970, pp. 146–147), and others before him, have pointed to the organization of the French National Assembly of 1789 as the historical referent for such representations:

> In 1789, when the French National Assembly convened, the nobles still retained sufficient respect to be given places of honor to the right of the president. The radicals took seats in the amphitheater as far away from the nobles as they could, placing themselves on the left. The moderates found themselves occupying the remaining seats in the center. Thus began the now familiar political dimension of left—center—right.

The landmark formal study of this spatial configuration as the structure within which political conflict and competition take place is, of course,

Anthony Downs's *An Economic Theory of Democracy* (1957).[34] The primary emphasis in Downs's initial treatment is on elections as devices by which democratic societies make social choices. Thus it is, in effect, a model of representative democracy.

In the Downsian model there are two categories of actors, citizens, and candidates for office. Each is assumed to behave rationally in the sense of possessing and acting upon well-defined, consistent goals. To the Downsian citizen the public sector is simply a source of goods and services, entailing both costs and benefits. He is assumed to have preferences about the different ways the collective weal (and its coercive potential) is distributed and used. He is cognizant of the effects of governmental activities on his well-being and thus has preferences for some bundles of collective choices as compared to others. He coordinates his political behavior with his political preferences in the sense that he decides whether or not to vote and for whom (as well as whether or not to engage in other forms of political activity) on the basis of his preferences. More specifically, the citizens of Downs's democratic polity are utility maximizers, assigning utilities to the various collective outcomes and choosing behaviors appropriate to the maximization of (expected) utility. In most instances this involves only deciding conditionally for whom to vote and then whether or not to vote at all, since the vote is the most widely distributed of political resources and typically is the *only* political resource for most citizens.

The candidates of Downs's polity are office-seekers. A candidate's electoral behavior is determined solely by its anticipated effect on the decisions of voters and of potential and actual competitors for office. "Politicians in our model are motivated by the desire for power, prestige, and income . . . their primary objective is to be elected" (1957, p. 30). A candidate may have policy preferences, but they are of marginal importance compared to his election goal. "Politicians . . . never seek office as a means of carrying out particular policies; their only goal is to reap the rewards of holding office, *per se*" (1957, p. 28).

Social choices emerge from a process of competition in which candidates are pitted against one another in a contest for the votes of the citizenry. The theoretical links between the choices of candidates, on the one

---

[34] Downs borrowed heavily, however, from some of his predecessors in economics, most notably Hotelling (1929) and Smithies (1941). Also it should be noted that Downs's study was initiated as a doctoral dissertation under Kenneth Arrow.

hand, and those of citizens, on the other, are the policy space and the voter distribution. The former is characterized well by Stokes (1963, p. 368):

> The root idea of Downs's model is that the alternatives of government action on which political controversy is focused can be located in a one-dimensional space, along a left-right scale. At least for illustration, Downs interprets this dimension as the degree of government intervention in the economy. . . . Each voter can be located on the scale according to how much government control he wants and each party [candidate] according to how much government control it [he] advocates.

Thus candidates compete for the people's vote, in true Schumpeterian form, by announcing their policy intentions, while citizens vote (or abstain) according to their evaluations of those announced intentions. Downs's conceptualization of electoral competition is *spatial* in the sense that a (one-dimensional) policy space, on which voters have well-defined preferences represented as single-peaked, von Neumann-Morgenstern utility functions, and appropriately correlated behaviors, provides the battleground for elections. Candidates locate themselves at distinct points in this space, intent upon winning, with an eye toward those "appropriately correlated behaviors" of voters. The relevant electoral parameter for them is the distribution of voter preferences in the space. The model, in effect, is a choice calculus both for candidates and voters.

Within this spatial framework Downs sought to identify "optimal" candidate behavior and "equilibrium" contingencies. A candidate's choice is *optimal* if, given his goals and the choices of his competitors, he has no incentive to change his choice. A competitive contingency is said to be in *equilibrium* if all competitors choose optimally. Since equilibrium requires that all candidates choose optimally (or, in game theoretic language, play optimal strategies), it will fail to emerge either if optimal courses of action do not exist, or, when they do, if they are not selected by some of the candidates. The latter possibility constitutes a violation of the principle of rational behavior and thus falls beyond the purview of a purportedly rational-choice model, so that the only threat to the emergence of equilibrium is the absence of optimal strategies.[35]

___

[35] I have said little about the distinction between irrational behavior and error. The former has been referred to earlier simply as random behavior. Erroneous behavior in the pursuit of goals, on the other hand, may not constitute irrational behavior; rather, it indicates an inappropriate or incorrect perception of means-ends relationships. Thus

Downs's spatial model, then, may be viewed as an attempt to identify electoral contingencies that yield nonempty sets of optimal strategies, and, hence, *equilibrium*.

To digress for a moment, it is important to observe an important strand of continuity relating the social choice analyses reviewed in the last two sections to spatial analyses. Optimal strategies will fail to materialize in the event that the preference configuration of the electorate generates cyclical majorities. If the electorate prefers policy X to policy Y, policy Y to policy Z, and policy Z to policy X, then no electoral strategy is optimal since a candidate can be defeated no matter which policy he announces. In such instances one might well witness near random maneuvering by the candidates. Thus the search for equilibrium contingencies in spatial analyses of elections is directly parallel to the search for the conditions necessary and/or sufficient to avoid the implications of Arrow's Impossibility Theorem.

Downs's principal result follows from the defining properties of a single-peaked preference configuration. For two-party systems, he shows that if voters have single-peaked utility functions and if everyone votes, then vote-maximizing (plurality maximizing) candidates will converge in their spatial position to the most-preferred point of the median voter. He further demonstrates (though not formally) that if abstention is allowed, or if more than two candidates compete, or if extremist voters choose to be future oriented (an example of "sophisticated" voting behavior), then the median of the distribution of voter most-preferred points may not be optimal for any candidate.

Downs's spatial analysis (1957, esp. chap. 8) is, of course, considerably more detailed and sophisticated than my brief summary statements indicate and must be read in its entirety to be appreciated. However, in a number of respects (and this is said with a good deal of hindsight working for me) the Downsian formulation is restrictive, and in some instances his analysis is wrong.

Part of the difficulty with Downs's *Economic Theory* follows from the theoretical language he settled on. Although his reliance on logic and deductive reasoning is novel for political science of the late 1950s, he de-

---

it is entirely possible for optimal strategies to exist but fail to be selected because of error in choice-making as well as irrationality. Error, however, is pretty tricky to handle without introducing a whole host of subsidiary propositions, e.g., assumptions about information collection and analysis, so it is ordinarily not treated in models of electoral competition. Empirical considerations will require that more attention be given to the information collecting and processing capabilities of political actors.

pends primarily upon English sentences to carry his argument. The resulting simple style makes for good reading, but occasionally leads to ambiguous argument and logical difficulties (I allude to some specific cases below). The style of Downs's discourse, then, has been a mixed blessing and has motivated much of the work following in its wake to rely on a more careful specification of concepts and valid use of deductive methods.

A second troublesome feature of Downs's model of electoral competition is its limited treatment or obvious omission of relevant aspects of the phenomena in question. Downs, for example, reifies a group—the political party—and treats it as a unified entity by assuming that it is, in effect, a *team* of activists with identical preferences. He thus successfully avoids the charge of false personification, but at the same time begs the rather interesting issue of intra-party conflict and its consequences. The simplification effected in Downs's treatment ignores the deviant behavior of the candidate whose official career depends on an electorate different from those of his party colleagues. This observation "underscores the limits to the empirical usefulness of models that assume that party leaders always act in common. . . . An awareness that party leaders (i.e. politicians) act for private motives ought to prompt an extension of models of rational behavior" (Schoenberger, 1969, pp. 520–521). Theoretical work addressed expressly to this issue as it manifests itself in primary elections and party conventions is found in Aranson and Ordeshook (1972), Brams (1973), Coleman (1971, 1972), and Davis and Hinich (1966, 1967) and is examined below.

Likewise, the whole set of issues involving participation, though acknowledged and informally treated, was not formalized by Downs. Riker and Ordeshook (1968) have shown (and McKelvey and Ordeshook, 1971, in more general form) that the decision to participate, as well as the form and direction of that participation, can be conceptualized in choice-theoretic terms. And Ordeshook (1969, 1970) and Hinich and Ordeshook (1969, 1970, 1971) have argued theoretically that participation (abstention) rates may depend in part on candidate behavior, and that the former may alter or entirely prevent equilibrium situations.

A third general area in which Downs covered much ground intuitively, but did not initiate a more formal treatment, is that of uncertainty. The political world is often inherently uncertain and at times is purposely made so by self-interested actors (see Shepsle, 1970, 1971, 1972a, 1972b). Uncertainty, whether its source is the Machiavellian ploys of clever politicians who campaign with ambiguous rhetoric or simply the data-deficient decisions of cautious candidates afraid to go out on a limb, is in need of formal conceptualization and treatment in theories of electoral choice (see Shepsle, 1972b).

Perhaps the weakest link in the Downsian analysis of electoral competition is, ironically, its spatial formulation. Downs's analysis focused on a *one-dimensional* policy space which simultaneously serves as an outcome set for voters and a strategy set for competing candidates. The implicitly ideological attributes of this dimension upset even the earliest critics of spatial modeling (see Stokes, 1963 and Converse, 1966 for excellent early treatments) who visualize a much more complex political world. Although Downs often alluded to the "packaging" of party platforms and the possibility of sets of "intense minorities" cooperating in such endeavors (1957, pp. 55–60), he never resolves the tension between these possibilities on the one hand and the unidimensional character of political conflict on the other.

Beginning with Davis and Hinich's seminal paper (1966), a number of scholars have addressed themselves to a more fully multidimensional basis for spatial competition. Since the multidimensional representation permits the treatment of other of Downs's omissions, I devote the remainder of this section to the massive reconceptualization of Downs's original analysis during the last several years.[36]

The general spatial model of electoral competition has, as its central feature, a multidimensional strategy space. The axes or dimensions of this space represent alternative criteria on which candidates are judged and voters express preferences. Some of these dimensions are truly spatial in the sense that they may be approximated by continuously variable parameters, e.g. dollars to be spent on primary and secondary education. Other of the dimensions are "lumpy"—what may be referred to as "valence issues." These are ordinarily not continuously variable and often are more resistant to strategic manipulation by candidates. Examples include the

---

[36] The researchers on this subject are extremely prolific, so a bibliographic note is appropriate before we begin. Three papers by Davis and Hinich (1966, 1967, 1968) initiated the search for electoral equilibria in a multidimensional policy space. In this context, abstention was first given serious formal treatment by Ordeshook (1969) and Garvey (1966). There then transpired an elaborate collaboration among Davis, Hinich and Ordeshook (1970), much of whose work is summarized in Riker and Ordeshook (1972, chaps. 11 and 12). For a summary of the most recent developments in this line of inquiry, see Hinich, Ledyard, and Ordeshook (1972, 1973).

party labels of the candidates and their personalities. Although most electoral situations involve dimensions of both sort, it is theoretically more manageable to restrict explicitly spatial analysis to those dimensions represented by continuous variables. Within this framework valance issues are introduced as biases in the choice calculus of voters and candidates.

Initially, then, the electoral space is represented by an n-dimensional Euclidean vector space, where n is any arbitrary integer denoting the number of continuously variable dimensions. Citizens (not necessarily voters) are "distributed" in this space according to their preferences on each of the spatial dimensions. Each citizen is represented by a point or vector in the space, $x^c = [x_1{}^c, x_2{}^c, \ldots, x_n{}^c]$, where $x_i{}^c$ is the most-preferred position of the cth citizen on the ith dimension. The distribution of citizen most-preferred points is the n-dimensional analogue of Downs's voter distribution. Candidates for office are represented in a similar fashion. Each candidate is identified by a vector $\theta^j = [\theta_1{}^j, \theta_2{}^j, \ldots, \theta_n{}^j]$, where $\theta_i{}^j$ corresponds to the position or perceived intention of the jth candidate on the ith issue dimension.

It is convenient, in reconstructing the multidimensional spatial model, to focus on four classes of assumptions: rules for citizen evaluation of candidates, rules of citizen participation, assumptions about the distribution of citizen preferences, and assumptions about candidate objectives. I treat each of these in turn, although an occasional overlap is unavoidable. My reconstruction closely follows the excellent treatment given in Riker and Ordeshook (1972, chaps. 11 and 12).

CITIZEN EVALUATIONS

The citizen's choice calculus is characterized by two distinct, but not independent, decisions. He must decide (conditionally) for whom to vote, if he votes at all; and then he must decide whether to cast a vote or to abstain. In order to deal with the first decision problem, we require some means of depicting the citizen's comparisons and evaluations of the candidates. Such means are provided, at a highly abstract level, by a general utility function whose arguments are the citizen's most preferred point, x^c, and the candidate's vector of intentions, θ^j. This is written as $u(x^c, \theta^j)$. A tautological consequence of this formulation—tautological because it is a defining characteristic of utility and (nonsophisticated) rational behavior—is that the citizen casts his vote for candidate j rather than j' (if he votes at all) if and only if θ^j is preferred to $\theta^{j'}$, i.e., if and only if $u(x^c, \theta^j) > u(x^c, \theta^{j'})$.[37]

Very little more can be said about voter choice without supplementing the general utility function with more specific properties. One such property, a rather mild one, evokes little controversy:

$$u(x^c, \theta^j) \text{ attains a maximum if and only if } \theta^j = x^c.$$

To posit equality between two vectors is to require equality in each of the respective components of the vectors. Thus, $\theta^j = x^c$ means that $\theta_i^j = x_i^c$ for all i.

This property might appropriately be called the *assumption of unimodality* for, as I have indicated, it restricts $u(x^c, \theta^j)$ to the family of functions in Euclidean n-space which possess unique global maximums. It is strikingly similar (though not identical) to the assumption of single peakedness. Although this is a relatively weak restriction on the more general form of the utility function, it is not without consequences. First, it restricts consideration to that family of functions that possesses maximum points, and within that family to functions having a unique global maximum. Second, it requires that all n-dimensions be salient for each voter, although it still allows considerable variations in salience among the dimensions.

Unfortunately, the class of unimodal utility functions is still not sufficiently restrictive to yield interesting deductions about electoral contingencies. At this point, a dilemma, not unusual in theoretical work, is encountered. On the one hand (or is it horn?), in the absence of empirical guidance on the properties of citizen utility functions, the appropriately cautious course to follow entails making few assumptions about those functions, and even then restricting oneself to those properties that have strong intuitive justification (as in the unimodality property). The result of following this course, however, is a paucity of theoretical deductions: a Spartan diet of assumptions yields precious few theoretical consequences of interest. On the other hand, the introduction of additional restrictions on $u(x^c, \theta^j)$, while providing a richer theoretical base from which to deduce consequences, may, on balance, be no more than a mean-

[37] For elections in which only two candidates compete, this consequence is consistent with sophisticated behavior as well. It is in multicandidate elections that sophisticated behavior may dictate casting a vote for a less-preferred, but presumably more viable, candidate. On this point, see the Casstevens-Kramer exchanges (1968, 1971). For the remainder of this essay, our concern will be with two-candidate elections.

ingless academic exercise. That is, the deductions that follow from the postulated properties, while logically true, may bear little resemblance to the empirical phenomena they purportedly explain.

The practical solution to this dilemma is, at first glance, a masochistic one, for it requires the investigator (to continue the metaphor) to impale himself, alternately, on one horn and then the other! Yet this procedure is not as perverse as it appears and, in fact, closely resembles the procedure of alternating between postulated and observed preference which I discussed in an earlier section of this essay. In the earlier papers by Davis and Hinich (1966, 1967, 1968), a very restrictive functional form was assumed for $u(x^c, \theta^j)$. Specifically, $u(x^c, \theta^j)$ was assumed to obey the equation for a version of the quadratic form:

$$u(x^c, \theta^j) = \lambda - (x^c - \theta^j)' A (x^c - \theta^j).$$

The utility for c of candidate j, $u(x^c, \theta^j)$, is at a maximum when $x^c = \theta^j$, and diminishes according to a quadratic loss rule as x^c and θ^j become increasingly disparate.[38] Combining the quadratic utility rule with a citizen participation rule (all citizens vote), a candidate motivational hypothesis (each candidate seeks a θ^j that is dominant, i.e., is a winning electoral strategy), and an assumption about the distribution of citizen preferred points in the space (the density of preferred points is normally distributed), Davis and Hinich prove (1966, pp. 182–185) that the vector of means[39] is an equilibrium electoral strategy.

Although we have gotten ahead of the story a little bit, the point I wish to make here is that a very significant theorem (a generalization of Downs's "convergence to the median" result of unidimensional spatial analysis) was proved on the basis of a rather restrictive assumption about the set of $u(x^c, \theta^j)$. Having proved this theorem, however, one is in a position to determine which of the features of quadratic utility functions were exploited to establish the result, and, by elimination, which features were extraneous. A process of generalization thus proceeds. That is, having been gored on the horn of highly restrictive assumptions, one struggles toward

[38] In this expression $(x^c - \theta^j)'$ is a $1 \times n$ vector, A is an $n \times n$ positive definite weighting (salience) matrix, and $(x^c - \theta^j)$ is an $n \times 1$ vector. According to the rules of matrix multiplication, the product of these three entities is a scalar which, upon subtraction from λ, yields $u(x^c, \theta^j)$. In their original formulation, Davis and Hinich represented the citizen's evaluation by a *loss function*, rather than a utility function. The former is simply the additive inverse of the latter (displaced perhaps by a constant) and the two representations are equivalent.

[39] The vector of means, $\delta = [\bar{x}_1, \bar{x}_2, \ldots, \bar{x}_n]$, is the vector whose i^{th} component, $\bar{x}_i$, is the mean of the ith component of all citizen's most-preferred vectors.

the horn of generalized forms, in the process hoping to establish results bearing on a host of empirical phenomena.

For the purposes of their analysis, Davis and Hinich (1966, 1967, 1968, 1972), and later Davis, Hinich and Ordeshook (1970) examined three alternative assumptions about $u(x^c, \theta^j)$, representing differing degrees of generality:

A1: $u(x^c, \theta^j)$ is concave

A2: $u(x^c, \theta^j)$ is represented by the quadratic form

A3: $u(x^c, \theta^j)$ is a monotonic function of the quadratic form
(quasi-concave)[40]

With A1, A2, or A3, one of the elements of the citizen choice calculus is specified: $u(x^c, \theta^j)$ allows the citizen to compare the alternative candidates and their intentions vis-a-vis his own preferences. To have political relevance, however, the citizen must *express* his evaluations by participating in some form. The forms of participation are many and varied and, ordinarily, are characterized by the expenditure of political resources. The most important of these resources at the citizen's disposal is the vote. While other resources, e.g. time, particular skills (especially in the tasks of organization and persuasion), money, and access, have productive uses, "the vote merits attention because it is one of the most widely distributed of all political resources, because all decisions in a democratic form of government rest ultimately on votes, and because it is perhaps the major mechanism for translating popular preferences into governmental decisions" (Keech, 1968, p. 3). To date spatial models have concentrated on voting as the means by which citizens express (or choose not to express) their evaluations.

CITIZEN PARTICIPATION

Perhaps the simplest rule to posit for citizen participation is one of universal activity:

B1: All citizens vote.

---

[40] A1 is a highly general class of functions; A2 is a considerably restrictive special case of A1; and A3 is somewhat more general, although the three are not quite comparable in terms of generality. This collection of assumptions concentrates on one aspect of the shape of $u(x^c, \theta^j)$. Other aspects, e.g. symmetry, have played a role in spatial analysis, too. However, I am following Riker and Ordeshook's (1972, chaps. 11 and 12) reconstruction of developments in the literature of spatial models for which it is convenient to concentrate exclusively on A1–A3 above.

In some democracies this rule has legal sanction, and, because of its analytical simplicity, B1 was employed in the initial work of Davis and Hinich. However, as the common lore of politics tells us, turnout is a crucial feature of electoral competition, having important consequences for the ultimate outcome—hence the large expenditures by candidates, parties, and interest groups on registration and canvassing activities (see Kramer, 1966, 1970, for a formal model of canvassing activities). Thus, a theory of voting participation is required.

The theoretical foundations of voter participation are provided by Riker and Ordeshook (1968) and further generalized by McKelvey and Ordeshook (1971). Assuming for the moment that, if a citizen votes, he votes for his most-preferred candidate, the utility of participation through voting is given by the following equation:

$$R = P\, B(\theta^j, \theta^{j\prime}) + D(\theta^j, \theta^{j\prime}) - C$$

where

R   is the citizen's expected utility of voting for his
       most-preferred candidate,

P   is the probability that his vote affects the final
       electoral outcome,

B   is the net benefit of having his most-preferred
       candidate win election,

D   is the utility of participation derived independent of the comparative evaluation of the candidates,

C   is the cost of voting.

In choosing from his action set $A = \{a_0, a_1\}$, where a_0 indicates abstention and a_1 indicates voting for his preferred candidate, the citizen acts as if he follows the dictates of the above equation: if R is positive he chooses a_1; if it is negative or zero he chooses a_0.

Notice that the B-term and the D-term in the expression for R are functions of candidate strategies. It is not unreasonable to assume that, *ceteris paribus*, the likelihood of citizen participation diminishes as θ^j and $\theta^{j\prime}$ approach one another, for in this event the citizen becomes increasingly *indifferent* about the final outcome. That is, the net benefit, B, of electing one's most-preferred candidate tends to zero where B is defined as $u(x^c, \theta^j) - u(x^c, \theta^{j\prime})$. Alternatively, it may be supposed that as both θ^j and $\theta^{j\prime}$ become increasingly distant from x^c, the likelihood of the *alienated* voter's participation will tend to diminish, even if he perceives some difference between the candidates. That is, even if $B > 0$, the alienated voter may well choose to stay at home. In this interpretation it is assumed that D is a decreasing function of the utility derived from the citizen's most-preferred candidate.

The following alternatives to assumption B1 (universal participation) are suggested:

B2: Citizens abstain because of indifference
B3: Citizens abstain because of alienation

The reader should note that abstention, whether from indifference or alienation, has been conceptualized in probabilistic terms (I have used the word "likelihood" quite intentionally in the above discussion). In an electorate composed of many citizens, it is of little consequence either for candidate calculations or electoral equilibrium whether citizen Jones votes or abstains. What is of consequence (again assuming a large citizenry) is the *participation rate of large collections of citizens* with preferences like Mr. Jones's. Thus, for theoretical purposes, a probabilistic representation of participation is sufficient.

THE PREFERENCE DISTRIBUTION OF THE ELECTORATE

The initial characterization of citizen preferences has been qualified, so far, in two distinct ways. At the outset a citizen's preference was represented by his most-preferred point, $x^c = (x_1^c, x_2^c, \ldots, x_n^c)$. Then additional structure, in the form of capabilities to compare alternative points in the space in terms of the citizen's x^c, was added via A1-A3. Finally, in B1-B3, a probabilistic representation of preference expression was introduced. What is needed to complete a description of the electorate is an *aggregate* representation of their preferences. After all, it is the aggregate of citizens which the candidate faces and appeals to for electoral support.

For this last task of description, the multidimensional spatial model incorporates an n-dimensional generalization of Downs's *voter distribution*. As was the case with the form of preference comparison and the manner of participation, alternative constructions of the voter distribution, of varying generality, may be posited. Assuming at the most fundamental level that the collection of citizen preferences is representable in a common electoral space, the simplest formalization of the electoral distribution, $f(x)$, is as a relative frequency function. That is, like a probability density, $f(x)$ is a function defined on the n-dimensional space that gives, for each point $x = (x_1, x_2, \ldots, x_n)$, the proportion of citizens with that as their most-preferred point:

C1: $f(x)$ is a density function.

Though quite general, C1 often suffices to prove results relevant to questions of electoral equilibrium, as we shall see below. In other respects, however, it is useful to assume specific properties for $f(x)$:

C2: $f(x)$ is a symmetric unimodal density function.

C3: $f(x)$ is a symmetric bimodal density function.

Property C2 applies to those electorates in which citizen-preferred points cluster around a single mode with points increasingly distant from that mode arising with diminishing frequency. The bell-shaped (or normal) distribution illustrates this feature. The unimodality characteristic reflects, in a sense, a consensual arrangement with electoral preferences focused about some central point. The symmetry characteristic restricts this representation of consensus considerably, but is included for the analytical simplicity it affords. Hopefully this latter feature will be relaxed in the future, thereby permitting a rather general characterization of consensus.

Property C3, in contrast to C2, reflects polarization in the electorate. Voter preferences cluster about two distinct points in this case. Again, though the bimodality characteristic may be taken as a general representation of conflict or dissension, the symmetry modifier circumscribes this generality rather severely.

With various combinations of A1-A3, B1-B3, and C1-C3, we have a very rich set of electoral structures. Were this analysis to proceed in the manner of the social choice literature reviewed in discussing Arrow's mathematical politics, then the question to motivate analysis would be: which point $x = (x_1, x_2, \ldots, x_n)$ should be taken as reflective of social preferences? Or alternatively: what preference ordering R_S or utility function u_S accurately reflects the preferences of the collection of citizens? While these kinds of questions are of importance, especially if one wishes to assess the fairness or representative character of alternative preference aggregation rules, a more positive analysis seeks to identify the policy vector that actually is chosen as a consequence of the choices of goal-seeking actors. The three sets of assumptions above provide a description of the citizen's choice calculus and the electorate's preference map. To complete the description of an election as a positive theory of social choice, the goals or motives of candidates seeking office must be specified.

CANDIDATE GOALS

While candidates run for office for a variety of reasons—some rather general and thus common to all candidates, others more idiosyncratic—it is assumed here that the primary motive for entering an electoral fray is to win election. Candidates, therefore, manipulate their choice variables, i.e., choose their electoral strategies, with an eye to ultimate electoral consequences. Since voters prepare evaluations and decide whether to participate on the basis of their own preferences on the one hand, and their perceptions of candidate intentions on the other, and since it is assumed (at least in the short run of the electoral campaign) that voter preferences are fixed, the candidate's strategic choice amounts to selecting a spatial position (reflective of his policy intentions), $\theta^j = (\theta_1{}^j, \theta_2{}^j, \ldots, \theta_n{}^j)$, and, perhaps altering his "image" on non-spatial, valence issues. Depending upon the rule of citizen participation (B1-B3), the choice of θ^j affects citizen evaluations, citizen participation probabilities, and, in the event that citizens abstain both for reasons of indifference and of alienation (B4), biases in participation probabilities.

In order to determine the basis on which candidates choose their respective θ^j's, it is necessary to specify more precisely the candidate goal of "winning." In the work to date in spatial modeling, two alternative statements of candidate objectives have been entertained:

> D1: Candidates maximize plurality.
>
> D2: Candidates maximize votes.[41]

With universal participation and two-candidate elections, D1 and D2 are equivalent. That is, in maximizing his votes a candidate is simultaneously maximizing his plurality as well. Under alternative participation rules, however, D1 and D2 may well lead to different results. In most democratic systems, D1 is probably a more accurate description of candidate motives than D2 since winning ordinarily requires that one simply get more votes than his opponent. However, D2 provides some comparative bases and, as Riker and Ordeshook point out, may provide a foundation for the analysis of multiparty proportional representation systems (where vote maximization is a more reasonable characterization of candidate goals). In addition, if the focus of analysis should shift from votes as the objective of optimal choice to a consideration of more generalized

[41] Aranson, Hinich, and Ordeshook (1972) examine six alternative formulations of candidate objectives in an attempt to ascertain general conditions in which these objectives are strategically equivalent.

resources (e.g., money, endorsements) then the maximization paradigm as stated in D2 may be an appropriate formulation.

This completes the statement of the structure of spatial models. To summarize, a spatial model of electoral choice is characterized by an n-dimensional issue space in which voter preferences are distributed and candidate intentions are located. Voter preferences and intentions are specified by A1-A3 and B1-B4, respectively. Collectively, their preferences are represented by a density function f(x), alternative formulations of which are provided by C1-C3. Finally, candidate choices are based on the motivation to win as specified by D1 or D2. This collection of assumptions generates seventy-two alternative models.[42] We turn now to an examination of some implications of this rich structure.

EQUILIBRIUM AND CONVERGENCE

Although a number of different questions are entertained in the context of one or another of the spatial models, the issue of equilibrium has occupied a central place in such analyses. This is not surprising in two respects. In the first place, the development and refinement of spatial models of electoral choice are closely related to the development of general theories of social choice as initiated in the work of Kenneth Arrow and Duncan Black. The chief concern of these latter attempts, as I have indicated in earlier sections, revolves around the search for equilibrium, i.e., a search for the conditions which insure that a social choice process is an SWF or an SDF, thereby avoiding the disequilibrium of voting paradoxes.[43] Thus, it is quite natural for spatial modelers to concentrate on that same hoary intellectual problem that has troubled theories of social choice generally.

In the second place, spatial models are offered to us as *positive* theories of electoral choice. They seek to provide "best" ways for actors to behave,

[42] Since some of the assumptions are special cases of others, the seventy-two models are not independently generated.

[43] A paper by Plott (1967) is something of a bridge between the social choice literature reviewed earlier and n-dimensional spatial models. Plott presented an n-dimensional generalization of the social choice problem, seeking to provide the necessary and sufficient conditions for rational social choice when the objects of choice are n-dimensional vectors. He demonstrated that the distribution of preferences of individuals in the society must satisfy rather extreme symmetry conditions in order to insure rational social choice. Plott's results, as well as those of others, are reviewed and analyzed in Kramer (1969). Also see note 44.

given their preferences and goals. Theoretically determined optimal behavior then serves as a prediction of actual behavior. The sense of "best" or "optimal" behavior is game-theoretic in nature: an individual choice is optimal if it secures for the individual a more-preferred outcome than any other choice he might make, given that other actors are behaving optimally vis-a-vis their own preferences. A collection of individual optimal choices defines *equilibrium*—no single actor has any incentive to behave differently. Thus, the search for equilibrium in spatial models of electoral choice is equivalent to a search for sets of optimal individual choices.

In its most recent formulation as a spatial model (see Hinich, Ledyard and Ordeshook, 1973), the process of electoral choice is framed as a noncooperative, two-person game defined on the n-dimensional issue space. The players of the game are the two candidates for office, whose "strategy" sets are the points (vectors) in the issue space. Voters, in this conceptualization, are *not* players in the game. Rather, their choice behavior (the result of individual maximization calculation) defines the payoff functions of the candidates. In this view, the search for equilibrium entails seeking answers to two questions:

1. Do vectors θ^A and θ^B exist such that θ^A is optimal when candidate B chooses optimally, and θ^B is optimal when candidate A chooses optimally? That is, does a strategy pair (θ^A, θ^B) exist that satisfies the definition of a Nash equilibrium?

2. If the answer to (1) is yes, then what are the properties of equilibrium pairs? For example, is $\theta^A = \theta^B$ (do the two candidates converge in strategy choice)? Is the mean (median) of the voter distribution $f(x)$ an optimal strategy for either or both of the candidates? Is the equilibrium pair (θ^A, θ^B) unique?

Having casually introduced the game-theoretic formulation, let me, before presenting some of the theorems of spatial models, sum up the noncooperative aspects of the electoral game:

1. *players:* the players of this game are the candidates for office, A and B.

2. *strategy sets:* each player chooses a point in the n-dimensional issue space. Candidate A's strategy is written as $\theta^A = [\theta_1{}^A, \theta_2{}^A, \ldots, \theta_n{}^A]$; B's strategy is $\theta^B = [\theta_1{}^B, \theta_2{}^B, \ldots, \theta_n{}^B]$. The strategy component $\theta_i{}^j$, then, is the position taken by the jth candidate (where j = A or j = B) on the ith issue (where i = 1, 2, \ldots, n).

3. *outcomes:* for each pair of strategy choices (θ^A, θ^B), an electoral outcome is determined. An outcome is an ordered pair (v_A, v_B), where v_A is the number of votes for candidate A, and v_B the number of votes for candidate B.

4. *determination of outcomes:* the outcome (v_A, v_B) is a function of candidate strategy selection: (v_A v_B) = M (θ^A, θ^B). The function M (the outcome function) may be alternatively formulated, depending upon the manner of comparative evaluation of candidates by voters (A1, A2, or A3), the probability that voters express their evaluations (B1, B2, B3, or B4), and the distribution of voter preferences (C1, C2, or C3).

5. *Criteria motivating candidate strategy selection:* candidates are assumed to have preferences over the set of outcomes (v_A, v_B). The manner in which preferences over outcomes are ordered is determined by D1 or D2. With D1, for example, candidate A prefers (v_A, v_B)$_1$ to (v_A, v_B)$_2$ if ($v_A - v_B$)$_1$ > ($v_A - v_B$)$_2$. Candidate B prefers the former to the latter if the inequality is reversed. With D2, on the other hand, outcome 1 is preferred to outcome 2 by A if (v_A)$_1$ > (v_A)$_2$, and is preferred by B if (v_B)$_1$ > (v_B)$_2$.

For a particular form of M (as determined by picking an assumption from A1-A3, from B1-B4, and from C1-C3), and a particular motivational criterion (either D1 or D2), it is of interest to determine whether optimal courses of action are available to the candidates.

At present only thirty of the seventy-two logical possibilities have been investigated, although results have been conjectured for twenty-six additional cases. In each of these cases the search for equilibrium is the motivating focus of the analysis. Four classes of solutions are isolated (Riker and Ordeshook (1972, chap. 12):

(i) in general no equilibrium exists,

(ii) an equilibrium exists such that the candidates converge but the point of convergence cannot be generally specified,

(iii) an equilibrium exists such that the candidates converge to the median or mean of f(x),

(iv) an equilibrium exists but the candidates may or may not converge—depending on the saliency of the issues.

The results are summarized in a table by Riker and Ordeshook:

		A₁				A₂				A₃			
		B_1	B_2	B_3	B_4	B_1	B_2	B_3	B_4	B_1	B_2	B_3	B_4
C_1	D_1	i	i^a	i^a	ii	i	i^a	i^a	ii	i	i^a	i^a	
	D_2	i^a	i^a	i^a	ii			ii					
C_2	D_1	i^a	i^a	i^a	iii	iii	iii	iii	iii	iii	iii	iii	iii^a
	D_2	i^a	i^a	i^a	ii	iii		iv	ii	iii		iv	
C_3	D_1	i^a	i^a	i^a	iii	iii	iii	iv^a	iii	iii		iv^a	
	D_2	i^a	i^a	i^a	ii	iii		iv^a	ii	iii		iv^a	

a: conjecture.

William H. Riker and Peter C. Ordeshook, AN INTRODUCTION TO POSITIVE POLITICAL THEORY, © 1972, p. 343, Prentice-Hall, Inc., Englewood Cliffs, N.J.

I do not propose to discuss each of these results in turn, since significant mathematical disgressions would be necessary. The reader may consult Riker and Ordeshook (1972, chap. 12), Davis, Hinich, and Ordeshook (1970), and Hinich, Ledyard, and Ordeshook (1973) for detailed summaries. Several comments, however, are in order. First, it should be noted that for a significant number of cases there is no equilibrium. The bulk of these instances (many of them conjectured) occur when A1 (the overly general assumption that individual utility functions are concave) is posited or when candidates are plurality maximizers and everyone votes (C1 and D1). In essence, this asserts that for every vector "played" by A, B has a non-equilibrium response. That is, B's "best" response induces A to change his vector, which in turn induces B to change again, . . . , *ad infinitum*. The process terminates at some arbitrary (θ^A, θ^B) when the campaign period ends at election day.

Perhaps the most nonobvious of the results in this category is the simple generalization of Duncan Black and Anthony Downs. As the first cell of the table (A1-B1-C1-D1) indicates, whereas the median of $f(x)$ is an equilibrium point in the unidimensional case, *there is, in general, no equilibrium for the multidimensional case*. This may be seen, with the aid of a diagram, in the case of two issues. In the figure shown the preferred points of three voters are identified (I, II, and III). Associated with each preferred point is a set of indifference contours represented, in this diagram, as segments of circles whose origins are the respective most-preferred points. Points on the same contour are of equal utility to the individual, while points on contours closer to his preferred point are strictly preferred by him to those on more distant contours. Thus, voter I

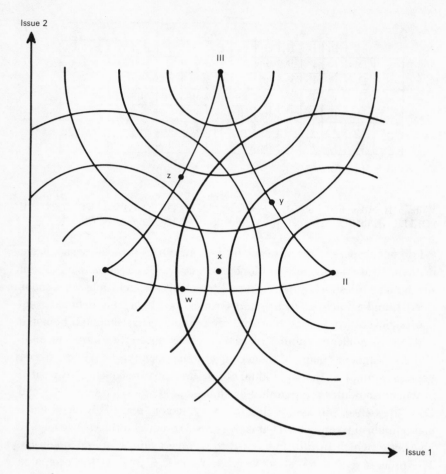

Figure 2

prefers W most, Z second, X third, and Y least. Voter II prefers Y first, X a close second, W third, and Z least. Finally, voter III prefers Z the most, Y second, X third, and W least. The lines joining the preferred points are the familiar contract loci of Edgeworth exchange models in economics. For any point on a contract locus, there exists no other point simultaneously more preferable for both of the players involved. Consider an arbitrary interior point X. By definition, there exist points on the contract locus of each pair of players preferred to X. The point Y, for example, is preferred by the coalition (II, III) to X. But the point Z falls on indifference contours for I and III closer to their respective preferred points. Hence Z is preferred by (I, III) to Y. However, by the same reasoning,

W is preferred by (I, II) to Z. And again by the same reasoning, X is preferred by (II, III) to W. Thus we have X preferred to W, which is preferred to Z, which is preferred to Y, which is preferred to X—a cyclical majority. In fact, only under highly restrictive symmetry conditions will this disequilibrium be avoided.[44]

Riker and Ordeshook have identified the contingencies in which there is generally no equilibrium as precisely those in which a "coalition of minorities" strategy is often employed. Oppenheimer (1971) has independently proven that a "coalition of minorities" strategy defeats the vector of means if and only if there is collective intransitivity, in which case the "coalition of minorities" strategy is not dominant either. From this it may be inferred that instances of widespread logrolling and vote trading, i.e., instances of coalitions of minorities, are inherently unstable; the outcomes in such situations are as much a consequence of institutional design as of preference patterns. (On "the paradox of logrolling"— that everyone may be less well off after logrolling than before it—see Riker, 1972.)

Where the assumption about the form of citizen evaluations is "strengthened" (A2 or A3), it is seen that equilibrium is far more prevalent, though convergence need not always occur and the point of equilibrium is not always determinate. With this category, convergence to the mean of $f(x)$ is the most prevalent outcome.

The array of theoretical deductions summarized in the table is, at the same time, impressive and disconcerting. The impressiveness of the theoretical structure is reinforced by the wide variety of uses to which it has been put. A simple, partial listing makes this point. Research on matters of substance in which an n-dimensional, spatial perspective is employed includes:

1. the "responsible parties" doctrine (Ordeshook, 1970; Riker and Ordeshook, 1972, chap. 12),

2. multiparty systems and coalition formation (Rosenthal, 1968a, b; Rosenthal and Sen, 1969, 1973; Axelrod, 1970),

3. alternative electoral systems (Aranson, 1971),

[44] This is precisely the theorem proved by Plott (1967). An equilibrium, if it exists, is a preferred point of one of the citizens. This point is an equilibrium point (for odd n) if and only if, for some partition of the remaining n-1 citizens into pairs, the contract loci of all of these pairs of citizens intersect at the preferred point of the nth citizen. Thus, a rather severe symmetry condition is both necessary and sufficient for equilibrium in the contingency described by A1-B1-C1-D1.

4. multistage elections (Aranson and Ordeshook, 1972; Coleman, 1971, 1972),

5. the effects of uncertainty (Shepsle, 1971, 1972a, b),

6. strategically-constrained competition (in which candidates face spatial or non-spatial constraints in their choice of electoral strategy) (Davis and Hinich, 1972; Shepsle, 1972b; Hinich, Ledyard, and Ordeshook, 1972, 1973),

7. the effects of competition from extremist candidates (Hinich and Ordeshook, 1969; Riker and Ordeshook 1972, chap. 12),

8. the effects on equilibrium of variations in the saliency of issues and the cost of voting (Hinich and Ordeshook, 1970; Riker and Ordeshook, 1972, chap. 12),

9. the consequences of multiple candidate objectives—the effect of a joint-maximization-of-electoral-resources strategy selection rule. (Riker and Ordeshook, 1972, chap. 12),

10. the welfare consequences of alternative spatial arrangements (Davis, DeGroot, and Hinich, 1972; Ordeshook, 1971; Kramer, 1969; Plott, 1971a; Shubik, 1970; Hinich and Ordeshook, 1971b; Davis and Hinich, 1966).

Suffice it to say that even in its infancy, the spatial model is sufficiently rich to permit widespread use in analyzing a whole host of substantive political phenomena.

It is precisely this richness, however, that is disconcerting as well as stimulating. The apparently wide net of the spatial model renders attempts at empirical verification especially illusive. For example, in their discussion of combinations of assumptions for which the theory predicts that candidates converge to the mean or median of $f(x)$, as discussed previously, Riker and Ordeshook write:

Candidates and parties, nevertheless, do differ significantly on many issues. Should these differences be interpreted as a refutation of the results we are discussing? Obviously, the validity of the theory can be reasserted by attributing the failure of candidates to adopt similar policies in real campaigns to the violation of the assumptions of the model, such as imperfect information or spatial mobility. Or, again, it may be said in excuse that a candidate can find it necessary to advocate policies off the mean in order to win the nomination of his party, and later find himself committed to these policies in the cam-

paign. Or, it may be said that candidates possess ideological preju-
dices which they may be unwilling or unable to forego. Finally, it
may be said simply that candidates err. These attempts to resolve an
apparent disparity between theory and empirical evidence, nevertheless, are not entirely necessary: Conditions can be found in spatial
analysis for which the candidates should provide distinct alternatives (1972, chap. 12).

My concern here is with the task of verification. It is not at all clear what
constitutes disconfirming evidence inasmuch as "conditions can be found
in spatial analysis" to remedy any disparity between theoretical prediction and observation. In the absence of empirical guidance as to which
of the many possible spatial models is appropriate for any given circumstance, verification and prediction both become a pretty tricky business.

One should not be unduly concerned about the initial difficulties involved in linking theory and empirical circumstance, however, since this
linkage has not received much serious attention yet. Initial empirical
research by Jackson (1972), Page and Brody (1972), Rabinowitz (1972),
Rosenthal and Sen (1973), Weisberg and Rusk (1970), and Rusk and
Weisberg (1971) suggest that alternative spatial models may serve
usefully to guide inquiry about the substance of politics. I should add,
however, that many empirical problems have yet to be resolved, and their
resolution will be no mean feat.

In the next section, I briefly examine some additional features of collective decision-making which might usefully be nested in a social choice
analysis. Some of these features have been given limited attention by
spatial modelers, and others have all but been ignored.

INSTITUTIONAL COMPLEXITIES

Throughout this essay, with only minor exception, I have examined
theories of collective choice in which the central component is the individual preference ordering. The simple, if naive, "syllogism" underlying
most of these theories is that individual behavior is determined by individual preferences, that collective outcomes are aggregations of individual
choices (behaviors), and hence that collective choices are determined by
individual preferences and rules of aggregation. The rules of aggregation
incorporated in analyses have typically been simple voting procedures
whose functions are the *weighting* of expressed preferences and the *deter-*
mination of winners and losers, i.e., outcomes, as a consequence of the

aggregated preferences. Rules, however, are complex entities; as well as aggregating preferences, they often affect the form in which preferences are *expressed,* if not their substance. And, after all, it is *expressed* preferences (or the anticipation of expressed preferences) that "really" determine collective choices.

A simple illustration of the effect of rules on *expressed* preferences was provided in the text pertaining to Figure I. There, it will be recalled, I showed that, despite single-peakedness, expressed preferences might well produce collective intransitivity. If one group misrepresents its preferences—and it has every incentive to do so—then the single-peakedness that characterizes the collectivity's (unexpressed) preferences fails to guarantee an "unconfused" result. That is, the simple, nonround robin, majority rule determines the collective choice by affecting the *form* in which preferences are expressed as well as by aggregating individual preferences, once expressed.

The problem of preference expression in institutional settings should not be underestimated. It has hounded economic analysis for years and poses a severe challenge to students of public policy and institutional processes. As I argued earlier in this essay, in institutional settings, as well as in abstract instances like the one illustrated above, it is surprisingly difficult to devise processes which elicit sincere expressions of preference from the actors involved. As a result it is often perplexing to infer preferences from behavior in actual decision-making settings. I have already alluded to the purposeful misrepresentation of preferences in sequential decision processes. To that may be added:

1. The problems encountered as a result of logrolling when several issues are simultaneously decided (see Oppenheimer, 1971; Riker, 1972; and Tullock, 1970b, for illustrations).

2. The problem of preference inference in simultaneous-choice settings. This is especially relevant in elections where issues are "packaged" in candidates and the latter are the objects of choice. Recent empirical interest in "Issue Voting" has, unfortunately, failed to deal with this matter adequately (see, for example, Boyd, 1972; Pomper, 1972; Kessel, 1972; and Brody and Page, 1972).

3. The understating of demand for public goods (see Buchanan, 1968; Frohlich, Oppenheimer, and Young, 1971; Olson, 1965; and Tullock, 1970a).

Farquharson (1969) has begun the analysis of the properties of institutions that encourage sincere expressions of preference. His study stands as a major contribution, though only a beginning, to the solution of this thorny set of problems. Kramer (1973) has employed some of Farquharson's results in his examination of the implications of different forms of preference expression for electoral equilibrium.

A second source of complication due to rules follows from the fact that rules confer roles and statuses on individuals. I use the terms "role" and "status" in a strategic, rather than in a sociological or psychological, sense. Roles and/or statuses constrain or expand an individual's behavioral alternatives. In the language of game theory, the "rules of the game" determine or specify the strategy sets available to each of the players.

The effect of rules on strategy sets is illustrated in simple economic models of exchange (see Shapley and Shubik, 1968). Consider a simple three persons—two commodity economy and an initial allocation of stocks of these commodities among the members. If trade is allowed among the members, and exchange in completely voluntary and unconstrained, then under certain conditions a competitive trading equilibrium obtains, where the latter is a final allocation of the stock of commodities which no group of two or more individuals jointly has any incentive to alter by voluntary trade. If, however, the rules had expressly prohibited *direct* trade between two of the players, the resulting equilibrium (if one exists) may well be different. In effect, the rules confer a monopoly status on the third player, permitting him, on the one hand, to serve as middleman in *indirect* trades between the two players and, on the other, to exploit his role as monopoly middleman (see Becker, 1971, 1972).[45]

Having observed that, in the abstract, rules not only define the stra-

---

[45] A variation on this theme is found in Luce's notion of *psi-stability* (see Luce and Raiffa, 1957, chap. 10). Luce argues that equilibrium in game situations may result (or fail to result) because of "social friction"—that underlying boundary limitations on communication and coalition formation, as well as preferences, may affect the existence of equilibrium. A game is said to be psi-stable if the only alterations in a given coalition structure that are "profitable" to the initiators of the alteration are infeasible alterations proscribed by the rules of coalition transformation. For example, a new coalition between the Communist party and one of the non-Gaullist parties of the right in France might be electorally "profitable," but is sociologically or ideologically infeasible. Indeed, coalitions with the Communist party, for many years in France, were explicitly denounced by all parties, despite the possibility of short-run electoral gain. If coalitions with the Communists were the only profitable alterations in a given coalition structure, then, because it is contrary to the rules of allowable coalition formation, the given coalition structure is psi-stable.

tegic context in which preferences are expressed, weighted, and aggregated, but also influence the form and substance of expressed preferences by laying sophisticated strategic possibilities bare and by determining roles and hence strategy sets, I find it useful to argue the same point about real-world, institutional processes as well. To take one example, consider institutions such as primaries and conventions—a complex of rules by which political parties nominate candidates. As Davis and Hinich have demonstrated (1966), a multi-stage collective choice process—in this instance a contest for nomination and then a general election—may possess optimal strategies for players at each stage, but the optimal strategy of the victorious player at one stage may be positively harmful for him at later stages. If "social friction" compels a victorious player at one stage to stick pretty much to his winning strategy in all subsequent stages, i.e., if strategic mobility is precluded, then he may well be constrained from behaving as he "should," if final victory is his goal. The voter distribution that a potential party nominee faces in his quest for the nomination differs markedly from the voter distribution he faces in the general election. Optimal behavior in the former, though necessary to qualify for the later stage, may thus preclude optimal behavior in the latter.

A second illustration of the effect of institutions on social choices falls under the rubric of "intergovernmental relations." The behavior of elected officials may be determined in part by their desire to win elections, but their goal-seeking behavior typically involves coordinating the behaviors of many individuals for whom the biennial or quadrennial bout with the electorate is less compelling or restraining. Chief among this latter group is the army of bureaucrats that mans the executive agencies. And, Niskanen (1971) suggests, the motives of individual bureaucrats are often at odds with the preferences of the citizens and their elected officials. Additionally, executive bureaucracies (and judicial institutions), often acting as advocates of particular points-of-view, contribute to the formulation of the agenda from which collective choices are made (on the role of gate-keeping, see for example, Cobb and Elder, 1972; Schattschneider, 1960; and Bachrach and Baratz, 1962, 1963).

What will emerge, I suspect, from an examination of the impact of rules and institutions on the definition of the collective agenda, on the specification of strategic alternatives and constraints, on the expression of preferences, and on the weighting and aggregating of expressed preferences, is a theoretical maze. The machinery of deductive logic, employed in most of the social choice theories discussed in this essay, may not serve well to uncover theoretical relationships. However, all need not be lost. The laws of motion were not repealed the first time an engineer became interested in the complex aerodynamics of a particular airplane wing design. When formal physical theory was insufficient, the engineer supplemented it by wind-tunnel experiments. In a similar vein, the social choice theorist will, in all likelihood, require computer simulations to supplement his deductive models when a richness of institutional detail is desired. (Needless to say, these observations hold a *fortiori* when dynamic dimensions are added.)

SOME CONCLUDING REMARKS

Two bodies of literature that have been completely ignored in this essay, despite their deserved inclusion in any definition of theories of collective choice, require some brief mention. The first is the theory of political coalitions and, more generally, the theory of n-person games. The reader is referred, of course, to Volume Four of the *Political Science Annual*, and especially to the lead essay by Brams (1973). Additionally, the classic work by Riker (1962), the essay by Rosenthal (1968a), and the collection of essays edited by Groennings, Kelley, and Leiserson (1970) provide some initial reading on the subject of coalition formation and its various applications.[46] On n-person games, the reader may consult the original formulation in von Neumann and Morgenstern (1964), the "standard" treatment in Luce and Raiffa (1957), and a readable elementary treatment by Rapoport (1970). Theories of bargaining are examined by Cross (1969) and Coddington (1968).

The second topic generally ignored in this essay is identified with the title of the widely cited book by Olson (1965): *The Logic of Collective Action*. This book, as well as others in a growing literature in political science (e.g., Olson and Zeckhauser, 1968; Frohlich and Oppenheimer, 1971; Frohlich, Oppenheimer, and Young 1971; Tullock, 1970a, b), deals with the congeries of problems varyingly called the problem of collective goods, the externality problem, or the free-rider problem. Within its purview falls a number of theoretical concerns related to the scope and appropriateness of collective institutions bound to raise the reader's ideological hackles. Since it is inappropriate to tackle so broad a set of con-

---

[46] A bibliography entitled "An Abbreviated Guide to the Literature on Theories of Conflict, Bargaining and Strategy with Special Emphasis on the Theory of Games and Its Relevance to the Study of Politics (and Other Sundry Topics)," covering literature through 1971, is available on request from the author.

cerns in summary fashion, I simply refer the reader to the above citations, to which I add Riker and Ordeshook (1972, chap. 10) where careful attention is given to many of the inherently political aspects of conflict over collective goods.

I conclude with a story, attributed to the economist George Stigler (and cited in Niskanen, 1971), known as the parable of the opera singers. Two opera singers, competing for a prize, were auditioned by a panel of judges. After hearing the first singer's performance, the judges unanimously awarded the prize to the second. The point of the parable is that "experts" often make choices among alternatives without really knowing or understanding the "operating characteristics" of the alternatives they choose. The aim of the theories of collective choice discussed in this essay is to understand and explain how collectivities go about determining their courses of action—to explicate the "operating characteristics" of alternative collective arrangements. A major thesis of the theories found in the preceding sections is that collective choices appear to be a direct consequence of rational goal-seeking by individuals in institutional settings. At this point in the development of these theories, it is fair to say that they have convincingly laid bare the complexities of the many problems involved in collective choice. Social choice theorists have also begun to integrate the many strands of theory that now exist. But the real task that still lies ahead involves coming to grips with reality. Hopefully, social choice theorists will begin to muster the intellectual energy to direct their theories toward the data of the everyday political world.

APPENDIX: RECENT ADVANCES IN CHOICE THEORY

In the body of this essay, I have chosen to present what might be called the "traditional view" of social choice and rationality. This view in economics grew up during the 1940s and 1950s and is associated with such names as Arrow, Blau, Inada, Vickrey, Black, Rothenberg, and others. More recently, however, an alternative conceptualization has been advanced by Fishburn, Hansson, Parks, Plott, Richter, and Wilson, to name a few. Their conceptualization differs from the traditional view in the way in which rationality is characterized and the manner problems of social choice are posed. These differences are the topic of this brief appendix.[47]

[47] Here I rely heavily on the excellent presentations by Plott (1971a, b, c, d) as well as on a detailed personal communication from him.

Early economic theory conceived of rational behavior as that which is compatible with some numerical representation of preferences. Thus, for the individual, rational behavior is characterized by the maximization of a utility function. Similarly, social rationality is exhibited in collective choices that maximize a social welfare function or benefit-cost ratio.

The key phrase here is "numerical representation" for, as I observed earlier in the text, there are at least three reasons why one might wish to relax or alter completely this particular specification of rational behavior. First, it is not always possible to provide a numerical representation. That is, some preferences, perfectly good in other respects, are simply not representable by a numerical function (see Debreu, 1954, and Richter, 1971, and their example of lexicographic preferences). Second, the numerical properties of preferences may well be superfluous for cogent explanation. Choice behavior is often given adequate account with an ordinal representation of preferences. Arrow, for example, represents individual preferences by *weak orders* (what Richter, 1971, calls a "regular relation")—complete, reflexive, transitive binary relations—rather than by numerical functions. Third, the object of representation—preferences —may be inappropriate. Whereas preferences are metaphysical, existing in people's heads perhaps, *choices* are observable. Indeed, except by assumption and introspection (see Plott, 1971b, note 12), our only knowledge of preferences is that which is *revealed* by choice behavior. Thus, the object of formal representation, whatever its mathematical form, probably should be choices rather than preferences.

The first two reasons above are, by this time, relatively uncontroversial. Although there are issues, such as matters of equitable distribution, the role of intensity of preference, etc., and circumstances, such as uncertainty, that still are problematic in the ordinal framework, the "ordinal revolution" is an accomplished and widely accepted fact. The third reason, however, is somewhat more controversial. In the remainder of this appendix I present in abbreviated form a framework for the study of collective decision-making that focuses on choice rather than on preference.

Some notation is needed before proceeding. Let S be the set of all social alternatives (or social states) and let $V = (v_1, v_2, \ldots, v_m)$ be a family of subsets of S, *i.e.*, for all i, $v_i \subseteq S$. Following Plott (1971a), V is called the *admissable agenda*. It serves as part of the domain of a social choice process in that it provides the collection of possible sets from which society must choose. A *society* is characterized by a vector of R_k-orderings $r = (R_1, R_2, \ldots, R_n)$, and the collection of *admissable societies* (the set of admissable r's) is labeled $\overline{R}$.[48] Finally, the process of social choice is represented by a *choice function* $C(v_i, r_j)$ whose domain is the elements $(v_i, r_j) \epsilon V \times \overline{R}$. The choice function is well-defined in two senses:

$$(1) \quad C(v_i, r_j) \neq \phi; \text{ and}$$
$$(2) \quad C(v_i, r_j) \subseteq v_i.$$

The first requires *decisive choice*—a chosen (set of) element(s) is always produced by the social choice process. The second requires *nonperverse* choice—the (set of) chosen element(s) is always from among the particular agenda of alternatives available (also note that the choice need not be a single element). The 4-tuple $[V, S, \overline{R}, C(v_i, r_j)]$ is referred to as a *constitution* (Arrow, 1971; Plott, 1971a), a *choice* (Richter, 1966, 1971), or a *choice structure* (Hansson, 1968b).

For a given constitution yielding decisive choices it is natural to focus on the properties of the choice process so constituted. In particular, one asks: Is it possible to constitute a collective choice process, with domain $V \times \overline{R}$, possessing properties A, B, C, . . . ? The obvious advantage of this approach is its direct emphasis on the evaluation of *social process*, an emphasis which leaves behind controversial (but in this view irrelevant) issues about the status of the "choosing agent," etc.

The first property of social process to be examined is rationality, itself. Here more recent choice theories distinguish themselves from the traditional idea of social rationality. A social process (read: a choice function) is *rational* if the elements chosen by this process can be viewed as "best" elements according to *some* binary "preference" relation. In particular, the binary relation R *rationalizes* $C(. , r)$ if, for all $v_i \epsilon V$, $C(v_i, r) = \{x \epsilon v_i / \text{for all } y \epsilon v_i, x \text{ R } y\}$. That this notion of social rationality differs from Arrow's is emphasized in the following remarks by Plott:

> A choice function is *rational* in case it can be *rationalized*. If a binary relation exists such that the chosen elements can *always* be viewed as the maximal elements, according to this binary relation, then the choice function is rational. Notice first that the concept of rational

[48] Two points need to be made here. First, in this formulation an individual is represented by a preference *ordering*. In light of Richter's work (1966, 1971), this representation may be relaxed, and individual rational behavior may be characterized by a much weaker binary relation than an ordering. Second, the set $\overline{R}$ of "admissable" societies may well include all conceivable societies. Some social choice processes, however, may only work in certain kinds of societies; or, alternatively, for some classes of societies specific kinds of social choice processes are possible. For example, if $\overline{R}$ contains only societies in which individual preferences are *single-peaked*, we know from the results of Black (1958) that an Arrowian process can be constituted.

refers to a *sequence* of choices—to the behavior of the choice function over part of its domain rather than its behavior at a single point. Notice also that the "chooser" need not be "purposeful" or "cognitive." In fact, a given choice function, if rational, may be rationalized by several different binary relations simultaneously. *Furthermore, a choice function may be rationalized by a binary relation which does not have the "usual" properties of "preference relations."* [emphasis added] . . . A social choice function is said to be rational in case, for given and fixed individual preferences, it chooses from the various agenda *as if* it used a binary relation, R, as a "criterion" and chose the "best" (R-maximal elements) accordingly (1971d, pp. 7–8).

Social choices are rational, then, if they may be rationalized by any binary relation. The binary relation need *not* be transitive (as in Arrow's Axiom II) and "society" need not be conceived of as a choosing agent, cognitive and purposeful, possessing preferences. This conception of rationality stands in stark contrast to the "consistent goal-seeking" notion discussed in the text above. Rationality, in the choice-theoretic sense, is simply a technical attribute of a process.

Perhaps the most surprising aspect of Plott's observation is the fact that rationality and transitivity are distinct properties of a process. Thus, one need not insist upon transitivity, which is often objectionable on other grounds, in order to characterize a process as rational. Consider the following illustration (Plott, 1971d, p. 9): Let $S = \{a, b, c\}$, $V = [v_1, v_2, v_3, v_4] = [\{a, b\}, \{a, c\}, \{b, c\}, \{a, b, c\}]$, and, for some fixed set of preferences r, let $C(\ . \ , r)$ be defined as:

$$(1) \quad C(\{a, b\}, r) = \{a, b\}$$
$$(2) \quad C(\{a, c\}, r) = \{a\}$$
$$(3) \quad C(\{b, c\}, r) = \{b, c\}$$
$$(4) \quad C(\{a, b, c\}, r) = \{a, b\}$$

From (1) we have a I b (*i.e.*, a R b and b R a); from (2) we have a P c; from (3) we have b I c; and from (4) we have a R b and a R c—since a is maximal—and b R a and b R c—since b is maximal. The rationalization a I b, b I c, a P c induces the choices given in (1)-(4) so that $C(\ . \ , r)$ is rational. *But notice that the rationalization fails to be transitive* (specifically, the equivalence part of the relation, I, is intransitive).

With this weaker notion of rationality in hand one may inquire about the (logical) possibility of constituting rational social choice processes that possess additional "desirable" properties. Notice that the nature of the question that motivated Arrow's work has changed. No longer is one concerned with finding processes consistent with a social *ordering* of alternatives. As Plott has observed, "One may argue that the concept of 'social preference' should play a *secondary role* in the analysis. Rather than one of determining 'social preference,' *the problem is one of designing processes for which the choice, C(v), has 'nice' features.* [Transitive] rationality properties may result from other restrictions but these other restrictions contain the properties which are to be appraised and not [transitive] rationality itself [emphasis added]" (1971c, p. 6).

It is perhaps best to begin by asking why Arrow required a *transitive* rationalization (Axiom II in this essay) in the first place.[49] Several philosophical justifications are provided in the previous section on Arrow and in Arrow (1963). The primary analytical justification is *independence of path:*

> . . . the choice [process] should have a type of "divide and conquer" property. One should be able to "split up" the alternatives into smaller sets, choose over each of these sets, collect the chosen elements, and choose over them. This done, he should be assured the outcome did not depend upon the arbitrary way he initially divided the alternatives for consideration (Plott, 1971c, p. 6).

Independence of path is one of those "nice" features a social process might have. Its presence assures a collectivity a great deal of institutional flexibility, for it allows decisions to be broken down into a number of sub-decisions thus encouraging efficiency and institutional specialization (as in a committee system). What it assures is "the independence of the final choice from the path to it" (Arrow, 1963, p. 120). Arrow believed that a transitive rationalization would insure independence of path. And, in fact, he is correct: A *sufficient* condition for independence of path is a transitive binary rationalization. But it is not necessary. Plott (1971c) proves this in Theorem 2, showing that "a choice function, C(.), can satisfy [independence of path] and have a total, reflexive rationalization without the relation being transitive."[50] Thus, if independence of path is a "desirable" criterion, it should be required directly; it is not necessary to assume a transitive social rationalization. The conclusion: "Without a solid motivation for requiring the existence of a social preference relation one feels little loss at dropping it" (Plott 1971b, pp. 28–29).

[49] This question is discussed in detail in Plott (1971d, pp. 23–30).

[50] Plott proves, however, that if, for all $v_i \epsilon$ V, $C(v_i, r)$ is a single element, then the Independence of Path condition implies a *transitive* rationalization (see 1971c, Theorem 5).

Perhaps we have moved too quickly in giving up on a social preference relation. A social preference relation assures (at least) two things:

1. independence of path; and
2. rationality (in the sense specified above).

We have just seen that a social preference relation is not necessary for (1), so we might as well assume (1) directly. But what about (2)? (2) is another "nice" property that one might wish to require of a social choice process. More specifically, if we give up on a social preference relation and assume (1) instead, does C(. , .) satisfy (2) as well? The answer is *no*. There are choice processes that satisfy independence of path but are irrational—not consistent with "any old" rationalization. It may be shown, however, that another property of processes, *extension,* together with (1), salvages (2).[51]

The property of *extension* (see Parks, 1971, and Plott, 1971c) requires that if some element in the agenda defeats all others in a series of binary comparisons, then it must be among the element(s) chosen from the entire set: A choice function satisfies extension if, for all $v_i \epsilon V$, $x \epsilon v_i$ and $x \epsilon C(\{x, y\})$ for all $y \epsilon v_i$ implies $x \epsilon C(v_i)$. Extension clearly rules out a plurality choice rule, for it may be the case that one alternative defeats all others in binary comparisons, but is not among the element(s) chosen from the entire set because it is not "most-preferred" by many voters. Plott shows that the properties of independence of path and extension are themselves independent conditions which jointly insure rational choice (in fact, they insure *quasi-transitive*[52] rational choice).

Let me summarize. The purpose of this appendix has been to illustrate two features of more recent theories of social choice. The first is a weaker conception of rationality than that propagated in the "traditional view." The second is the form taken by questions about consistent social choice. Rational choice, in this view, is choice compatible with *some* binary relation. Questions about consistent social choice are really questions about *the possibility of constituting social choice processes possessing (ethically) desirable properties (of which rationality is only one).* Here I have only discussed three such properties: rationality, independence of path, and extension. Others, such as independence of irrelevant alternatives,

[51] Notice that the research tactic remains that of positing desirable properties of choice processes (rather than postulating something like a social preference relation which raises a host of philosophical issues) and inquiring into their consistency.

[52] The binary relation R is quasi-transitive if its associated P-relation is transitive. Quasi-transitivity allows intransitive indifference.

neutrality, anonymity, Pareto optimality, are fully discussed in the literature, so I shall not dwell on them here. Nor shall I dwell on the theoretical consequences of this particular approach except to note that various possibility and impossibility results have been produced for a number of social choice domains, V X $\overline{\text{R}}$. Many of these results are collected in Plott (1971a) and will not be repeated here.

Hansson's message (1969b) is a suitable, though perhaps anti-climactic, conclusion to this appendix: "When one interprets the import of Arrow's result, one must remember that tentative group decision functions are ruled out not only by . . . explicitly mentioned conditions, but also by the way of posing the problem." By posing the problem in a significantly different form, recent choice theorists have arrived at some different answers than those offered by Arrow. The interested reader is urged to consult their work, namely: Fishburn (1970, b, c); Hansson (1968b, 1969a, b); Parks (1971); Plott (1971a, b, c, d, 1972); Richter (1966, 1971); and Wilson (1969, 1972a, b).

BIBLIOGRAPHY

ADAMS, ERNEST W. "Survey of Bernoullian Utility Theory," in Solomon, Herbert, ed., *Mathematical Thinking in the Measurement of Behavior*. Glencoe: Free Press, 1960, pp. 151–269.

ARANSON, PETER H. "Political Participation in Alternative Election Systems," paper presented at the Annual Meeting of the American Political Science Association, Chicago, 1971.

———, and ORDESHOOK, PETER C. "Spatial Strategies for Sequential Elections," in Niemi and Weisberg (1972).

———; HINICH, MELVIN J.; and ORDESHOOK, PETER C. "Election Goals and Strategies: Equivalent and Non-Equivalent Candidate Objectives," paper presented at the Annual Meeting of the American Political Science Association, Washington, D.C., 1972.

ARROW, KENNETH J. "Alternative Approaches to the Theory of Choice in Risk-Taking Situations," *Econometrica*, 19 (1951), pp. 404–437.

———. "Utilities, Attitudes, Choices: A Review Note," *Econometrica*, 26 (1958), pp. 1–23.

———. *Social Choice and Individual Values*. 2nd ed. New York: John Wiley, 1963. First published 1951.

———. "Public and Private Values," in Hook, Sidney, ed., *Human Values and Economic Policy*. New York: New York University Press, 1967, pp. 3–21.

———. "Control in Large Organizations," in Arrow, Kenneth J., ed., *Essays in the Theory of Risk-Bearing*. Chicago: Markham, 1971, pp. 220–239.

AUMANN, ROBERT. "A Survey of Cooperative Games Without Sidepayments," in Shubik, Martin, ed., *Essays in Mathematical Economics in Honor of Oskar Morgenstern*. Princeton: Princeton University Press, 1967, pp. 3–27.

AXELROD, ROBERT. *Conflict of Interest*. Chicago: Markham, 1970.

BACHRACH, PETER, and BARATZ, MORTON. "Two Faces of Power," *American Political Science Review*, LVI (1962), pp. 947–953.

———. "Decisions and Non-Decisions: An Analytical Framework," *American Political Science Review*, LVII (1963), pp. 632–642.

BADGER, WADE W. "Political Individualism, Positional Preference and Optimal Decision Rules," in Niemi and Weisberg (1972).

BAUMOL, WILLIAM J. *Welfare Economics and the Theory of State*. 2nd ed. Cambridge: Harvard University Press, 1965.

BECKER, GORDON M., and McCLINTOCK, CHARLES G. "Value: Behavioral Decision Theory," *Annual Review of Psychology*, 18 (1967), pp. 239–286.

BECKER, ROBERT A. "On a Theorem of Rader," unpublished paper, Washington University, 1971.

77

————. "Some Results on Three Person Indirect Exchange Games," unpublished paper, Washington University, 1972.

BLACK, DUNCAN. "On the Rationale of Group Decision-Making," *Journal of Political Economy*, 56 (1948), pp. 22–34.

————. *The Theory of Committee and Elections*. Cambridge: Cambridge University Press, 1958.

————. "On Arrow's Impossibility Theorem," *Journal of Law and Economics*, 12 (1969), pp. 227–248.

————, and NEWING, R. A. *Committee Decision with Complementary Valuation*. London: William Hodge, 1951.

BOWEN, BRUCE D. "Toward an Estimate of the Frequency of Occurrence of the Paradox of Voting in the U.S. Senate Roll Call Votes," in Niemi and Weisberg (1972).

BOWEN, HOWARD R. "The Interpretation of Voting in the Allocation of Economic Resources," *Quarterly Journal of Economics*, 58 (1943), pp. 27–48.

BOYD, RICHARD. "Popular Control of Public Policy: A Normal Vote Analysis of the 1968 Election," *American Political Science Review*, LXVI (1972), pp. 429–449.

————. "Rejoinder," *American Political Science Review*, LXVI (1972), pp. 468–470.

BRAMS, STEVEN J. "Positive Coalition Theory: The Relationship Between Postulated Goals and Derived Behavior," in Cotter, Cornelius P., *Political Science Annual, IV*. Indianapolis: Bobbs-Merrill, 1973.

BRODY, RICHARD A., and PAGE, BENJAMIN I. "Comment," *American Political Science Review*, LXVI (1972), pp. 450–458.

BUCHANAN, JAMES M. "An Individualistic Theory of Political Process," in Easton, David, ed., *Varieties of Political Theory*. Englewood Cliffs: Prentice-Hall, 1966, pp. 25–37.

————. *The Demand and Supply of Public Goods*. Chicago: Rand McNally, 1968.

————, and TULLOCK, GORDON. *The Calculus of Consent*. Ann Arbor: University of Michigan Press, 1962.

CAMPBELL, COLIN, and TULLOCK, GORDON. "A Measure of the Importance of Cyclical Majorities," *Economic Journal*, 75 (1965), pp. 853–857.

CAMPBELL, DONALD E. "Social Choice and Intensity of Preference," *Journal of Political Economy*, 81 (1973), pp. 211–218.

CASSTEVENS, THOMAS. "A Theorem on Voting," *American Political Science Review*, LXII (1968), pp. 205–208.

————. "Communication," *American Political Science Review*, LXV (1971), pp. 187–188.

CHAPMAN, DAVID E. "Models of the Working of a Two-Party Electoral System, I," in Tullock, Gordon, ed., *Papers on Non-Market Decision Making, III*. Charlottesville: Thomas Jefferson Center, 1967, pp. 19–39.

————. "Models of the Working of a Two-Party Electoral System, II," *Public Choice*, 5 (1968), pp. 19–38.

CHIPMAN, JOHN S. "The Foundations of Utility," *Econometrica*, 28 (1960), pp. 193–224.

COBB, ROGER W., and ELDER, CHARLES D. *Participation in American Politics: The Dynamics of Agenda-Building.* Boston: Allyn and Bacon, 1972.

CODDINGTON, ALAN. *Theories of the Bargaining Process.* Chicago: Aldine, 1968.

COLEMAN, JAMES S. "The Possibility of a Social Welfare Function," *American Economic Review,* 56 (1966), pp. 1105–1122.

————. "The Possibility of a Social Welfare Function: A Reply," *American Economic Review,* 57 (1967), pp. 1311–1317.

————. "The Positions of Political Parties in Elections," in Niemi and Weisberg (1972).

————. "Internal Processes Governing Party Positions in Elections," *Public Choice,* 11 (1971), pp. 35–60.

CONVERSE, PHILIP E. "The Problem of Party Distances in Models of Voting Change," in Jennings, Kent M., and Zeigler, Harmon L., eds., *The Electoral Process.* Englewood Cliffs: Prentice-Hall, 1966, pp. 175–207.

CROSS, JOHN G. *The Economics of Bargaining.* New York: Basic Books, 1969.

CURTIS, RICHARD B. "Decision Rules and Collective Values in Constitutional Choice," in Niemi and Weisberg (1972).

DAVIS, OTTO, and HINICH, MELVIN. "A Mathematical Model of Policy Formation in a Democratic Society," in Bernd, Joseph, ed., *Mathematical Applications in Political Science, II.* Dallas: Southern Methodist University Press, 1966, pp. 175–208.

————, and HINICH, MELVIN. "Some Results Related to a Mathematical Model of Policy Formation in a Democratic Society," in Bernd, Joseph, ed., *Mathematical Applications in Political Science, III.* Charlottesville: University Press of Virginia, 1967, pp. 14–38.

————, and HINICH, MELVIN. "On the Power and Importance of the Mean Preferences in a Mathematical Model of Democratic Choice," *Public Choice,* 5 (1968), pp. 59–72.

————, and HINICH, MELVIN. "Spatial Competition Under Constrained Choice," in Niemi and Weisberg (1972).

————; DEGROOT, MORRIS; and HINICH, MELVIN. "Social Preference Orderings and Majority Rule," *Econometrica,* 40 (1972).

————; HINICH, MELVIN; and ORDESHOOK, PETER C. "An Expository Development of a Mathematical Model of the Electoral Process," *American Political Science Review,* LXIV (1970), pp. 426–449.

DEBREU, GERALD. "Representation of a Preference Ordering by a Numerical Function," in Thrall, R. M., Coombs, C. H., and Davis, R., eds., *Decision Processes.* New York: John Wiley, 1954, pp. 159–165.

————. *Theory of Value: An Axiomatic Analysis of Economic Equilibrium.* New York: John Wiley, 1959.

DeMEYER, FRANK, and PLOTT, CHARLES R. "The Probability of a Cyclical Majority," *Econometrica,* 38 (1970), pp. 345–354.

DOWNS, ANTHONY. *An Economic Theory of Democracy.* New York: Harper-Row, 1957.

DUMMETT, MICHAEL, and FARQUHARSON, ROBIN. "Stability in Voting," *Econometrica,* 29 (1961), pp. 33–42.

EDWARDS, WARD. "The Theory of Decision Making," *Psychological Bulletin,* 51 (1954), pp. 380–417.

————. "Behavioral Decision Theory," *Annual Review of Psychology,* 12 (1961), pp. 473–498.

FARQUHARSON, ROBIN. *Theory of Voting.* New Haven: Yale University Press, 1969.

FIORINA, MORRIS. "Representatives and Their Constituencies: A Decision Theoretic Analysis," paper presented at the Annual Meeting of the Political Science Association, Washington, D.C., 1972.

FISHBURN, PETER C. "Utility Theory," *Management Science,* 14 (1968), pp. 335–378.

————. *Utility Theory for Decision Making.* New York: John Wiley, 1970a.

————. "Intransitive Individual Indifference and Transitive Majorities," *Econometrica,* 38 (1970b), pp. 482–489.

————. "The Irrationality of Transitivity in Social Choice," *Behavioral Science,* 15 (1970c), pp. 119–123.

————. "The Theory of Representative Majority Decision," *Econometrica,* 39 (1971a), pp. 273–285.

————. "Should Social Choice Be Based on Binary Comparisons?," *Journal of Mathematical Sociology,* 1 (1971b), pp. 133–142.

FRIEDMAN, MILTON. *Essays in Positive Economics.* Chicago: University of Chicago Press, 1953.

————. "Value Judgements in Economics," in Hook, Sidney, ed., *Human Values and Economic Policy.* New York: New York University Press, 1967, pp. 85–93.

FROHLICH, NORMAN, and OPPENHEIMER, JOE A. *An Entrepreneurial Theory of Politics.* Unpublished doctoral dissertation. Princeton, N.J.: Princeton University, 1971.

————; OPPENHEIMER, JOE A.; and YOUNG, ORAN R. *Political Leadership and Collective Goods.* Princeton: Princeton University Press, 1971.

GARMAN, MARK B. and KAMIEN, MORTON I. "The Paradox of Voting: Probability Calculations," *Behavioral Science,* 13 (1968), pp. 306–316.

GARVEY, GERALD. "The Theory of Party Equilibrium," *American Political Science Review,* LX (1966), pp. 29–39.

GLESER, LEON. "The Paradox of Voting: Some Probabilistic Results," *Public Choice,* 7 (1969), pp. 47–64.

GOLDBERG, ARTHUR S. "Social Determinism and Rationality as Bases of Party Identification," *American Political Science Review,* LXIII (1969), pp. 5–25.

GRAAF, J. DEV. *Theoretical Welfare Economics.* Cambridge: Cambridge University Press, 1957.

GROENNINGS, SVEN; KELLEY, E. W.; and LEISERSON, MICHAEL, eds. *The Study of Coalition Behavior.* New York: Holt, Rinehart, and Winston, 1970.

GROFMAN, BERNARD. "Some Notes on Voting Schemes and the Will of the Majority," *Public Choice,* 7 (1969), pp. 65–80.

HALMOS, PAUL R. *Naive Set Theory.* Princeton: Van Nostrand, 1960.

HANSON, NORWOOD RUSSELL. *Patterns of Discovery*. Cambridge: Cambridge University Press, 1958.

HANSSON, BENGT. "Fundamental Axioms for Preference Relations," *Synthese* 18 (1968a), pp. 423–442.

———. "Choice Structures and Preference Relations," *Synthese*, 18 (1968b), pp. 443–458.

———. "Group Preferences," *Econometrica*, 37 (1969a), pp. 50–54.

———. "Voting and Group Decision Functions," *Synthese*, 20 (1969b), pp. 526–537.

HARSANYI, JOHN C. "Rational-Choice Models of Political Behavior vs. Functionalist and Conformist Theories," *World Politics*, 21 (1969), pp. 513–538.

HILDRETH, CLIFFORD. "Alternative Conditions for Social Orderings," *Econometrica*, 21 (1953), pp. 81–94.

HINICH, MELVIN J., and ORDESHOOK, PETER C. "Abstentions and Equilibrium in the Electoral Process," *Public Choice*, 7 (1969), pp. 81–107.

———, and ORDESHOOK, PETER C. "Plurality Maximization vs. Vote Maximization: A Spatial Analysis with Variable Participation," *American Political Science Review*, LXIV (1970), pp. 772–791.

———, and ORDESHOOK, PETER C. "Transitive Social Preference and Majority Rule with Separable Probabilistic Choice Functions," mimeo, 1971a.

———, and ORDESHOOK, PETER C. "Social Welfare and Electoral Competition in Democratic Societies," *Public Choice*, 11 (1971b), pp. 73–88.

———; LEDYARD, JOHN O.; and ORDESHOOK, PETER C. "Nonvoting and the Existence of Equilibrium Under Majority Rule," *Journal of Economic Theory*, 3 (1972), pp. 143–153.

———; LEDYARD, JOHN O.; and ORDESHOOK, PETER C. "A Theory of Electoral Equilibrium: A Spatial Analysis Based on the Theory of Games," *Journal of Politics*. 35 (1973), pp. 154–193.

HOMANS, GEORGE C. *Social Behavior: Its Elementary Forms*. New York: Harcourt, Brace, & World, 1961.

HOTELLING, HAROLD. "Stability in Competition," *Economic Journal*, 39 (1929), pp. 41–57.

INADA, KEN-ICHI. "Alternative Incompatible Conditions for A Social Welfare Function," *Econometrica*, 23 (1955), pp. 396–399.

———. "A Note on the Simple Majority Decision Rule," *Econometrica*, 32 (1964), pp. 525–531.

———. "The Simple Majority Decision Rule," *Econometrica*, 37, (1969), pp. 490–506.

———. "Majority Rule and Rationality," *Journal of Economic Theory*, 2 (1970), pp. 27–40.

JACKSON, JOHN E. "The Importance of Issues and Issue Importance in Presidential Elections: A Test of the 'Rational Model,'" paper presented at the meetings of the Public Choice Society, Pittsburgh, 1972.

JEFFREY, RICHARD. *Formal Logic, Its Scope and Limits*. New York: McGraw-Hill, 1967.

KATZNER, DONALD W. *Static Demand Theory*. New York: Macmillan, 1970.

KEECH, WILLIAM. *The Impact of Negro Voting: The Role of the Vote in the Quest for Equality.* Chicago: Rand McNally, 1968.

KENDALL, WILLMORE, and CAREY, GEORGE W. "The 'Intensity' Problem and Democratic Theory," *American Political Science Review,* LXII (1968), pp. 5–24.

KESSEL, JOHN H. "Comment," *American Political Science Review,* LXVI (1972), pp. 459–465.

KLAHR, DAVID. "A Computer Simulation of the Paradox of Voting," *American Political Science Review,* LX (1966), pp. 384–390.

KRAMER, GERALD H. "A Decision Theoretic Analysis of a Problem in Political Campaigning," in Bernd, Joseph, ed., *Mathematical Application in Political Science, II.* Dallas: Southern Methodist University Press, 1966, pp. 137–160.

———. "Communication," *American Political Science Review,* LXII (1968), pp. 955–956.

———. "On a Class of Equilibrium Conditions for Majority Rule," Cowles Discussion Paper No. 284, 1969.

———. "The Effects of Precinct-Level Canvassing on Voter Behavior," *Public Opinion Quarterly,* 34 (1970), pp. 560–572.

———. "Communication," *American Political Science Review,* LXV (1971), pp. 188–189.

———. "Sophisticated Voting Over Multidimensional Choice Spaces," *Journal of Mathematical Sociology,* 3 (1973).

KRANTZ, DAVID H.; LUCE, DUNCAN R.; SUPPES, PATRICK; and TVERSKY, AMOS. *Foundations of Measurement.* New York: Academic Press, 1971.

KUHN, THOMAS S. *The Structure of Scientific Revolutions,* 2nd ed. Chicago: University of Chicago Press, 1970.

LAZARSFELD, PAUL F. "Notes on the History of Quantification in Sociology: Trends, Sources and Problems," in Woolf, Henry, ed., *Quantification.* Indianapolis: Bobbs-Merrill, 1961, pp. 147–203.

LITTLE, I. M. D. *A Critique of Welfare Economics.* Oxford: Clarendon Press, 1950.

LUCE, DUNCAN R., and RAIFFA, HOWARD. *Games and Decisions.* New York: John Wiley, 1957.

MACRAE, DUNCAN. "Preference and Welfare in Political Economy," paper presented at the Seminar on Mathematical Theory of Collective Decisions, Harbour Town, South Carolina, 1971.

MAJUMDAR, TAPAS. "Choice and Revealed Preference," *Econometrica,* 24 (1956), pp. 71–73.

MARSCHAK, JACOB. "Rational Behavior, Uncertain Prospects and Measurable Utility," *Econometrica,* 18 (1950), pp. 110–141.

McKELVEY, RICHARD D. *Some Extensions and Modifications of a Spatial Model of Party Competition.* Unpublished doctoral dissertation, University of Rochester, 1972a.

———. "Policy Related Voting and Its Effect on Electoral Equilibrium," paper presented at the Annual meeting of the Political Science Association, Washington, D. C., 1972b.

————, and ORDESHOOK, PETER C. "A General Theory of the Calculus of Voting," in Bernd, Joseph, ed., *Mathematical Applications in Political Science, VI.* Charlottesville: University Press of Virginia, 1971.

MUELLER, DENNIS C. "The Possibility of a Social Welfare Function: Comment," *American Economic Review,* 57 (1967), pp. 1304–1311.

MURAKAMI, YASUSUKE. *Logic and Social Choice.* New York: Dover, 1968.

VON NEUMANN, JOHN, and MORGENSTERN, OSCAR. *Theory of Games and Economic Behavior,* Science ed. New York: John Wiley, 1964. First published 1944.

NIEMI, RICHARD G. "Majority Decision-Making With Imperfect Agreement on Norms," *American Political Science Review,* LXIII (1969), pp. 488–497.

————. "The Occurrence of the Paradox of Voting in University Elections," *Public Choice,* 8 (1970), pp. 91–100.

————, and WEISBERG, HERBERT F. "A Mathematical Model for the Probability of the Paradox of Voting," *Behavioral Science,* 13 (1968), pp. 317–323.

————, and WEISBERG, HERBERT F. "The Effects of Group Size on Collective Decision Making," in Niemi and Weisberg (1972).

————, and WEISBERG, HERBERT F., eds. *Probability Models of Collective Decision Making.* Columbus: Charles Merrill, 1972.

NISKANEN, WILLIAM A. *Bureaucracy and Representative Government.* Chicago: Aldine-Atherton, 1971.

OLSON, MANCUR. *The Logic of Collective Action: Public Goods and the Theory of Groups.* Cambridge: Harvard University Press, 1965.

————, and ZECKHAUSER, RICHARD. "An Economic Theory of Alliances," in Russett, Bruce M., ed., *Economic Theories of International Politics.* Chicago: Markham, 1968.

OPPENHEIMER, JOE D. "Relating Coalitions of Minorities to the Voters' Paradox or, Putting the Fly in the Democratic Pie," mimeo, University of Texas, 1971.

ORDESHOOK, PETER C. *Theory of the Electoral Process.* Doctoral dissertation, University of Rochester, 1969.

————. "Extensions to a Mathematical Model of the Electoral Process and Implications for the Theory of Responsible Parties," *Midwest Journal of Political Science,* 14 (1970), pp. 43–70.

————. "Pareto Optimality in Electoral Competition," *American Political Science Review,* LXIV (1971), pp. 1141–1145.

OSTROM, ELINOR, and OSTROM, VINCENT. "Public Choice: A Different Approach to the Study of Public Administration," *Public Administration Review,* 31 (1971), pp. 203–216.

PAGE, BENJAMIN I., and BRODY, RICHARD A. "Policy Voting and the Electoral Process: The Vietnam War Issue, "*American Political Science Review,* LXVI (1972), pp. 979–996.

PARK, R. E. "The Possibility of a Social Welfare Function: Comment," *American Economic Review,* 57 (1967), pp. 1300–1304.

PARKS, ROBERT P. "Rational Choice, Extending Choice, and Choice Paths," paper presented at the Seminar on Mathematical Theory of Collective Decisions, Harbour Town, South Carolina, 1971.

PATTANAIK, PRASANTA K. *Voting and Collective Choice*. Cambridge: University Press, 1971.

PLOTT, CHARLES R. "A Notion of Equilibrium and Its Possibility Under Majority Rule," *American Economic Review*, 57 (1967), pp. 787–806.

———. "Recent Results in the Theory of Voting," in Intrilligator, Michael, ed., *Research Frontiers in Quantitative Economics*. Amsterdam: North Holland Publishing Company, 1971a, pp. 109–129.

———. "The Relevance of Social Choice Theory to Models of Economic Policy," mimeo, California Institute of Technology, 1971b.

———. "Social Choice and Social Rationality," mimeo, California Institute of Technology, 1971c.

———. "Rationality and Relevance in Social Choice Theory," paper presented at the Seminar on Mathematical Theory of Collective Decisions, Harbour Town, South Carolina, 1971d.

———. "Individual Choice of a Political-Economic Process," in Niemi and Weisberg (1972).

POMERANZ, JOHN, and WEIL, ROMAN. "Calculation of Cyclical Majority Probabilities," unpublished paper, University of Chicago, 1968.

POMPER, GERALD. "From Confusion to Clarity: Issues and American Voters, 1956–1968," *American Political Science Review*, LXVI (1972), pp. 415–428.

———. "Rejoinder," *American Political Science Review*, LXVI (1972), pp. 466–467.

PZEWORSKI, ADAM. "Party Systems, Electoral Mobilization and the Stability of Capitalists Society," mimeo, Washington University, 1971.

RABINOWITZ, GEORGE. "A Spatial Look at U.S. Politics," presented at the meetings of the Public Choice Society, Pittsburgh, 1972.

RABUSHKA, ALVIN, and SHEPSLE, KENNETH A. *Politics in Plural Societies: A Theory of Democratic Instability*. Columbus: Charles E. Merrill, 1972.

RAE, DOUGLAS W. *The Political Consequences of Electoral Laws*. New Haven: Yale University Press, 1967.

———. "Decision-Rules and Individual Values in Collective Choice," *American Political Science Review*, LXII (1968), pp. 40–56.

RAPOPORT, ANATOL. *N-Person Game Theory*. Ann Arbor: University of Michigan Press, 1970.

RAWLS, JOHN A. *A Theory of Justice*. Cambridge: Harvard University Press, 1972.

RICHTER, MARCEL. "Revealed Preference Theory," *Econometrica*, 34 (1966), pp. 635–645.

———. "Rational Choice," in Chipman, John S. *et al.*, eds., *Preferences, Utility, and Demand*. New York: Harcourt, Brace, Jovanovich, 1971, pp. 29–58.

RIKER, WILLIAM H. "Events and Situations," *Journal of Philosophy*, 54 (1957), pp. 57–70.

———. "The Paradox of Voting and Congressional Rules for Voting Amendments," *American Political Science Review*, LII (1958), pp. 349–366.

———. "Causes of Events," *Journal of Philosophy*, 56 (1959), pp. 281–291.

———. "Voting and the Summation of Preferences: An Interpretive Bibliographic Review of Selected Developments During the Last Decade," *American Political Science Review*, LV (1961), pp. 900–912.

———. *The Theory of Political Coalitions*. New Haven: Yale University Press, 1962.

———. "Arrow's Theorem and Some Examples of the Paradox of Voting," in Claunch, John, ed., *Mathematical Applications in Political Science*. Dallas: Southern Methodist University Press, 1965, pp. 41–60.

———. "A Paradox of Voting Trading," paper presented at the Annual meeting of the American Political Science Association, Washington, D.C., 1972.

———, and ORDESHOOK, PETER C. "A Theory of the Calculus of Voting," *American Political Science Review*, LXII (1968), pp. 25–42.

———, and ORDESHOOK, PETER C. *Positive Political Theory*. Englewood Cliffs: Prentice-Hall, 1972.

ROSENTHAL, HOWARD. "Voting and Coalition Models in Election Simulations," in Coplin, William D., ed., *Simulation in the Study of Politics*. Chicago: Markham, 1968a, pp. 237–285.

———. Political Coalition: Elements of a Model and the Study of French Legislative Elections," in *Calcul et Formalisation dans les Sciences de l'Homme*. Paris: Editions du C.N.R.S., 1968b, pp. 269–282.

———, and SEN, SUBRATA. "Candidate Selection and Voting Behavior in France," *Public Choice*, 6 (1969), pp. 71–92.

———, and SEN, SUBRATA. "Electoral Participation in the French Fifth Republic," *American Political Science Review*, LXVII (1973), pp. 29–54.

ROTHENBERG, JEROME. *The Measurement of Social Welfare*. Englewood Cliffs: Prentice-Hall, 1961.

RUSK, JERROLD G., and WEISBERG, HERBERT F. "Perceptions of Presidential Candidates: A Midterm Report," paper presented at the Annual meeting of the American Political Science Association, Chicago, 1971.

SAMUELSON, PAUL A. "Arrow's Mathematical Politics," in Hook, Sidney, ed., *Human Values and Economic Policy*. New York: University Press, 1967, pp. 41–51.

———. "Maximum Principles in Analytical Economics," *Science*, 173 (September 10, 1971), pp. 991–997.

SCHATTSCHNEIDER, E. E. *The Semi-Sovereign People: A Realist's View of Democracy in America*. New York: Holt, Rinehart and Winston, 1960.

SCHOENBERGER, ROBERT A. "Campaign Strategy and Party Loyalty: The Electoral Relevance of Candidate Decision-Making in the 1964 Congressional Elections," *American Political Science Review*, LXIII (1969), pp. 515–520.

SCHOFIELD, NORMAN J. "Is Majority Rule Special?" in Niemi and Weisberg (1972).

SCHWARTZ, THOMAS. "Rationality and the Myth of the Maximum," presented at the Public Choice Society meetings, Pittsburgh, 1972.

SEN, AMARTYA. "Preferences, Votes and the Transitivity of Majority Decisions," *Review of Economic Studies*, 31 (1964), pp. 163–165.

――――. "A Possibility Theorem on Majority Decisions," *Econometrica,* 34 (1966), pp. 491–499.

――――. "Quasi-Transitivity, Rational Choice and Collective Decisions," *Review of Economic Studies,* 36 (1969), pp. 381–393.

――――. "The Impossibility of a Paretian Liberal," *Journal of Political Economy,* 78 (1970), pp. 152–157.

――――. *Collective Choice and Social Welfare.* San Francisco: Holden Day, 1971.

SHAPIRO, MICHAEL J. "Rational Political Man: A Synthesis of Economic and Social-Psychological Perspectives," *American Political Science Review,* LXIII (1969), pp. 1106–1119.

SHAPLEY, LLOYD, and SHUBIK, MARTIN. "On Market Games," RM-5671-PR, RAND Corporation, Santa Monica, 1968.

SHEPSLE, KENNETH A. *Essays on Risky Choice in Electoral Competition.* Unpublished doctoral dissertation, University of Rochester, 1970.

――――. "Uncertainty and Electoral Competition: The Search for Equilibria," presented at the Seminar on Mathematical Theory of Collective Decisions, Harbour Town, South Carolina, 1971.

――――. "Parties, Voters, and the Risk Environment: A Mathematical Treatment of Electoral Competition Under Uncertainty," in Niemi and Weisberg, (1972a).

――――. "The Strategy of Ambiguity: Uncertainty and Electoral Competition," *American Political Science Review,* LXVI (1972b), pp. 555–569.

SHUBIK, MARTIN. "Voting or a Price System in a Competitive Market Structure," *American Political Science Review,* LXIV (1970), pp. 179–181.

SIMON, HERBERT. *The Sciences of the Artificial.* Cambridge: MIT Press, 1968.

SMITHIES, ARTHUR. "Optimum Location in Spatial Competition," *Journal of Political Economy,* 49 (1941), pp. 423–439.

SNOW, C. P. *The Masters.* New York: Scribner's, 1951.

STIGLER, GEORGE. "The Development of Utility," *Journal of Political Economy,* 58 (1950), pp. 307–327, 373–396.

STOKES, DONALD E. "Spatial Models of Party Competition," *American Political Science Review,* LVII (1963), pp. 368–377.

SUPPES, PATRICK. *Introduction to Logic.* Princeton: Van Nostrand, 1957.

TAYLOR, MICHAEL. "Proof of a Theorem on Majority Rule," *Behavioral Science,* 14 (1969), pp. 228–231.

――――. "Review Article: Mathematical Political Theory," *British Journal of Political Science,* 2 (1971), pp. 339–382.

――――. "The Theory of Collective Choice," in Greenstein, Fred I., and Polsby, Nelson W., eds., *Handbook of Political Science,* forthcoming.

TINGSTEN, HERBERT F. *Political Behavior.* Totowa, N.J.: Bedminster Press, 1963. First published, 1937.

TULLOCK, GORDON. "The General Irrelevance of the General Impossibility Theorem," *Quarterly Journal of Economics,* 81 (1967a), pp. 256–270.

――――. *Toward a Mathematics of Politics.* Ann Arbor: University of Michigan, 1967b.

———. *Private Wants, Public Means.* New York: Basic Books, 1970a.

———. "A Simple Algebraic Logrolling Model," *American Economic Review,* 60 (1970b), pp. 419–426.

VICKREY, WILLIAM. "Utility, Strategy, and Social Decision Rules," *Quarterly Journal of Economics,* 74 (1960), pp. 507–535.

WADE, LAWRENCE L., and CURRY, ROBERT L. "Economics of Decision-Making," in Cotter, Cornelius P., ed., *Political Science Annual, Volume VI.* Indianapolis: Bobbs-Merrill, forthcoming.

WALSH, VIVIAN CHARLES. *Introduction to Contemporary Microeconomics.* New York: McGraw-Hill, 1970.

WARD, BENJAMIN. "Majority Voting and Alternative Forms of Public Enterprise," in Margolis, Julius, ed., *Public Economy in Urban Communities.* Baltimore: Johns Hopkins University Press, 1965, pp. 112–126.

WEIDENBAUM, MURRAY L. "Institutional Obstacles to Reallocating Government Expenditures," in Haveman, Robert H., and Margolis, Julius, eds., *Public Expenditures and Policy Analysis.* Chicago: Markham, 1970, pp. 232–245.

WEISBERG, HERBERT F., and NIEMI, RICHARD G. "Probability Calculations for Cyclical Majorities in Congressional Voting," in Niemi and Weisberg (1972).

———., and RUSK, JERROLD G. "Dimensions of Candidate Evaluation," *American Political Science Review,* LXIV (1970), pp. 1167–1185.

WILLIAMSON, OLIVER, and SARGENT, THOMAS. "Social Choice: A Probabilistic Approach," *Economic Journal,* 77 (1967), pp. 797–813.

WILSON, ROBERT B. "An Axiomatic Model of Logrolling," *American Economic Review,* 59 (1969), pp. 331–341.

———. "The Game-Theoretic Structure of Arrow's General Possibility Theorem," *Journal of Economic Theory,* 5 (1972a), pp. 14–20.

———. "Social Choice Theory Without the Pareto Principle," *Journal of Economic Theory,* 5 (1972b), pp. 478–486.

The Impacts of Public Policy

KENNETH M. DOLBEARE*

Political scientists have long endorsed the Lasswellian definition of politics as "who gets what, when, how." But we have been far more interested in exploring "how" than in identifying "who" actually got "what" or "when." The recent surge of research activity directed at the impacts of public policy thus marks a shift of focus. It has come in the context of a more general revival of interest in the substance of public policy, in turn brought about by increased awareness of social problems and large-scale government efforts at amelioration. Governments at all levels have sought the aid of social scientists in coping with a wide variety of demanding problems, and both social and scholarly motivations have led numbers of political scientists back into the sometimes grubby world of public policy studies.

For several reasons, detailed critical assessment of even the "impact studies" component of the revived analysis field is simply not possible here. It is a rapidly developing subfield with few shared definitions or boundaries. Depending on one's definition, there are between one and four thousand impact studies of varying quality by various social scientists already published or stored in government warehouses. The area of impact studies is, to understate the matter somewhat, in a state of rapid flux—so rapid that today's categories are outmoded before they can be subjected to critical examination. In this paper, therefore, I shall attempt no more than an essay on the state of the art, sacrificing comprehensiveness and detail for breadth (and, let us hope, depth) of analysis of problems and prospects. I shall assess the subfield of impact studies from the perspective of political science, emphasizing the work of political scientists and its place within that discipline. I shall identify or review the literature in this field only as specific works illustrate my points, and

* I wish to acknowledge the very considerable assistance of my colleagues Trevor Chandler, Philip Meranto, and David Schuman in the development of this essay.

consider my bibliographical obligations discharged by reference to comprehensive sources available elsewhere.

The plan of the essay is as follows. First, I consider the troubling problem of defining "public policy," a term with almost as many different meanings as "democracy." In this section, I also explore the meaning of "impact," and review the various purposes with which social scientists have studied "policy impact." Next, I employ a very loose categorization derived from this first section to present an overview of the kinds of policy impact research undertaken by political scientists. Finally, I attempt a critical evaluation of the problems and prospects of this direction of research. The reader should probably be warned at this point that I am not sanguine about this research focus. Indeed, and in part from experience, I believe not only that policy impact studies *have not* contributed much of value, but also that for a variety of reasons *it may not be possible for them to do so.*

DEFINITIONS AND PURPOSES IN "POLICY IMPACT" STUDIES

PUBLIC POLICY

A simple definition of public policy is "what governments *do.*" The problem is that many different people at many different places among the various layers of government *do* many different kinds of things. And politicians, journalists, and social scientists at various times describe a wide variety of these things rather indiscriminately as "public policy." (For a useful discussion of the problems involved in defining public policy, and some cogent suggestions, see Meehan, 1972.) We may speak of government policies in the sense of general goals (prosperity in a peacetime economy, equality of opportunity), or broad statutes associated with general goals (the Employment Act of 1946, the Civil Rights Act of 1964), or in terms of specific provisions (particular titles or sections of statutes, court decisions). At the same time, "policy" may mean the actual practices of officials whose discretionary behavior may be more determinative of what is actually done than is framing legislation or voting for its enactment. Examples of the foregoing readily come to mind: desegregation guidelines formulated by HEW, investigative practices regarding violations, criteria for prosecution of violations, and so on. Or "policy" may take the form of the creation of new forms of governmental organization (new agencies, reapportioned legislatures) or new jurisdictions for established units of government (new rights and remedies enforceable in the courts). Or "policy" may be seen in durable patterns of government expenditure—supplemented by specific inducements, grants-in-aid, withdrawals, etc., which may in turn be conditioned on specific circumstances.

This catalogue does not begin to exhaust the uses of the term "policy," for it has touched only upon dimensions of primary relevance to impact studies, i.e., distinctions having to do with the *substance* of policy, of *what it is* that the government in question is *doing*, and *to whom*. Many other uses of the term, and numerous classification efforts, are grounded in differences in the institutional source of policies, the intent behind them, or the general goals or subject areas involved. If anything, there is overawareness of the multiple forms that "policy" takes, and an excess of classificatory schemes (not always clearly linked to purpose or evidence), in the literature of political science.

For the most part, however, students of "policy impact" have gone ahead and done their research, unencumbered by a felt need for *a priori* classification of either categories of impacts or characteristics of policies. While I applaud the decision to repress or defer the urge to classify until more evidence is collected about characteristics of impact, some clarification of what is meant by "policy" is surely overdue. Lack of clarity about the nature of policy may greatly limit the dimensions of policy impact which are explored or may build flawing premises into the inquiry from the start. In later sections we shall see evidence of these and other problems stemming in part from imprecision about the nature of "policy." For the moment, let me indicate how I shall distinguish among uses of the term, and how such an approach may help in an analytical review of impact studies.

Without embarking upon another classificatory effort, I want to note the obvious, i.e., that there is a broad distinction to be made among types or levels of policies (or, perhaps, uses of the term "policy") that has relevance for impact studies. This corresponds roughly to a continuum ranging from fundamental directions and structures to specific outputs; even more roughly, it is akin to the distinction between ends and means. At one pole, we have "policy" as a set of priorities and directions, themselves grounded in basic societal values, ideology, and the basic elements of our economic and social systems. Institutional structures and procedures, Constitutional provisions and practices, major aspects of political style and expectation, and the general goals of government action flow coherently from such underpinnings and make up one level of "policy." Paramount among priorities and directions (or "fundamental policies") at this level is that of preserving the basic outlines of the economic and social systems and the values supporting them—in effect, of promoting the continued growth and viability of the American enterprise. Secondary priorities include equality, procedural regularity, etc. Change in such fundamental matters does not come readily, and the process is qualitatively distinguishable from that characteristic of less fundamental policies.

At the other extreme are policies that fully assume the basic propriety and/or continuity of existing systems, structures, and directions, and essentially involve only accommodations or adjustments within that framework. These may be termed "output policies," to underscore their subordinate status. There is still conflict among interests, of course, and much at stake in the allocations of burden and benefit accomplished by the policies in question, but it all occurs within the range set by established values and structures and the more or less fixed priorities and directions of fundamental policies. Most government action, and most policy studies, perhaps understandably, are near this end of the continuum. Structural issues may be involved, such as the form or powers of new or reconstituted agencies or state governments (as in reapportionment or voting rights policies developed by the national government). And there may well be striking differences in the scope and character of coverage, or the precision with which specific policies seek to intervene in social processes (such as the difference between national fiscal policy and the Head Start program in St. Louis, both of which fit near this end of the continuum). But what is shared among such policies is a narrower focus, a more limited and more specifiable set of goals, a more particular content, more identifiable objects, fewer intervening variables, and hence potentially researchable consequences. These are the kinds of policies that, at least at first glance, appear to provide useful grist for the new field of impact studies. The important point to note here, however, is that such policies *necessarily* reflect *both* the broader "fundamental policies" *and* the more specific goals that are explicit or implicit in their formulation. Separation of the purposes, content, or consequences of output policies from the larger framework of fundamental policies and the general social context is thus very difficult if not impossible.

Establishment of this rough continuum may permit us to locate certain other uses of the term "policy," or at least to understand more clearly what we mean by some familiar uses. No hard and fast division between fundamental and output policies is either necessary or practical—indeed, as just noted, most policies may well include aspects of each. But it does seem possible to say that "foreign policy" (for example) is locatable on the fundamental side, and "transportation policy" on the output side. The former involves relatively more of general directions and purposes, such as the protection of the American social and economic system and the furtherance of its interests abroad, and relatively less specifiable goals, content, or objects—more intervening factors, and less researchable consequences. The latter may be more readily disaggregated into components, such as subsidies, grants-in-aid, regulations, and other inducements, each of which has relatively more specifiable goals and objects whose responses may be studied. It should be clear that the distinction is one involving both the character of the policies and the feasibility of research. The probabilities of successful empirical research increase as one approaches the output pole of the continuum; but so do the prospects of unexamined assumptions and of difficulty in addressing the larger issues of politics.

To summarize, most policy impact studies involve output policies on the domestic scene, i.e., occasions where governments have acted in the form of subordinate agency forms, to achieve particular (and limited) goals. Substantive components of these policies are isolated and employed as the independent variable, and policy in the larger sense is either ignored (or considered impractical) as a research focus—or incorporated without recognition. This may be an unavoidable concomitant of research resources and capabilities, but it may also be due in part to lack of precision in defining (or recognizing) "policy" in its various forms and levels.

IMPACT

What is it about policies that is to be explored under the rubric of "impact"? The previous allusion to use of policy content as the independent variable implies a substantial shift of focus. It is quite in contrast to the now well-established use of policy content as the dependent variable in efforts to understand the relative significance of various elements of the decision-making process and its environment. Here, questions are addressed not to *why* the policy has the form that it does, but to *what difference it makes* to people and problems. Clearly, policies have distinguishable stages of "impact," extending from the immediate effects upon primary objects through ever widening circles of second- and third-order consequences. Such broader consequences may be intended or unintended, direct or indirect, behavioral or attitudinal, short or long term, mediated or unmediated, convergent with other policies or at odds with them. And every policy is but a limited intervention into an ongoing and dynamic social context, in which a large number of powerful forces (mostly "private," some public) are operative. What is the scope of the concept of "impact," and what boundaries does it acknowledge? In part, this is a function of the purposes of the researcher, to which I shall shortly turn. However, some further discussion of the problem of defining "impact" may be in order first.

A strict usage of the term "impact" suggests demonstrable behavioral or attitudinal response which can be causally linked to components of the policy in question. Only a few researchers have been content with such self-limitation, however, and so the concept has been expanded to mean much more, and the terms "impacts," "effects," and "consequences" have come into use. The further one seeks to trace "consequences," of course, the more mediating and contextual variables become relevant and the less likely it is that causal connections with policies can be shown. Researchers thus face a serious dilemma between the desire to be rigorous and evidential and the desire to be comprehensive and meaningful. It seems clear that strict usage of "impact" in the limited, direct sense would be unsatisfying to all but the dedicated laboratory experimentalist. Henceforth, I shall use the term as if it were plural or interchangeable with "consequences," and return later to the problem of developing tolerance levels for various sorts of departures from desirable standards of rigor, evidence, and causal linkage.

But difficulties with the concept of "impact" are not yet exhausted. No policy, however disaggregated and isolated, ever exists by itself. In the most rigorous empirical study of the impact of an output policy, the effects of fundamental policies—and particularly the effects of symbolic acts and words of key officeholders—are likely to be involved. Not even the carefully controlled experimental study is proof against this probability, for fundamental policies and symbolic activity may have effects when combined with tangible applications of output policies that they do not have for control groups. The implication seems to be that all impact studies must involve, to a greater or lesser degree, consequences attributable to fundamental policies and symbolism as well as the consequences attributable to the (perhaps) more specific effects of the output policy under investigation. This situation may become acute when the impacts to be explored are attitudinal, long term, or indirect. Consider the problem of analyzing the impact of court-developed policy regarding bussing where necessary to achieve racial balance: official "policy" after President Nixon's nationally-televised address of March 1972 attacking school bussing and pledging opposition was exactly as it had been before, but thousands of school boards and millions of individuals faced a totally revised context. What had been building in law and practice for nearly two decades was now called into question from the White House itself. On a much lesser scale, and not necessarily including mid-process changes of course, similar symbolic auras and fundamental policy directions enter into the background of many output policy impact processes.

This review suggests that the impacts of output policies take place in a context of the broader effects of fundamental policies, i.e., that the former are lesser included elements in the general directions set by the latter. Perhaps it also suggests a way of understanding where impact studies fit in the literature of political science. For years, we have studied demand and decision-making processes, right up to the point where policy emerges. We then skipped all the way to public opinion and voting studies, which are grounded *in part* in popular reactions to *both* fundamental *and* output policies. In effect, we have been studying policy impact for decades, albeit the broadly diffused long-term consequences of various levels of policy and symbolic activity as they are perceived in changing social context. What the new generation of policy impact studies seeks to do is to fill the gap between policy enactment and the ultimate stages of generalized feedback, to fill in the linkages between policy content, specific impacts, tangible distributive effects, and spreading attitudinal, ideological, and value reactions.

THE PURPOSES OF INQUIRY

Patently, selection of a particular breadth or scope for analysis of "impact" depends upon the purposes to be served by inquiry. Keeping in mind the above-described gap that impact studies might seek to fill, four purposes with ever-widening foci may be identified. First is the relatively limited goal of identifying the objects of policies and the nature of the effects of the policies on them, i.e., simple description of what happens, who actually wins and loses by virtue of particular policies. Second is the goal of understanding the political processes by which policies or problem-solving efforts of governments are implemented/effectuated/deflected or otherwise absorbed into the ongoing social context and process. Third is the attempt to assess the extent to which policies achieve stated or other goals, to forecast effects of policies, select among alternative policies, and generally maximize government capacity to solve problems. This would include both previous purposes, and direct them toward evaluative ends. Finally, some seek to build theories of politics through exploration of the many dimensions of feedback—in effect, to fill in all the gaps noted in the previous paragraph—but without concern for application of such understanding to the amelioration of social problems or the evaluation of either specific policies or the workings of the larger system itself.

At the risk of implying far more symmetry than really obtains, I want to suggest that relationships exist between the purposes of inquiry, the scope and character of "impact" analyzed, and the mix of levels involved in the "policy" employed as a focus. The table following attempts to

Relationships Among Purposes of Inquiry, Scope, and
Character of "Impact" and Mix of Levels of "Policy"

Category	Purpose of Study	Scope and Character of "Impact" Involved	Mix Among Levels of "Policy" at Focus
1.	Identification of winners and losers from policy, burden/benefit patterns ("What happened?")	(a) Immediate, direct, short-term, few mediating factors (b) Behavioral rather than attitudinal	Chiefly output, with residuum of fundamental
2.	Understanding implementing processes in context ("Why did things happen this way?")	Immediate and secondary, direct and indirect, longer term, more mediating factors; larger role for attitudinal responses and power context of implementing agencies	Principally output, particularly forms of agencies, but substantial component of fundamental
3.	Evaluation of goal attainment, exploration of alternatives, problem solving ("How might things be done better?") (" 'Better' in what sense?")	All above, plus intended consequences traced from and contrasted with stated goals of policymakers and/or "needs" derived from assessments of problems themselves; unintended consequences, mediating and contextual factors, 2nd and 3rd order consequences also emphasized	Roughly equal parts output and fundamental, with policy packages (e.g., "housing policy") disaggregated into specific researchable components
4.	General theories of feedback processes ("What does it all mean for general explanations of politics?")	Long-term, diffused, attitudinal, ideological, systemic consequences, broad patterns of aggregate distributive effects	Chiefly fundamental, interspersed with occasional salient output issues

indicate some of these relationships, and recapitulates much of this section in the process. The scope of "impact" needed for inquiry designed to serve the first purpose noted earlier is the most limited, tangible, and empirically demonstrable—and the most fully focused on output policies. The second and third categories involve broadening purposes, expanding scope to the definition of "impact" employed, and increasing proportions of fundamental policies—along with certain other shifts of emphasis and focus. The final category merges with long-familiar public opinion studies, as noted earlier.

With substantial allowance for diversity within categories and no intention of drawing sharp boundaries between them, we may employ the categories of this Table as a means of organizing a review of what political scientists have done in the way of impact research. The accomplishments and prospects of this research will profit from review in terms of these relationships. For simplicity's sake, I shall use the short-form question contained in the Table to represent each category. It may also be worth noting explicitly how much of the work of various social scientists has been pushed to the periphery by these definitions. Political scientists' usage of policy content as a dependent variable is not relevant, for example, nor is their work involving the impact of structural or procedural change *within* the decision-making processes, or even research focused on the impact of institutions as such. (In the latter two cases, as already noted, it may not really be possible to exclude certain effects, but research focused primarily on their consequences would not meet the criteria of impact on people or problems outside of government.) In the process of delineating the subfield of policy impact studies we have, by definition, excluded large areas. But much remains, and may now be analyzed.

POLITICAL SCIENCE AND POLICY IMPACT RESEARCH: AN OVERVIEW

WHAT HAPPENED?

The first coherent body of empirical impact research appears to have been developed by scholars in the field of public law, in the form of studies of the impact of Supreme Court decisions. Because the political impact field still bears the imprint of its public law origins and orientations, the reasons for development of impact studies in the public law setting are worth review. At least four seem probable, and all may have played some part in spurring (and shaping) impact research in its early stages. First, public law scholars tend to see the Supreme Court in terms of its historical tradition, which continually confronts them with occasions when decisions were obeyed only partially or not at all. Second, the Court's pronouncements were, for many, hallowed symbols of justice and the rule of law, and failure to follow them on the part of reluctant elements of the population was regarded a serious failure of responsible citizenship and a threat to the integrity of the Court. A normative concern was thus added to the recurring fact of noncompliance. Third, the behavioral revolution created multiple opportunities to apply new research tools and perspectives: some picked up the tools enthusiastically and devoted themselves to the relatively narrow field of judicial behavior; many others sought wider scope and integration with the larger concerns of political science—and some found such possibility in studies of post-decision processes. Fourth, and perhaps most important of all, public law retained a healthy concern for the substance of what government *did*, for the *content* of decisions, statutes, and regulations making up the body of law, during the period when other political scientists were exclusively engaged in the study of *processes*.

Judicial impact studies are not only first in point of time, but perhaps simplest in character, in the impact research field. They involve a single discrete policy stimulus (a court decision), identifiable objects (parties to the case or officials charged with enforcement responsibilities), and readily dichotomizable responses (compliance or noncompliance). From the beginning, inquiry was motivated by the question of whether the decision of the court (always the Supreme Court, until quite recently) was having its intended effect. Later, interest broadened to include more general efforts to specify who did what (if anything) as a result of the decision, and thereby to say what difference it made that the Court had decided in a certain way. These studies may be reviewed in three groups of increasing scope and complexity: first are analyses of the impact on other government officials charged with enforcement responsibilities (and thus indirectly upon the intended segment of the public); next are studies of impact directly upon some intended segment of the public; and finally research which views court decisions in a larger context of ongoing social processes.

Intragovernmental impact

Consistent with the Constitutional lawyer's traditional concerns, major law reviews from time to time summarized state court or Congressional responses to Supreme Court mandates in particular cases. Postdecision behavior by lower courts was brought to the attention of political scientists by Walter Murphy (1969) in a well-known article pointing out the capabilities of lesser judges at deflecting, delaying, or frustrating a Supreme Court order. The lack of visible effect of the Court's desegregation rulings of 1954 and 1955 no doubt reemphasized the long-standing awareness that "impact" was highly variable and uncertain, even at this first level of application. The lack of affirmative response to the *Brown* case also inspired a larger study by Jack Peltason (1961) of the effects of the case upon the courts and lives of federal judges in the South. Others have shown the effects of particular decisions, mainly the *Brown* case, upon the workload and decision-making patterns of trial and appellate courts.

Another range of studies explores the impact of Court decisions upon national and state legislative bodies. This body of research also draws upon earlier law review-type summaries of Congressional reversal or evasion of Supreme Court decisions, and expands toward more general analyses of the interactions between the two institutions. Pritchett (1961) and Murphy (1962) explore responses to different sorts of cases in some detail, and several subsequent articles add additional dimensions. (See also Stumpf, 1966; and Beaney and Beiser, 1964.) Perhaps the largest body of impact studies directed at legislatures was spawned by the reapportionment cases. Most of these examine only changes in the legislatures themselves, however, and do not relate such changes to modifications in the outputs of such legislatures—and thus do not link the Court decision even indirectly with effects upon people or problems outside of government. Robert Dixon's massive summary (1968) brings these studies together, and gives them their most coherent meaning.

Direct impact upon segments of the public
Schoolhouse religion cases appear to have provided much of the early impetus toward political scientists' studies of impact upon persons outside of government. This series begins with articles by Gordon Patric (1957) and Frank Sorauf (1959), which explore the degree of compliance by school systems with two different Supreme Court decisions on released time for religious education. Each rests upon questionnaire responses from school superintendents. Later studies by Katz (1965) and Birkby (1966) expand upon this data base, with a focus on the same decision and a more or less stimulus-response model in mind.

The development of judicial impact research profited at this stage from several still-useful essays by nonpolitical scientists regarding methods and purpose. Law professor Arthur Miller's trenchant "On the Need for 'Impact Analysis' of Supreme Court Decisions" (1965) effectively made the case for result-conscious jurisprudence; his own work (particularly 1968) serves as an example of aggregated-impact research, though not systematically empirical in character. Sociologist Richard Schwartz's "Field Experimentation in Socio-legal Research" (1961) both opened a long-enduring argument with respect to methods of impact research and pointed to the developing field of "sociology and law" or "law and society" as an area from which political scientists might draw inspiration and instruction. Law professor Ernest M. Jones offered further proposals for impact research within the sociology of law framework in an article in the *Wisconsin Law Review* (1966). The still-untied knots involved in causal linkage in impact research were reviewed and suggestions made by sociologist Richard Lempert in the first issue of *The Law and Society Review* (1966), a journal initiated in part for the development of greater sharing of research results among political scientists, sociologists, and lawyers; impact research in its various forms has been a continuing concern in the pages of this journal throughout its history.

By the mid and late 1960s, judicial impact research had broadened well beyond the initial focus on school and religion cases, although these have continued to make up a very large proportion of the research undertaken. Obscenity cases provided the focus for several studies, as did certain defendants' rights decisions, particularly the *Miranda* case requirement that police officers warn defendants of their right to silence before soliciting confessions (Levine, 1969; Milner, 1968). The impact of numbers of decisions made by state and federal trial courts has also been studied (Dolbeare, 1967a).

Impact in a context of ongoing social processes

The broadening of impact studies occurred not only with respect to the types of cases used as the focus, but also with respect to scope—more variables were involved in analyzing an outcome removed in time and immediacy from the policy-stimulus. In effect, a sense of process began to replace the quicker snapshot; many actors were seen as involved in a more complex process leading in time to a wide variety of responses no longer dichotomizable as compliance or noncompliance. Some illustrations of this broadening appear in William K. Muir, Jr., *Prayer in the Public Schools: Law and Attitude Change* (1967) and Richard Johnson, *The Dynamics of Compliance: Supreme Court Decisionmaking From a New Perspective* (1967a). Muir concentrated on the responses of a limited number of teachers and principals, exploring their actions as part of their personal psychological and social situations. Johnson contrasted two small towns in which different ultimate responses emerged. Neal Milner (1968) compared police response to *Miranda* in four towns, and several teams of lawyers and law students investigated a variety of other cities in regard to the same ruling.

Other scholars soon began to try to set explorations of the effects of judicial decisions against a backdrop of public opinion concerning the Court and the issues involved. Public opinion studies concerning the Court and its work had been long foreshadowed by commentators' frequent assertions about the symbolic role of the Court, and their concern for the Court's "standing" in the eyes of the people. Some early (and small-scale) studies were already available by 1966 (Kessel) and 1967 (Dolbeare, 1967b), but these were soon overshadowed by a larger and more definitive inquiry undertaken by Murphy and Tanenhaus (1969). The first to employ systematic public-opinion data in legal impact research, however, was Harrell Rodgers's study of responses in Iowa to the enforcement of school attendance rules upon Amish children (1969). This is a tight little study involving several types of data, and is focused on enforcement of state statute rather than judicial decisions as such. In a substantially looser way, Dolbeare and Hammond (1971) integrate public opinion data, elite behavior at various levels, and local behavior to characterize the process of response to another in the series of school prayer decisions.

Four major sources collect, synthesize, and interpret the findings of this now large body of judicial impact research, the parameters of which have been sketched here. Theodore Becker's edited *The Impact of Supreme Court Decisions* (1969) collects excerpts from seventeen leading impact studies, including several not readily available elsewhere. Stephen Wasby's *The Impact of the United States Supreme Court* (1970) synthesizes the available literature in a most comprehensive manner, reviewing a multitude of findings and emerging with 134 hypotheses regarding the factors that shape the impact of Supreme Court decisions. Martin Shapiro, in a brief essay entitled simply "The Impact of the Supreme Court" (1971), provides an incisive short course in judicial impact research. Walter Murphy and Joseph Tanenhaus perform a similar distinctive service in ten pages of their recent *The Study of Public Law* (1972). All of these authors see the study of judicial impact as representing a major developing area of the field of public law and perhaps the discipline itself. Becker (1969, p. 3), for example, refers to impact studies as "the second important breakthrough in the modern study of the Supreme Court," and Murphy and Tanenhaus (1972, p. 58) declare, "It would seem that the first and greatest contribution of political scientists to the study of public law would be a set of explanations of what—and how—forces shape the impact of judicial decisions on the governmental system."

There is relatively little critical evaluation of the methods, concepts, or theoretical contributions of this body of research in these sources, however, although both Shapiro and Murphy-Tanenhaus recognize the problems stemming from the fact, set forth in the previous section, that impact research must of necessity take place in the context of the effects of fundamental policies and institutional symbolism. The closest that impact-oriented political scientists have come to assessing the problems and uses of this research is Stuart Nagel's very brief "Some New Concerns of Legal Process Research Within Political Science" (1971). Referring to impact research as "the main post-behavioral or policy-behavioral development within public law," Nagel goes on to suggest that there are already "old" and "new" versions of impact research. The first proceeds from an "effects perspective" and details the consequences of the single (usually Supreme Court) decision involved, frequently upon other government officials. The second proceeds from an "optimizing perspective," in which evaluation of various types of policy is attempted, and the concern is with effects upon the ultimate consumer rather than government officials. Nagel may be too polite to suggest that the "old" impact studies have some serious limitations, but he has clearly caught (however implicitly conveyed) a significant shift in research focus away from judicial impact toward much more general *policy* impact studies. Students of public law do not continue to have any distinctive claims to expertise in the area, although a considerable portion of the work is still done by scholars with such interests.

It may be, as some of the early students of judicial impact hoped, that the broadening of impact studies has indeed resulted in the potential integration of that branch of public law with the larger concerns of political science. It seems clear at least that such broader impact research brings one into contact with scholars of different orientations and different disciplines. The effects of government expenditures and other economic actions continue to be a central concern of many economists; the tools of cost/benefit analysis, PPBS, and various aggregate monitoring devices, though their utility is controverted in many situations, have generally been taken as placing economists in positions where they can advise authoritatively on policies. Sociologists also have long been in that business; the Coleman Report (1966) is only one example. Contact with the orientations and research of policy-oriented scholars from these and other disciplines cannot fail to have a further broadening impact upon political scientists. As we shall see, this process may already be well under way.

HOW AND WHY DID IT HAPPEN THIS WAY?

The threshold between the last group of context-sensitive judicial impact studies and those in this second category is not sharply definable. But here we shall review research that acknowledges multiple sources of the policy "stimuli" that are to serve as the independent variable, and focuses on policies that often involve one or more implementing agencies charged with oversight and enforcement. Moreover, inquiry is directed at indirect or later consequences, well after the policy intervention has been converted into one of several forces at work upon some ultimate "consumers" of that policy to (perhaps) alter certain social patterns in their lives. We shall review and illustrate these studies in two broad categories distinguished chiefly by the purposes for which the research was undertaken. The first, and closest to the public law orientations of the judicial impact studies, may be termed the "law and change" group. Here the interest of researchers is on the process by which the new policy (conceived of as "law") enters and causes changes in the lives of numbers of people. The underlying purpose is as much to understand the role of law in the process of social change as it is to learn about the effects per se. The second group of studies is less tied to public law interests, and is more simply characterizable as "policy effects." Here, the legal character of the policy is unimportant—the focus is on the effects of law/agency/practice (combined) upon consumers, and the purpose is to explain why one or another result came about.

Law and change

The role of law in the process of social change has been a subject of enduring fascination for all manner of social theorists and commentators. Much of the literature is either normative or impressionistic; some of the best recent work of this sort is collected by Grossman and Grossman in their recent *Law and Change in Modern America* (1971). Perhaps because the subject is so difficult to come firmly to grips with, there is still more interest and enthusiasm than solid empirical research. The great problem of desegregation, and race relations generally, placed this subject inescapably on the research agenda in the mid-1950s, however, and has led to a number of studies.

For most, the issue of *whether* law can change attitudes and values as well as behavior has long been decided in the affirmative; the absorbing question for research is *how* and *under what circumstances*. Jack Greenberg's well-known work (1959) effectively states the case for the first and goes on to frame the second of these questions for the area of race relations. The United States Commission on Civil Rights and the Southern Regional Council have each produced an invaluable series of publications measuring various aspects of change in race relations in the South. Systematic, empirically-grounded explanations of the hows and whys of the process by which law effects various sorts of change—as opposed to mere summaries of data indicating differences in conditions which may or may not be related to some origin in law—nevertheless remain severely limited in number. Two recent works deserve mention, however, in part because they illustrate sharply contrasting approaches.

In *Law and Social Change: Civil Rights Laws and Their Consequences* (1972), Harrell Rodgers and Charles Bullock have integrated a vast array of quantitative data to present a thorough and revealing portrait of the effects of a decade and a half of national government civil rights actions upon the Southern states. First setting up the law as it stands on the books in Washington, they proceed to depict the actual state of affairs and extent of movement toward that legal standard in each of five major areas: voting, public accommodations, school desegregation, employment, and housing. In each area, they seek understanding of the factors contributing to change (or lack of change), and of the consequences of such impacts. They find increasing divergence between laws on the books and actual outcomes among the five areas in the order stated earlier, i.e., conformity with the law is greatest in the voting area, least in housing. The principal thrust of their subsequent analysis and explanation is that the nature of federal enforcement pressure decisively shapes actual outcomes. They document effectively that pressure has been more uneven and uncertain in the areas in which there has been less change in existing practices. The work concludes with some useful synthesis and observations concerning the ways in which law can and cannot succeed in inducing change in aggregate behavior patterns.

Frederick Wirt's *Politics of Southern Equality: Law and Social Change in a Mississippi County* (1970) justly merits the honorable mention Woodrow Wilson Award it received from the APSA. It is almost the complete inverse of the Rodgers and Bullock study: it is grounded in exhaustive interviewing of all population strata in a single county, and focuses on the *subjective* aspects of the *process* of law-induced change along with the more tangible modifications of behavior. Effectively integrating quantitative data with a subtle sense of the texture of life in Panola County, Wirt emerges with a solid characterization of people under stress and moving gradually toward new social relationships. Federal intervention is the major explanatory factor here also, but now joined to and weighed together with a congery of other factors.

Policy effects

Studies in this subgroup are less—or not at all—concerned with adding to understanding of the role of law as such. They seek instead to define the effects of given government policies and/or the effects of a particular administrative agency's structure or practices. Once again, a definitional exclusion is operative in this review: political scientists have produced many studies of the character, activities, or political context of agencies of government, but the criterion of relevance here is the existence of systematic empirical investigation of impacts upon people or problems—and relatively few meet that standard. Examples of works that employ selected impact data to more effectively characterize problems and practice in a broad area of government activity are readily available, of course. Martin Anderson's *The Federal Bulldozer* (1964) is typical of several works attacking urban renewal: Leonard Freedman is less strident but no less effective in his *Public Housing* (1969), and the same might be said for Gilbert Steiner's *The State of Welfare* (1971). Each of these contrasts intentions with results in broad terms, as do the many other works for which they stand as examples, but none sets about to compile a comprehensive empirical catalogue of impacts or to use impacts as the focus of analysis and explanation. The critique of existing policy that they make in almost all cases is based chiefly upon analysis of policy content and intent, and/or agency characteristics and practices.

The move toward systematic investigation of impacts as a central feature of policy analysis research in political science appears to date from the mid-1960s. Davis and Dolbeare's study of Selective Service (1968) contains a chapter in which several kinds of impact data are used to show the effects of the draft upon the people of one state. Gary Orfield's *The Reconstruction of Southern Education: The Schools and the 1964 Civil Rights Act* (1969) is more comprehensive and more fully linked to impact data. It traces the federal policy from its initiation through administrative implementation, then across a period of time in its local impact state, and finally to the point of feedback and change at the national level.

Considerable impetus toward further research directed at policy effects was generated in the mid to late 1960s by the discipline's reawakening to policy analysis generally. "Policy analysis" is a term that apparently covers practically anything related to public policy, to judge by the alacrity with which political scientists have billed themselves as such and the range of works proposed for inclusion under that rubric. But the specific thrusts that set off the current wave of policy-popularity were two in number. Students of urban and local politics were led by the salience of urban policy problems to seek explanations of them as well as understanding of the processes by which governments sought to cope with them. James Wilson used a panel at the 1966 APSA meetings as a focus and then drew those papers together with some scattered previous work to produce a seminal volume entitled *City Politics and Public Policy* (1968). In part, the papers drew upon the older tradition of municipal reform, and asked what difference it made that different cities had different forms of government. But Wilson's purposes also had to do with "making public policy a central concern" of political scientists' research, in order "to explain why one goal rather than another is served by government, and the consequences of serving that goal, or serving it in a particular way" (Wilson, 1968, p. 3). The papers collected dealt with a variety of aspects of policy, but some undertook to use policies as the independent variable and then explore policy impacts in such areas as desegregation (Crain and Vanecko, 1968), law enforcement (Gardiner, 1968), and wage garnishment (Jacob, 1968). Others employed impact data to investigate the significance of government forms, such as Eyestone and Eulau, Lineberry and Fowler, and Greenstone and Peterson.

The second major impetus toward policy analysis, including policy impact, came from two conferences and associated papers sponsored by the SSRC Committee on Governmental and Legal Processes. These papers were collected by Austin Ranney, then chairman of the committee, and published as *Political Science and Public Policy* (1968). The title accurately suggests the principal concern of the conferences: what could the discipline of political science do with respect to public policy analysis that would be consistent with professional standards and proprieties? The principal opportunity seen was that of employing policy contents as the dependent variable and thus weighing the relative significance of various aspects of the decisional process and environment. The development of classifications of policy content and hence improved decisional analysis was secondary. The danger envisioned was that of losing professional detachment and standards of evidence and rigor amidst the temptation involved in a return to policy-prescriptive efforts. Only two papers in the collection deal with policy impacts as such, one on water resources and one on Selective Service.

A subsequent edited volume compiled by Ira Sharkansky, one of the pioneers in policy analysis using expenditures as the dependent variable, accurately reflects the emphases of this strand of the return to policy analysis.[1] Published in 1970 as *Policy Analysis in Political Science*, the Sharkansky collection includes models and classifications of policies, a large assortment of articles under the heading of "determinants" of public policy, and a final section entitled "evaluation of public policy." Four articles are included in the section on policy evaluation—one on program budgeting, one on political feasibility in policymaking, one on post-reapportionment changes of influence among members of a state legislature, and only one involving actual data concerning the effects of policies upon people outside of government. In the otherwise exhaustive bibliography with which the book closes, entries under the heading of "Evaluation of Public Policy" include only two books involving such data, one of which is the Wilson collection reviewed previously; other works are either studies of administrative agencies, policymaking, PPBS, or urban politics generally.

These points are made not to disparage those political scientists who study, write, or teach about public policy, but simply to stress certain key features about the emergence of the subfield of policy impact studies. First, they emerged as a small and contrastingly focused component of the larger field of policy analysis. Constrained at first by overwhelming emphasis upon process as the focus of research and analysis, and then by concern for empirical rigor and professional limitations, there was considerable delay in recognizing either their relevance or their potential. Considerable credit may be due to David Easton's address as President of the APSA, later published as "The New Revolution in Political Science" (1969), in which Easton emphasized (and legitimized) a "postbehavioral revolution" that would use empirical techniques to fill in the "feedback loop" between policy and demands and supports, in part as a means of serving social needs.

The second feature worth stressing about the emergence of policy impact studies is that they have not only surfaced very recently in political science, but owe their rapid blossoming to those very social needs that Easton stressed. Underlying the goals that Wilson and his associates had in mind, and ever-present as a source of destructive temptations in the minds of the SSRC conferees, were the pressing social problems of the United States in the late 1960s. It was no quirk or coincidence that led

[1] See Wade (1971) for a useful review essay on all of these early ventures in policy analysis.

Sharkansky to caption the final section of his collection "Evaluation of Public Policy." The multiplication of government social programs in the 1960s led to a desperate need for evaluation of existing programs and development of alternative policies demonstrably more likely to achieve goals. Political scientists were almost literally pulled into advisory-prescriptive roles by the needs of government. Many other social scientists were at work in this field, and political scientists arrived at a very late stage. As we examine impact studies under the larger rubric of policy evaluation, however, we shall see that there is not a great deal of conceptual or methodological ground to be made up.

TO WHAT EXTENT ARE GOVERNMENT PROGRAM GOALS BEING ACHIEVED?
HOW MIGHT THINGS BE DONE BETTER?

Studies in this category involve many of the same research tasks as do the more limited impact studies reviewed in the two previous sections. But they are undertaken from the perspective of seeking to measure levels of attainment of the goals of the policy, and with an eye to specifying how those goals might be better realized. Problems immediately arise with respect to such a goal-centered approach. It may be difficult to specify precisely what the goals or priority among goals of the relevant policymakers were. Or the goals themselves may be subject to challenge, if the researcher proceeds (as many do, and no doubt should) in the context of assessing the needs of persons confronting a particular problem. Another range of problems inheres in the fact that most government social programs are such that political scientists have no special claim to the subject area expertise, and their work must be undertaken in conjunction with members of other disciplines. Not least are the serious problems of concept and method that must be solved before evaluative research can establish itself on solid grounds. Each of these (and other) problems will become more tangible as we proceed. In this subsection, I shall first touch upon some of the few examples of evaluative research as yet completed by political scientists, and then (because it is so relatively new) undertake a brief survey of the field of evaluative research generally in terms of some of its major problems.

Political scientists in the evaluative arena

The work of a political scientist may of course be loaded with evaluative implications whether or not "policy evaluation" as such was explicitly in the researcher's mind as the project was first designed. Herbert Kaufman's study of the forest service (1960), or Gary Wamsley's observation of local draft boards (1969), for example, carry powerful evaluative implications. I am concerned with studies which seek to assess the present or probable results of particular policies as such, however, rather than their implementing agencies, upon people outside of government—and they are far fewer.

One example of evaluation-for-the-sake-of-prescription that was at least sponsored by a political scientist is Theodore Marmor's *Poverty Policy* (1971), which may serve to illustrate several characteristics of this genré. This is a collection of analyses of *need* (the characteristics of poverty), the workings of the current welfare system, and a series of proposals for cash transfer (welfare reforms, negative income tax, etc.) which are based on evidence about both current need and current policy consequences. Marmor's own essay sets up criteria and contributes effectively to the ability to choose among the available alternatives. The contrasting goals and biases of the various contributors (none of the rest of whom are political scientists) are clear, and the collection stands as confirmation of the hopes of some that evidence and sophisticated analysis would be brought to bear on the solution of social problems—as well as of the fears of others that policy research would end by engaging social scientists in research where conclusions depend upon value preferences rather than data. Engagement in evaluation, of course, can mean no less than substantial involvement with value preferences, if only in the form of policy-makers' goals.

The work of Frances Fox Piven also stands out in drawing policy prescriptions out of evaluative research. Her recent *Regulating the Poor* (1971, with Richard Cloward) employs several data sources regarding current impacts to build a prescription for reform. An essay entitled "The Urban Crisis: Who Got What, and Why?" (1973) is more fully devoted to tracing the consequences of policies (particularly expenditures) and less to prescription.

Policy evaluation (such as those last noted) obviously need not involve heavy doses of the researcher's preferences, and in most cases it does not. The primary purpose is merely to measure in some satisfactory way the extent to which policies are attaining the goals set for them by policy-makers, and if possible to identify flaws or obstacles which prevent them from doing so. In discussing the nature of the governmental and social need for understanding of the effects of policies, Bertram Gross framed the task in this fashion:

> Proper testing, therefore, first requires careful identification of the problem, followed by some plausible approach to scale. Proper testing also requires such elementary provisions as the following:
> 1. The development of specific criteria for success and failure;
> 2. The collection of reliable information;
> 3. The evaluation of performance both by those handling a project and by more impartial (even if less intimate) observers; and
> 4. The release for public scrutiny of the evaluations and supporting information (Gross, 1966, p. 16).

He then went on to say bluntly, "We know of no case where these requirements have been met." Since then, studies have multiplied, and some have begun to measure up to those deceptively simple criteria.

One of the best illustrations of tightly constructed evaluative research —and a valuable short course on some of the problems of policy evaluation—is Martin Levin's "Policy Evaluation and Recidivism" (1971). This is a report on an experimental analysis of alternative sentencing policies, in which Levin carefully weighs the strengths and weaknesses of various approaches to evaluation and assesses the relative uncertainties in specific policy implications emerging from this and similar studies. I am not aware of works by political scientists which exhibit greater sensitivity to the problems of establishing causal relationships between policies and consequences.

Much impetus has been given to the study of policy consequences, however, by the needs for evaluation of a variety of social programs. The result is a very rapid expansion of research effort and a sharp quickening of concern for issues of concept and method. In no area of policy research is characterization more rapidly out of date. As this essay was written, for example, two conferences brought political scientists and various other social scientists, in and out of government, together and added new substance to the available literature. The SSRC, once again under the leadership of Austin Ranney, sponsored a series of papers on the impacts of public policies in December of 1971. Issues of concept and measurement are discussed in general terms by James Coleman (1971). The impacts of civil rights laws and federal manpower policy are examined by Gary Orfield (1971) and Paul Puryear (1971) respectively, while comparative dimensions are added by studies of the impact of air pollution legislation in Britain (Scarrow, 1971) and old age pensions in Britain and Sweden (Heclo, 1971). A series of papers given at the 1972 public policy workshop of the Midwest Political Science Association evidence a similar burst of interest. The latter session more directly focused on evaluation for prescriptive and problem-solving purposes; the former, consistent with its origins and disciplinary focus, on concepts, methods, and general explanatory purposes. Such formal sessions devoted to aspects of policy evaluative research are now occurring at the rate of five or six per year.

Evaluative research generally: some problems of concept and method

In this subsection I shall attempt a brief sketch of a multidisciplinary field encompassing literally thousands of studies. I have not read most studies in this area and I am probably not even aware of many. The sketch will be organized in terms of the problems of concept and method in the field. I do not think the job can be done in any other way. Materials are widely scattered; the best evaluative studies are to be found in the reports of government commissions (particularly staff studies) or in the contract research done for government agencies. Many of these receive little circulation, even within the government, and are filed away in the Federal Clearinghouse[2] under any of a large number of whimsical catalogue classifications. What follows is based on reasonable diligence, much good advice (and some bad), and considerable stubbornness.

Evaluative research had a respectable history before the current wave of felt need for social reform purposes. Such research for the purpose of aiding government action, however, presents special problems. Many of these are well reviewed in Joseph Wholey's *Federal Evaluation Policy* (1970), which may serve as a useful primer. Predictable problems surround the time demands of government agencies and the political constraints experienced in developing and using reliable evidence. Perhaps less predictable ones involve the organization and orientation of social science research resources and personnel for purposes of policy research. All of these are well presented and analyzed in a lively and informative case study by Walter Williams (1972), an economist and a former member of OEO's research and evaluation staff. Entitled *The Struggle for a Negative Income Tax*, this brief (56 pp.) study shows the problems in generating and employing evaluative data in a timely manner, both in agency deliberations and in executive-legislative decisionmaking. It is an

[2] U.S. Department of Commerce, Clearinghouse for Federal Scientific and Technical Information, which publishes the *Government-wide Index to Federal Research and Development Reports,* and a journal, *U. S. Government Research and Development Reports.*

excellent teaching device because of the breadth of topics covered. The substantive merits of various negative income tax alternatives is one of the more important topics which Williams covers.

Political scientists, however, are likely to be more aware of the problems of securing action within national government institutions and that these problems, when soluble at all, are such chiefly on an ad hoc basis and by major political actors. In other words, they are not very much under the control or the responsibility of social scientists doing evaluative research. But problems of concept and method in the doing of that research *are,* and despite much attention many such problems seem to endure.

Conceptual problems. Many of the problems encountered in this area are not unique to evaluative research, but are common to social science generally. When applied to evaluative research, however, normally limiting elements may become destructive of useful results. An example is the enduring tendency of social scientists to see social problems exclusively from the perspective of policymakers. In evaluative research, this means that only policymakers' goals are taken as legitimate, and results are assessed with this yardstick in hand.[3] In the process, the probably quite different perspectives, goals, preferences, etc., of the clientele may be totally ignored. Or a single factor of paramount importance to policymakers (for example, the ratio of costs to perceived benefits) may be elevated into the chief basis of evaluation; much of the unfortunate application of cost-benefit methodology to evaluative results of social programs is related to this approach.[4]

A somewhat different problem also arises out of the tendency to adopt policymaker's perspectives and conduct top-down analyses from that vantage point. This is the compartmentalization and fragmentation that re-

[3] It is obviously very difficult for social scientists *not* to do so, for their natural perspective is that of the policy advisor. Goals stated very generally are translated into specifics, the needs of clientele are acknowledged rhetorically and then reduced to secondary status in practice, and so forth. See, e.g., Evans (1969). Even the best of the new generation of administrative practitioners are susceptible to this narrowness at times. See Marini (1971).

[4] The availability of cost-benefit analysis as a tool apparently led to its nearly-exclusive use in the early stages of *evaluation of outputs,* as distinguished from its obvious utility in *monitoring ongoing expenditures* and *comparing alternative methods of implementation.* Social policy cannot be measured exclusively by tangible economic data, of course. For an early discussion of this point, see Freeman and Sherwood (1965), and Orcutt and Orcutt (1968).

sults from taking one policy at a time and seeking to trace its effects upon its objects. Analysis that focuses on a single policy and its implementation is bound to exaggerate the importance of that policy and ignore other policies, limiting or enabling conditions, etc., and generally lead to failure to address objects of policies "wholistically," or in terms of their entire life situation.[5]

Such policy-focused, compartmentalized conceptualization may also contribute to one of the most frequent problems, that of failure to characterize pre-policy social circumstances and to combine policy-effects analysis with analysis of the effects of ongoing changes in social conditions and the impact of various other public and private policies. In the late 1960s, OEO commissioned eight major evaluative studies of the Community Action Programs (CAP) in a like number of areas.[6] Reputable social science organizations (universities and private research centers) were employed, and were allowed to establish their own concepts and methods. Although massive reports were written and filed, they appear almost useless. If personal experience may be drawn upon, I served as one of a three-member team of social scientists at the Institute for Research on Poverty at the University of Wisconsin which sought to synthesize and interpret the findings for OEO. After several months of effort, the task had to be abandoned as impossible. No policy prescriptions could be generated, because there was insufficient basis for confidence that the effects of the CAP had been "evaluated." Most studies made no effort whatsoever to establish any baseline description of social conditions prior to implementation of the policies involved; without knowing the "before," it is hard to know how the "after" differs from it. Most studies made no effort to describe what agencies did and how policies were applied; without such knowledge, one cannot tell *whether* "changes" in the status of objects of policies are related to policy-implementing actions—or *how*. Most studies made no effort to describe the major forces at work in the social environment of the objects of policies, so that it was impossible to tell whether "changes" were due to CAP actions or other public or private factors. What emerged from this mutimillion dollar investment in evaluative research were some scattered and often illuminating descriptions, a

[5] For an argument for "wholistic" analysis drawn from the area of educational policy evaluation, see Tumin (1970).
[6] The studies were set in Austin, Tex.; Atlanta, Ga.; Baltimore, Md.; Lexington County, Ky.; Knox County, Va.; Kansas City, Kans.; San Diego, Calif.; and Seattle, Wash. All are available in multi-volume form from the Clearinghouse for Federal Scientific and Technical Information, Springfield, Va.

great deal of precise statistical analysis of some very shaky numbers—and many lessons about the need for coherent, integrated, contextual, and time-sensitive research.

Attention to context has not yet moved to the point of systematically taking up the perceptions of the consumers of the policy themselves, which it must do. There is often a wide disjunction between what policy-makers perceive and desire, and what the individuals who are the objects of their policies perceive and desire. Coming from different class backgrounds, experiencing totally different life styles and situations, the latter's world views, goals, and perceptions are understandably far from those of policymakers. Nor is it sufficient for policymakers to rely upon analyses made from the top-down and from the middle-class perspectives of social science to make up for this disjunction, as William Ellis has shown at length in his *White Ethics and Black Power* (1969). There are examples in which such "consumers' perspectives" have been faithfully represented, and thus we know that it can be done; but ironically this insight is owed more to psychologists such as Keniston (1968) or Coles (1971, 1972) or journalists such as Terkel (1970) or Gitlin (1970), than to social scientists (with certain exceptions, such as Herbert Jacob, 1969).

With all these major conceptual flaws, however, social science seems to be well ahead of some newcomers to the problem of evaluating the effects of public policies. The general field of technology assessment, which seeks to understand the probable impacts of various alternative uses of technology, has made some bold and welcome calls for major investment in developing evaluative methodology.[7] But the approach so far is superficial, technology-focused to an extreme (with all the predictable flaws detailed above in regard to policy-foci), and socially and politically naive. Such studies as have been made tend to provide extended "laundry lists" of things to consider, but end up assuming continuity in practically all aspects of life except what the particular technology happens to touch. This appears to be an area where good intentions have yet to come to grips with the hard realities of in-depth social research. Little guidance is yet to be found here, but there is correspondingly great opportunity for political scientists to show what is needed. [The Environ-

[7] United States House of Representatives, Committee on Science and Astronautics, *A Study of Technology Assessment* (Washington, D.C.: U.S. Government Printing Office, 1969), and *Technology: Processes of Assessment and Choice* (Washington, D.C.: U.S. Government Printing Office, 1969). The former is the Report of the Committee on Public Engineering Policy, National Academy of Engineering, and the latter the Report of the National Academy of Sciences.

mental Protection Act's requirement of an "environmental impact statement" in connection with every major project is enforceable in court, and the preparation and review of such statements opens up a major field for social scientists.]

Methodological problems. The boundary between a conceptual problem and a more technical or methodological problem is far from clear, but in neither is the distinction crucial. I mean to include here those types of problems of measurement and procedure that might endure after a more comprehensive conceptualization was achieved. Many of them, of course, are closely related to problems of conceptualization.

The most salient issue in evaluative methodology is probably the controversy between experimental and exploratory approaches. These issues are well joined and discussed in the exchange between Weiss and Rein and Donald T. Campbell (1970). (See also Cain and Hollister, 1969; Levitan and Taggart, 1971). It should be apparent that I have reservations about certain aspects of the experimental approach (policy focus, compartmentalization, noncontextuality, absence of the consumers' perspective, etc.). Weiss and Rein (1970) have stated some of these concerns well, although in a narrower frame of reference. I do not believe that the only alternative is unsystematic, impressionistic, or unreplicable exploratory meandering.[8] A panel approach, for example, with sufficient numbers of interviewees, sufficient depth of analysis, and sufficient time duration, combined with systematic top-down policy analysis including some experimental elements where appropriate, could prove to be a viable synthesis amounting to a third methodology.

A related problem is that of adequately attributing causality to the components of the policy being evaluated. This is, to be sure, one of the continuing difficulties of social science; the fact that change of the sort sought follows the implementation of a policy does not necessarily show that it came about *because* of the policy. But this standard problem is exacerbated in evaluative research by failure to consider other contextual factors and possible explanations, and by researchers' failure to try to relate consequences to specific components of policies. This becomes crucial under circumstances where policymakers' choices of alternative policies depend on knowledge of which components operate to bring about which specific consequences. Undoubtedly such precision in dem-

[8] For some alternatives, see Coles (1971, 1972), Ellis (1969), Gitlin and Hollander (1970), Keniston (1960, 1968), Terkel (1970), U.S. House Committee on Science and Astronautics (1969a b), and Yancy (1969).

onstrating causal linkages depends on the availability and character of data, but this is partly a function of investigators' methods. The National Advisory Commission on Selective Service (1967), for example, succeeded in establishing that nonuniformity in application of national conscription standards was attributable to the local board structure, while discrimination between men of different economic levels was brought about by the substance of criteria for various deferment categories. Demonstrated in detail and with precision as to subordinate aspects, such findings helped make possible policy modifications appropriate to achieve a different desired mix of consequences.

One way in which social scientists have in effect sought to avoid the difficulties of attributing causality in specific situations is through turning to large-scale quantitative studies. From a larger body of comparative data, it may appear that correlations establish causal relationship at sufficient levels of confidence. Experience in such data collection, however, gives clear reason for skepticism. The NORC evaluation of CAP (Vanecko, 1969), for example, depends on very uncertain indicators, employs imprecise definitions, and derives findings from sketchy data. Problems of reliability, comprehensiveness, and subtlety remain to be overcome in quantitative research, and the need for careful and contextual observation of such complex phenomena as individual responses to government social intervention probably must be accepted for the foreseeable future (Levitan and Taggart, 1971).

Another range of problems in contemporary methodology is encountered when evaluators begin tracing the effects of a given policy, no matter how sensitively. Initially, they must devise ways of assessing the mediating roles played by policy implementors, such as administrative agencies[9] or intervening levels of government.[10] Characteristics of agencies, the style of political administration, internal ideologies of organizations, and soon all may play a major role in shaping the effects of policies. These are very difficult to measure, of course, but cannot be ignored. Equally hard to trace and to measure are the secondary and tertiary effects of policies, which may well be more consequential for the individual, the economy, and the society, than the original impact upon policy objects.[11] Unintended consequences are also part, but only part, of this problem. There

[9] Davis and Dolbeare (1968) focus on this sometimes ignored aspect of policy implementation.
[10] See, for example, Derthick (1970).
[11] A thoughtful call for such consideration may be found in LaPorte (1971). For an example of how secondary and tertiary effects may differ from apparent intentions and primary beneficiaries, see Piven (forthcoming).

appears to be no quick or convenient means of including such important dimensions in an evaluation, and we are again directed toward detailed field study focused on (or emanating from) a body of the individuals who are the objects of policies.

A final range of problems involves the organization of resources to do evaluative research, and effects upon the field situation of the presence of evaluators. Walter Williams (1971) has shown the gaps between academic social scientists' capabilities, experience, and orientations and the needs of operative agencies, as well as the kinds of constraints under which government evaluators must work. Many of these difficulties are translated into inadequacies of design or method in the field, haste in preparation of reports, conditioning of findings in anticipation of various uses, etc. These combine with such naturally frustrating problems as harmonizing quite contrasting images of what is occurring on the part of informants[12] and other data sources to lend a heavy aura of uncertainty to the task of accurately characterizing a specific social reality and evaluating a particular policy intervention. Not least of the obstacles in the way of effective policy evaluation is the problem of the multiple participants in research activities and multiple audiences for whom reports are intended. Cain and Hollister (1969) make this point effectively. Maintaining a consistent and intelligible design under such conditions may become very difficult.

I shall summarize and discuss these and other problems of contemporary evaluative research in the final section of this essay, where the implications of such problems can be elaborated further. Not noted here, for example, is the earlier stressed problem of different levels of policy (fundamental *and* output) involved in any given evaluative research project, no matter how narrow in scope; I am not aware that existing evaluative studies take it into account in any substantial way. Let us first complete our review of approaches to policy impact research by moving to our fourth category, which will be very brief.

WHAT DOES THIS ALL MEAN FOR GENERAL THEORIES
AND EXPLANATIONS OF POLICIES?

As already suggested, political scientists have long studied the late stages of policy impact, in the sense that public opinion, socialization, and voting studies reflect, in part, accumulated effects of fundamental

---

[12] American Technical Assistance Corp. (1969) presents the problem in terms of volunteers' information. For a much more comprehensive discussion, see Ferman (1969).

and output policies over time. David Easton was understandably quick to see the uses of impact studies for general theory purposes. What would be new here would be studies of the way in which policy consequences led to changes in general supports and/or specific demands—in other words, studies which sought to close the feedback loop or otherwise relate policy effects to the character of the evolving political system. Policy consequences could and should be used to say what difference it makes who governs, or to generate explanations of political change, but few studies exist that actually fill such gaps. In a series of articles, Norton Long (e.g., 1970) has suggested ways in which policy consequences could be used to build explanatory theory. Seeking to build a base for both evaluation of system components themselves and for understanding of political change processes, Dolbeare (1970) urged many of the same things in his "Public Policy Analysis and the Coming Struggle for the Soul of the Post-Behavioral Revolution." One of the few actual studies done in this area is an imaginative little work by Hayes (1972), who used policy consequences as a means of identifying elements of the power structure of Oakland, thus avoiding the dilemmas and controversies of elitist-pluralist concepts and methods. Matthews and Prothro's well-known *The Negro in the New Southern Politics* (1967) also fits in this category in many ways.

But it seems clear that a major gap still exists between policy enactment and the ultimate stages of their effects upon demands and supports. No doubt research designed to help fill this gap is already underway. Whether it can succeed in doing so, however, is another question. Standing in the way of fulfilling the goals marked out by Easton, Long, Wilson, and others is the fact that the building of general theory requires research into the effects of fundamental—not just output—policies. I doubt that we can sufficiently broaden our frameworks to fully encompass fundamental policies, and still do empirical research. This is the great dilemma underlying the whole field of policy consequences research, not just research with theory building purposes (though it is particularly visible here). Consideration of this question is the main burden of the next section.

PROBLEMS AND PROSPECTS: A CRITICAL EVALUATION

I shall first summarize the problems of concepts and methods in policy consequences research, then consider possible solutions, and finally assess the implications of those "solutions"—or lack of them. In noting the problems of evaluative research in the penultimate subsection, it should be clear, we were also raising questions about the less ambitious impact studies necessarily included within the ambit of evaluative research. I use the still more inclusive term "policy consequences research" now in order to include the broader purposes of the subsection just completed; in other words, I am now talking about problems common to all policy effects studies, undertaken for whatever purpose.

MAJOR PROBLEMS: A SUMMARY

The top-down perspective establishes policymakers' views of the nature of problems, and their goals, as controlling. Moreover, it causes gross exaggeration of the importance of a single policy and eliminates a vast array of factors more powerfully affecting the life situation of the objects of the policy—thus effectively preventing wholistic analysis and understanding.

Focus on a single policy from any perspective encourages ignorance of process and context. Without understanding of what conditions were like before a policy intervention, what forces were at work, creating what changes in social relationships, how those forces shape the lives of people, and related questions, analysts cannot hope to understand the effects of policies.

The consumers' perspective on both problems and policies is unrepresented—still another spin-off from social scientists' top-down, noncontextual approach. The world as it is seen and felt from below is not the world that social scientists and policymakers experience and prescribe for; which world is relevant for policy consequences research?

Linkages between policy components and particular consequences is very hard to demonstrate evidentially. Even the more precisely constructed experimental studies have loopholes and limitations, and there is usually neither time nor opportunity nor resources to undertake experimental research.

Second- and third-order consequences, or indirect effects, may be more important than immediate impacts. But the diffusion, accomplished as policies radiate out in their effects, time passes, and mediating and intervening factors operate, effectively prevents precise identification of such consequences.

Fundamental policies are always involved to some extent, whether mixed in with the subjective consequences of output policies or more directly and independently. But they are difficult to conceptualize, harder to operationalize, and perhaps impossible to research except at a scale and with resources too vast to be practical—at least if one insists upon empirically measurable indicia as evidence.

These are by no means all the problems of policy consequences research, but they will do to focus our discussion.

POSSIBLE SOLUTIONS

Substantial steps could be taken to resolve a number of aspects of the first three problems. For example, we could simply abandon the top-down approach and self-consciously adopt the perspective of people who experience problems. If we start from thorough understanding of the nature and causes of problems, both objectively and subjectively as experienced by people, and conduct all analyses of policy consequences from that ground-up vantage point, our findings and interpretations might more fully reflect social reality as people know it—and more harmoniously articulate with ultimate consequences for political demands and supports. At the same time, of course, we would have to abandon the single-policy focus and seek to understand the total context—the nature of the interplay of all the forces that converge to create contemporary social dynamics—of the individual objects of policies. We would be seeking to develop integrated, comprehensive understanding of the social situation of those individuals. In viewing the policy world from the ground up, both public and "private" forces that operate on individuals would be relevant. Thus, an old-fashioned "political economy" or some similar integrated conceptual framework would have to be evolved —one that enabled the analyst to see both public and private forces operating upon people in tandem, a single intermeshed system of forces.

As I intimated in the earlier discussion of these problems, one way to counter the difficulties of much contemporary research and to operationalize the suggestions just made might be to introduce the panel method into the study of policy consequences. If researchers could bring themselves to first understand the social context and world view of members of a broadly representative panel, it might then be possible to see the social forces and policy interventions of the times through their eyes. In other words, the integration and comprehensiveness we need might be obtainable by starting from the relevant point at which all these forces and factors converge—the individual, who experiences them in integrated form in his personal life. In studying the effects of policies on members of the panel, researchers would be seeking to understand all the effects of all the policies in the context of all the forces that bear upon the life situation of those individuals. There is no other way in which the relative weights of various forces can be sorted out and policies seen in their true context. This approach would go a considerable way toward resolving problems stemming from the top-down approach and the single policy focus; it would assure the presence of baseline characterizations, consumers' perspectives, and contextual and processual understanding; and it might help to alleviate some of the uncertainties produced by diffusion of policy consequences and the involvement of fundamental policies.

But it may be totally impracticable, at least on the scale necessary to do the job properly. How large a panel, how many social scientists, how long a time would it take? The payoffs would be much greater for general policy-consequences-based explanations of politics than for immediate government policy evaluation needs. They would also be greater for the considerably reconstructed social science that would emerge, to say nothing of the expanded conceptual approach to the nature of "politics" that would be implied. Consideration of payoffs is precipitate, however.

Many of the problems summarized above would remain untouched even after such a drastic reorientation of approach. Moreover, efforts to solve them lead directly *away* from the wholistic emphasis underlying those suggestions. The problem of demonstrating linkage between policy components and their consequences, for example, requires narrowing rather than enlarging of the framework within which research is conducted. It requires that every possible step be taken to isolate the policy under analysis and analyze its effects with all other variables rigorously controlled; experimental research thus tends toward the study of only the immediate tangible impacts of limited forms of explicity framed output policies in confined social settings. Government needs for evaluative research of this kind will continue to force such narrow-gauge analysis, not to mention acceptance of the top-down perspective and policymakers' definitions of problems and goals.

We are thus faced with a substantial dilemma. To meet established standards of empirical demonstrability, we must adopt limiting premises, narrow the focus, and exclude as many factors from the analysis as possible. But doing so means that we are obliged to build in inescapable flaws and biases. And it assures that we shall not either accomplish wholistic analysis or be able to include fundamental policies in our analysis. The dilemma is acutely focused when we imagine attempting research into the consequences of fundamental policies: by the time such policies are disaggregated into specific researchable components, and the direct tangible impacts compiled with the precision demanded by empirical research, the quality and character of fundamental policy itself has been lost. The concepts and methods of empirical social science force particularism upon us, and particularism prevents true—wholistic—social understanding.

Some accommodations are imaginable. We could establish some looser standards of tolerance for what evidence is sufficient to create inferences of causal linkage, for example, and we could rely upon very gross aggregate data to assess the effects of broad policy packages. But these kinds of middle grounds are not likely to satisfy those committed to professional standards of rigorous logic and proof.

PROSPECTS

Where does this leave the field of policy consequences studies? The nature of this dilemma suggests two not very satisfactory prospects. One is a continued development of evaluative research of increasing empirical "rigor." This rigor, of course, can only be obtained at the cost of maximizing the distortions I have characterized as problems of this type of research. Policymakers need evaluations of the effects of the policies for which they are responsible, to be sure. Perhaps even a narrow technocratic study replete with such distortions is an improvement over nothing, although I am not at all confident of that; it might well be better on occasion *not* to lend false encouragement about ways of attaining illusory goals with respect to misunderstood problems.

The other direction would involve the effort to develop the kind of understanding of policy consequences that would lead to general explanatory theories of politics. As implied above, I do not see how this can be done with what we currently understand as empirical social science. I have discussed the serious conceptual reorientation that would be required, and the probably disabling practical problems of the scale of research needed to encompass the wide scope of factors relevant to properly conceptualized inquiry. Even if such major obstacles were overcome, however, we would still be faced with trying to apply a set of tools applicable to hard data in laboratory situations to the dynamics of a complex and interconnected social system and process. In order to understand some aspect of that system and process, our social science tells us to abstract it from the larger context which is essential to its meaning, and what we then come to "understand" is something different from what actually exists.

This problem is not unique to policy consequences research, of course, nor will it prevent further efforts to study policy consequences. I think it is more acute in this area than in some others, however, because policy consequences lead to evaluations of the workings of both policies and the political system itself—and thence to political actions that affect people in important ways. If we do not see the serious limitations of our research approaches, concepts, and methods, we run the risk of doing great harm when we innocently think we are doing good. It is said that medicine reached the point where doctors began to do more good than harm to their patients sometime around 1920. If we seek confidence that we have passed a similar point, we might start by reexamining—and perhaps reconstructing—the social science that we employ.

BIBLIOGRAPHY

ALBERTA, DAVID S. *A Plan for Measuring the Performance of Social Programs.* New York: Praeger, 1970.

AMERICAN TECHNICAL ASSISTANCE CORP. *Measuring the Impact of VISTA on Poverty Communities.* Washington, D.C.: U. S. Government Printing Office, 1969.

ANDERSON, MARTIN. *The Federal Bulldozer.* Cambridge: MIT Press, 1964.

BEANEY, WILLIAM M., and BEISER, EDWARD N. "Prayer and Politics: The Impact of *Engel* and *Schempp* on the Political Process," *Journal of Public Law,* 13 (1964), pp. 475–503.

BECKER, THEODORE L., ed. *The Impact of Supreme Court Decisions.* New York: Oxford University Press, 1969.

BIRKBY, ROBERT H. "The Supreme Court and the Bible Belt: Tennessee Reaction to the 'Schempp' Decision," *Journal of Political Science,* 10 (1966), pp. 304–315.

BLAUSTEIN, ALBERT, and FERGUSON, CLARENCE. *Desegregation and the Law.* New Brunswick: Rutgers University Press, 1957.

CAIN, GLEN G., and HOLLISTER, ROBINSON G. "The Methodology of Evaluating Social Action Programs." Madison, Wisc.: Institute for Research on Poverty, discussion paper series, 1969.

CAMPBELL, DONALD T. "Reforms as Experiments," *American Psychologist,* 24 (1969), pp. 409–429.

———. "Considering the Case Against Experimental Evaluations of Social Innovations," *Administrative Science Quarterly,* 15 (1970), pp. 106–113.

———, and Ross, H. LAURENCE. "The Connecticut Crackdown on Speeding: Time-series Data in Quasi-Experimental Analysis," *Law and Society Review,* 3 (1968), pp. 33–54.

COHEN, DAVID. "Politics and Research: The Evaluation of Social Action Programs in Education," *Review of Educational Research,* 40 (1970), pp. 213–238.

COLEMAN, JAMES S. *Equality of Educational Opportunity.* Washington, D.C.: U. S. Government Printing Office, 1966.

———. "Problems of Conceptualization and Measurement in Studying Policy Impacts," unpublished paper delivered at the Virgin Islands SSRC Conference on the Impacts of Public Policy, 1971.

COLES, ROBERT. *Children in Crisis.* Boston: Little, Brown & Co., 1972.

———. "Understanding White Racists," *New York Review of Books,* 17 (1971), pp. 12–15.

CRAIN, ROBERT L., and VANECKO, JAMES J. "Elite Influence in School Desegregation," in Wilson (1968).

DAVIS, JAMES W., JR., and DOLBEARE, KENNETH M. *Little Groups of Neighbors: The Selective Service System.* Chicago: Markham, 1968.

The Impacts of Public Policy   125

DERTHICK, MARTHA. *The Influence of Federal Grants: Public Assistance in Massachusetts.* Cambridge: Harvard University Press, 1970.

DIXON, ROBERT G. JR. *Democratic Representation: Reapportionment in Law and Practice.* New York: Oxford University Press, 1968.

DOLBEARE, KENNETH M. *Trial Courts in Urban Politics: State Court Policy Impacts and Functions in a Local Political System.* New York: John Wiley, 1967a.

———. "The Public Views the Supreme Court," in Jacob, Herbert, ed., *Law, Politics, and the Federal Courts.* Boston: Little, Brown & Co., 1967b.

———. "Public Policy Analysis and the Coming Struggle for the Soul of the Post-Behavioral Revolution," in Green, Philip, and Levinson, Stanford, eds., *Power and Community: Dissenting Essays in Political Science.* New York: Pantheon Press, 1970.

———, and HAMMOND, PHILIP E. *The School Prayer Decision: From Court Policy to Local Practice.* Chicago: University of Chicago Press, 1971.

EASTON, DAVID. "The New Revolution in Political Science," *American Political Science Review,* LXIII (1969), pp. 1051–1061.

ELLIS, WILLIAM W. *White Ethics and Black Power.* Chicago: Aldine, 1969.

EVANS, JOHN W. "Evaluating Social Action Programs," *Social Science Quarterly,* 50 (1969), pp. 568–581.

EVERSON, DAVID H., ed. *The Supreme Court as Policy-Maker: Three Studies on the Impact of Supreme Court Decisions.* Carbondale, Ill.: Public Affairs Research Bureau, Southern Illinois University, 1968.

FERMAN, LOUIS. "Some Perspectives on Evaluation Social Welfare Programs," *The Annals,* 385 (1969) pp. 143–156.

FREEDMAN, LEONARD. *Public Housing.* New York: Holt, Rinehart & Winston, 1969.

FREEMAN, HOWARD E., and SHERWOOD, CLARENCE C. "Research in Large-Scale Intervention Programs," *Journal of Social Issues,* 21 (1965), pp. 11–28.

———. *Social Research and Social Policy.* Englewood Cliffs: Prentice-Hall, 1970.

GARDINER, JOHN A. "Police Enforcement of Traffic Laws: A Comparative Analysis," in Wilson (1968).

GITLIN, TODD, and HOLLANDER, NANCI. *Uptown: Poor Whites in Chicago.* New York: Harper & Row, 1970.

GREENBERG, JACK. *Race Relations and American Law.* New York: Columbia University Press, 1959.

GROSS, BERTRAM, and MARIEN, MICHAEL. "The President's Questions—And Some Answers," in Gross, Bertram, ed., *A Great Society?* New York: Basic Books, 1966, pp. 3–31.

GROSSMAN, JOEL B., and GROSSMAN, MARY H., eds. *Law and Change in Modern America.* Pacific Palisades, Cal.: Goodyear Publishing Co., 1971.

HAYES, EDWARD C. *Power Structure and the Urban Crisis: Who Rules in Oakland?* New York: McGraw-Hill, 1972.

HECLO, H. HUGO. "Old Age, Inequality, and Political Conjunctures in Britain and Sweden," unpublished paper delivered at the Virgin Islands SSRC Conference on the Impacts of Public Policy, 1971.

JACOB, HERBERT. "Wage Garnishment and Bankruptcy Proceedings in Four Wisconsin Cities," in Wilson (1968).

———. *Debtors in Court: The Consumptions of Government Services.* Chicago: Rand McNally, 1969.

———, and LIPSKY, MICHAEL. "Outputs, Structures, and Power: An Assessment of Changes in the Study of State and Local Politics," *Journal of Politics*, 30 (1968), pp. 510–538.

JOHNSON, RICHARD M. *The Dynamics of Compliance: Supreme Court Decision-Making From a New Perspective.* Evanston, Ill.: Northwestern University Press, 1967a.

———. "Compliance and Supreme Court Decision-Making," *Wisconsin Law Review*, (1967b), pp. 170–185.

JONES, ERNEST M. "Impact Research and the Sociology of Law: Some Tentative Proposals," *Wisconsin Law Review*, (1966), pp. 1–9.

JONES, MARTIN V. *A Technology Assessment Methodology: Some Basic Propositions.* Washington, D.C.: The Mitre Corporation, 1971.

KATZ, ELLIS. "Patterns of Compliance with the Schempp Decision," *Journal of Public Law*, 14 (1965), pp. 396–405.

KAUFMAN, HERBERT. *Forest Ranger: A Study in Administrative Behavior.* Baltimore: Johns Hopkins, 1960.

KENISTON, KENNETH. *The Uncommitted: Alienated Youth in an Alienating Society.* Princeton: Princeton University Press, 1960.

———. *Young Radicals: Notes on Committed Youth.* New York: Harcourt, Brace & World, 1968.

KESSEL, JOHN H. "Public Perceptions of the Supreme Court," *Midwest Journal of Political Science*, 10 (1966), pp. 167–191.

LAMB, W. CURTIS; STARR, EMILY S.; and SPENCE, JOHN D. *National Evaluation of CAP's.* Report Number 2. Cambridge: Barss, Reitzel and Associates, 1970.

LAPORTE, TODD R. "The Context of Technology Assessment: A Changing Perspective for Public Organizations," *Public Administrative Review*, 21 (1971), pp. 63–73.

LEMPERT, RICHARD. "Strategies of Research Design in the Legal Impact Study," *Law and Society Review*, 1 (1966), pp. 111–132.

LERNER, MAX. "Constitution and Court as Symbols," *Yale Law Journal*, 46 (1937), pp. 1290–1319.

LEVIN, MARTIN A. "Policy Evaluation and Recidivism," *Law and Society Review*, 6 (1971), pp. 17–46.

———. "An Empirical Evaluation of Urban Political Systems: The Criminal Courts," in Kilpatrick, Sam, and Morgan, David, eds., *Urban Politics: A System Analysis.* Glencoe, Ill.: Free Press, 1972, pp. 17–46.

LEVINE, JAMES P. "Constitutional Law and Obscene Literature: An Investigation of Bookseller Censorship Practices," in Becker, Theodore L., ed., *The Impact of Supreme Court Decisions.* New York: Oxford University Press, 1969.

———. "Implementing Legal Policies Through Operant Conditioning: The Case of Police Practices," paper presented at the meetings of the American Political Science Association, Los Angeles, 1970.

LEVINE, ROBERT A. *The Poor Ye Need Not Have With You: Lessons From the War on Poverty.* Cambridge: MIT Press, 1970.

LEVITAN, SAR, and TAGGART, ROBERT, III. *Social Experimentation and Manpower Policy: The Rhetoric and the Reality.* Baltimore: Johns Hopkins Press, 1971.

LONG, NORTON. "Indicators of Change in Political Institutions," *The Annals of the American Academy of Political and Social Sciences,* 388 (1970), pp. 35–45.

MARINI, FRANK, ed. *Toward a New Public Administration: The Minnowbrook Perspective.* San Francisco: Chandler Publishing Co., 1971.

MARMOR, THEODORE R., ed. *Poverty Policy: A Compendium of Cash Transfer Proposals.* Chicago: Aldine-Atherton, 1971.

MARRIS, PETER, and REIN, MARTIN. *Dilemmas of Social Reform.* New York: Atherton Press, 1967.

MATTHEWS, DONALD, and PROTHRO, JAMES. *The Negro in the New Southern Politics.* New York: Harcourt, Brace & World, 1967.

McKAY, ROBERT B. "With All Deliberate Speed: A Study of School Desegregation," *New York University Law Review,* 31 (1956), pp. 991–1090.

MEDALIE, RICHARD J.; ZEITZ, LEONARD; and ALEXANDER, PAUL. "Custodial Police Interrogation on Our Nation's Capital: The Attempt to Implement Miranda," *Michigan Law Review,* 66 (1968), pp. 347–1422.

MEEHAN, EUGENE J. "Policies and Inventories: An Analysis," unpublished paper, Center of Community and Metropolitan Studies, University of Missouri-St. Louis, 1972.

MILLER, ARTHUR S. "On the Need for 'Impact Analysis' of Supreme Court Decisions," *Georgetown Law Journal,* 53 (1965), pp. 365–401.

———. *The Supreme Court and American Capitalism.* New York: Free Press, 1968.

MILNER, NEAL. "The Impact of the *Miranda* Decisions in Four Wisconsin Cities." Madison, Wis.: unpublished doctoral dissertation, University of Wisconsin, 1968.

MUIR, WILLIAM K. *Prayer in the Public Schools: Law and Attitude Change.* Chicago: University of Chicage Press, 1967.

MURPHY, WALTER F. "Lower Court Checks on Supreme Court Power," *American Political Science Review,* LIII (1959), pp. 1018–1031.

———. *Congress and the Court.* Chicago: University of Chicago Press, 1962.

———, and TANENHAUS, JOSEPH. *The Study of Public Law.* New York: Random House, 1972.

———, and TANENHAUS, JOSEPH. "Public Opinion and the United States Supreme Court: Mapping of Some Prerequisites for Court Legitimation of Regime Change," in Grossman, Joel B., and Tanenhaus, Joseph, eds., *Frontiers of Judicial Research.* New York: John Wiley & Sons, 1969.

NAGEL, STUART S. "Some New Concerns of Legal Process Research Within Political Science," *Law and Society Review,* 6 (1971), pp. 9–16.

NATIONAL ADVISORY COMMISSION ON SELECTIVE SERVICE. *In Pursuit of Equity: Who Serves When Not All Must Serve?* Washington, D.C.: U.S. Government Printing Office, 1967.

NATIONAL SCIENCE FOUNDATION. *Knowledge Into Action: Improving the Nation's Use of the Social Sciences.* Washington, D.C.: Government Printing Office, 1969.

ORCUTT, GUY H., and ORCUTT, ALICE G. "Incentive and Disincentive Experimentation for Income Maintenance Policy Purposes," *American Economic Review*, 58 (1968), pp. 754–772.

ORFIELD, GARY. *The Reconstruction of Southern Education: The Schools and the 1964 Civil Rights Act.* New York: John Wiley & Sons, 1969.

————. "The Impact of Civil Rights Laws," unpublished paper delivered at Virgin Islands SSRA Conference on the Impacts of Public Policy, 1972.

PATRIC, GORDON. "The Impact of a Court Decision: Aftermath of the McCollum Case," *Journal of Public Law*, 6 (1957), pp. 455–464.

PELTASON, JACK W. *Fifty-Eight Lonely Men: Southern Federal Judges and School Desegregation.* New York: Harcourt, Brace & World, 1961.

PIVEN, FRANCES FOX. "The Urban Crisis: Who Got What, and Why," in Wolff, Robert Paul, ed., *1984 Revisited.* New York: Knopf, 1973, pp. 165–201.

————, and CLOWARD, RICHARD. *Regulating the Poor: The Function of Public Welfare.* New York: Pantheon Books, 1971.

PRITCHETT, C. HERMAN. *Congress Versus the Supreme Court.* Minneapolis: University of Minnesota Press, 1961.

PURYEAR, PAUL L. "The Measurement of Manpower Policy Impacts in the Black Community: Income Mobility, Occupational Status, and Political Support," unpublished paper delivered at the Virgin Islands SSRC Conference on the Impacts of Public Policies, 1971.

RANNEY, AUSTIN. *Political Science and Public Policy.* Chicago: Markham, 1968.

RIVLIN, ALICE M. *Systematic Thinking for Social Action.* Washington, D.C.: The Brookings Institution, 1971.

RODGERS, HARRELL R. *Community Conflict, Public Opinion, and the Law.* Columbus: Charles E. Merrill, 1969.

————, and BULLOCK, CHARLES S., III. *Law and Social Change: Civil Rights Laws and Their Consequences.* New York: McGraw-Hill, 1972.

ROSENTHAL, ROBERT. "Teacher Expectations for the Disadvantaged," *Scientific American*, 218 (1968a).

————, and JACOBSON, LENORE. *Pygmalion in the Classroom.* New York: Holt, Rinehart, and Winston, 1968b.

ROSS, H. LAURENCE; CAMPBELL, DONALD T.; and GLASS, GENE V. "Determining the Social Effects of a Legal Reform: The British 'Breathalyser' Crackdown of 1967," *American Behavioral Scientist*, 13 (1970), pp. 493–509.

SCARROW, HOWARD A. "The Impact of British Air Pollution Legislation," unpublished paper delivered at the Virgin Islands SSRC Conference on the Impacts of Public Policy, 1971.

SCHUBERT, GLENDON. *Reapportionment.* New York: Charles Scribner & Sons, 1965.

SCHWARTZ, RICHARD D. "Field Experimentation in Socio-Legal Research," *Journal of Legal Education*, 13 (1961).

————, and ORLEANS, SONYA. "On Legal Sanctions," *University of Chicago Law Review*, 34 (1967), pp. 274–300.

SHAPIRO, MARTIN. "The Impact of the Supreme Court," *Journal of Legal Education*, 23 (1971), pp. 77–88.

SHARANSKY, IRA. *Policy Analysis in Political Science.* Chicago: Markham, 1970.

SORAUF, FRANK. "*Zorach* v. *Clauson:* The Impact of a Supreme Court Decision," *American Political Science Review*, XLIII (1959), pp. 777–791.

STEINER, GILBERT Y. *The State of Welfare.* Washington, D.C.: The Brookings Institution, 1971.

STUMPF, HARRY P. "The Political Efficacy of Judicial Symbolism," *Western Political Quarterly*, 19 (1966), pp. 293–303.

SUCHMAN, EDWARD A. *Evaluation Research.* New York: Russell Sage, 1967.

TERKEL, STUDS. *Hard Times: An Oral History of the Great Depression.* New York: Pantheon, 1970.

TUMIN, MELVIN M. "Evaluation of the Effectiveness of Education: Some Problems and Prospects," *Interchange*, 1 (1970), pp. 96–109.

U.S. HOUSE OF REPRESENTATIVES, COMMITTEE ON SCIENCE AND ASTRONAUTICS. *A Study of Technology Assessments.* Washington, D.C.: U.S. Government Printing Office, 1969a.

———. *Technology: Processes of Assessment and Choice.* Washington, D.C.: U.S. Government Printing Office, 1969b.

VANECKO, JAMES J. *Community Mobilization and Institutional Change: The Influence of the Community Action Programs in Large Cities.* Chicago: National Opinion Research Center, 1969.

WADE, LAWRENCE. "Political Science and Public Policy: A Review Essay," *Policy Sciences*, 2 (1971), pp. 321–334.

WAMSLEY, GARY. *Selective Service in a Changing America.* Columbus, Ohio: Charles E. Merrill, 1969.

WASBY, STEPHEN L. *The Impact of the United States Supreme Court: Some Perspectives.* Homewood, Ill.: Dorsey Press, 1970.

WAY, H. FRANK, JR. "Survey Research on Judicial Decisions: The Prayer and Bible Reading Cases," *Western Political Quarterly*, 21 (1968), pp. 189–205.

WEISS, ROBERT S., and REIN, MARTIN. "The Evaluation of Broad-Aim Programs: Experimental Design, Its Difficulties and an Alternative," *Administrative Science Quarterly*, 15 (1970), pp. 97–105.

WHOLEY, JOSEPH S. *Federal Evaluation Policy.* Washington, D.C.: Urban Institute, 1970.

WILLIAMS, WALTER. *Social Policy Research and Analysis: The Experience in Federal Agencies.* New York: American Elsevier, 1971a.

———. "The Capacity of Social Science Organizations to Perform Large-Scale Evaluative Research," Public Policy Paper No. 2, Institute of Governmental Research, University of Washington: Seattle, Washington, 1971b.

———. "The Struggle for a Negative Income Tax," Public Policy Monograph No. 1, Institute for Governmental Research, University of Washington: Seattle, Washington, 1972.

WILSON, JAMES Q., ed. *City Politics and Public Policy.* New York: John Wiley, 1968.

WIRT, FREDERICK M. *Politics of Southern Equality: Law and Social Change in a Mississippi County.* Chicago: Aldine, 1970.

YANCEY, WILLIAM L. "Intervention as a Strategy of Social Inquiry," *Social Science Quarterly,* 50 (1969), pp. 582–597.

YALE LAW JOURNAL, eds. "Interrogations in New Haven: The Impact of Miranda," *Yale Law Journal,* 76 (1967), pp. 1521–1648.

Organizational Constraints and Public Bureaucracy

LAWRENCE C. PIERCE*

Individuals make choices. They choose what to have for dinner, whom to marry, and where to go on vacations. They also choose how much to spend on city streets, policies to protect the environment, and how many missiles are needed to defend the country. The first group of decisions is normally made privately by an individual and affects only the individual and possibly a few others. The second group of decisions is normally made collectively and affects many people. By organizing to make decisions, individuals benefit from the specialized abilities that others can add to their individual decision calculus. But collective decision-making also imposes costs on individuals. Organizations are designed therefore not only to take advantage of the benefits of collective action but also to reduce their costs. The purpose of this chapter is to review the organizational literature for clues on how organizations act to control the costs of collective choice.[1]

To look at the way in which organizational variables constrain collective choice (particularly the effects of standard operating procedures on choice) seems eminently reasonable. This common sense approach is seldom considered in the decision-making literature, however. (The most

* The author wishes to acknowledge the support of the Center for the Advanced Study of Educational Administration during a portion of the time he devoted to the preparation of this chapter. CASEA is a national research and development center which is supported in part by funds from the United States Office of Education, Department of Health, Education and Welfare. The opinions expressed in this chapter do not necessarily reflect the position or policy of the Office of Education and no official endorsement by the Office of Education should be inferred.

[1] This chapter deals primarily with public organizations. The author assumes, however, that large public and private organizations may be viewed in similar terms. (See Wildavsky, 1965, for a persuasive case to this effect.) Furthermore, since much of the public choice literature which will be reviewed focuses on private organizations, it will be necessary to use some examples from the private sector.

notable exceptions are Cyert and March, 1953; March and Simon, 1958; and Feldman and Kanter, 1965.) For example, conventional economists tend to deal with collective choice as if organizational variables were unimportant.[2] The theory of the firm and the theory of investment, for instance, are built on the assumption that if you know an organization's goals and the state of its environment, you can predict with relative certainty its pricing, product, and investment decisions. (For reviews of the psychology and economics literature on decision-making, see Edwards, 1954, 1961, and Simon, 1959.) Even political scientists, who are supposed to be experts on political behavior, frequently overlook the effects of organizational variables on public choice. The behaviorialists in political science emphasize the socio-psychological correlates of individual political behavior and pay little attention to formal rules and the policy consequences of that behavior. And when political scientists have looked at the relationship between structural variables and public policy, they have generally correlated such system level variables as interparty competition, division of party control, voter participation, malapportionment, and policy choices. From these analyses they have concluded that the political process has little to do with policy choices (Dawson and Robinson, 1963; Dye, 1966; Hofferbert, 1966, 1972; and Sharkansky, 1968).

The failure of social scientists to adequately consider or find relationships between organizational variables and collective choices results, I believe, from looking at the wrong organizational variables and not from the absence of important relationships. Consequently, this essay begins on the assumption that organizational rules and decision-making procedures do affect organizational decisions. Just as a defendant's substantive rights in a court of law are no better than his procedural rights, this chapter will show that an organization's decisions are in large part a function of the rules and procedures that produce those decisions.

One final introductory note. The chapter deals only with the organizational constraints that affect a single organization's choices. It does not deal with the many institutional constraints, such as federalism, the separation of powers, bicameralism, judicial review, etc., which affect the performance of the entire American political system. It is restricted, in other words, to variables that have an immediate bearing on the environment of a public organization and on the way individuals or-

---

[2] As we will see later, a small group of public choice economists have begun to analyze the effect of organizational rules on collective choices.

ganize themselves to accomplish the organization's goals. The review is divided into four sections: collective choice and organizational constraints, environmental constraints, internal constraints, and an agenda for future research.

COLLECTIVE CHOICE AND ORGANIZATIONAL CONSTRAINTS

One view of public organizations is that they are collections of individuals who voluntarily join together to make collectively binding or authoritative decisions. They are specifically designed to improve the decision-making abilities of individuals which comprise the organization. In order that the organization's decision-making processes actually serve the interests of its members, a number of constraints (or controls) are imposed by the members of the organization on the manner in which the organization selects a course of action to accomplish its goals. In much the same way that a computer program guides the analytic task of the computer, organizational constraints guide the decision-making processes in organizations.

The focus here on organizational choice and the organizational constraints which affect those choices is not a widely used approach for studying organizational decision-making. The dominant approach is to view organizations as patterns of interrelated behavior, and to emphasize the effects of the organization's system of *roles* on individual behavior. Typical of the dominant social psychological approach to organizational decision-making is the work of Robert Kahn and his colleagues at the University of Michigan (Kahn et al., 1964; Katz and Kahn, 1966).

For Kahn and many other social psychologists, organizations are conceptualized as stable patterns of interrelated behavior, or as role systems. The individual's role consists of his part in the total pattern of activity. The effect of organizational structure on an individual may be approached, therefore, through the role behavior of organizational members. Any particular individual's role behavior is determined primarily by the behavior of other members of the organization with whom he has direct contact. They become his role set. As Kahn et al. point out:

> It is a key assumption of this approach that the behavior of any organizational performer is the product of motivational forces that derive in large part from the behavior of members of his role set, because they constantly bring influence to bear upon him which

serves to regulate his behavior in accordance with the role expectations they hold of him (1964, p. 35).

The focus of attention is on the determinants of an individual's role behavior and his personal adjustment to the demands made by his role set. These determinants are illustrated in figure 1.

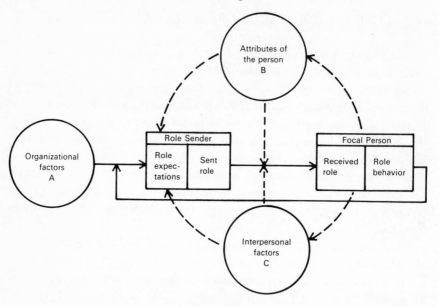

Figure 1: Role Episode

Reprinted from Robert L. Kahn et al., *Organizational Stress*, (John Wiley: 1964, p. 30), by permission of the author.

This conceptualization suggests that a person's behavior is determined primarily by the communications he receives from his role set. The role messages the focal person receives may or may not be the same as the messages sent him, depending primarily on the congruence of the messages with his own role expectations. Furthermore, the messages sent to the focal person depend on the expectations that role senders have for the focal person, which in turn depends on various organizational realities, their perception of specific attributes of the focal person, and the quality of their interpersonal relationships to the role incumbent.

Significantly, there is little in this approach that helps us understand choices made by public organizations. There is an implicit assumption that organizational choice consists of the "accumulated behavior" of all role players. But since every individual has a different role set, many of which overlap one another, it is impossible to aggregate individual behavior into organizational behavior.

Since the social psychological approach to organizational decision-making does not actually address itself to the determinants of organizational choice or policies, I had to look elsewhere for an appropriate theoretical structure for this chapter. One possibility was to focus on a new body of literature that is developing which deals with the organization and its environment (Lawrence and Lorsch, 1967; J. Thompson, 1967, for example). Another possibility was to look at the growing body of literature on public choice (Buchanan and Tullock, 1962; Downs, 1957; Niskanen, 1971). The advantage of the public choice literature is that it is built upon a theoretical explanation for the provision of collective goods. Perhaps the best way to demonstrate the utility of the public choice approach to organizational decision-making is to examine the public choice explanation of why individuals engage in collective choice and of the particular kinds of problems collective choice poses for individuals.

The theory of public choice rests on the assumption that individuals freely choose to accomplish some activities collectively because they expect to benefit by doing so. Or stated in another way, individuals choose to make decisions collectively because they expect the alternative, decisions made individually, to be relatively more costly.

A useful conceptualization of the relative advantages and disadvantages of individual and collective choice is provided by Buchanan and Tullock (1962, pp. 43–84). They identify two kinds of costs resulting from any decision-making activity. First, "there are costs that an individual expects to endure as a result of the actions of others over which he has no direct control" (p. 45). These are called *external costs* and include the costs that the actions of others impose on an individual, such as the discomfort from industrial pollution, the loss suffered when someone steals your car, or the extra taxes required to support governmental programs you dislike. External costs also include opportunity costs (or benefits foregone) arising when only private action is used, such as when no, or too little, organized fire protection is available. Secondly, "there are costs which the individual expects to incur as a result of his own participation in an organized activity" (p. 45). These are called *decision-making costs* (individuals also incur decision-making costs when they act individually, but they are relatively small, and Buchanan and Tullock limit decision-making costs to the costs resulting when two or more people are required to reach agreement). In this schema, the individual, in deciding between individual and collective activity, must weigh the external costs of private choice against the sum of external costs and decision-making costs of collective choice. The rational individual selects that form of activity which minimizes the total costs.

In what situations will collective action be selected? It is clear that for those few activities in which the external costs can be reduced to zero, it would not be rational for an individual to provide them collectively. Collective choice would impose unnecessary decision-making costs. A necessary condition for collective choice, therefore, is the presence of external costs. But it is only when the external costs plus the decision-making costs of collective activity are less than the external costs of private activity that collective activity is preferred. The existence of external costs, or externalities, is not, in other words, a sufficient condition for collective activity. Furthermore, in seeking to reduce the external costs of private activity, individuals may join together in private contractual organizations, such as business organizations, or in public organizations. Again, the choice of the form of collective organization should be based on the individual's calculation of which kind of organizations minimizes total costs (see Olson, 1965). The theory of constitutions developed by Buchanan and Tullock describes how individuals behave collectively. It also has prescriptive implications by showing the effects of alternative decision rules on an individual's decision calculus.

Having decided that it is to his advantage to have certain kinds of decisions made collectively, the rational individual still tries to minimize the total costs of collective decision-making. This can be done by either reducing the external costs of collective choice or reducing the decision-making costs of collective choice or both. The rest of this paper will be concerned with the ways this is done. Before discussing the specific constraints on organizational choice, however, a few more remarks are needed about the general relationship between organizational constraints and collective choice.

To minimize the total costs of collective choice, individuals can first of all try to reduce or minimize external costs. External costs result when an organization makes a decision which deviates from the preferences of those affected by the decision, or when an organization makes a poor decision—that is when it selects the wrong alternative to accomplish its goals. In very summary terms, the literature suggests two ways of reducing external costs. The first is to adopt a more comprehensive decision model which requires the specification of goals, the listing of alternative means for achieving the goals, the analysis of the consequences of each alternative, and the selection of the alternative that most nearly accomplishes the goals. This approach, which is implicit in much of the planning literature, the PPB movement, and systems analysis, is directed at reducing external costs by reducing the chances of an organization making the wrong or poor decisions. The process of comprehensive decision-making is outlined clearly by Feldman and Kanter:

> The decision problem is that of selecting a path which will move the system—individual, computer program, or organization—from some initial state to some terminal state. A problem may have one or more initial states and one or more terminal states, and there are usually many paths emanating from each initial state. Which path will be chosen? One criterion is that of selecting the path which will achieve the most preferred terminal state. The only procedure which can guarantee that this "best" path will be found is one which generates the entire decision tree, i.e., all alternative paths and the consequences of each terminal state for all relevant goals (1965, p. 615).

The more alternatives considered—the more comprehensive and decision-making process—the less likely an organization is to make a poor decision, and the less are the expected external costs incurred.

The second approach to reducing the external costs of organizational decisions is to increase the participation in the decision-making process of those people likely to be affected by the decision. Democratic theory is based largely on this principle, that if you permit people to participate in government, they will ensure it is responsive to their preferences. Rather than being concerned with organizations selecting a poor alternative, this approach focuses on the problem of organizations making decisions that deviate from the preferences of those affected by them. Buchanan and Tullock (1962) have formalized the relationship between the costs a person expects to incure as the result of actions of others and the number of individuals required to agree before a final decision is made in what they call the "external-cost function" (1962, p. 64). In the geometric representation of the "external-cost function" in figure 2, this function decreases as the number of people required to agree increases. "When unanimous agreement is dictated by the decision-making rule, the expected costs on the individual must be zero since he will not willingly allow others to impose external costs on him when he can effectively prevent this from happening" (p. 64). On the other hand, if a single individual has the authority to make decisions for the entire collectivity, the expected external costs are much higher.

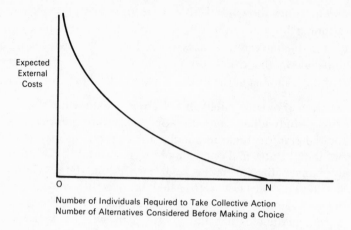

Number of Individuals Required to Take Collective Action
Number of Alternatives Considered Before Making a Choice

Figure 2: External Cost Function

As figure 2 suggests, the expected external costs of an organizational decision can be reduced either by establishing procedures requiring that additional alternatives be considered before selecting a course of action, or by adopting a decision rule that increases the number of people required to agree on a course of action. Unfortunately, both strategies increase decision-making costs—the expenditure of time, effort, resources, and opportunities foregone in decision-making. In fact, whereas external costs are a decreasing function of both the number of alternatives considered and number of people making decisions, decision-making costs are positively related to both of these variables. For even moderately complex problems, the comprehensive decision model, requiring the consideration of all possible alternatives, is simply not feasible (see Braybrooke and Lindblom, 1963). According to Feldman and Kanter, the comprehensive model is not feasible, first, because the size of the decision tree is very large even for simple problems; second, because the alternative paths and rules for generating them are probably not available; and third, for most problems the consequences of alternatives are difficult to estimate (Feldman and Kanter, 1965, p. 615). Similarly, the adoption of a unanimity rule or extra-majority rule would greatly increase the amount of bargaining time required to make collective decisions. Consequently, to avoid inaction, individuals must find some way to achieve an optimal balance between external costs and decision-making costs.

Figure 3 shows the relationships among total costs, the two single cost functions, and the number of alternatives considered or number of people required to make a decision.

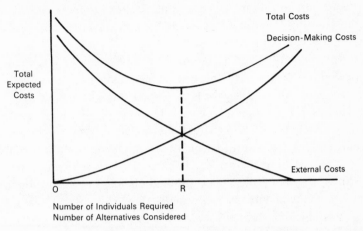

Figure 3: Total Cost of Collective Choice

To arrive at point R where the sum of external costs and decision-making costs are minimized, individuals must somehow limit the number of people who participate in decision-making and/or the number of alternatives considered. Limiting the number of decision makers is done by establishing rules to govern who participates and how decisions are made.[3] The rules, procedures, or routines, which Buchanan (1967, p. 216) calls "constitutional" decisions, are choices about how future "operational" decisions will be made. According to Buchanan, when decision-making costs become very large

> even idealized individual choice need not require simultaneous determination of all values for the choice variables. In this context, it may become rational for the individual to consider his choice among rules or institutions independently from his own particular choices to be exercised within the operation of these institutions or rules. In other words, it may become rational for the individual to discuss his choice among alternative institutions under which subsequent choices will be made independently from these later choices or his predicted reactions to them (1967, p. 215).

[3] Limiting the number of alternatives is done by adopting standard operating procedures or routines for handling problems.

Constitutional rules, or organizational constraints, as they are called in this paper, are not completely inflexible. In fact, they are likely to change periodically in response to longer-run feedback from the organization's environment, usually according to some even more general rules. In other words, organizations have the capacity to learn from their behavior, and this learning is reflected in adaptations to the rules and procedures governing the choice process.

In conclusion, organizations consist of a set of more or less stable rules and procedures to simplify the task of responding to immediate operating problems. Or, in the words of Cohen, March, and Olsen, "an organization is a collection of choices looking for problems, issues and feelings looking for decision situations in which they might be aired, solutions looking for issues to which they might be the answer, and decision makers looking for work" (1972, p. 2). It is with these rules and procedures, whether called constitutional choices or organizational constraints, that this chapter is concerned.

Organizational constraints vary greatly in the kind and amount of control imposed. Organizational goals, at one extreme, provide a general guideline for organizational activities. At the other extreme is an econometric model for forecasting the demand for an organization's services, which provides a complete prescription of the decision-making process.

For the purposes of this chapter, organizational constraints are divided into constraints imposed by the organization's environment and those imposed by the actions of the organization itself. The first set, which are called *environmental constraints,* are designed primarily to insure that the external costs of the organization's decisions are held to a minimum. They describe the limitations imposed by nonmembers and noncontrollable factors on the solutions available to the organization. The second set, which are called *internal constraints,* consists of rules and procedures adopted by the organization to simplify the comprehensive decision model so that decisions can be made at reasonable cost and in a reasonable amount of time. They are designed primarily to reduce the decision-making costs of collective choice.

ENVIRONMENTAL CONSTRAINTS

Decision makers in organizations are not free to select any course of action that maximizes their personal interests. Their choices are limited by a number of constraints imposed primarily by the organization's environment to reduce the external costs of collective action. These environmental constraints vary in the manner in which they limit organizational choice. General social norms usually affect decision makers indirectly. Expenditure limitation imposed by a legislature, on the other hand, directly affects the alternatives an organization can consider. Environmental constraints also vary in terms of the ease with which they can be changed by the organization. Social norms regarding sex education have proved difficult to change. On the other hand, school administrators frequently try to change particular legal requirements by lobbying for a change in the law. Environmental constraints, in other words, are not immutable limitations on organizational choice. They change over time and are subject to some manipulation by organizational members—particularly when a constraint stands in the way of the organization accomplishing its purpose. Nevertheless, in the short term, decision makers in organizations must work within the limitations imposed by environmental constraints. To ignore them in considering alternative courses of action is to depart from the real world.

One useful classification of environmental constraints is provided by Eckstein (1961). He considers physical constraints, legal constraints, political constraints, financial or budget constraints, and traditional, social, and religious constraints. Our discusssion follows Eckstein's classification of constraints but modifies the order of consideration to look first at constraints that have a direct effect on an organization's outputs. Next it considers constraints that have more indirect effects.

PHYSICAL CONSTRAINTS

The physical constraints on organizational choice refer to the state of the knowledge about and technology available for relating the physical inputs and outputs of an organization. For many years dreamers and engineers wanted to fly faster than the speed of sound. Not until jet engines and lightweight, heat-resistant metals were developed did it become physically possible to do so.

The failure of public programs to accomplish their objectives also results from a lack of knowledge about the social production functions involved (Schultze, 1968, pp. 57–64). In some cases it is a matter of not knowing the effects of program activities on the desired outcomes. The government, for instance, continues to pump more money into ghetto schools despite considerable evidence that its expenditures have not improved the quality of education in the schools (Coleman, 1966). In other cases, such as with the federal water pollution control program and government programs dealing with the maternal and child health care (see Schultze, 1968, pp. 57–58), knowledge of the consequences of program has been constrained, not so much by the technical questions involved, but by the interaction of institutional, economic, and technical factors which complicate the relationship between inputs and outputs. The physical constraint imposed by complexity can be minimized in part by systematic analysis. Nevertheless, public suspicion of government programs is increasing in part because many believe that government decision makers proceed too quickly with half-thought-out and costly programs, that they do not recognize the physical constraints on their ability to do good.

Finally, where there are choices between projects, or about the size or timing of projects, physical constraints may be involved. A particular factor of production may be available in one place and not another; or its limited supply may simply preclude a large project or multiple projects. As the adage says, you can't squeeze blood from a stone, and decision makers who are aware of the physical constraints facing the organization won't try.

RESOURCE CONSTRAINTS

Every organization is faced with resource constraints, which are reflected in the prices it must pay for the men, money, and materials (the factors of production) needed to supply a particular good or service. In general terms, for a given level of demand for a good or service, the more scarce a particular factor of production—and consequently the higher its price—the less of the good requiring that particular factor will an organization produce. The resource constraints, in other words, have a direct relationship to the supply of an organization's output as long as the people using that output are free to spend their income as they wish.

An important question for students of public organizations is whether resource constraints affect public organizations differently than private organizations. This question is dealt with in Niskanen's recent book, *Bureaucracy and Representative Government* (1971). Some of Niskanen's arguments are summarized in this section and the one following on demand constraints.

For the most part, resource scarcity affects public organizations in about the same way as private organizations. Both hire employees, borrow money, and purchase materials in free markets. Since most public and private organizations are not so large that their use of a factor increases its price appreciably, those organizations using like factors pay approximately the same price for them. The relationship between the prices paid for factors of production and the output of an organization are reflected in an organization's "cost-output function." According to Niskanen, "any point on this function represents the minimum total payment of factors necessary to produce a given output, given the factor prices and available production processes; the cost-output function represents the relation among these points" (pp. 31–32).

For an organization that sells its services on a per unit basis, the average cost curve (or long term supply function) is arrived at by dividing the cost-output function by the quantity produced. It shows how much an organization will supply of a good or service at various prices. In a competitive situation, deviation from the price and output relationship indicated by the supply function will force a private firm into an unprofitable position.

Public bureaus are not as constrained by the cost-output relationship as private organizations. This is because the supply of a bureau's service is determined by the size of the budget it receives and not directly by its supply curve. This is not to say that bureaus ignore costs. To the contrary, as we will see later, budget maximization for most bureaus depends on keeping costs as low as possible. It is only to say that if the legislative body which gives a bureau its budget wants, it can provide for a level of service which is higher or lower than the demand and supply conditions would permit in the private sector.

A somewhat less important difference between the impact of resource scarcity on public and private organizations is that it is still possible in some instances for public bureaus to exercise factor price discrimination. Public bureaus may discriminate against factors when they are the only users of those factors such as with career military personnel. Some believe that, for the same reason, local governments and hospitals discriminate in hiring personnel (Devine, 1970). Public bureaus may also discriminate against certain factors which are considered to be a part of the public domain (Niskanen, 1971, p. 31). Governments pay nothing for the use of public lands, congested air space, and the electronic frequency spectrum. They also pay less than a fair market price for young men drafted to fight wars, and for nuclear material.

In summary, the owners of the needed factors of production (resources) constrain organizational choices by charging a price for use of those factors. If factors are purchased in free markets, there are no external costs imposed on the owners of those factors. They simply do not make the particular factor available if the organization does not pay them what they want. When an organization can limit the availability of alternative uses for a factor or when it can expropriate factors, such as drafting men into armies or taking control of the airways, the constraint imposed by resource scarcity acts imperfectly in protecting the owners of factors from incurring external costs. The extent of the external cost imposed is equal to the difference between the price paid for the factors and what they would receive if they were free to sell the factor elsewhere.

DEMAND CONSTRAINTS

Organizations are also constrained by the demand for their products or services. For private competitive organizations which attempt to maximize profits, the demand constraint limits output to a level at which the return from selling an additional unit of output equals the additional cost of producing that unit of output. Since individual consumers are free to buy or not to buy the service, no external costs are incurred by the public. External costs of private activity are limited primarily to costs incurred by people who do not participate in either the factor market or product market for the service, but suffer some unpleasantness resulting from the production of the service.

The demand constraint on the output of public bureaus is much more complex. For the most part, public services are paid for with taxes and not on a fee for service basis. Since taxes are compulsory and public services are delivered without charge, the consumer has no direct way of avoiding the costs of public services he does not want. The major limitation on the output of a specific bureau is the size of the bureau's budget. As Niskanen demonstrates with some care, however, the budget is an imprecise instrument of control and one that leads to relatively large external costs for the public.

Niskanen is primarily concerned with the effects of the relationship between the organization that approves a bureau's budget (which he calls the sponsor) and the bureau, on a bureau's budget and output. As mentioned above, a bureau does not normally sell its services to consumers on a per unit basis. Instead, a bureau offers a proposed set of activities and unexpected outcomes to a sponsoring body in return for a budget (Niskanen, 1971, p. 25). The sponsor, in turn, obtains its money from tax revenues. The primary financial constraint facing a public bureau, therefore, is the size of the budget it receives. A less direct constraint is the proportion of personal income the public is willing to turn over to the sponsor for public services. A bureau is dependent on the sponsoring organization since it has no alternative source of income. Consequently, the personal preferences of the officials in the sponsoring body are more likely to be considered in preparing a bureau's program and budget than are the preferences of the clientele the bureau is supposed to serve.

The relationship between the sponsoring body and bureau is not a typical superior-subordinate relationship, however. In fact, a bureau is in a very good position to dominate the relationship and to obtain benefits for itself in the process. It is true that the sponsoring organization (legislature) which is usually elected, exercises some control since it reviews the budget, monitors the bureau's performance and procedures, and usually ratifies the selection of the bureau's head. The power of the bureau relative to the sponsoring organization arises from the latter's dependence on the bureau as the only supplier of a given service. According to Niskanen, the monopoly position of a bureau gives it a clear bargaining advantage:

> Under many conditions it gives a bureau the same type of bargaining power as a profit-seeking monopoly that discriminates among customers or that presents the market with an all-or-nothing choice. The primary reason for the differential bargaining power of a monopoly bureau is the sponsor's lack of a significant alternative and its unwillingness to forego the services supplied by the bureau. Also . . . the interests of those officers of the collective organization responsible for reviewing the bureau are often best served by allowing the bureau to exploit this monopoly power (Niskanen, 1971, p. 25).

From the viewpoint of the bureau the preferences of the sponsoring organization are summarized in a budget-output function. "Any point on this function represents the maximum budget the sponsor is willing to grant to the bureau for a specific expected level of output" (Niskanen, 1971, p. 25). The budget output relationship is such that the sponsors are willing to provide a larger budget for a higher level of expected output. The sponsors are also willing to provide a larger budget per unit of output for a smaller expected output than a larger expected output. (This means that the sponsors' marginal budget-output function, or demand function, is negatively sloped.) The important point is that it is the sponsors' demand for the bureau's output that determines the size of the bureau's budget and not the public demand for the service. The public has some say indirectly through the electoral process and through the internal decision process of the sponsor, but it is unlikely, for reasons that will become clear later, that the preferences of the two groups are identical.

If we assume, as do a number of analysts of bureaucratic behavior (Parkinson, 1957; Downs, 1967; Niskanen, 1971), that bureaucrats are motivated to maximize the size of their agencies' budgets, then it is possible to illustrate how the budget review process limits the budget and output of a bureau. To review, the bureau being described purchases the factors of production competitively. It is considered to be a monopoly supplier of a particular service, but the sponsor is assumed not to exercise its monopoly position as the single buyer of the service. Under these demand and cost conditions, Niskanen suggests that a bureau will submit to the sponsor a budget "which maximizes the expected approved budget subject to the constraint that the approved budget must be sufficient to cover the costs of the output expected by the sponsor at the budget level" (p. 46). In other words, the bureau will not promise more than it can deliver at the agreed upon total budget, since to do so would tend to make the sponsors reduce the bureau's budget in the future (see Wildavsky, 1964).

The expected level of output of a bureau at the approved budget level is illustrated in figure 4 under two demand situations. Under the lower demand condition, where the sponsors' marginal valuation of the bureau's services is represented by V_1, the output of the bureau will be in what Niskanen calls the budget constrained region, where ea_1gh equals ecfh.

At this level of output, Q_1, the total budget just covers the cost of producing the expected output. The bureau, however, will be producing at a level of output where the marginal benefits enjoyed, gh, are much less than the marginal cost, hf, or at a level well above the optimal output level where marginal value equals marginal costs. This occurs, of course, because under a majority vote rule, those sponsors who have a high demand for the bureau's services will be able to pay off or bargain with those with relatively low demand. (For a fuller explanation of why this occurs under majority rule, see Wagner, 1971, pp. 7–13.) The bargaining can continue up to a point where all the net benefits that would accrue from an optimal level of service (represented by the triangle ca_1i) are wiped out by the net costs of operating above the optimal level (represented by the triangle, ifg). In other words, when a bureau

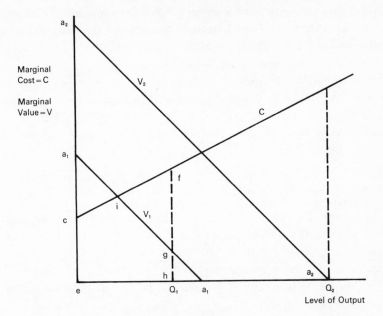

Figure 4: Equilibrium Output of a Bureau

is operating in the budget constrained region, the marginal voter among the sponsors is indifferent between producing nothing and Q_1.

When the demand for a bureau's service is very high relative to its cost, or under the high demand condition, V_2, the bureau will operate in what Niskanen calls the "demand-constrained" region, where the marginal value of output is zero, or at Q_2. Unlike in the budget-constrained region where a bureau can only maximize its budget by producing at the lowest possible cost, in the demand-constrained region there is no immediate incentive to operate at minimum cost. In this region the output of a bureau is constrained only by demand conditions, and changes in costs will not change the budget. Again the output of the bureau is above the optimal level.

In terms of the socially efficient allocation of resources, the public budget constraint on the supply of public goods is even less adequate than it appears, because a sponsoring body, whether it is an appropriations subcommittee or a city council, is likely to both overrepresent high demand groups in society and to overrepresent the suppliers of important factors to the bureau. To the extent that this happens, the marginal valuation functions shown in figure 4 will be higher than would the functions reflecting the public's demand for the same service.

After determining the output level of a bureau under both low and high demand conditions, Niskanen goes on to compare the supply of a bureau's services with that provided by profit-seeking forms of organization. What he finds is summarized in four hypotheses (Niskanen, 1971, pp. 64–65):

1. A bureau will supply an output up to twice that of a competitive industry faced by the same demand and cost conditions.

2. At the equilibrium level of output, a bureau will generate smaller net benefits than a competitive industry, but, in the absence of factor price discrimination, a larger factor surplus. This suggests that the owners of specific factors will be stronger advocates of the bureaucratic supply of a service than will most beneficiaries of the service.

3. At the equilibrium level of output, a bureau may appear to be nearly as efficient as a competitive industry (in terms of the average cost per unit of output), but this average cost is realized only at the higher output level, where the marginal value of the service is less than the marginal cost.

4. The minimum marginal cost function of a bureau, like that of a profit-seeking monopoly, will not be revealed by its budget and output proposals. The budget and output combinations proposed by a bureau will suggest that marginal costs decline with output, regardless of the slope of the minimum marginal costs.

If Niskanen's analysis is correct, he then joins Buchanan in believing that governments tend to overproduce nearly all "public goods" (Buchanan, 1967). Or stated in terms we have used before, the overproduction of public services imposes external costs on the public, the extent of which would be measured by the opportunities foregone by not allocating resources optimally. This position is not shared by all economists, however. Two very well-known scholars, John Kenneth Galbraith and Anthony Downs, have argued the opposite case, that governments in democracies produce too few public goods (Galbraith, 1958; Downs, 1960). They both believe that the public fails to support public services because they are less aware of the benefits of public services than their costs. Regardless of which is true, this disagreement reflects the fact that the public budgetary process is not nearly as precise an instrument for controlling the supply of public goods and services as is the competitive market mechanism for controlling the output decisions of private organizations.

LEGAL CONSTRAINTS

As Buchanan points out, at any moment in time there is a political constitution which greatly limits the manner in which organizations make decisions (Buchanan, 1967, p. 287). The political constitution constrains organizational choice by specifying the kinds of activities that shall be carried out by public and private organizations, by specifying the forms of organizational arrangements in both the public and private sectors, by establishing the qualifications of people who may participate in organizations, and by specifying the goals and procedures organizations must use in selecting a course of action.

The laws and legal decisions that make up a country's political constitution determine to a large degree the kinds of activities performed by public or private organizations. Activities involving national security, law enforcement, welfare, and education are restricted for the most part to the public sector. Furthermore, within the public sector the United States Constitution gives the Federal government responsibility for protecting national security, while leaving major responsibility for law enforcement, welfare, and education to state and local governments.

The laws also govern the form that both public and private organizations may take. Antitrust laws constrain the use of monopolies in the private sector. At the same time, statutes restrict competition in the public sector, thereby encouraging public monopolies.[4] Legislation specifies the conditions under which profit or nonprofit organizations may and may not be formed.

In limiting the form that organizations may take, law makers try to minimize the total costs that certain forms of organization may impose on society. Unfortunately, we still have a very imperfect understanding of the advantages and disadvantages of alternative institutional arrangements, or of the conditions under which one kind of organization is superior to another. Economists, such as Thomas Marschak, have com-

[4] Some economists, such as Milton Friedman, Anthony Downs, and William Niskanen have suggested reforms to induce more competition among bureaus in the public sector.

pared the performance of decentralized and centralized decision-making arrangements (1965, pp. 436–445). Niskanen has also compared the level of output, revenues, costs, profits, collective surplus and factor surplus for private monopolies, competitive enterprises, and public bureaucracies (1971, p. 61). Lawmakers are still unable, however, to assess accurately the benefits and costs to different kinds of organizations. Consequently, the legal form of public organizations is likely to be based on historical precedents.

A third way that the political constitution constrains organizational choice is by saying which groups of people may participate in organizations and the qualifications they must have to participate. Laws restrict the political activity of public officials and the political contributions of corporate officers. When the Penn Central Railroad filed for reorganization under the Bankruptcy Act in June 1970, federal legislation was enacted providing government loans to the company and placing certain restrictions on the management of the company's affairs. Governments also establish rules on the qualifications of participants. Plumbers, real estate salesmen, stockbrokers, doctors, and many other workers must be licensed to ply their trades.

Finally, organizations are constrained by laws specifying the goals they must pursue and the procedures they must follow in making choices. The Employment Act of 1946 directed the federal government to use all "means consistent with its needs and obligations. . . . in a manner calculated to foster and promote maximum employment, production and purchasing power." The act also established the qualifications of the President's economic advisors and outlined a number of procedural requirements the President must follow in carrying out the provisions of the legislations (Pierce, 1971). Laws constrain the behavior of private decision makers as well. An example of such constraints is furnished by Clarkson (1962) in his study of investment portfolio selection. The laws regulating trust departments of banks restrict the kinds of securities that may be considered. As a result of this restriction a procedure has been adopted that limits the selection of securities to those which have been purchased by national banks.

Some of the most interesting work on the effects of legal constraints on organizational choice has focused on the impact of alternative decision rules (Wicksell, 1958; Pigou, 1932; Coase, 1969; Buchanan and Tullock, 1962). The analysis of the consequences of decision rules (rules for aggregating individual choices into social decision) was pioneered by Knut Wicksell. He suggested that efficient budgets will be chosen only under a rule of near unanimity. His analysis was supported by Pigou's writings on welfare economics, in which he postulated that under a majority rule, decisions will be made without regard to the costs or benefits incurred by those in the minority, that is, without consideration of the total social benefits and costs involved. Since externalities are excluded, a majority will supply an inefficiently large or small amount of a public service (Pigou, 1932, pp. 183–184). Coase, and Buchanan and Tullock have taken issue with Pigou's conclusions on the basis that if those suffering from another's acts can make bribes or make side payments, then majority voting may not generate inefficient budgets (Coase, 1969, pp. 1–44; Buchanan and Tullock, 1962, pp. 147–169). Any limits on side payments, however, increases bargaining costs or serves to prevent the negotiation of efficient outcomes under a majority rule.

POLITICAL CONSTRAINTS

Solutions available to decision makers in organizations are also constrained by the need to gain support for a proposed action. While decision makers in private organizations must increasingly consider the reactions of outsiders to their acts, the reactions of outsiders are compelling for public officials. The importance of political reality for public decision makers is argued most forthrightly by the philosopher Paul Diesing:

> . . . the political problem is always basic and prior to the others.
> . . . This means that any suggested course of action must be evaluated first by its effects on the political structure. A course of action which corrects economic or social deficiencies but increases political difficulties must be rejected, while an action which contributed to political improvement is desirable even if it is not entirely sound from an economic or social standpoint (1962, p. 228, as quoted in Wildavsky, 1966).

The need for support or approval of people outside the organization constrains an organization's choices in several ways. First, decision makers usually need the support of outsiders to approve a course of action. To gain their support, decision makers incur a variety of exchange costs. Every politician and every economist knows there is no such thing as a free lunch; that he must pay for the support of others by using up resources in the form of side payments, promises of reciprocal support, or threats to get even. Unpopular and controversial proposals incur more exchange costs than do popular and noncontroversial actions. Some decisions must be rejected, in other words, because the political costs of enacting them would be too high; other decisions must be compromised to reduce the political costs of enactment; almost no decisions will be acceptable to everyone. (For an analysis of how political constraints affect the formulation of fiscal alternatives see Pierce, 1971, pp. 108–124.) Since there are always exchange costs, a political decision

> . . . never is based on the merits of a proposal but always on who makes it and who opposes it. Action should be designed to avoid complete identification with any proposal and any point of view, no matter how good or how popular it might be. The best available proposal should never be accepted just because it is best; it should be deferred, objected to, discussed, until major opposition disappears. Compromise is between a good and a bad proposal (Diesing, 1962, p. 232).

Second, policy choices are constrained by their electoral consequences for decision makers. The electoral costs of governmental choice has been explored most thoroughly by Anthony Downs. Downs assumes that government organizations are made up of self-interested individuals who voluntarily choose to pursue common objectives. Since they must also win elections in order to pursue their ends, Downs postulates that their choices are solely influenced by the expected reaction of voters to alternative choices. Rather than choosing policies to maximize some welfare criteria, Downs says the vote calculus is more important.

> Because government in our model wishes to maximize political support, it carries out those acts of spending which gain the most votes by means of those acts of financing which lose the fewest votes. In other words, expenditures are increased until the vote-gain of the marginal dollar spent equals the vote-loss of the marginal dollar financed (Downs, 1957, p. 52).

The need to be reelected, for instance, accounts for the difficulty of increasing taxes and controlling expenditures in an election year. As Freeman points out, "since 1950 Congressional authorizations (for water resource projects) in election years have exceeded those in odd-numbered years by a ratio of 7 to 1" (1967, p. 331).

Finally, decision makers must consider the effects of various alternatives on the ability of the organization to make future decisions. It may be possible to gain the necessary outside support by not revealing the likely consequences of the proposed action, or by expending a great deal of effort in behalf of the proposal (putting all your eggs in one basket). The likely result, however, would be a loss of confidence in the organization, making it more difficult to gain acceptance of proposals in the future. Decision makers must consider, in other words, the political opportunity costs of their acts—what they must forego, both now and in the future, to gain support for a particular action—in addition to the exchange costs of gaining acceptance. Political rationality, as Wildavsky emphasizes, requires that the preservation and improvement of decision structures become as important a criteria to decision makers as criteria to produce economic efficiency (1966, p. 78–82).

NORMATIVE CONSTRAINTS

A final group of environmental constraints can be categorized as normative constraints. These are a more or less permanent set of shared expectations about how organizations should behave and how they should carry out their business. There are many cultural, social, and religious norms which make many economically feasible solutions unacceptable. Cultural values regarding the value of work make the dole suspect but subsidies for limiting agricultural acreage acceptable. Achievement, hard work, efficiency, progress, and individualism are still honored by many Americans, and policies which ignore them are more difficult to sell.

Many actions that are economically and politically sound are made less acceptable because they violate various notions of equity. To pass legislation favoring one region of the country over another creates political problems for legislators from the disadvantaged regions; to redistribute income from the poor to the rich violates accepted standards of equity. The outcry against millionaires who pay no taxes arises from the norm that people with equal income should pay equal taxes, and those with higher incomes should pay a proportionately larger tax bill. (For a discussion of various distributional criteria see Weisbrod, 1970.)

Normative constraints influence the choices of decision makers by requiring them to follow previously agreed upon patterns of behavior. In legislative bodies norms regarding hard work, doing one's apprenticeship, courtesy, or keeping one's word are best followed if one hopes to be an effective legislator (Bullitt, 1959; Pierce et al., 1972). In bureaucracies subordinates are expected to defer to their superiors and generally do what their superiors expect. Thompson (1961) and Tullock (1965) point out the negative behavioral consequences of such norms in large organizations. Nevertheless, much of society's resources are spent teaching young people similar norms so that they may survive in an organizational society.

Despite their limiting nature, environmental constraints are often helpful to organization members. Without them, decision makers would have almost unlimited freedom to choose possible courses of action, because there are always many things that might be done. The environmental constraints mentioned here bring organizational decision makers' imaginations back to reality, to what is feasible for the situations within which they operate. While environmental constraints greatly simplify the decision makers' tasks and greatly reduce the external costs of proposed actions, most organizations are still inclined to adopt rules and procedures to simplify their choice problems even further. These rules and procedures adopted by organization members themselves will be discussed next.

INTERNAL CONSTRAINTS

In this chapter, organizations are viewed as collections of self-interested individuals who join together to accomplish a variety of objectives. Since the number of possible actions organization members may take to reach their objectives is very large, the process by which choices are made must be constrained if decisions are to be made in a reasonable amount of time and at a reasonable cost. Outsiders facilitate an organization's control problem by imposing limitations on its behavior. These environmental constraints tend to eliminate alternatives that might be beneficial to individuals in an organization, but that would hurt or work to the disadvantage of those on the outside. But the constraints imposed by outsiders are not enough to guarantee that an organization will accomplish the objectives of its members and do it at least cost to those participating. Further restrictions are imposed by the members themselves to insure that the costs of decision-making do not outweigh the benefits gained by the members from taking collective action.

This section deals with the constraints imposed by the organization itself on the decision-making process. These internal constraints consist primarily of rules and porcedures that direct the component parts of the organization toward their common objectives. The specific rules and procedures adopted depend, however, on various characteristics of the decision situation. For instance, the more mechanized the decision-making process, the more interdependent the component parts of the decision-making system, and the more available satisfactory solutions, the more specific will be the organization's rules and procedures and the more constrained the decision-making process (Feldman and Kanter,

1965, p. 619). Conversely the more an organization relies on people with previous experience and specialized knowledge, the more independent the subsystems of the organization, and the less agreement there is on the appropriate response to problems, the more general will be the organization's rules and procedures and the less constrained the decision-making process.

More specifically, a review of the literature on decision-making reveals at least four distinct explanations of how individuals organize themselves to make collective choices. For the purpose of this discussion, these explanations will be referred to as programmed decision-making, process decision-making, systems decision-making, and political decision-making. The two variables related to the decision situation that seem to account for the differences in the rules and procedures adopted under each of the patterns of decision-making are the level of agreement among decision makers on what needs to be done (the goals to be achieved) and the level of agreement on how to do it (the appropriate responses to problems).[5] The relationships between these variables and an organization's decision-making procedures are outlined in figure 5.

The Level of Agreement on Appropriate Responses

	High	Low
High	PROGRAMMED DECISION-MAKING Use predetermined responses. Performance Programs Standard Operating Procedures	SYSTEMS DECISION-MAKING Use goal-oriented problem-solving techniques. Program Budgeting Systems Analysis Benefit-Cost Analysis
Low	PROCESS DECISION-MAKING Use standardized search and estimating procedures. Incremental Routines	POLITICAL DECISION-MAKING Use conflict resolution procedures. Competition, Bargaining Coalition Formation

(Left margin label: The Level of Agreement on Problems and Organizational Goals)

Figure 5: Patterns of Organizational Decision-Making

[5] See James D. Thompson (1967) for a similar typology of organizational strategies.

The general argument to be pursued is that the greater the agreement among organization members on what needs to be done and the way to do it, the more specific will be the rules and procedures used in decision-making. Decision-making will be highly constrained in the sense that few deviations are permitted from the programmed response to specific stimuli. On the other hand, when there is little agreement among organization members on what needs to be done and the way to do it, organizational rules will be less specific and constraining. They may, as in the case of political bargaining, consist of informal rules of the game on how organizational members bargain with one another to resolve their conflicting views of what the organization should do.

PROGRAMMED DECISION-MAKING

When organizations are confronted with highly repetitive demands in which the nature of the problem and appropriate response to it are known, they typically react with standardized or routinized responses. The decision-making process in such cases is either abridged or completely eliminated. Situations in which a particular event evokes a program of activity without an intervening period for decision-making are common in all organizations. For example, a job application sets off a predetermined review process. No decision has to be made about how to deal with the application. A request for information, a report that supplies are low, an appeal from a promotion decision, all are usually dealt with in routine or programmed ways. This kind of programmed decision-making accounts for a very large part of the behavior of individuals and units within all organizations. Since their effect on organizations does not seem to be as important, however, they have not received as much attention as have more complex forms of problem solving.

Programmed (or routine) decision-making is discussed by March and Simon (1958). They characterize any predetermined set of responses to specific stimuli as performance programs. Performance programs include both sets of activities that follow directly from some stimuli, such as the dispatch of a fire engine when the fire alarm sounds, and sets of activities that are conditional on information that is independent of the initial stimuli. An example is a taxi company's choice of which taxi to send to an address depending on the present deployment of available taxis. As March and Simon point out:

> We will regard a set of activities as routinized, then, to the degree that choice has been simplified by the development of a mixed re-

sponse to defined stimuli. If search has been eliminated, but a choice remains in the form of a clearly defined and systematic computing routine, we will still say that the activities are routinized (1958, p. 142).

March and Simon are particularly interested in the content of performance programs and in the conditions under which program content varies. The content of performance programs may include rules or instructions on the kind of product or service to be delivered, on the kind of activities to be carried out in supplying a service, and on the timing or sequence of organizational activities. In the limiting case of a performance program consisting of a computerized response to an external demand, all three kinds of program specifications are included. The organizational response, in this case, is completely constrained, and little or no decision-making costs are involved.

The increasing application of computer programs and automated processes by organizations indicates the breadth of situations in which decision-making can be highly routinized. Many tasks, however, cannot be machine programmed but are still susceptible to routinization. The extent of routinization, or program specification, will vary according to characteristics of the decision-making situation. Specifically, March and Simon expect program content to be "a function of the ease of observing job activities, the ease of observing job output, and the ease of relating activities to output" (1958, p. 145). They expect programs to contain activity specifications in preference to output specifications to the extent that "the activity pattern is easily observed and supervised; the quantity and quality of output are not easily observed and supervised, and the relationship between activity pattern and output are highly technical" (p. 145).

Cyert and March (1953) likewise emphasize the extent to which organizations employ standard responses to recurring situations. They are more concerned, however, with the range of activities that are constrained by standard operating procedures and the functions performed by them. Task-performance rules, records and reports, information-handling rules, and plans and planning rules influence an organization's choices in a number of ways. Task-performance rules, for instance, consist of instructions to members on how to carry out tasks assigned to them. They exist in considerable detail at all levels of organizations and permit some apparently complex decision problems, such as engineering problems, to be handled simply and with a minimum of uncertainty. Task-performance rules permit the transfer of past learning to new members of an organization. They also insure that the many different people in an organization carry out the same tasks in similar ways making the performance of the organization predictable. Rules specifying how records and reports are to be prepared help control individual performance by making each person accountable for his behavior. They also help an organization predict its environment by giving the organization information about the relationship between past and future events (Cyert and March, 1953, pp. 103–113).

In summary, programmed decision-making takes place whenever there are repetitive situations facing an organization, and there is general agreement on the goals and actions applicable in those situations. To reduce the costs of handling repetitive and noncontroversial problems, organizations adopt "performance programs" or "standard operating procedures" which permit the organization and its members to respond quickly and predictably.

While standard rules and procedures do simplify decision-making considerably, such constraints can produce undesirable results. The most frequently cited disadvantage of rules is the tendency of organization members to forget or ignore the intent of the rules and emphasize instead compliance with them. This phenomenon referred to as the "displacement of goals" or the "internalization of rules" has been thoroughly discussed in the literature of Merton, 1940; Blau, 1955; and March and Simon, 1958, pp. 340–347. Another problem arises in getting organization members to comply with the rules. An extensive literature on organizational socialization, incentives, and acceptance of constraints has developed around this problem (Barnard, 1938; Simon, 1945; and Simon, Smithburg, and Thompson, 1950).

PROCESS DECISION-MAKING

Despite the prevalence of situations in which programmed responses are used, organizations must make other decisions for which no ready answers are available. They must engage in some problem solving activity to select an appropriate course of action. Ideally, as was pointed out earlier, the responsible administrator would like to employ a comprehensive decision model and consider all values involved, all possible alternatives for solving the problem and their likely outcomes, and then select that alternative which maximizes his values. In most situations the consideration of all possible alternatives is simply impossible, however. For the reasons already mentioned, it is necessary to simplify the decision process. As March and Simon point out, "Rational behavior involves substituting for the complex reality a model of reality that is sufficiently simple to be handled by problem solving processes" (1958, p. 151).

There are two general models for reducing the complexity of the comprehensive-decision model. The first, which we have entitled the process model, starts with an agreed upon set of decision-making procedures and works toward a decision within the limits imposed by the procedures. According to Feldman and Kanter the "working forward model" (which we are calling the process model) "enables the system to move from an initial state to a terminal state by exploring outward from the initial data in a limited fashion" (1965, p. 617). If the appropriate decision rules and search and decision strategies can be agreed on, and the agreed upon process is working properly, then it is assumed that the decision process will lead to desirable results. (For a rationalization of this approach see Lindblom's discussison of "Muddling Through," 1959).

The other general model, the systems model, starts with the desired end states and considers only those alternatives that lead to the agreed upon goals.

> The working-backward procedures is a device for limiting the amount of search required to find a path by examining only those paths which will lead to the desired state. The path is generated by considering what means are required to accomplish the terminal state (end). (Feldman and Kanter, 1965, p. 617.)

The distinction between process and systems decision-making is made clear by Allen Schick.

> The salient feature of process politics is the activity by which bargains are struck and allocations negotiated—the so-called rules of the game and the strategies of the contestants. There is a presumption that if the process is working properly, the outcome will be favorable. Hence, there is no need itself to determine its performance and desirability. The sine qua non of systems politics is the outcome, not the activity, but what results from it. Take away this component and you do not have a system (1969, p. 137).

Each of these approaches for simplifying problem solving will now be explored.

The process model constrains the comprehensive-decision model, then, by establishing agreed upon rules and procedures for generating alternative solutions for a problem. Since generating and evaluating alternatives are costly for an organization (and assuming that rational organizations will limit their consideration of alternatives when the expected value of additional information gathered is less than its costs) they will first try to identify those alternatives that have the best chance of solving the problem facing them. The analysis of strategies organizations employ to generate alternatives is a relatively new concern of organizational theorists (Cyert and March, 1953; Lindblom, 1959; Downs, 1967). Most students of decision-making have focused on the procedures used to select the best alternative among those being considered. But since only few are considered, the process for selecting alternatives may have as an important effect on the organization's decisions as the process of choosing among them.

Occasion for search

According to the process model, the consideration of alternatives is constrained by limiting the occasion for search, by limiting the sources of alternative solutions, and by simplifying the methods for evaluating alternatives and choosing among them.

Most recent literature suggests that organizations seriously search for alternatives only when they become dissatisfied with their present course of action (March and Simon, 1958, pp. 172–177; Cyert and March, 1953, pp. 120–122; Downs, 1967, pp. 168–191; and Sharkansky, 1972, pp. 59–60). Cyert and March emphasize that search for alternatives is motivated by the recognition of a problem.

> A problem is recognized when the organization either fails to satisfy one or more of its goals or when such a failure can be anticipated in the immediate future. So long as the problem is not solved, search will continue (p. 121).

The other principal occasion for search, according to Cyert and March, is when a crisis or problem must be found to justify the adoption of a favorite solution (p. 121).

Downs' basic model of organizational search assumes there is a more or less continuous process of search for alternatives and evaluation of organizational goals. (For a similar approach to this subject see Etzioni's discussion of mixed-scanning, 1967). According to Downs, an individual in an organization engages in a continuous search of the organization's environment regardless of the organization's present performance. The general level of search continues as long as no alternative pattern of behavior is found that produces more utility at less cost than present behavior. Only when the present performance fails to meet the organization's expectations is the responsible official motivated to intensify his search for forms of behavior which will improve the organization's performance.

> He will designate the difference in utility he perceives between the actual and the satisfactory level of performance as the performance gap. The larger this gap, the greater his motivation to undertake more intensive search. He is already engaging in some search just by being alive; but in this case, dissatisfaction leads him both to intensify his normal search and to direct it specifically at alternatives likely to reduce the causes of his dissatisfaction (Downs, 1967, p. 169).

Sharkansky, drawing more heavily from the psychological literature on cognitive dissonance, adds to Downs's formulation the qualification that organizations begin an intensive search for alternatives only when a certain level of dissatisfaction is reached. Some dissatisfaction is always present and tolerable. Only when the problems become sufficiently severe to cause a tension do administrators feel compelled to respond. "Tensions can be thought of as a screening device between an administrative unit and its environment; the members of the unit use it to determine when unmet demands are so severe as to require a response" (Sharkansky, 1972, p. 59).

Search strategies

Once the search for alternatives begins, organizations further simplify their problem-solving task by limiting the kinds of alternatives considered. Cyert and March (1953) claim that organizations use simple-minded search strategies in that they (1) "search in the neighborhood of the problem symptom" and (2) "search in the neighborhood of the current alternative" (p. 121). They do this to provide continuity with present behavior, and because of the difficulty of anticipating the consequences of any radical changes. (For a similar analysis see Lindblom, 1959.) Downs (1967) believes that organizations first consider familiar alternatives and then proceed to expand their search in discrete steps out from those most familiar to them. "The search continues until he [a bureaucrat] either finds an alternative that restores him to the satisfactory level [or puts him onto some even higher level], or the cost of further search exceeds the cost of accepting a level of performance below his satisfactory level" (Downs, p. 170).

Search strategies are frequently institutionalized into what Sharkansky calls "routines." "Routines are decision rules that specify which of the numerous inputs that might be relevant are actually considered in making decisions" (Sharkansky, 1972, p. 61). Sharkansky describes three routines that prevail in the public sector decision-making: incremental budgeting, regional consultation, and the spending-service cliche. Incremental budgeting is probably the most frequently discussed routine in the political literature (see Wildavsky, 1964; Lindblom, 1959; Schultze, 1968; Davis, Dempster and Wildavsky, 1966; and Webb, 1972). It suggests that decision makers consider only the increments of change proposed in budget requests and evaluate these requests in terms of the short-term consequences for the goals embodied in an agency's existing program. Regional consultation refers to the practice of state and local bureaucrats of searching for solutions in the experience of their immediate neighbors. They justify this practice by saying something is a local problem or a regional problem. The spending-service cliche equates spending level with service provided. All of these routines, or norms for search behavior, reduce the number of factors decision makers must consider and thereby simplify decision-making.

The results of limited search procedures are discussed by Downs (1967). He indicates that, other things being equal, the following types of alternatives are more likely to be considered than their opposites.

1. Those that provide "side benefits" which are unrelated to the problem requiring a solution.

2. Those that are relatively simple and easy to understand.

3. Those that involve small changes from existing patterns of behavior.

4. Those that do not depend on highly uncertain variables requiring accurate estimates of future consequences. (Downs, 1967, p. 170.)

Evaluating alternatives

Finally, in the process model alternative solutions are evaluated, not in terms of their likely consequences for some predetermined goals, but in terms of their political acceptability. Lindblom (1959) argues that public administrators do not distinguish ends from means clearly and that therefore means-ends analysis is an inappropriate basis for selecting alternatives. The test of a good policy is agreement among organizational members that it is a good policy. The result, admits Lindblom, is that important outcomes are neglected, potential policies are ignored, im-

portant affected values are neglected, and theory is ignored. (For a justification of political feasibility as a decision criteria see Wildavsky, 1966,
and Meltsner, 1972.)

Sharkansky adds some additional details to the process of mutual adjustment described by Lindblom. He says that the procedures for ranking
and selecting alternatives include:

> the delegation of decision making to subunits; the representation
> in subunits of spokesmen for various interests; reluctance to view
> any part of one's own position as inflexible; a willingness to bargain
> with a protagonist; the expectation that protagonists will negotiate
> in good faith and relinquish part of their demands in exchange for
> one's own concessions; and the view that goal formation and policy-
> making is a continuing process, so that desires that are not satisfied
> in one period may be realized some time in the future (Sharkansky,
> 1972, p. 60).

In process decision-making, in other words, the discussion of goals is
discouraged, decisions are made in response to problems, familiar solutions are analyzed first, and decisions are made on the basis of consensus.
The model assumes that decision makers are generally satisfied with the
way the organization is performing, share a high level of agreement on
actions appropriate for the organization, and have no necessary prior
agreement on the goals being pursued.

SYSTEMS DECISION-MAKING

The systems model of decision-making also consists of a set of procedures designed to simplify the comprehensive decision model (see
Feldman and Kanter, 1965, pp. 617–618; and Schick, 1969). Unlike the
process model, however, it presupposes agreement on goals or requires
that they be specified before alternatives are evaluated. It simplifies decision-making by considering only those alternatives that can be related
to desired results, and only those procedures that relate means to ends.

The development of systems procedures for organizational decision-
making resulted in part from dissatisfaction with the results of process
decision-making and a belief that better results can be obtained with
systematic analysis. The failures of process decision-making, at least as
practiced in the public sector, have been discussed by several authors
(Schultze, 1968; Schick, 1969). Schick argues that the process model of
decision-making, which draws on the theory of competitive economic
markets, has many of the same deficiencies of pure competition (1969,

pp. 137–151). Schultze tries to show how systematic analysis can improve process decision-making. He argues that specific programs cannot be evaluated directly in terms of political values as Lindblom suggests. Participants must have some idea of the consequences of programs before they know what values will be affected. This requires knowledge of the relationship between inputs and outputs. He goes further to say that the relationship between inputs and outputs has become increasingly complex in recent years making the careful analysis of "social production functions" all the more important (Schultze, 1968, pp. 55–57). What Schultze and Schick are saying, in effect, is that decisions arrived at through a political process alone impose unsatisfactory external costs, particularly costs arising from the unintended consequences of organizational decisions.

The systems model of decision-making constrains organizational decision-making primarily by requiring the specification of objectives or goals, and by imposing procedures for systematically analyzing the relationships between programs and their consequences.

Goals

Goals are the most general kind of constraint which face systems decision makers. They usually establish the minimum criteria that an alternative must meet to be considered. As long as organizations are conceived of in terms of a single decision maker and a single goal, the problem of goal setting is not very important. The economic theory of the firm is an example. A single decision maker, the firm's chief executive officer, is assumed to act to maximize profit.

As soon as organizations are viewed as consisting of many decision makers each with his or her own set of goals, then goal setting becomes more difficult and the delimitation of goals has a greater influence on the organization's choices. Goals, rather than being a statement of personal preferences, become the end product of a process of interaction between individuals and groups in the organization. They change as membership in the organization changes and as pressures, both inside and outside the organization, change. Organizational goals, looked at in this way, can be described as a more or less agreed upon set of constraints on the organization, arrived at through processes of bargaining, competition, conflict, and cooperation among its members, and modified over time by changes in the internal and external situation that the organization faces (see Cyert and March, 1953).

Organizational decisions are not only constrained by the content of the organization's goals but also by the intensity of its goal commitment. For example, the federal government is committed to a goal of full employment. It also has a number of other objectives and must take into account the costs of programs to reduce unemployment in terms of these other objectives which would have to be foregone to pursue the programs. The result is that contrary to many normative theories of organizational choice which assume that organizations try to maximize their goals by finding the best alternative for achieving a specific goal, organizations, as a number of empirical studies indicate, follow a "satisficing" strategy in the pursuit of their goals (Simon, 1959). They seek some satisfactory level of performance based on their level of aspirations. The most important variables in determining an organization's level of aspiration are the organization's past goals, its past performance in achieving them, and to some extent, the performance of other comparable organizations.

A major attempt to require that government agencies make decisions in terms of specific goals was the introduction of program budgeting. President Johnson announced on August 25, 1965, that he was asking every agency to begin a revolutionary system of program budgeting. Every agency would define goals and then the most effective and least costly way of accomplishing them would be found. The general idea of program budgeting is that decisions should be made in terms of output categories instead of cost categories like personnel, equipment, and capital expenditures. (For a complete set of articles on program budgeting see Novick, 1965.) Critics of recent government attempts to make decision-making more systematic have attacked program budgeting for being unworkable, for distorting the true preferences of the American people, and for being too time consuming and costly (Wildavsky, 1966; Merewitz and Sosnick, 1971).

Estimating consequences

The procedures used to estimate the consequences of alternatives is an important part of the systems model of decision-making. They determine in large part how individuals structure the problems facing an organization and how they evaluate the consequences of alternatives for the organization's goals. There are two important problems involved in estimating the consequences of alternatives for organizational goals. One is the problem of forecasting the future, and the other is the problem of drawing inferences from current data about future consequences.

Forecasting future events requires a simplified model of the present situation facing an organization, and some rules for predicting what changes are likely to occur at specific times in the future. Forecasting models may be very crude, such as a simple description of the present state of affairs, or very complex, such as a 200 equation model of the U.S. economy. (For a general discussion of econometric models see Kuh, 1965; and Suits, 1962.) Once the present situation is described, there are several ways of extrapolating the present to the future. The simplest procedure is to say that the future will be like today. Another procedure is to project trends from the past into the future. This in effect says that things will change in the future as they have in the past. A more complex procedure is to estimate independently the magnitudes of factors affecting the model in the future and then to compute forecasts of future behavior by analyzing the interrelated effects of each important variable.

The second problem, and somewhat the easier of the two, is to compute the effects of alternatives for the organization's goals, given a forecast of the future. For example, if the government assumes that unemployment will be at 6 percent a year from now, then it is a relatively easy task, given modern econometric models, to analyze the effect on the employment rate of increasing government spending by $10 billion, given the forecast.

During the last thirty years both public and private organizations have employed a number of analytical procedures for estimating the consequences of alternative proposals on an organization's goals. During World War II operations research techniques were developed to discover how the military could get the most out of its stock of equipment. The most familiar techniques associated with operations research are linear programming, game theory, and Monte Carlo methods. Systems analysis (Quade and Boucher, 1968) overlaps operations research, but is generally less quantitative than operations research and allows for more uncertainty. Systems analysis focuses on the system of relationships among the most important variables affecting a situation. The model allows analysts to vary not only the alternative policies but also alternative objectives or end states.

With the introduction of the planning-programming-budgeting system into governmental agencies, benefit-cost analyses were required as part of program evaluation. Benefit-cost analysis consists of a set of procedures for evaluating the long-term social benefits and costs of a program so that resources can be allocated efficiently. The aim of these procedures is to maximize the present value of all benefits and costs subject to a number of legal, political, budgetary, and normative constraints (Prest and Turvey, 1966). Critics argue that benefit-cost procedures are very costly, biased in favor of what is measureable and against what is unmeasurable, and are too simplistic to account for the complexities and uncertainties of modern society (Merewitz and Sosnick, 1971; Wildavsky, 1966).

The systems model of decision-making, in summary, constrains the comprehensive decision-making model by forcing prior agreement on objectives and then limiting the consideration of alternatives to those which lead to the desired end results. The systems model restricts the decision-making by requiring that certain kinds of analytic procedures be used to estimate the consequences of alternatives on the organization's goals. Particular attention is given to problems of uncertainty or to avoiding the uncertainty of future events.

POLITICAL DECISION-MAKING

When individuals in organizations cannot agree on the goals and problems of the organization or on the appropriate kinds of responses to make, they engage in political decision-making. Since there is no apparent way for the members to reach agreement on the course of action to take, the problem in political decision-making becomes one of finding a process by which the members can resolve their differences. This usually involves attempts to segment the decision-making process so that only a few people are allowed to participate on any one issue, but at the same time to increase the opportunities for trading support between issues.

The processes of political decision-making have been analyzed in greatest detail by Dahl and Lindblom (1953). They describe four basic processes for resolving differences among organization members. They include the price system, hierarchy, polyarchy, and bargaining. Under the price system, conflicts are left unresolved, in that each member is permitted to pursue his own objectives according to his ability to pay for them. Within an organization a price system may work in situations where the consequences of individual decisions for others are either small or nonexistent. In hierarchical decision-making processes, differences among members are resolved by a single leader or leaders of the organization. Presumably, if the leaders act consistently in ways contrary to the interests of most of the other members of the organization, those members will object or choose to leave the organization (see Hirschman, 1970). Polyarchy is another form of centralized decision-making in which nonleaders rule leaders. Bargaining refers to a number of methods for resolving differences among members by making mutually beneficial exchanges.

Whereas the primary purpose of programmed decision-making, process decision-making, and systems decision-making was to simplify decision-making and thereby reduce decision-making costs, the purpose of political bargaining is to expand the opportunities for interaction among organizational members so that mutually beneficial decisions can be reached. Bargaining can take a number of forms (see Froman, 1967; and Mitchell and Mitchell, 1969). It may involve persuasion, that is an attempt to convince others of the worth of one's position. It may result in compromise in which both parties to the exchange agree to settle for something less than each would prefer. Bargaining frequently involves trading support across issues or promising support on some future issue in return for support on the present issue. In some cases a person may simply try to compensate the person whose support is needed for the loss that person thinks will be incurred if the decision in question is made. The important point is that bargaining is a very time-consuming and costly activity. Nevertheless, it is frequently the only way decisions can be reached in organizations when there are large differences among organization members on both goals and actions.

SUMMARY

Internal constraints are imposed on the organizational decision-making process by the members themselves to simplify and thereby reduce the costs of making decisions. The particular kinds of rules and procedures adopted depend, however, on the kind of situation in which decision makers find themselves. Most demands made of organizations are highly repetitive. It would be a waste of time to treat such requests individually. Consequently, organizations develop predetermined or programmed responses which either minimize or completely eliminate decision-making activity. If decision makers cannot agree on the goals they are pursuing, it is still possible in some cases to agree on the process by which problems are resolved. Instead of considering all alternatives affecting all possible values, decision makers agree to maintain the status quo as long as there is not too much pressure to change. When the level of dissatisfaction with the organization's performance begins creating problems, familiar alternatives are sought that will solve the problem. In the process model of decision-making, changes tend to be small and are selected on the basis of their acceptability among decision makers. Dissatisfaction with process decision-making has created a demand for a more rational, means-ends approach to problem solving. If goals can be agreed upon, then a number of techniques can be used to estimate the consequences of alternatives in terms of those goals. Such techniques as linear programming, systems analysis, and benefit-cost analysis allow decision makers to handle relatively complex problems more easily. These are ways of structuring complex problems so that only the most important aspects of the problem have to be considered. Finally, if decision makers cannot agree on either decision-making procedures or the organization's goals, then the focus of decision-making shifts to the processes by which agreement on these questions can be resolved.

AGENDA FOR FUTURE RESEARCH

Research on organizations and organizational decision-making is vast and growing (March, 1965; Alexis and Wilson, 1967; Cooper et al., 1964). Nevertheless there are still some important gaps that need to be filled. As was pointed out earlier, one of these gaps is in our knowledge of the effects of organizational structure on behavior within organizations and on the supply of organizational services to the public or its clientele.

A good start has been made on the effects of bureaucratic organization on the internal decision-making process (Tullock, 1965; Downs, 1967). Downs has compiled the most complete set of generalizations about the effects of bureaucratic structures on organizational decision-making. For the convenience of the reader he presents a summary of the major hypotheses in the last chapter of the above-mentioned book.

With respect to the consequences of organizational behavior, an important beginning has been made with the publication of Niskanen's recent book (1971). He not only demonstrates, as was described earlier, that the budgets of bureaus tend to be too large, but also analyzes the effects of bureaucratic supply on the consumers of public services. By assuming, for instance, that high income groups in the society are willing to pay a uniformly higher tax price than low income groups and that the aggregate tax charges of all levels of government are approximately proportional to the income of each group, Niskanen is able to show that under a majority-decision rule, groups with high demand for public services receive greater benefits than those with low demand.

A government characterized by the bureaucratic supply of public services and majority rule yields positive net benefits only to the high-demand group, most of whom have relatively high incomes, primarily because this group controls the formulation of alternatives. Around 60 percent of the total benefits of government accrue to the 40 percent of the population that pays around 50 percent of the taxes. Within the high-demand group, the individuals who benefit most are those who also have low incomes and thus pay low taxes (Niskanen, 1971, p. 178).

He then goes on to analyze the effects of bureaucratic supply with a two-thirds rule, competitive supply with majority rule, and "optimal government with endogenous tax shares." In each case the resulting distribution of benefits and costs are somewhat different.

The greatest need in decision-making research, I believe, is for more work of the kind Downs and Niskanen have begun. One reason why government, in particular, has been reluctant to consider many suggestions for change is that there has been very little evidence on the consequences of the proposed changes. One may be justified in criticizing local government, for instance, for not meeting its responsibilities. But to infer from the failures of local government that the federal government would do the job better is wrong unless evidence to that effect is provided. When society and government are relatively simple, a proposed change can be experimented with and accepted or rejected on the basis of the experiment. But the costs of experimentation in the federal bureaucracy or national political institutions are very great. Experimentation is costly, not only because the proposed program may involve substantial costs, but also because programs and organizations tend to create supporters both inside and outside of the government, making them extremely difficult to get rid of if the program is unsuccessful. Consequently, few changes designed to improve organizational performance will be made unless social scientists can develop more complete and more accurate models of the effects of proposed institutional changes. If experimental evidence is impossible to obtain, decision makers will at least want sound logical reasons for supporting institutional change.

High on the research agenda are studies of changes to improve the performance of existing organizations. How can the reward system in organizations be changed to give managers greater incentive to be efficient? How can the political-review process be altered to make bureaucrats more responsive to the President, the President more responsive to the Congress, and the Congress more responsive to the American people?

What effects would lengthening the term of the President, making Senators run at large nationally, or requiring a two-thirds vote on all bills have on the supply of public services?

Research is also needed on alternative forms of public and private organizations. Both formal models and empirical research are needed to analyze the consequences of greater decentralization of decision-making at all levels of government. Some work is presently being done in the area of educational administration, welfare programs, and tax reform. But much remains to be done if organizations are going to serve the needs both of their members and their clientele.

BIBLIOGRAPHY

ALEXIS, MARCUS and WILSON, CHARLES Z., eds. *Organizational Decision Making.* Englewood Cliffs, N.J.: Prentice-Hall, Inc., 1967.

ARROW, KENNETH J. "Alternative Theories of Decision-Making in Risk Taking Situations," *Econometrica,* 19 (1951), pp. 404–437.

BARNARD, CHESTER I. *The Functions of the Executive.* Cambridge, Mass.: Harvard University Press, 1938.

BLAU, PETER M. *The Dynamics of Bureaucracy.* Chicago: University of Chicago Press, 1955.

BOULDING, KENNETH E. *Conflict and Defense.* New York: Harper & Row, 1962.

BRADFORD, D. V. "Constraints on Public Action and Rules for Social Decision," *American Economic Review,* 60 (1970), pp. 455–467.

BRAYBROOKE, DAVID, and LINDBLOM, CHARLES E. *A Strategy of Decision.* New York: The Free Press of Glencoe, 1963.

BUCHANAN, JAMES M., and TULLOCK, GORDON. *The Calculus of Consent.* Ann Arbor, Mich.: University of Michigan Press, 1962.

————. *Public Finance in Democratic Process.* Chapel Hill, N.C.: The University of North Carolina Press, 1967.

BULLITT, STIMSON. *To Be A Politician.* New York: Doubleday, 1959.

CLARKSON, GEOFFREY P. E. *Portfolio Selection: A Simulation of Trust Investment.* Englewood Cliffs, N.J.: Prentice-Hall, 1962.

COASE, RONALD H. "The Problem of Social Cost," *Journal of Law and Economics,* 3 (1969), pp. 1–44.

COHEN, MICHAEL D.; MARCH, JAMES G.; and OLSEN, JOHAN P. "A Garbage Can Model of Organizational Choice," *Administrative Science Quarterly,* 17 (1972), pp. 1–25.

COLEMAN, JAMES S. "Collective Decisions," *Sociological Inquiry,* 1 (1964), pp. 166–181.

————. "Foundations for a Theory of Collective Decisions," *American Journal of Sociology,* 71 (1966), pp. 615ff.

————, et al. *Equality of Educational Opportunity.* Washington, D.C.: U.S. Government Printing Office, 1966.

COOPER, WILLIAM H.; LEAVITT, HAROLD J.; and SHELLY, MAYNARD W. II. *New Perspectives in Organization Research.* New York: John Wiley, 1964.

CYERT, RICHARD M., and MARCH, JAMES G. *A Behavioral Theory of the Firm.* Englewood Cliffs, N.J.: Prentice-Hall, 1953.

DAHL, ROBERT A. and LINDBLOM, CHARLES E. *Politics, Economics, and Welfare.* New York: Harper, 1953.

DAVIS, OTTO A.; DEMPSTER, M. A. H.; and WILDAVSKY, AARON. "A Theory of the Budgetary Process," *American Political Science Review,* LX (1966), pp. 529–547.

DAWSON, RICHARD E. and ROBINSON, JAMES A. "Inter-Party Competition, Economic Variables, and Welfare Policies in the American States," *Journal of Politics*, 25 (1963), pp. 265–289.

DEVINE, EUGENE. *Analysis of Manpower Shortages in Local Government.* New York: Praeger, 1970.

DIESING, PAUL. *Reason in Society.* Urbana, Ill.: University of Illinois Press, 1962.

DOWNS, ANTHONY. *An Economic Theory of Democracy.* New York: Harper & Row, 1957.

———. "Why the Government Budget is Too Small in a Democracy," *World Politics*, 12 (1960), pp. 541–563.

———. *Inside Bureaucracy.* Boston: Little, Brown, 1967.

DYE, THOMAS R. *Politics, Economics, and the Public: Policy Outcomes in the American States.* Chicago: Rand McNally, 1966.

ECKSTEIN, OTTO. "A Survey of the Theory of Public Expenditure Criteria," in Buchanan, James M., ed., *Public Finances: Needs, Sources and Utilization.* Princeton, N.J.: Princeton University Press, 1961.

EDWARDS, WARD. "The Theory of Decision Making," *Psychological Bulletin*, 51 (1954), pp. 380–417.

———. "Behavioral Decision Theory," *Annual Review of Psychology*, 12 (1961), pp. 473–498.

ETZIONI, AMITAI. "Mixed-Scanning: A 'Third' Approach to Decision-Making," *Public Administration Review*, 27 (1967), pp. 385–392.

FELDMAN, JULIAN, and KANTER, HERSCHEL E. "Organizational Decision-Making," in March, James G., ed., *Handbook of Organizations.* Chicago: Rand McNally, 1965.

FREEMAN, A. MYRICK. "Six Federal Reclamation Projects and the Distribution of Income," *Water Resources Research III* (Second Quarter, 1967).

FROMAN, LEWIS A., JR. *The Congressional Process.* Boston: Little, Brown, 1967.

GALBRAITH, JOHN KENNETH. *The Affluent Society.* Boston: Houghton Mifflin, 1958.

HIRSCHMAN, ALBERT O. *Exit, Voice, and Loyalty.* Cambridge: Harvard University Press, 1970.

HOFFERBERT, RICHARD I. "The Relation Between Public Policy and Some Structural and Environmental Variables in the American States," *American Political Science Review*, LX (1966), pp. 73–82.

———. "State and Community Policy Studies," *Political Science Annual*, III. Indianapolis: Bobbs-Merrill, 1972, pp. 3–72.

KAHN, ROBERT L., et al. *Organizational Stress: Studies in Role Conflict and Ambiguity.* New York: John Wiley, 1964.

KATZ, DANIEL, and KAHN, ROBERT L. *The Social Psychology of Organizations.* New York: John Wiley, 1966.

KUH, EDWIN. "Econometric Models: Is a New Day Dawning?" *American Economic Review*, 55 (1965), pp. 362–369.

LAWRENCE, PAUL R., and LORSCH, JAY W. *Organization and Environment.* Boston: Graduate School of Business Administration, Harvard University, 1967.

LINDBLOM, CHARLES E. "The Science of 'Muddling Through'," *Public Administration Review*, 18 (1959), pp. 79–88.

————. *The Policy-Making Process*. Englewood Cliffs, N.J.: Prentice-Hall, 1968.

MARCH, JAMES G., ed. *Handbook of Organizations*. Chicago: Rand McNally, 1965.

MARCH, JAMES G., and SIMON, HERBERT A. *Organizations*. New York: John Wiley, 1958.

MARSCHAK, JACOB. "Efficient and Viable Organizational Forms," in Haire, Mason, ed., *Modern Organization Theory*. New York: John Wiley, 1959, pp. 307–320.

MARSCHAK, THOMAS A. "Economic Theories of Organization," in March, James G., ed., *Handbook of Organizations*. Chicago: Rand McNally, 1965, pp. 423–450.

MELTSNER, ARNOLD J. "Political Feasibility and Political Analysis," *Public Administration Review*, 33 (1972), pp. 859–867.

MEREWITZ, LEONARD, and SOSNICK, STEPHEN H. *The Budget's New Clothes*. Chicago: Markham, 1971.

MERTON, ROBERT K. "Bureaucratic Structure and Personality," *Social Forces*, 18 (1940), pp. 560–568.

MITCHELL, JOYCE, and MITCHELL, WILLIAM C. *Political Analysis and Public Policy*. Chicago: Rand McNally, 1969.

NISKANEN, WILLIAM A., JR. *Bureaucracy and Representative Government*. Chicago: Aldine-Atherton, 1971.

NOVICK, DAVID, ed. *Program Budgeting*. Cambridge: Harvard University Press, 1965.

OLSON, MANCUR. *The Logic of Collective Choice*. Cambridge: Harvard University Press, 1965.

OSTROM, ELINOR. "Some Postulated Effects of Learning on Constitutional Choice," *Public Choice*, 5 (1968), pp. 87–104.

OSTROM, VINCENT, and OSTROM, ELINOR. "Public Choice: A Different Approach to the Study of Public Administration," *Public Administration Review*, 31 (1971), pp. 203–216.

PARKINSON, C. NORTHCOTE. *Parkinson's Law and Other Studies in Administration*. Boston: Houghton Mifflin, 1957.

PIERCE, LAWRENCE C. *The Politics of Fiscal Policy Formation*. Pacific Palisades, Calif.: Goodyear, 1971.

————; FREY, R. G.; and PENGELLY, S. *The Freshman Legislator: Problems and Opportunities*. Portland, Ore.: Binfords and Mort, 1973.

PIGOU, A. C. *The Economics of Welfare*, 4th ed. London: Macmillan, 1932, pp. 183–184.

PREST, A. R., and TURVEY, R. "Cost-Benefit Analysis: A Survey," American Economic Association, *Surveys of Economic Theory; Resource Allocation*, Vol. III. New York: St. Martin's Press, 1966.

QUADE, E. S., and BOUCHER, W. I., eds. *Systems Analysis and Policy Planning*. New York: American Elsevier, 1968.

RIKER, WILLIAM H. *The Theory of Political Coalitions*. New Haven: Yale University Press, 1962.

SCHICK, ALLEN. "Systems Politics and Systems Budgeting," *Public Administration Review*, 29 (1969), pp. 137–151.

SCHULTZE, CHARLES L. *The Politics and Economics of Public Spending.* Washington, D.C.: The Brookings Institution, 1968.

SHARKANSKY, IRA. "Regionalism, Economic Status and the Public Policies of American States," *Social Science Quarterly*, 49 (1968), pp. 9–26.

———. *Public Administration*, 2nd ed. Chicago: Markham, 1972.

SIMON, HERBERT A. *Administrative Behavior.* New York: The Macmillan Co., 1945.

SIMON, HERBERT A.; SMITHBURG, DONALD W.; and THOMPSON, VICTOR A. *Public Administration.* New York: Alfred A. Knopf, 1950.

———. "Theories of Decision Making in Economics and Behavioral Science," *American Economic Review*, XLIX (1959), pp. 253–283.

SUITS, DANIEL E. "Forecasting and Analysis With an Econometric Model," *American Economic Review*, 52 (1962), pp. 104–132.

THOMPSON, JAMES D. *Organizations in Action.* New York: McGraw-Hill, 1967.

THOMPSON, VICTOR A. *Modern Organization.* New York: Alfred A. Knopf, 1961.

TULLOCK, GORDON. *The Politics of Bureaucracy.* Washington, D.C.: Public Affairs Press, 1965.

WAGNER, RICHARD E. *The Fiscal Organization of American Federalism.* Chicago: Markham, 1971.

WEBB, RICHARD. "Earmarking in a Formal Model of Oregon's Budgetary Process," unpublished paper, Department of Political Science, University of Oregon, 1972.

WEISBROD, BURTON A. "Collective Action and the Distribution of Income: A Conceptual Approach," in Haveman, Robert H., and Margolis, Julius, eds., *Public Expenditures and Policy Analysis.* Chicago: Markham, 1970.

WHITEHEAD, CLAY T. *Uses and Limitations of Systems Analysis.* Santa Monica: The RAND Corporation, 1967.

WICKSELL, KNUT. "A New Principle of Just Taxation," in Musgrave, Richard A., and Peacock, Alan T., eds., *Classics in the Theory of Public Finance.* London: Macmillan, 1958, pp. 72–118.

WILDAVSKY, AARON. *The Politics of the Budgetary Process.* Boston: Little, Brown, 1964.

———. "Private Markets and Public Arenas," *American Behavioral Scientist*, (1965), pp. 33–37.

———. "The Political Economy of Efficiency: Cost-Benefit Analysis, Systems Analysis, and Program Budgeting," *Public Administration Review*, 26 (1966), pp. 292–310.

WILLIAMSON, OLIVER E. "Hierarchical Control and Optimum Firm Size," *Journal of Political Economy*, 75 (1967), pp. 123–138.

The Decision-Making Culture Of
American Public Education

HARMON ZEIGLER, M. KENT JENNINGS,
*AND G. WAYNE PEAK**

Only within the past decade has educational policy-making come to be widely recognized as a political process. If systematic studies of educational decision-making are still rare, it is because students of politics have traditionally directed their attention toward the more obviously "political" institutions of society, e.g., political parties, interest groups, the courts, and legislatures. There is certainly no reason to argue that schools are not political. Even when nobody noticed them, they were performing distinctly political functions (Easton, 1957; Zeigler and Peak, 1970). The past decade—with its student protests, teacher strikes, and taxpayers' revolts—has thrown the schools into political focus. As one student of educational administration observed:

> We "educationalists" find it most amusing to observe the contemporary discovery of local school systems by political and social scientists. It is as if thirty-five thousand local units of government have popped up unexpectedly (Cunningham, 1964).

In all fairness, there were a few political scientists who recognized the political centrality of schools. Eliot's plea of 1959 stands out most clearly. He argued for:

> Analysis not only in terms of political institutions . . . but in terms of voting behavior, ideological predispositions, the clashing interests, decision-making, and the impact of individuals and organizations on

* The authors wish to acknowledge the support of the Research and Development Division, Center for Educational Policy and Management during a portion of the time they devoted to the preparation of this paper. The Center for Educational Policy and Management is funded under a contract with National Institute of Education, Department of Health, Education and Welfare. The research reported in this paper was conducted as part of the research and development of the Center.

nationwide trends in educational policy. Of those only the first two have been examined at all extensively (and then usually by social scientists whose primary concern is not politics) and even those have not been the source of any noticeable amount of published material (Eliot, 1959).

The available evidence about educational decision-making is sparse, and generalizations made from the evidence are not very firm. With this *caveat*, we proceed to try to fit the pieces together.

POLICY LEVELS

School policy is made by a variety of participants at *all* levels of government. The federal government—while not usually providing direct financial support—affects lower education through such activities as subsidizing teacher training, giving aid to federally impacted areas, supporting demonstration and innovative projects, providing the "hot lunch" program, sponsoring research, and overseeing such controversial national policies as desegregation. State legislatures finance education to the tune of between twenty and fifty percent of the educational expenditure of local school districts. State boards of education establish—to a greater or lesser degree depending upon the state—curriculum and text requirements, and certification procedures. Local boards of education and superintendents are "legally" in charge of the basic educational program of a district; and the local electorate sometimes makes policy through referenda voting. School principals must interpret district-wide policy, and the classroom teacher (in most cases effectively shielded by the classroom door) must instruct within the guidelines established by this multi-layered decisional apparatus.

If we are to discuss decision-making culture in depth, it is obvious that we will have to eliminate some levels of decision-making. We have elected to concentrate on the local level for two reasons. First, this is the level with which we are most familiar, as a result of our own research. Second, despite evidence of growing nationalization, most of the important routine and episodic decisions still seem to be made at the local level. Although one hears increasing demands for "decentralization" and "community control," American schools, compared with those of other Western nations, *are* decentralized. Out of a variety of diffuse historical trends (including the deep commitment to localism on the part of the Pilgrims), the "traditional" American pattern of school governance emerged: a weak state education department providing limited leadership to a very large number of local units (Walker, 1972). In spite of the decline in the number of districts, this pattern remains intact. We feel justified, therefore, in concentrating upon local school districts.

POLICY ACTORS

The differentiation of hierarchical levels is a helpful initial step in our narrowing-down process. Now we need to know who is *usually* most active in local decision-making. Obviously the school board and superintendent are constantly involved. Additionally, however, and in various degrees, so are organized interest groups, teachers, students, and informal community power elites. While this is not an exhaustive list, it does include the most visible participants. A major task of this essay will be to indicate the way in which these participants influence local education policies. Because of its unique role the electorate will not be considered here.

TYPES OF DECISIONS

It is clear—by reason of common-sense and empirical evidence—that the influence of specific participants in a decision varies with the nature of the decision. School systems, like all organizations, must make decisions of diverse magnitudes and impacts. Organizational theorists have attuned themselves to the problem of types of decision with varying degrees of clarity. In all cases, the goal is to classify decisions along a continuum ranging from almost purely routine to fundamental goal-altering decisions. Downs, for example, uses the notion of "depth of change." There are minor changes in everyday behavior, which can be made without changing organizational goals. However, new organizational purposes require (theoretically) changes in day-to-day behavior (Downs, 1967, pp. 167–168). A similar, if dichotomous, distinction is offered by Agger, Goldrich, and Swanson:

> An *administrative* demand or decision-making process is regarded by its maker or participants as involving relatively routine implementation of a prior, more generally applicable decision; it implicates relatively minor values of a relatively few people at any one time and has 'technical' criteria available to guide the technically trained expert in selecting one or another outcome as *the* decision. A *political* demand or decision-making process is thought to involve either an unusual review of an existing decision or an entirely new decision, it implicates relatively major values of a relatively large

number of people and has value judgments or preferences as the major factors in determining selection by "policy-makers" of one or another outcome as *the* decision (Agger, Goldrich, and Swanson, 1964, p. 45).

As applied specifically to schools, Martin has distinguished between "internal" (e.g., administrative) and "public" (e.g., political) decisions (Martin, 1962, p. 61).

Most decisions made in school districts are administrative, routine, or internal. As we shall see, the routinization of decision has considerable impact upon the influence of various participants.

POWER AND EXCHANGE

Having defined the policy arena, listed the potential participants, and outlined the range of possible decisions, we are left with the task of presenting a theory of the way in which participants are linked with issues— a theory of influence. One of the most fruitful contributions to understanding political influence has been made by the exchange theorists, especially Blau (1964), Cartwright (1965), Gamson (1968), and Zald (1969). Their argument is that potential power is a function of the amount of political resources contributed by a participant. The conversion of potential power to actual power is dependent upon the nature of the decision and the skills of the participants. The conversion process involves the mobilization of one's resources and their subsequent application toward the attainment of a desired objective.

Our use of exchange theory should be distinguished from bargaining or choice theory, in that it is much less explicit about the properties of an "exchange." As used by Homans (1961), exchange means no more than "interaction" or "transaction." Blau (1964) is equally unconcerned, preferring to move directly into conditions influencing the outcome of exchanges rather than exploring what an exchange looks like. The clearest referent is by Waldman (1972), who asserts that the focus of exchange theory is how a person gains rewards from another person. Explicit application of exchange theory to political events appears to describe exchanges more in terms of *function* than concepts (Salisbury, 1970, p. 1–32). For the purposes of this essay, consider an exchange as an interaction involving the effort of at least two people to transform values into policy.

When two or more participants are vying for decisive influence over the same outcome, the exchange of resources is similar to primitive economic bargaining. In the situation under consideration here, for instance, formal control of educational policy rests with the school board. The board appoints the superintendent and may remove him at any time. The superintendent is an administrative officer similar to a city manager (Snow, 1966; Martin, 1962, p. 62). In most instances, the school board is the elected representative body speaking for "the public." Even when the board is appointed, its function is still a representative one. However, as is often the case when elected officials confront their administrative employees, the legal and the actual distribution of influence varies considerably. It is frequently the case that the resources of the superintendent are of sufficient value to cause the board to defer to him in the actual exercise of authority. The "rank" authority of the board loses out to the "technical" authority of the superintendent (Minar, 1964, pp. 132–133). Technical decisions—those involving merely the implementation of a prior, more goal-altering decision—are the domain of the superintendent.

Clearly, if school boards were to maximize their fundamental resource—formal authority—there would be no question of their supremacy. Nor would there be much point in continuing this essay. Obviously, as will become clear, this resource is underutilized.

Another potential school-board resource is *representative* responsibility. From the normative view of lay control of education, school boards speak for "the people." In a society in which symbols associated with popular sovereignty have high salience, the mere act of representation is a potential resource. If the school board is perceived—at least by the superintendent—as being a potential mobilizer of various publics, its power is enhanced. The amount of public, or external, support available to a board varies with a number of factors. Among these are: the recruitment pattern of a particular board, the visibility of the board to its public, and the salience of and satisfaction with educational policy.

Although legal authority and the representative function are the most universal of the potential resources available to school boards, others may exist in specific districts. In their study of a rural community in upstate New York, for instance, Vidich and Bensman discovered that the school board was closely allied with prevailing community elites (1960). Others have found this to be the case in communities characterized by an allegedly monolithic elite structure (Kimbrough, 1964). The whole question of utilization of political elites by school boards is complex, and needs further explanation than is possible here. Our assessment is that the interaction between community political elites and educational decision makers has been exaggerated. Gittell and Hollander's comparative analysis of six urban districts (1968) finds little evidence of *interaction*, much less efforts and influence between educational decision makers and other more generalized political actors.

Still, the question should be dealt with, because so many students of educational administration have followed sociologists and political scientists—uncritically—into the thicket of "power structure" research. Early studies suggested that major educational decisions were shaped directly by "prime movers" in the community. Hence, school boards could mobilize key members of the power system to do battle (if need be) with the superintendent. By the same token, key influentials were said to set the major policies of the educational system. Obviously, the lack of reliable support for this most popular hypothesis does not mean that educational decision-making is completely autonomous. What *is* suggested is that the political elite(s) of a community may—depending upon the issue, the community, the style of the board—be unavailable as a board resource.

The superintendent's potential resources are more limited in scope but potentially more effective in an exchange. His *primary* resource is his professional reputation for expertise in matters pertaining to education. The exchange between bureaucratic experts and elected laymen is hardly unique to school boards. The analogies which come most readily to mind are city council and city manager, and legislative committee and executive department. The medium of bargaining is similar to all these situations, yet there is something both unique and puzzling about the resources of the superintendent of schools. We have a tradition of "lay control." The existence of local school boards—almost uniquely American—attests to this tradition. In contrast with, say, England, the popular assumption that laymen should influence educational policy-making is viable. Simultaneously, however, we accord greater deference to superintendents than is true of most other public "professionals" (Martin, 1962, p. 50). This curious ambivalence actually strengthens the value of expertise, since there are virtually no institutional controls on superintendents other than accountability to the board. Superintendents, then, use their expertise in a disguised fashion, insisting that they are held in check by an alert board while usually holding a far superior advantage, sometimes a near-monopoly, on technical skills and information. As Minar notes:

> The technical expert, the district superintendent, is likely to flourish in those community settings where expertise and division of labor are assigned intrinsic value. . . . Where his "employers" on the board

and in the community trust and value *expertise* [the superintendent] is likely to have much more discretion and initiative, right up to the highest policy level (Minar, 1964, p. 141).

The claim for expert status by the superintendent is buttressed by another belief which can be used as a resource: the widely-held norm of separation of education and politics, and the consequent insulation of educational decision-making from broader based political conflict. The "reforms" of 1890–1910—initiated in response to the growing influence of urban political machines—produced a conventional wisdom which is still intact among administrators: the separation of policy-making from administration, and concentration of authority in the office of the superintendents. Keeping schools out of politics also meant minimizing the legitimacy of political conflict, and hence the legitimacy of "outside" influence as represented by pressure groups (Salisbury, 1967). In contrast to overtly political bodies, such as state legislatures or city councils, school boards and administrators define pressure groups as outside the proper influence system (Hess and Kirst, 1971). The "normal" resource of an interest group is the perception by a decision maker of its legitimacy (Zeigler and Baer, 1969). Admittedly, perceptions of legitimacy vary from group to group and issue to issue, but there is a general assumption on the part of most politicians that groups have a right to be heard. Superintendents do not share in this assumption (Crain, 1968, pp. 115–128). Further, only about half the school-board members accept the legitimacy of group-originated demands (Jennings and Zeigler, 1971). When the claim for expertise is successful, interest group influence will be minimal, as in New York:

In the last two decades, education in New York City has become amazingly insulated from political and public controls. One could accurately describe the situation as an abandonment of public education by key forces of political power within the City. . . . Weber's theory of the emergence of a specialized bureaucracy monopolizing power through its control of expertise characterizes the role of the education bureaucracy in New York City. The claim that only professionals can make competent judgments has been accepted. Civic and interest groups have responded ambivalently. On the one hand they accept the notion of the professional competence of the bureaucracy, but at the same time express a hopelessness regarding their ability to change the system (Gittell, 1967, p. 209).

To a lesser degree, teachers suffer from a comparable denial of legitimacy. They are *employees* of the school district. Employees, runs the official argument, have a right to be heard but not to participate. If teachers accept the employee role, their organizational influence will be minimal. Similarly, students (and parents) have not yet been accorded a legitimate voice as the consumers of the educational product. They are accorded considerably less voice than consumers normally exercise. They are not free to "vote with their feet." Since their choices are limited, their resources are largely confined to protest. Protest normally isolates the protesters from sources of power, thus proving to be an inefficient mechanism (Lipsky, 1968; Wilson, 1961).

THE MARKET PLACE: STRATEGIES OF INFLUENCE

We have described the most persistent actors and their resources. We now turn to another key concept: the market place or arena of exchange. The point here is that the existence of a new potential resource does not warrant the conclusion that it will necessarily be used in political exchange. Power requires, in addition to resources, the ability of the resource holder to convert the resources, and that the resources be relevant to the stakes of the exchange. A market, then, is more than a physical or conceptual space within which transactions take place; it is also a set of norms which govern these transactions. One type of market norm is that which provides criteria by which resources are evaluated. Since there are no conventional standards of evaluation within political markets comparable to that of money in economic markets, conversion rates for comparing the relative value of resources may vary widely from market to market. The goal of the participants is thus to arrange for issues to be defined in such a way that their particular resource will be highly valued. The superintendent seeks to achieve a definition of *all* issues as "technical." He seeks to routinize decision-making by constructing the agenda for board meetings and establishing himself, and his staff, as the most reliable source of information. Since boards typically do not have staffs, they usually have fewer alternative sources of information.

The board, to counter the information and expertise monopoly of the superintendent, must perceive the issues as nonroutine, or external, so that the superintendent's resources are deflated. The most obvious way to accomplish this goal is to keep the agenda loaded with problems of resource allocation rather than resource utilization, thus engaging the interest of organized groups. Thus, while the superintendent's best strategy is to constrict the range of debate, the board's best strategy is to expand the range of debate, arousing the public passions, and embedding the decision-making process within the general framework of the representational process or, if need be, community conflict.

A key component in this description of exchange is that of *perception*. In order for a resource to be applied, the potential user must view it as appropriate. Perceptions are not easily explained, but we do have some clues. The two factors to be relied upon are recruitment and environment. We shall direct our attention to patterns of recruitment, images of representative obligations, and response to "outside" influences. We shall then turn our attention to general patterns of interaction between school boards and superintendents. Finally, we shall address ourselves to the policy outcomes of such interactions.

RECRUITMENT

The recruitment of board members illustrates how well the reformers' dream of an insulated educational system has been realized. Prior to the reform of the turn of the century, board members were frequently supported by parties and elected on a ward basis. In some urban areas, there were between thirty and fifty boards with members (hundreds of them) elected from districts. Seats on boards were hotly contested; and the decentralization and partisanship of these elections contributed to the success of lower-middle class aspirants to the boards (Cronin, n.d.; Stelzer, 1971). With the institutional insulation of school districts from community politics the upper-class domination of school boards began. Nonpartisan at large elections fostered the hegemony of the upper-middle class. By 1927 Counts concluded that school boards were manned by a homogeneous business-professional class. Although all governmental bodies are underrepresentative of various ethnic and social minorities, school boards are unusually so. When compared to the general public, board members have the qualities that are—rightly or wrongly—more valued and esteemed in American society. Specifically, they are more male, white, middle-aged; longer residents of their communities; much better educated and better placed occupationally; more Protestant, more devout, and more Republican (Jennings and Zeigler, 1969b). Although the fallacy of inferring attitudes and behaviors from the social origins and positions of public officials is by now well established, social characteristics are important in demonstrating that certain perspectives or *Weltanschauung* are inevitably underrepresented on governing bodies by virtue of their status bias. Thus, while specific decisions or policies might not be attributable to a middle- and upper-class ethos, it does seem likely that the agenda of problems and possible solutions as well as the style of decision-making are affected by composition factors (Minar, 1966b; Masotti, 1968).

186   POLITICAL SCIENCE ANNUAL

The upper-class bias of school boards is hardly unique; indeed *all* governmental bodies exhibit such a bias. Nor is it surprising that school boards attract a disproportionate share of people who, along with their families, have been associated with education. What *is* unique is the isolation of board members from political involvement. Since the governing of schools is part of the political process, we might expect board members to spring disproportionately from politicized homes. Such is not the case (Jennings and Zeigler, 1972b). Board members are no more likely to come from homes where public affairs assume a high profile than is the general public. For all the usual findings about the political backgrounds of political elites, the pattern obviously does not apply to local elites in education. Thus the recruitment process provides more evidence of a recurrent theme of this essay: the "apolitical" character of school politics.

Another way we can discern the insulation of school board members is by looking at the positions held by board members *prior* to being elected. Most members serve an apprenticeship in public affairs; either in civic-business, political-governmental, or educational spheres (Jennings and Zeigler, 1972b). While all three avenues to the school board are used, the civic-business path emerges as the most prominent. The senior position of civic-business apprenticeship is, again, not unique, as a variety of community studies have shown. Such organizations as the Chamber of Commerce are prominent actors in the drama of local politics. Yet boards of education provide an even more congenial destination than, say, city councils or state legislatures. What could be better preparation for service in a "nonpolitical" agency than proven ability in the civic-business world?

There are, obviously, other paths to the school board. One alternative path of considerable theoretical interest is the political. Those board members whose careers interface with the community's manifest political process are likely to approach their jobs with markedly different attitudes than those whose career is in civic and business organizations. Boards with strong political orientations (when they can be found) stand in stark contrast to the "normal" board. Crain notes that:

> . . . . the appropriate model for studying school board recruitment is one of conflict between the two most powerful groups in the city— the political party and the civic leadership. . . . this is simply a continuation of the pressures which divided those two groups over fifty years ago, when the industrial cities of the North developed professional politicians who could use ethnic and class conflict as a resource to compete with Yankee money (1968, p. 196).

Crain went on to assert that boards recruited from the civic-business sector were more sympathetic to desegregation demands, hence were high on "reform orientation." This conclusion fits well with what we know of upper-class attitudes, but hides some other consequences of recruitment patterns. Jennings and Zeigler (1972b) found that board members with strong links to the political process (20 percent) are more likely to 1) have been originally elected to a board; 2) have attracted the support of various publics during the campaign; 3) be desirous of instituting changes in the educational program; 4) have differed seriously with their opponents; and 5) be more unhappy with the role of the board in making decisions.

On every one of these dimensions, the civic-business oriented board members (32 percent) ranked considerably lower. Such persons, while perhaps satisfying the reform values of being "above politics" hardly satisfy requirements for meaningful lay control: contested elections, issue differences, challenging the *status quo*, and looking back over one's shoulder at the mood of the constituency:

.... of all those board members with prior public affairs experience the civic notables are the blandest and gained office in the least competitive fashion (Jennings and Zeigler, 1972b, p. 54).

It need hardly be added that political paths and civic-business paths occur in reasonable correlation with the institutional relationship between the school and the political community. Political careers occur more often in partisan districts with ward elections; civic-business careers abound in nonpartisan, at large districts.

Adding to the noncompetitive nature of the recruitment process is the strong tendency of boards to perpetuate themselves. Elections to school boards are only moderately competitive. Only about half of the board members were elected in a contest with an incumbent (Jennings and Zeigler, 1971, p. 29). We stress the importance of challenging incumbents because those who do so are likely to stress ideological concerns and specific issues as opposed to symbolic euphorisms such as "better schools." Still, most board members can cite only one difference with their electoral opponents, and such differences are not likely to relate directly to the educational program.

In addition to self perpetuation by default, there is deliberate self perpetuation (Crain, 1968; Cronin, n.d.; Goldhammer, 1964; Jennings and Zeigler, 1971). The best way for any elected body to perpetuate its style and policies is to handpick its successors. True, such designees do not always fulfill the promise of their supporters. Moreover, the lone dissident or two might be most active in encouraging others to run. Over the long pull, however, it seems probable that board members encourage like-minded individuals to join them and that those who are successful prove compatible with existing board members. Adding to this probability is the socialization of new members into the norms and folkways of the board. If the new entrant initially considers diverging from his fellow members, such deviance is quickly attenuated by the socialization process, especially since the new member owes his position on the board to the instigation of board personnel. If one adds to the recruitment by the board, the activity of the PTA (closely identified with the "establish-ment"), superintendents and teachers, about one-half of the members of school boards are the products of self-perpetuation. To a substantial de-gree the pool of eligibles comes to be those people recognized by local educational elites as potential board members.

It is not surprising that school boards are WASPish; what does bear directly upon resource utilization is the low-keyed, self-perpetuating selection process which minimizes conflict. Such a selection process sub-verts the notions of lay control and hence the "public" orientation of board members. Orthodoxy and tradition are cherished, controversy is not. There is little intensive lay, or group, involvement in elections. Thus boards emerge as relatively impermeable. The early educational re-formers have succeeded too well: politics (i.e., partisan) and education are normally separate. Thus, the superintendent's basic resources—tech-nical skills, information monopoly, expertise—are not matched by an equally resourceful board. As we continue to describe the decisional culture of school systems, the lack of a balance of power between board and superintendent will become apparent.

Superintendents, too, have a clear—even more homogeneous—recruit-ment pattern. Like school board members, they are WASPish, Repub-lican, and devout. Here, however, the similarity ends. Superintendents are far more likely to have been reared in a small town, and to have a lower-middle class background. Very few of them are urban and profes-sional in origin (Carlson, 1972, pp. 7–37; Crain, 1968, pp. 116–117). For most school board members, board service is neither a route or end goal of upward mobility. Very few seek to better themselves politically. For superintendents, the job represents the culmination of a struggle out of the lower-middle class.

To be a superintendent, one must first be a teacher. To survive as a teacher—or become an administrator—one must learn to understand and accept occupational norms. The norm for teachers—less now, but certainly so when today's administrators were teachers—is quiescence, acceptance of authority, and conservatism (Corwin, 1966; Jennings and Zeigler, 1969a). Those that cannot accept the norms drop out (Zeigler, 1967). Surviving long enough to become an administrator requires more than an "employee" orientation. In addition to "knowing one's place," male teachers (superintendents are universally male), have to face the financial and psychological deprivations of existing in a highly feminized occupation (Clark, 1964). Ninety percent of all elementary teachers and about half of high school teachers are female. It is not surprising that only about 10 percent of the male teachers last longer than five years. The pool of eligibles is thus reduced considerably to those male teachers who, through keeping free of controversy, are able to survive. As Carlson notes: sheer *perseverance* seems to be a contingency of the career path of the superintendent (Carlson, 1972, p. 9).

It is perhaps here as a teacher—or more specifically as one of the few male teachers who survive—that future superintendents first develop their suspicion of lay control. In competition with parents for the obedience of the child, teachers develop defensive reactions: opposition to para-professionals, resentment of parental interference, belief in certification, methods courses, etc. Surviving male teachers, buffeted by the misfortunes of their jobs, *tend* to become more politically conservative and to develop an unusually high need for respect, an exaggerated concern for authority, and a personal rigidity and a fear of risk-taking behavior (Zeigler, 1967, p. 28; Brown, 1970, p. 97).

The occupational recruitment of superintendents—coupled with their unusually high small-town representation and working-class origins—helps considerably in understanding their view of boards which are usually composed of upper-middle class laymen. Given the humble origins of superintendents and their tendency to develop a defensive response to criticism, overcompensation is virtually guaranteed. Thus, the development of expertise as a resource comes naturally. Curiously, the militant defense of education expertise comes from an occupational group academically quite undistinguished. Among graduate students in seventeen fields attending universities which grant doctoral degrees, those in educational administration have the lowest mean score on the Miller Analogies test (Carlson, 1972, p. 25).

Taken together, these various strands of the recruitment process add up to the superintendent's giving his role a "narrow and defensive" definition (Crain, 1968, p. 117). Superintendents are intolerant of "lay" criticism and frequently unwilling to engage in dialogue with "outsiders."

Criticisms are answered with either complete disagreement or with irrelevant replies loaded with trivial detail (Crain, 1968, p. 117). For superintendents, then, expertise is not only a resource, it is a way of life learned early and necessary for psychic and *occupational* survival. Small wonder that superintendents use their resources more relentlessly than do school boards.

LINKAGE: THE ENVIRONMENT AND THE SCHOOLS

This relatively closed educational system is one which the various articulate publics have found remarkably impermeable. At the risk of redundancy, it is worth repeating that American education is symbolically democratic. As we have seen, however, few insiders pay more than lip service to the concept of lay control and many actively oppose it. Martin, perhaps most severe among those who expose this conflict between symbols and reality, laments:

> Thus is the circle closed and the paradox completed. Thus does the public school, heralded by its champions as the cornerstone of democracy, reject the political world in which democratic institutions operate (Martin, 1962, p. 89; see also Salisbury, 1967, pp. 408–420).

Legitimacy—the key to successful negotiation between elected officials and various publics—is difficult to establish. Information—a basic resource in the arsenal of the lobbyist—is hard to pry loose from the iron grip of the superintendent. Clearly, the opening of school districts to environmental demands hinges upon the extent to which educational decision makers conceive their role as legitimately entailing acknowledgment of and response to such demands. On this score, we find that the mass public, in keeping with its attachment to the symbols of democracy, is less inclined than board members and superintendents to accept the notion that school board members should follow their own judgment. The respective proportions are one-half, two-thirds, and three-fourths (Jennings and Zeigler, 1969b).

Of course, such categories of role orientations as delegate and trustee are well known and well worn. They provide, at best, a clue about linkages between governing elites and public demands. Obviously, school boards and superintendents do interact with agents of the community. To get more precisely at the nature of this interaction, Jennings and Zeigler (1971) categorized school boards according to the legitimacy and responsiveness accorded to group demands and individual demands.

While it is possible for boards to be equally responsive to both types of demands, in fact the two response styles are negatively correlated. Further, group responsive boards and individual responsive boards differed appreciably along a variety of dimensions. The conditions that lead boards to be responsive to group demands are those that *lessen* the responsiveness to individual sources of preferences and cues. Boards are considerably more group-oriented in the complex environments of metropolitan areas. Demands originating from individuals receive more sympathy in small towns. It seems that the ambience of small towns is conducive to the sort of informal, almost casual inputs of information so characteristic of our images of hinterland America (Vidich and Bensman, 1958, pp. 194–201). Even if these constituents are formal group spokesmen, they are not recognized in this fashion. They are seen as fellow merchants, farmers, luncheon club or church members, former high school classmates, relatives, friends, or perhaps just some residents with whom to pass the day. The exchange is nonthreatening, and the intensity is low.

It is only when one moves into the complexities of urban life that there is any appreciable exchange between formal organizations and elected and appointed school officials (Jennings and Zeigler, 1972a). Not only do such officials have a positive affect toward groups (e.g., accord them legitimacy), but they see more of them. However, even in those urban, group-oriented districts, interest-group activity is sporadic at best. Indeed, urban districts are "groupy" only in comparison to small town and rural ones. A sizeable portion of the districts are hardly boiling cauldrons of interest activity. To the contrary, they seem to be functioning with a minimum of formal group life (Jennings and Zeigler, 1972a).

Whereas Jenning's and Zeigler's conclusions about the paucity of group life are based upon comparative surveys, Smoley's (1965) study of pressures on the Board of School Commissioners in Baltimore provides corroboration by an exhaustive case study. Using minutes of the board and some additional published sources, he considered 2,389 issues during a seven-year period. Smoley revealed that even in a large city, interest groups are largely uninvolved:

> Of the 2389 issues considered by the Board of School Commissioners, only 207 included participation by outside groups—less than ten percent! Furthermore, much of the participation which did take place contained no hint of attempted influence, but was action in the performance of official functions to provide service to the Baltimore school system (Smoley, 1965, p. 180).

Smoley's analysis also provides insight into how superintendents can use their resources to minimize external demands. Superintendents usually set agendas for board meetings, and load them with trivia—nuts and bolts problems of administration which neither boards nor interest groups can understand. At first glance, the inclusion of administrative tasks in the agenda may seem risky, but the strategy is successful. Immersed in trivial administrative matters rather than major issues of educational policy, boards do not provide a forum for interest arbitration. Over 2,000 of the 2,389 decisions concerned staff personnel and the school building program. Only a handful related to instructional affairs. Most issues were routine and quickly resolved. The skillful use of trivia is a powerful weapon.

Further evidence of isolation appears when we probe into the *distribution* of activity among types of groups. The results are unequivocal: the most active voice is that of the PTA, followed (distantly), by teachers (Smoley, 1965; Gross, 1958; Jennings and Zeigler, 1972a). Almost two-thirds of the board members in the Jennings and Zeigler study cited the PTA; about one-third recalled demands by teacher groups. After these two, the list declines through civil rights groups (29 percent); various business, professional and service clubs, down through the much feared (but relatively quiescent) right-wing groups (13 percent), to the rarely active labor organizations (3 percent). PTA's and teachers are most active, and we will return to them for a more thorough analysis. At this point, let us note anew that most of the interest-group action is controlled by "in-house" organizations whose major thrust is to create a climate in which the *status quo* goes unchallenged. There is an "establishment" tinge to the group spectrum.

If the usual decisional climate is ideologically cool, there is no gainsaying the fact that it does, on occasion, become quite heated. When issues lose their routine, technical flavor, and strike deeply at emotions, then the superintendent may find himself in the midst of group-dominated conflict. Such conflicts surrounding the resolution of episodic issues are rare but usually spectacular.

Granted that schools are now commonly described as the center of turmoil (teacher strikes, student revolts, taxpayer revolts, bussing, community control), even in the 1960s relatively placid districts probably outnumbered the tempestuous ones. Some districts cope with their problems over a long period of time with a minimum of strife. Others—those which capture the imagination of the mass media—seem to be caught up in perpetual conflict. What may best characterize school district phenomena of this type is a model of episodic crisis (Iannaccone, 1967; Campbell, 1968). Most districts experience crises and unrest at one time or another; the difference is that some few are marked by frequently recurring episodes whereas most enjoy rather long periods of calm between crises.

What happens when episodic crises erupt? When the district population becomes antagonized, support for school policy dwindles and group demands increase (Jennings and Zeigler, 1971; Jennings and Zeigler, 1972a). Imagine, for example, a school beset by scandal or fiscal chaos. As popular support dwindles, an increase in group demands sets in. As public confidence in the school continues its descent, the loss of confidence is articulated and given explicit focus by interest groups. They pinpoint, according to their own objectives and interests, the specific aspects of discontent to which they will address their efforts. The decline in popular support becomes less generalized as group activity increases. Groups clearly thrive in an atmosphere of conflict between the governed and the governors. Such a condition of stress is a precipitant condition for group activity, irrespective of the social complexity of the community. The board and superintendent are in a state of siege.

The threatening environment of group activity surely sets educational governance apart from other public decision-making processes, where group activity is normal and considerably lower keyed. School boards, unlike most governmental bodies, are (in normal times) accustomed to individual exchanges, consisting of cues rather than demands (Summerfield, 1971). Such cues may have affective content, but quite often simply consist of feedback to the board, signals about the reception of their actions. When individual cuing does consist of preferences on pending policies, such preferences are not seen as vigorously made demands. Since individual, unattached communications are typical of communities with a high level of satisfaction with educational policy, the content of the communications is usually supportive and not directed toward alterations in basic policy.

Group communications, more often reflecting the *ressentiment* of the masses, are addressed toward serious ideological conflict (except when coming from supportive organizations such as PTA's). Can organizations translate their anger into observable phenomena? If not, their activity would make little difference, since school boards and superintendents would have little evidence of the state of public opinion. The evidence is that group activity is strongly associated with financial defeats, teacher firings, and superintendent turnovers (Jennings and Zeigler, 1972a).

Small wonder that they are feared! Of particular interest is a strong association between the activities of political organizations and superintendent turnovers. When superintendents insist that education and politics do not mix, they are not just mouthing platitudes. Again, there is strong incentive for superintendents to use their resources to buffer themselves against the assault of "outside" groups.

In addition to their control of the agenda—and their studied use of trivia—superintendents have the advantage of an institutional structure designed, as we have seen, to insulate schools from the erratic winds of community conflict. Such devices as at-large, nonpartisan elections serve to *minimize* the link between public anger and group demands. Although it makes intuitive sense to argue that large electoral units increase social heterogeneity and hence exacerbate group conflict, the opposite is true. Ward elections (a minority phenomenon in school district organizations) increase the likelihood that interest groups will provide a clearer focus for grievances which are likely to be neighborhood based. Similarly, partisan elections place the educational decision-making process squarely within mainstream, conflictual politics, thus providing a visible target for interest groups.

Linkage opportunities are also reduced appreciably by the self-perpetuating recruitment pattern characteristic of school boards. When, as is frequently the case, incumbent board members are able to perpetuate their influence by bringing like-minded colleagues to the board, interest-group activity (and individual communications as well) tapers off considerably. Boards in these circumstances appear almost akin to closed corporations, insulating themselves from the hue and cry of interest-group politics. Popular uprisings or expressions of discontent come slowly to the attention of the board, since cues are internally generated. Boards and superintendents value a public display of unity, generally eschew identification with group-originated values, and avoid public conflicts. About 90 percent of the votes observed by Lipham, Gregg, and Rossmiller (1967), in twelve Wisconsin districts, were unanimous.

The only groups welcomed into such dynasties are PTA's and, less often, teachers. Their comparative acceptance stems from their semi-official status.

The PTA—with its membership strongly biased in favor of the social characteristics not comparable to those of school boards—functions not as a demand-generating group, but rather as a buffer or defense mechanism. It does not translate mass hostility into specific demands, but rather communicates the policy of the board and superintendent to its clientele.

It coopts potentially disruptive parents, defusing conflicts before they begin (Dahl, 1961, p. 155; Koerner, 1968, p. 26).

Teachers' organizations (the local affiliates of the National Education Association and of the American Federation of Teachers) occupy a curious place in the array of group activity. Of all the groups engaging—however sporadically—in efforts to influence the content of educational policy, teachers have the highest legitimacy. They are not outsiders. Furthermore, they generally confine their activity to narrowly defined issues, such as teacher hirings, firings, conditions of work, and salaries. Yet teachers' organizations are a distant second in group activity (Jennings and Zeigler, 1972a). In spite of some very visible political activities, teachers' organizations are apparently no more influential today than they were more than a decade ago. In 1956, Griffiths concluded that "Teachers as a group have little or no say in the formulation of school policy" (Griffiths, 1956, p. 106). In 1969 Rosenthal wrote ". . . . they [teachers' organizations] play a negligible part in determining school policies. . . ." (Rosenthal, 1969, p. 154).

Why is this the case? A variety of explanations for the weak position of teachers have been advanced. Most relate, directly or indirectly, to the occupational norms of teaching, and the authority structure of the school system. Most prominent among the explanations are: 1) the employee status and orientation of teachers, 2) the nonpolitical tradition of education, as it translates into organizational quiescence, and 3) the administrative domination of schools and teachers' organizations. Each will be examined briefly.

Teachers—and especially teachers' organizations—use the word "profession" to the point of abuse, but it is difficult to agree with this self-concept. Among other attributes, professions are presumed to have some degree of autonomy in exercising their special competence. Yet, teachers cannot exercise much independent authority even within the classroom to which they are assigned. Nor do they control entry into teaching or assessment of colleagues' performance. Legally, they are employees, not professionals. More importantly, most teachers are *emotionally* employees. Traditionally, superintendents, principals, and other administrators have made decisions for teachers with the expectation that "teachers would be grateful for the generosity bestowed upon them" (Goldhammer, Suttle, Aldridge, and Becker, 1967). The upsurge in "militancy" should not obscure the fact that *most* teachers accept the employee orientation, which requires a basic loyalty to the "boss." Some teachers—and the number appears to be growing slowly but inexorably—have adopted a genuinely professional orientation, which impels them to seek to expand the power of teachers at the expense of administrators and lay authorities. However, Corwin's general conclusion is that teachers find the employee role more compatible. Two-thirds of the teachers he studied claim that they:

> Make it a practice of adjusting their teaching to the administration's views of good educational practice and are obedient, respectful and loyal to the principal: that they *do* look primarily to the judgment of the administration for guidance in cases of disputes in the community [over a textbook or speaker]. . . . Approximately one half of the sample, too, agreed that their school's administration is better qualified to judge what is best for education. . . . one half of the sample agreed that teachers who openly criticize the administration should go elsewhere. . . on the other hand, less than half of these believed that the ultimate authority over major educational decisions should be exercised by professional teachers (Corwin, 1966, p. 107).

Corwin estimates that only about 10 percent of teachers have enough nonemployee characteristics to qualify them as militant. Zeigler (1972) found that going on strike was not considered professional by most teachers. Even collective bargaining is viewed with suspicion (Doherty and Oberer, 1967). The fact that most teachers are not militant should not be taken to minimize the "teacher revolt." Obviously, some teachers are seeking more power and, equally obviously, administrators are resisting. While the number of "work stoppages" (e.g., strikes) underwent an "irregular but gradual decline" from 1945 to 1966 (Lieberman and Moskow, 1966), they began to surge upward around 1968 (National Education Association, 1968).

Nevertheless, predictions of increased militancy must be taken into account. This is especially true since school boards and superintendents regularly issue statements about dealing with teacher militancy (whether or not they have experienced it). Also what we know about militancy may lead us to speculate about the future. Teachers are far more willing to challenge established authority in big cities and in the Northeast and West, than they are in small towns and in the Midwest and South (Zeigler, 1972). Not surprisingly, large city school districts are more likely to experience teacher strikes. Further, popular support for strikes is also greatest in these areas. Indeed, segments of the public—particularly those with union affiliations—are more sympathetic to teachers than has popularly been assumed (Almy and Hahn, 1971). However, opportunities to form coalitions with various outside groups are constricted by the nonpolitical tradition of the teaching profession and the dominant position of administrators. In sum, *one* reason why teachers are not more active is that they do not wish to be. They are comfortable in their employee station. Even when strikes occur, the issue to be contested is usually salary and working conditions, not authority.

Closely related to the acquiescence which accompanies the employee image is the acquiescence of the nonpolitical organization. Of the two teacher organizations, the older, larger, still dominant National Education Association stands clearly in the nonpolitical tradition in contrast with the smaller, urban-oriented American Federation of Teachers. NEA local affiliates have—until recently—opposed strikes and eschewed political activity of any kind. The official ideology of the NEA was that the "professional" stature of teachers would suffer if the organization became involved in the rough and tumble world of politics. Hess and Kirst (1971) report, for example, that only tiny fractions of teachers openly discuss school board elections, much less try to influence their outcomes. Although leaders of NEA locals are more politically inclined than followers (Luttbeg and Zeigler, 1966), they are partially immobilized by a nonstable membership (Clark, 1964).

Finally, there is administrator dominance of schools and associations. The National Education Association, in addition to stressing professionalism, stresses "unity." Administrators and teachers, therefore, are in the same organization. Administrators have—until very recently—controlled the NEA policy-making machinery, and they still dominate most locals. Pressure on teachers to join the NEA is fairly wide-spread, with administrators proudly announcing that their school is "100 percent" (Doherty and Oberer, 1967). The role of administrators in the NEA parallels their role in schools, and even parallels the influence of the administrative point of view in schools of education. Schools of education are typically more authoritarian, and products of such schools more acquiescent, than is true of other portions of the university (Lazarsfeld and Thielens, 1958; Jennings and Zeigler, 1970). Further, there is a strong relationship between acquiescent behavior and administrative approval within the school (Jennings and Zeigler, 1969a). The cry for unity, therefore, serves the administration well, and the NEA is the vehicle which enforces the ideology.

The AFT—which represents a minority of teachers—has a more militant, less acquiescent membership. It excludes administrative personnel from membership and has traditionally supported political action. Its success in winning representation elections in large cities—notably New York—has spurred the NEA to a substantially more militant position (so much so that administrators are considering pulling out). Still, the NEA is the major teachers' organization, and it does speak more authoritatively for "unity" (e.g., administrative dominance) than for teachers. Administrators are even more opposed to teacher militancy than are school boards (especially where teachers' revolutions have actually taken place), and are almost obsessed with authority. As the American Association of School Administrators puts it: "We pledge to resist any effort to displace the superintendent and his authority in matters affecting the interest and welfare of school personnel" (cited in Rosenthal, 1969, p. 19).

THE BOARD-SUPERINTENDENT EXCHANGE

We are left, then, with an analysis of the exchange between the school board and superintendent. In *most* cases, understanding this exchange is the key to unravelling the "causes" of local educational policymaking.

Superintendents, like city managers, are products of the demand for efficiency, and the increasing complexity of educational policy. In the early years of the public school system, the authority to manage schools was in the hands of school boards. Boards had leaders, raised money, selected texts, and even interviewed prospective students (Callahan, 1966). However, in the middle of the nineteenth century, schools rapidly became compulsory and free. Simultaneously, the country leaped enthusiastically into the Industrial Revolution with its accompanying population explosion and urbanization. As schools grew in complexity, it became apparent that lay boards did not have time or inclination to continue management. Various schemes (including the currently popular "community school"—the division of large cities into small districts, each with its own board) were tried; but finally the boards gave up. In the latter half of the nineteenth century boards began to hire professional administrators who slowly and inexorably began to assume not only administrative but policy-making authority (James, 1967). Around 1895 a rearguard action on the part of boards was conducted in an effort to prevent the abolition of boards. Superintendents proposed that responsibility for instructional policy be turned over to them. Once appointed, superintendents were to be independent of boards. Boards—patronage oriented and imbedded in the partisan politics of the community—managed to win this fight, retaining their authority to hire and fire superintendents. Thus, the shape of educational policy-making was set: each contestant retained some resources (Callahan, 1966). Indeed, noting the erosion of board powers, Carlson maintains that the board's most important function is selecting a superintendent (Carlson, 1972).

Winning the fight to retain legal authority over the hiring and firing of superintendents did not do much more than keep retreat from turning into rout. The decline in the number of districts (thereby increasing the centralization of policy-making) continued to be a major component of the ideology of "scientific management." Since 1932, four-fifths of the school districts in the United States have disappeared, while pupil populations have risen by 15 million. The ratio of board members to student population has increased from one to forty-six in 1932 to one member to three hundred pupils in 1967 (James, 1967). Further, superintendents predict—and approve—even more centralization in the future (Andes et al., 1971). Since complexity works to the advantage of superintendents, these movements should increase the power of the superintendent.

Hines' (1951) fifty-year history of the Eugene, Oregon school board illustrates the trends which James and Callahan outlined. His study shows the gradual assumption by superintendents of the responsibility for the instructional program, then for the selection and supervision of the professional staff. From these beachheads the superintendent expanded his domain to budget preparation and fiscal control, purchasing, school site selection, plant management, and public relations. The assumption of board powers was gradual and sometimes contested. Conflict erupted at each new expansion of superintendent's authority, and was not necessarily resolved during the incumbency of the superintendent that initiated the "power grab." But the general thrust of the change is unmistakable when viewed over the long sweep of time.

According to Hines, the first erosion of board power occurs when the superintendent (and central office staff) assumes control over the instructional, or educational, program. Curiously, the educational program is the one area where boards have theoretical legitimacy: yet it is the first to go. In virtually all studies classifying issues coming to the attention of the board, matters bearing upon the quality of the educational program rank last in the attention devoted to them by the board:

> It is common knowledge that boards of education devote little time and thought to the problems of the educational program per se (Greider, Pierce, and Rosenstengel, 1961, p. 198).

A systematic study of a national sample of school districts by Zeigler and Jennings with Peak (1974) provides clear support for the earlier generalizations. In this study, it was assumed that the superintendent would have a well-developed idea of an appropriate educational program for his district, and that the board's function would be to *react* (much in the manner of Congress reacting to the initiative of the "chief legislator," the President). Accordingly, we examined the extent to which boards were able and/or willing to muster significant (e.g., close to a majority) opposition to the superintendent about the content of the educational program. About one-fourth of the boards qualified. However, we further reasoned that—given the agenda-setting authority of the superintendent—overt opposition would give us only a partial image of board-superintendent exchanges. Policy may be controlled by preventing conflict over a threatening issue from ever being joined. We found that only 4 percent of the boards exercised independent agenda-setting authority.

As one superintendent in an earlier study candidly put it, referring to the board members and the educational program:

> They don't know anything about it; but the things they *know* they talk about, like sidewalks, sites, and so forth. I let them go on sometimes because I don't want them to talk about curriculum (Kerr, 1964, p. 51).

This is an example of an adept superintendent avoiding overt board disagreement over a potentially controversial issue by the practice of non-decision-making. On the other hand, the occasional superintendent who is passive or dominated by his board may anticipate board opposition and avoid an issue (in spite of his preferences) because of his expectation of defeat. To minimize these pitfalls, we constructed a composite measure consisting of degree of opposition, and the subjective probability which board members attribute to the likelihood of the superintendent winning an overt contest between himself and the board over the content of the educational program.

According to the theory outlined at the beginning of the essay, a crucial variable in the exchange between school board and superintendent is each party's definition of the issues to be resolved, their perceived appropriate role, and the resources accompanying each perception of roles and decisions. The basic resource of the board is its *representative* capacity. However, we have seen that relatively few boards have been able to escape superintendent domination, and (presumably) assert their representative resources. How does it come about that the representative resource is underutilized? Clearly, some clues can be found in the self-perpetuating recruitment process, and its attendant suspicion of out-siders. Yet a more fundamental contributing factor is simply the board's image of its opportunities. Dykes states that "what the school board does depends in large measure on the board's view of itself in relation to its responsibilities" (Dykes, 1965, p. 11).

Basically, we see Dykes's assertion as allowing us to classify boards along a continuum according to the degree to which they accept a repre-sentative or "professional" role. A board which sees itself principally as a mechanism through which various segments of the community can participate in the formation of educational policy will behave much dif-ferently from one that views its role as being a protective buffer between the professionals who run the schools and the public whose children are educated in them. In the former instance, public('s) support or opposi-tion will be a salient input for the board. In the latter case, the *profession-ally* oriented board is less inclined to perceive and act upon expressions of popular values. Such boards will place greater reliance on technical expertise. The board which subordinates its representative responsibili-ties to what it perceives to be its responsibilities to professional educators is likely to accept an administrative definition of its job.

Gross, Mason, and McEachern's seminal study of school boards and superintendents in Massachusetts (1958, p. 225) makes it clear that, from the point of view of the superintendent, the two roles are incompatible and the professional role is preferred. One of the items used to ascertain degree of professionalism is: "In deciding issues the board members vote as representatives of important blocs or segments." The modal superin-tendent response was "absolutely must not" and 68 percent of the board members agreed with their superintendent.

Our assumption led us to ask the direct question: "Do you ever feel any conflict between your responsibility to the public and to the school administration?" Each board was given a score to reflect the percent of its members who responded negatively. Thus, high scores indicate rela-tively high degrees of professionalism in school board orientations, whereas low scores are indicative of representative boards. The mean score was 60.15 indicating a distribution skewed in favor of a "profes-sional" role. Our use of this question as a surrogate for professionalism is based upon our understanding of the values of superintendents to in-sulate the school. Hence, more "representative" responses indicate a link-age with the community, or a nonprofessional attitude.

The distribution of scores indicates that a majority of American school boards tend to perceive their roles as being consistent with the values of professional educators. In terms of the language of the theory guiding the essay, the majority of boards define educational markets in such a way as to give superintendents the advantage. Rather than serving as a conduit to channel popular views to the administrators, boards came to define their job as "selling" the administration's program to segments of the community.

Not surprisingly, there is a significant positive correlation (.35) between board professionalism and superintendent dominance: superintendents win (partially) because boards *want* them to. As Lipham, Gregg, and Rossmiller (1969, p. 2) put it, "board members [tend] to engage in role avoidance—delegating the decision-making power to the superintendent of schools." Lipham and his colleagues found, for instance, that 90 percent of all school board members thought that they should not serve as spokesmen for segments of the community; yet slightly over one-fourth of the citizens thought this was a good idea (Lipham, Gregg, and Rossmiller, 1969).

The McCarty and Ramsey report (1971) contains a graphic description of a typical professional board:

> The superintendent of schools made certain that no issue came up that would raise the ire of any board member. . . . Therefore, there was very little in the way of controversy, argument, debate, or the like. . . . School board meetings were very short since they were confined to approving the recommendations of the superintendent. . . . Much of [the superintendent's] work was done behind the scenes. He frequently contacted board members. . . . and probably knew exactly how every vote would be beforehand. This allowed him the option of failing to bring up issues that might lead to a confrontation or raise some question regarding his authority.
>
> The school board members felt that Dr. X knew school matters well. He had a doctor's degree and long experience with the schools. Why should they question him. Or, as it was more often put, "Who am I to question him?" Improvements were made, but conspicuous issues such as sex education . . . were brought up only after the superintendent was relatively assured that everyone agreed on them. . . . The counselors, administrative assistants, principals, or any person involved in any way in school policy were all hand-picked by the superintendent.
>
> Perhaps the key issue in the decision-maker role is that of selecting board members. . . . The school board itself urged people to run . . . and they usually did so unopposed. . . . Candidates were always suggested by the superintendent . . . in terms of their name,

the person's prestige in the community, his talent for being down to earth on crucial issues, and his compatibility with the other board members (McCarty and Ramsey, 1971, pp. 173–174).

If this type of board-superintendent exchange is a victory for expertise and the erosion of representation, there are still variations in this pattern: representative roles do, occasionally, become articulate and superintendents occasionally lose. In looking for explanatory factors in exploring this variance, we can address ourselves to the character of the board, the level of conflict in the community, and the nature of the issues (whether routine or episodic).

A beginning clue as to when we might expect to discover exceptions can be found in the well-worn (but still interesting) idea of *status*. We are, of course, accustomed to expect an association between social status and political behavior, but Minar has given the concept of status a more refined definition:

> The differences in decision-making we would suppose to derive from differences in conditioning to, understanding of, and outlook on expertise and the division of labor [are] . . . differences rooted in the experience of status groups. Thus the better educated and those in professional and managerial occupations are those who respect and understand specialization and delegation, those who see it in their own life routines (Minar, 1966b, p. 832).

The higher-status professional's respect for technical skill can be observed operating throughout the history of school (and municipal) reform. As Hofstadter notes (1955), municipal (and school) reformers sought to attack the partisan bias of ethnic politics by the application of modern business methods, especially scientific management. "Efficiency" and reform were virtually synonymous terms. Accordingly, administrators began to assume the role of business manager (Callahan and Button, 1964, p. 80).

The middle-class respect for expertise results in a curiously ambivalent exchange with the superintendent. As we noted, opposition to the superintendent is relatively scarce. However, it is strongly associated with social status. Higher-status boards are far more likely to oppose the superintendent than are lower-status boards (Zeigler and Jennings with Peak, 1974). Initially, this finding contradicts the assumptions of Minar (see also Gross, Mason, and McEachern, 1958, p. 95). Further, Bowman (1963) found higher-status boards considerably more inclined than lower-status ones toward permissiveness and granting decision-making latitude to the superintendent. Why, then, do our higher-status boards appear less "professional" than they should be?

Higher-status boards have—in their status itself—a resource (Zald, 1969, pp. 105–106). Higher-status persons are generally more informed, articulate, and have a more coherent ideology than do lower-status persons. Thus, while they respect expertise, they also possess more of it than lower-status board members (but not necessarily superintendents). However, while they oppose the superintendent more often, they are ultimately less successful as antagonists: compared with lower-status boards they are less likely to win when they oppose the superintendent (Zeigler and Jennings with Peak, 1974). Their opposition, then, is relatively easily overcome; they lack the tenacity of lower-status boards. The latter, although less likely to challenge the superintendent, are more likely to persist as the conflict becomes heated. They are less persuadable.

Aroused lower-status boards usually spell trouble for the superintendent. They are, as we have noted, not clear in their understanding of the division of labor between superintendent and board. Thus, there is a negative association ($-.20$) between board status and desire to maintain close supervision over the superintendent (Zeigler and Jennings with Peak, 1974). Lower-status boards spend more time on routine, internal issues at the expense of the educational program. The emergent picture of the lower-status boards is one of overconcern with administrative detail, failure to delegate authority over routine matters to the superintendent, and forfeiture of responsibility to oversee the general educational program. The opposite is true of higher-status boards. However, their inability to ride out a conflict minimizes the effects of their concern with general educational policy.

Although efforts to link the decision-making style of boards and superintendents to the structure of influences in a community have yielded ambiguous results, there is still the possibility that the decision-making style of a board will affect the exchange with the superintendent. If, for example, the board is immersed in bitter factional conflict, it may have little opportunity to contest the superintendent. Political scientists who study collective decision-making assume the existence of factional conflict and concentrate upon bargains and strategies of influence. When one examines school boards, it is important to understand that intraboard conflict is not considered legitimate in the eyes of professional educators. As Dykes says, "Factions exist in hundreds of school boards throughout the country. In every instance they present obstructions to the proper functioning of the board and to the work of the superintendent" (Dykes, 1965, p. 152).

One might well wonder why this is the case, and the answer is not difficult to ascertain. Factions are "bad" because they contradict the administrative ideological tenet of "unity." Salisbury captures well the essence of the ideology:

> Educators have tried very hard to achieve and maintain consensus among all those engaged in the educational enterprise. Unity is a prerequisite to a reputation for expertise, and it thus adds to the bargaining power of schoolmen as they seek public support. Unity inside the school helps justify independence from "politics" (Salisbury, 1967, p. 417).

In spite of the official ideology, school boards do have intragroup disagreement. In order to tap the nature of this disagreement, we constructed a threefold typology of school boards based upon: 1) the extent of the disagreement, and 2) the development of reasonably permanent coalitions. Boards in which the majority of members perceived little or no disagreement, were characterized as *consensual*. Those in which the majority perceived relatively frequent disagreement but no stable coalitions are described as *pluralistic*. The remainder, which have both frequent disagreements and stable coalitions fell within what we term the *factional* category. The figure following indicates the resulting distribution of boards in the sample.

Distribution of School Boards
by Decision-Making Style

Type of Board	No. of Boards	Percent
Consensual	24	22.4
Pluralistic	57	53.6
Factional	26	24.0

As we can see, about one-fourth of the boards resemble "little legislatures," i.e., have stable factions. On the other hand, the ideology of unity does not prevent the entirely human characteristic of arguing. The majority of boards are pluralistic, with frequent disagreements, but none serious enough to produce enduring friction. Finally, quite a few boards are quite harmonious. The basic question is: Are superintendents justified in their fear of conflict? Do consensual boards provide more freedom for superintendents? The answer is not as unequivocal as we might expect.

It is true that consensual boards behave pretty much according to the expectations of the superintendent. They are exceptionally high in "professional" orientation and quite likely to be dominated by the superintendent (Zeigler and Jennings with Peak, 1974). Yet the factional boards are even more likely to defer to the superintendent, even though their acceptance of the professional role is not quite as high as is the case for consensual boards. What probably happens is that factional boards would like to take a poke or two at the superintendent but are debilitated by the rigidity of their factions and seriousness of disputes. Energy is directed inward. Given the high level of tension in such boards, their inability to control the superintendent might disappear if a coalition were able to achieve a working majority. From the superintendent's point of view the consensual board is preferable to the factional one—despite the latters' slightly greater acquiescence—because of the lower potential for upheaval.

Pluralistic boards are clearly the most difficult for superintendents to dominate. Their frequent squabbles but infrequent coalitions suggest a board engaged to some degree in debates over the substance of educational policy yet capable of resolving conflict. In these boards, the lowest level of superintendent dominance is found. Such boards represent the most serious short-run threat to the superintendent. They can keep him off balance with shifting alliances and the articulation of diverse points of view.

Our view of the superintendent-board nexus as a small social system incorporates the more general view of forces affecting educational policy. The interaction among board members and the superintendent produces forces affecting behavior which are beyond, and in some cases independent of, forces emanating from the community (Charters, 1953). Such forces contribute to the continuity and stability of the small social system and serve to insulate it from the larger political community.

Who shapes these group norms? The superintendent or the board? Superintendents frequently express an interest in socializing board members into their own definitions of the situation, as evidenced in their frequent use of phrases such as "orienting new members," "educating the board," or "making the board more professional." We know that most boards fit well into the superintendents' definition of the situation, but we do not know how much work he has to do to achieve a "professional" board.

The most extensive treatment of the socialization of board members is by Kerr (1964). Kerr was particularly interested in illustrating how the older board members and superintendents inducted new members into the system—by applying to them the status of "freshmen," and by using the common sanctions of humiliation and criticism, and ultimately social and intellectual isolation if the new member persisted in deviant behavior. Kerr documented the process whereby new members of the board (even those members who had displayed close attention to the educational program during the campaign) came to accept the view that concern for the instructional program was not their affair, but rather lay within the province of the administration.

Kerr, given the limitation of his data, gives the impression that the superintendent is the major socializer and that he always wins. Certainly, the conventional doctrine of superintendents virtually requires that they treat boards as in need of education. The *raison d'etre* of the institution of the superintendency places board members in the position of pupils:

> The superintendent should expect the board to look to him for leadership in the educational affairs of the district. . . . He alone is in a position to see the total picture, and, furthermore, he must carry the responsibility implicit in the role of chief school officer (Ashby, 1968, p. 48).

There is, in addition to frequent professional repetition of the liturgy of the expert, considerable emphasis upon the *political* role of the superintendent by a growing group of students of educational administration, most of whom (in an effort to explode the argument of neutrality) describe the superintendent as a skillful manipulator in the tradition of Lyndon Johnson. Actually, his ability to coopt the board is constrained by the resources available in the exchange. Peak has summed up the dangers of the overactive superintendent:

> Not only is he violating the norm of keeping education out of the arena of political conflict, but he is also likely to find himself in a contest with the board over the mobilization of political resources. The exchanges . . . would involve but one type of currency—political support. In a sense, the superintendent would be competing with the board on the latter's "home turf". . . . the superintendent would be engaged in an out-and-out contest to see whether he or the board (assuming, of course, that the board wished to compete) could muster the most political clout (Peak, 1971, pp. 154–155).

These assumptions suggest that the best strategy for superintendents is to avoid "meddling in board politics as such." Some findings in support of Peak's statement are: 1) superintendents who intervene openly in the election of board members are more likely to encounter opposition, 2) the results of superintendents' efforts to "educate" board members, or to build private coalitions of community support, are mixed at best. In large cities and suburbs, there is a strong *negative* association between conscious indoctrination and superintendent dominance; the reverse is true in small towns. Thus, a heavy-handed approach succeeds in antagonizing board members in larger places. Further, there is no discernible effect on superintendent dominance of the effort to build external political coalitions, except in large cities, where it has a small positive effect (Zeigler and Jennings with Peak, 1974). In fact, the *more* superintendents engage in overt efforts to muscle boards, the *less* likely they are to dominate them!

Not only does "playing politics" in a manifest fashion reduce the value of the superintendent vis-a-vis the board; he may very well find himself in the job market if he does so. Superintendents can keep their jobs and their influence, by ignoring the pleas of political scientists and students of education and politics that they recognize their "true" status as politician. If selecting a superintendent is the most important job of the board, superintendents should be wary of giving them this opportunity. Superintendent turnover is clearly related to levels of conflict on the board. The more opposition to the superintendent within the board, the greater is the turnover. Also, thre is evidence that superintendent turnover is linked to *board* turnover, i.e., the rapid infusion of new members into a stable system (Walden, 1967; Iannaccone, 1967; Zeigler and Jennings with Peak, 1974); in turn, there is some evidence that board turnover is linked to community political instability (Goldhammer and Farner, 1964). We shall return to the question of linkages between board-superintendent interactions and community conflicts; but for the moment it is sufficient to observe that community political instability is largely beyond the control of the superintendent. His only option—and frequently this option closes quickly—is to stay clear of conflict (Browder, 1970). Superintendents *can*, however, avoid *starting* a community conflict by minimizing the visibility of the school system (Charters, 1953; Zeigler and Peak, 1970).

The insulation of the schools from the larger framework of community politics cannot be guaranteed. Community tension does have some clear spillover into the exchange between board and superintendent. The structure of board decision-making is remarkably attuned to levels of perceived community tension: consensual boards are associated with very low levels of tension ($\overline{X} = -.49$), pluralistic boards are unaffected

($\overline{X} = -.01$), and factional boards are strongly associated with high levels of community tension ($\overline{X} = .48$).

The factional board, with its stable coalitions of antagonists, reflects the hostilities of the community; the consensual board, with its pattern of harmony and unanimity, mirrors the placidity of the community environment. Not surprisingly, consensual boards are found most often in small cities.

The level of tension in a community also translates into board-superintendent conflict, but not necessarily in a diminution of superintendent influence. No matter what kind of community we consider, the higher the level of community tension, the greater the tendency of the board to oppose the superintendent. The translation is most immediate in large cities. Yet in those very places, increased tension in the community actually strengthens the hand of the superintendent in his exchange with the board. One reason for his improved position is the probability that the board will become factional and direct its energy inward. Further, the complexity of the educational system in large cities makes it difficult for the board to challenge the superintendent efficiently. The complexity of the system renders it almost impervious to change (Rogers, 1968). However, in spite of his ability to overcome opposition (perhaps *because* of it), the superintendent leaves himself open to the only possible challenge: the right of the board to fire him. The battle then becomes one in which the use of "the ultimate weapon" is the only possible strategy.

Boards in smaller districts behave quite differently. On the one hand, there is a less direct translation of community tension into opposition to the superintendent. On the other hand, when opposition does develop, it is likely to be nearly unanimous and effective. Usually in the large cities, the board divides more or less evenly into opponents and supporters. In smaller areas, there is usually consensus either for or against the superintendent. Unlike large city boards, small town ones are willing and able to overcome the technical expertise of superintendents. Small town boards, as Vidich and Bensman (1958) note, are likely to conceal conflict if they can, but are also likely to devalue the resources of the superintendent if they elect to respond to high levels of community tension (Alford, 1960). Small towns are, after all, characterized by greater homogeneity of values and political leadership (Bidwell, 1965). In such an atmosphere, the expertise of the superintendent actually may be a hindrance: he appears as the alien expert and may remain unintegrated with the community.

The translation of the mood of the community, then, into the characteristics of the board-superintendent exchange is partially dependent upon the nature of the community. Although tension about schools is generally low, an increase in tension heralds an upheaval in the exchange between board and superintendent (Minar, 1967; Masotti, 1967).

The nature of the issue to be resolved is, as we have argued, a crucial variable. The currency of the expert applies only when the issue is technical; hence superintendents try to define *all* issues as technical. We can contrast the resource-utilization process of boards and superintendents in two areas, one generally regarded as technical (curriculum) and one which, from the point of view of nearly everyone but the superintendent, is not (racial conflict).

Concerning curriculum, the American Association of School Administrators is unequivocal:

> Curriculum planning and development is a highly technical task which requires special training. . . . Board members do not have and cannot be expected to have the technical competence to pass on the work of expert teachers in this field. . . . Nor can the board pass upon specific textbooks (quoted in Eliot, 1959, p. 1037).

Obviously, such claims for a scientific curriculum run into occasional trouble. The perennial battles over sex education and the new math bear witness to the fact that even the most allegedly scientific issue can arouse passions. Further, curriculum decisions are faddish. As Kirst and Walker (1971) note, when immigration was a national issue, "Americanization" was a curriculum goal. Since World War II, when various forms of totalitarian government have challenged American international superiority, "democracy" has been the focus. When Sputnik wounded American pride, math and science became the objects of curriculum reform. Nevertheless, curriculum issues rarely become sufficiently freighted with an emotional content to plunge them into a community-wide conflict.

Although there are no national governmental units establishing curriculum, there is remarkable similarity in the curriculum of public schools, due largely to the influence of accrediting associations. Accrediting agencies, though private, have universal influence with administrators because they can assert the *imprimatur* of professional support for a curriculum, thus helping to neutralize potential board-level opposition. National testing services also constrain local initiative, since schools strive to best the national norm. To do so, schools must emphasize subjects which testing services deem important (Koerner, 1968). University entrance requirements and state departments of education also limit local options (Kirst and Walker, 1971). There is, in brief, a well-integrated curriculum "establishment" beyond the reach of local school officials or publics. With the recent entry of the National Science Foundation, U.S. Office of Education, and Office of Economic Opportunity into the curriculum business, further nationalization is occurring. Finally, of course, the large publishing houses have had a nationalizing effect on the curriculum.

Nationalization of interest-group activity parallels the nationalization of curriculum policy. Local interest groups do not view curriculum as a salient issue (Jennings and Zeigler, 1971). The Council for Basic Education, a group stressing the traditional curriculum, is almost never seen locally. Other organizations—NAACP, AFL-CIO, John Birch Society— are only occasionally concerned. As Kirst and Walker (1971, p. 502) observe: "these not specifically educational interest groups would probably be relatively weak forces in normal policy-making, but extremely powerful in crisis policy-making." The professional strategy is, naturally, to exclude groups rather than compete with them. Further, "lay" knowledge of curriculum is minimal. Numerous polls have revealed that the public knows almost nothing about the substance of education. Discipline bothers the lay community, but curriculum does not. However, although the public is ignorant of the control of education, there is suggestive evidence that they would *like* to know more (Gallup, 1969, p. 2).

The evidence suggests, then, that curriculum experts prevent the development of external, or episodic issues by reducing the flow of information to potentially active publics (Kirst and Walker, 1971). Curriculum issues are clearly a reservoir for episodic issues (Martin, 1962). Children are "sacred objects"; the possibility of conflict is ever present. School boards do not fare any better than individuals or organizations. As we have seen, they have been declared incompetent, and they usually accept this judgment. Election campaigns, as bland as they are, almost never emphasize curriculum and rarely initiate discussions of it during board meetings: ". . . . research has shattered the myth of lay control of schools . . . in the area of curriculum" (Kirst and Walker, 1971, p. 481).

Superintendents and their staffs, then, are (except as they feel intimidated by nonlocal sources) unchallenged in curriculum policy-making. The curriculum-centered bureaucracy is expanding: even small districts are hiring curriculum specialists, and courses in curriculum planning are increasing in colleges of education. Thus, not only boards and interest groups are excluded. In most cases teachers (who are not curriculum specialists) are uninvolved. In more bureaucratically complex school systems, even the superintendent defers to the experts.

Racial conflict is the "external" issue par excellence. One is tempted to describe racial conflicts as episodic, but in this case the episodic has become almost routine. The racial issue in public education has always been a question of how the school system will respond to external demands. The Court system, followed belatedly by Congress and the U.S. Office of Education, has required that schools achieve integration, even if pupils must be bussed from one school to another. The issue is one that superintendents and school board members would not have raised; it is one to which they have no option but to respond. It arouses fierce antagonism, propels interest groups into the educational policy-making process, and provides little opportunity for professional resources to be exchanged. School finance and racial problems stimulate more intense interest group activity than do any other issues (Jennings and Zeigler, 1974). On race, unlike most issues, the federal government is—through the legal system—providing a serious challenge to the insularity of school systems. Superintendents see federal intervention as a seriously disruptive force, even more of a threat than militant civil rights organizations (Zeigler and Boss, 1974).

The response to such pressure is usually avoidance. Both boards and superintendents prefer to believe that they have no problem *until it is brought to their attention by external groups* (Zeigler and Boss, 1974). Not surprisingly, racial conflict is closely linked to the social composition of the district: the more racially heterogeneous the student population, the greater the probability of racial conflict. However, boards respond more quickly to the racial environment than does the superintendent, and they are more likely to be aware of the problem than is the superintendent (Zeigler and Boss, 1974).

Crain's explanation for the superintendent's reluctance to engage the problem is persuasive. Due to a variety of factors linked to recruitment and professional image, superintendents are likely to reject the demands of civil-rights groups without consulting the boards (Crain, 1968). Their reaction to racial strife is to treat it as a "normal" issue. They assert themselves to be "color-blind," stress a narrow definition of the function of schools as "educational" rather than "social," and stress the illegitimacy of the claims of external groups (Crain, 1968). In short, they try to use their traditional resources, defining the issue in such a way that they are likely to maintain their authority by reason of their expertise. When confronted with demands by civil rights organizations, superintendents react defensively and hostilely, not so much because of racial bias, but because they "literally do not speak the same language" (Crain, 1968, p. 123). Thus, what the administration might want to treat as a routine matter balloons into a confrontation when the resources of the superintendent have no value (Zeigler and Boss, 1974). The more hostile superintendents become, the more expansive becomes the conflict.

As the superintendent loses control of the conflict, the school board increases its power and ultimately takes the responsibility for racial policy away from the superintendent. Crain identifies a point when, in most cases, "the major decision which most influences the outcome of the integration issue was made not by the superintendent but by the board" (Crain, 1968, p. 124). Superintendents do not have political resources and are, therefore, unskilled in the use of such resources. Their expertise is not a useful resource for integration policy. Thus race as an issue poses a dilemma for them.

CONCLUSIONS

The decisional culture of the schools is, to generalize, insulated from the political process, routinized, and dominated by the administration. Is such a culture "normal" or "functional" for a society? Viewed as an essentially *conservative* institution (Key, 1963; Lane and Sears, 1964; Zeigler and Peak, 1970), one that stresses consensus values, minimizes tensions, and thus homogenizes the oncoming generation, the educational system has worked rather efficiently. However, there is a reasonably strong probability that the apolitical view of educational policy-making is coming to an end and that the governing pattern—as described here— will be modified. There are several conspicuous symptoms of change: first, there is the gradual reduction of routine at the expense of external issues; demands for increased participation on the part of traditionally disfranchised groups are increasing, and the issues they raise usually are not technical (e.g., student rights). Second, pressures are building from both the national and sublocal levels against the monopolization of influence by the central administration of local school districts (Coleman, 1970; Fantini, Gittell, and Magot, 1970). In some cases, national and sublocal coalitions are forming abetted by such strategems as the Office of Economic Opportunity's support of experimental voucher plans. Third, there appears to be a gradual fragmentation of values in the society (Toffler, 1971), making it increasingly difficult for schools to make authoritative decisions.

If our premise that schools, insulated in most cases from ebb and flow of community conflict, "encapsulate the past" (Lane and Sears, 1964, p. 25), then some conspicuous research need appear. A brief discussion of the past and present will assist us in suggesting paths for future research.

Research on educational politics is relatively new to political science, but has been conducted by professors of educational administration since the turn of the century. The merging of two research disciplines has been slow and painful and has produced—at best—an uneasy alliance.

Early research in educational decision-making was hampered by the traditional separation of education and politics. More often than not, educational administration texts concerned themselves exclusively with proposed methods of implementing the key concepts of the reform movements: centralization, expertise, professionalization, nonpolitical control, and efficiency (Wirt and Kirst, 1972, p. 7).

Commitment to "apolitical" schools guided the selection of research topics. Iannaccone (1967) asserted that the "politics preferred by peda-gogues" and the goals of administrators were mutually reinforcing. Since the manpower flow between schools of educational administration and administrative positions was (and is) considerable, the incentives for research on politics and education were lacking (Kirst and Mosher, 1969, p. 625). At least in terms of research there was (and, to a lesser extent, is) an educational "establishment" which sponsored research *politically* beneficial to administrators, even though the research was "nonpolitical" (Tyler, 1965).

The winds of change were felt in the late 1950s and early 1960s. The factors contributing to the emerging interest in the political aspects of educational systems are impossible to unravel. One can, however, point to certain milestones. David Easton (1957), as a consequence of his interest in political socialization, argued that the educational system can be understood as a subsystem of a general political system. This was hardly a novel or original conclusion, but it did (to the extent that it was noticed by political scientists) awaken researchers to the obvious target of opportunity provided by school systems. Most political scientists, however, followed Easton's theory into empirical studies of the acquisition of political values rather than the governance of schools. Eliot (1959)— while less conceptually precise—articulated the necessity for understanding local school politics.

Political events at this time probably had more to do with the destruction of the boundaries between education and politics than did the pleading of scholars. The Russian launching of Sputnik in 1958 prompted not only widespread public concern, but also the first serious criticism of American education from "outsiders" such as James Conant. Shortly thereafter the federal government unlocked the treasury and, as is usually the case, there was no shortage of proposals of how to study the politics of education.

As one must expect, there was no single theory to guide such efforts. Indeed, as Kerlinger (1965) lamented, most research was descriptive and narrative, rather than explanatory. Gradually, researchers became frustrated at description and began finding areas for some theories or explanations. A broad net was cast, but we can classify the theoretical schemes which emerged in the following manner:

1. Theories based upon an explicit systems model, e.g., theories which consciously borrow from Easton's work;

2. Explanations inspired by systems theory *heuristically* but with little or no explicit reliance upon its propositions, e.g., studies of community-school linkages;

3. Theories derived from sociology rather than political science, e.g., role theory and exchange theory.

The first kind of theoretical argument is best typified by Scribner's essay on school boards (1966) and Wirt and Kirst's (1972) synthesis. Easton (1957, p. 309) suggested that one might examine "the way in which educational institutions organize in groups to bring their interests to bear upon the various governmental structures of which they are a part . . . and . . . the effect . . . that this . . . participation has upon the organization of education. . . ." However, the part of Easton's work that caught the imagination of researchers was his formulation of the idea of input-conversion-output. Scribner relies more upon Almond (1958, 1965) than upon Easton, but his concepts are pure systems theory. Empirically, Scribner simply examined the public records of school board meetings, classifying communications according to whether they were inputs (extractive or symbolic) or outputs (rule-making, rule application).

Significantly, the net result of systems theory—in this case—was categorization rather than explanation.

Wirt and Kirst (1972) took systems theory a bit further as a device for integrating a disparate collection of information, rarely deviating from two essential components: how are values allocated in the educational system and how does the educational system link to the larger political system? As one would expect from previous efforts to use Easton's theoretical outline, virtually everything written on the general topic of education and politics can be located under one or both of these topics. As is the case in political science generally, one can use, or decline to use, systems theory without gaining or losing very much. Stroufe (1969) asserted that educational administration had used systems theory as "window dressing," rather than as a genuine conceptual scheme, largely because systems theory is not a theory in that it offers no propositions to be tested. Other equally familiar criticisms were leveled, e.g., systems theory guides one toward a focus on stability rather than change.

If systems theory led educational researchers into a cul-de-sac, it nevertheless served as a stimulus requiring researchers to attempt to describe (and, occasionally offer explanations for variations in) linkages between the educational and political systems. In addition to the systems emphasis there emerged a focus on the "power" or "power structure" approach. Mills and Hunter, rather than Dahl, provided the inspiration. The reasons for the failure of the pluralist model of community power to engage the attention of educational researchers is possibly explained by the tradition which the writers on power in education were trying to overcome: that of the separation of education and politics. Educational researchers attempted to assert a clear relationship between the distribution of political influence within a political community and the style of educational policy-making.

Initial studies argued that decisions in schools are effectively controlled by a small group of men drawn from the dominant economic institutions of the community. The monolithic elite explanation suffered the same fate in educational research that it did in political science: it was replaced by more varied explanations (e.g., competing elites). However, the emphasis upon linkages remained. The method of research—as is typical of research on education and politics—was largely the case study of a single community, a method that makes it easy to conclude that school government is simply an extension of a more general social and political process (Goldhammer, 1955a, 1955b). Further, when comparative investigation was undertaken, it was usually overstated or a bit overzealous in linking the school and the community. In one study of fifty-one districts, the proposition was made that the distribution of influence in the community (dominated, factional, pluralistic, or inert) is directly reflected in the internal structure of decision-making on the school board (dominated, factional, status congruent, or sanctioning). The linkage was successfully made, but the data were collected in such a manner as to question the possibility of a genuine test. Field teams of graduate students, fully aware of the hypotheses, judged both the power structure and the decision structure in group discussions after two days of interviewing in each community (McCarty and Ramsey, 1971).

Gradually, after the necessity to demonstrate a link was reduced in intensity, evidence supporting the *insulation* of school systems began to accumulate (Bloomberg and Sunshine, 1963, pp. 70–71; Pellegrin, 1968, p. 13; Crain, 1968).

Simultaneously with the rise and fall of a community power structure approach, a radically different methodology was developed—yet one heuristically reliant upon systems theory. Dye (1969), and Sharkansky and Hofferbert (1969)—with appropriate declarations of reliance upon Easton—assembled vast amounts of data about the aggregate character-istics of states and communities, leading to the now familiar conclusion that economic rather than political variables predict educational (and other) expenditures. By minimizing the conversion process, they never-theless (at least tacitly) asserted the belief that the educational system is part of the larger social system. However, James, Kelley, and Gans, (1966) apparently unknown to Dye and other policy-oriented political scientists (and vice-versa), reached exactly the same conclusions without *mentioning* Easton (or Dye, for that matter). Further, the mere fact that those who have money spend it seems beyond dispute and offers little in the way of guides for more explicit propositions.

The final grasping for theories—those derived from sociology—has been equally frustrating. Role theory, which burst upon the scene with Gross, Mason, and McEachern's careful 1958 investigation of motivation and perception of board members, produced little replication and refine-ment but did (along with the appearance of studies of representation by political scientists) inspire a number of inquiries into the "trustee" or "delegate" orientation of board members (Christie, 1966, p. 41; McCarty, 1959; Abbott, 1960). These studies inadvertently linked with exchange theory in that they addressed themselves directly to the question of the permeability of the educational system. Beyond this, however, their util-ity is limited by their failure to link roles and behaviors.

Tracing these strands of research leads us to conclude—as have others —that research on educational decision-making has followed a variety of avenues, most of which have led to dead ends. The body of knowledge is poorly attended by causal theories. Yet before we succeed in explaining what is, we are forced to come to grips with what will be. Just as we have—hopefully—provided some tentative descriptive statements about how decisions are made, we find ourselves in the midst of relentless social change.

Irrespective of the blandishments of theoreticians, schools have been unresponsive and isolated. The rhetoric of change has disguised an unyielding and rigid bureaucracy (Goodlad, 1970). Consequently, the assault on the schools is beginning to worry administrators who (even if they have read the work of researchers) have not prepared themselves for coping with widespread demands for change.

The press for change is in the same direction: a reallocation of power. Demands for "community control" are a moderate form of the response to insulation. Demands for "deschooling society" (such as represented by the voucher plan) are a more intense form of the response.

Educational research needs to shift from efforts at explanation (even though the task is hardly begun) toward efforts at predicting the probable consequences of reallocation of power or decentralization. The literature on community control is promising and should be made more systematic. In the early 1960s, almost desperate efforts toward decentralization and community control were made in an effort to cool off the growing alienation of minority groups, with no articulation of the underlying value conflict between professional expertise and lay control. We know, from the few scattered bits of evidence available, that most efforts in the direction of increased lay control have failed. Is the failure one more bit of supporting evidence for the iron law of oligarchy? How might we offer guidelines for districts which are facing decentralization demands? What are the costs and benefits of alterations in the power balance? Researchers should, then, address themselves to the problems of forming reliable images of what relevant aspects of the future might be; forecasting probable differential effects of action called for by alternative policies; and providing preference evaluations between alternative consequences (Helmer, 1967).

To achieve these goals means supplementing case studies and surveys with the development of techniques—such as Delphi* and simulation— for reliable estimates of probable results of a given course of action.

As a beginning, we can address ourselves to the question of the "goals of education" but in a more systematic way than has been true of past research. For instance, we know that rich school districts spend more for education than poor ones, yet we rarely ask what we get for our money

---

* Delphi is a technique for forcing group consensus about a future state of events from a panel of experts who are unknown to each other.

in rich or poor districts. Silberman (1970) says we get "education for docility," and he is probably right. Yet who has asked whether we *really* want to educate for docility? Where, in other words, is the linkage between the lament of Silberman and the "system maintenance" (or socialization function) of schools? In the perspective of community control, it is quite probable that the increase of, for instance, parental power would increase education for docility.

A particularly valuable target of opportunity is the voucher plan—currently attracting widespread attention because of its appeal to a broad spectrum of intellectuals ranging from Ivan Illitch (1970) through Christopher Jencks (1970) to Milton Friedman (1962). Although details of the various plans differ, all provide for direct payment (voucher) to parents who then have a wide range of alternative ways of spending the money for education (Jencks, 1970); opportunity for the study of public and individual choice will be virtually unlimited as districts (such as San Jose, California) begin experimental vouchers.

The opportunity is for the study of a system in the midst of change. Unfortunately we have little in our past that indicates that we are very good at researching dynamic systems.

BIBLIOGRAPHY

ABBOTT, MAX G. "Values and Value-Perceptions of School Superintendents and Board Members," *Administrator's Notebook,* 9 (1960), pp. 1–4.

AGGER, R. E.; GOLDRICH, D.; and SWANSON, B. E. *The Rulers and the Ruled: Political Power and Impotence in American Communities.* New York: John Wiley, 1964.

ALFORD, R. E. "School District Reorganization and Community Integration," *Harvard Educational Review,* XXX (1960), pp. 350–371.

ALMOND, GABRIEL. "A Developmental Approach to Political Systems," *World Politics,* XVIII (1965), pp. 183–214.

———. "A Comparative Study of Interest Groups and Political Process," *American Political Science Review,* LII (1958), pp. 270–282.

ALMY, TIMOTHY A., and HAHN, HARLAN. "Public Perceptions of Urban Conflict: The Case of Teacher Strikes," *Education and Urban Society,* III (1971), pp. 440–452.

ANDES, JOHN O.; JOHNS, ROE L.; and KIMBROUGH, RALPH B. *Changes in Organizational Structures of Large School Systems With Special Reference to Problems of Teacher Militancy and Organizational Conflict.* Gainesville, Fla.: University of Florida, 1971 (Litho.).

AREEN, JUDITH, and JENCKS, CHRISTOPHER. "Education Vouchers: A Proposal for Diversity and Choice," *Teachers College Record,* 72, 3 (1971).

ASHBY, LLOYD W. *The Effective School Board Member.* Danville, Ill.: The Interstate Printers & Publishers, 1968.

BIDWELL, CHARLES E. "The School as a Formal Organization," in *Handbook of Organizations,* March, James G., ed. Chicago: Rand McNally, 1965.

BLAU, PETER M. *Exchange and Power in Social Life.* New York: John Wiley, 1964.

BLOOMBERG, W., JR., and SUNSHINE, NORRIS S. *Suburban Power Structures and Public Education.* Syracuse, N.Y.: Syracuse University Press, 1963.

BOWMAN, T. R. "Participation of Superintendents in School Board Decision-Making," *Administrator's Notebook,* XI (1963), pp. 1–4.

BROWDER, LESLIE A. "A Suburban School Superintendent Plays Politics," in Kirst, Michael W., ed., *The Politics of Education at the Local, State, and Federal Levels.* Berkeley, Calif.: McCutchan, 1970, pp. 191–194.

BROWN, JULIUS S. "Risk Propensity in Decision Making: A Comparison of Business and Public School Administrators," *Administrative Science Quarterly,* XV (1970), pp. 473–481.

CALLAHAN, RAYMOND E., and BUTTON, H. WARREN. "Historical Change of the Role of the Man in the Organization: 1865–1950," in Griffiths, Daniel E., *Behavioral Science and Educational Administration Yearbook, Part II.* Chicago: University of Chicago Press, 1964.

————. *The Superintendent of Schools; An Historical Analysis.* St. Louis, Mo.: Washington University Press, 1966.

CAMPBELL, ALAN K. "Who Governs the Schools?" *Saturday Review*, 64 (1968), pp. 50–52.

CARLSON, RICHARD O. *School Superintendents: Careers and Performance.* Columbus, Ohio: Chas. E. Merrill, 1972.

CARTWRIGHT, DORWIN. "Influence, Leadership, Control," in *Handbook of Organizations*, March, James C., ed. Chicago: Rand McNally, 1965, pp. 1–47.

CHARTERS, W. W., JR. "Social Class Analysis and the Control of Public Education," *Harvard Educational Review*, 23 (1953), pp. 268–283.

————. *A Bibliography of Empirical Studies of School Boards, 1900–1951, 1952–1968.* Eugene, Oregon: Center for the Advanced Study of Educational Administration, 1968.

————. *School Board Research Revisited.* Eugene, Oregon: Center for the Advanced Study of Educational Administration, forthcoming.

CHRISTIE, S. G. "Political Pressure on the School Board Member." San Diego, Calif.: Unpublished Master's dissertation, San Diego State College, 1966.

CLARK, BURTON R. "Sociology of Education," in Faris, Robert E. L., ed., *Handbook of Modern Sociology.* Chicago: Rand McNally, 1964, pp. 734–769.

COLEMAN, JAMES S. "The Struggle for Control of Education," in Bowers, C. A.; Housego, Ian; and Dyke, Doris, eds., *Education and Social Policy: Local Control of Education.* New York: Random House, 1970.

CORWIN, RONALD G. *Staff Conflicts in the Public Schools.* Columbus, Ohio: Department of Sociology and Anthropology, Ohio State University, 1966.

COUNTS, GEORGE P. *The Social Composition of Boards of Education.* Chicago: University of Chicago Press, 1927.

CRAIN, ROBERT L. *The Politics of School Desegregation.* Chicago: Aldine, 1968.

CRONIN, J. M. "The Superintendent Selection Patterns of Large City School Boards." Mimeo, n.d.

CUNNINGHAM, LUVERN L. "Community Power: Implications for Education," in Cahill, Robert S., and Hencley, Stephen P., eds., *The Politics of Education in the Local Community.* Danville, Ill.: The Interstate Printers & Publishers, 1964.

DAHL, ROBERT A. *Who Governs?* New Haven, Conn. & London: Yale University Press, 1961.

DOHERTY, ROBERT E., and OBERER, WALTER E. *Teachers, School Boards, and Collective Bargaining: A Changing of the Guard.* Ithaca, N.Y.: New York State School of Industrial & Labor Relations of SUNY, 1967.

DOWNS, ANTHONY. *Inside Bureaucracy.* A RAND Corporation Study. Boston: Little, Brown, 1967.

DYE, THOMAS R. "Government Structure, Urban Environment, and Educational Policy," *Midwest Journal of Political Science*, II (1969), pp. 265–288.

DYKES, ARCHIE R. *School Board and Superintendent: Their Effective Working Relationships.* Danville, Ill.: Interstate Printers & Publishers, 1965.

EASTON, DAVID. "An Approach to the Analysis of Political Systems," *World Politics*, 9 (1957), pp. 383–400.

ELIOT, THOMAS H. "Toward an Understanding of Public School Politics," *American Political Science Review*, LII (1959), pp. 1037–1051.

FANTINI, MARIO D.; GITTELL, MARILYN; and MAGOT, RICHARD. *Community Control and the Urban School.* New York: Praeger, 1970.

FRIEDMAN, MILTON. *Capitalism and Culture.* Chicago: University of Chicago Press, 1962.

GALLUP, GEORGE. *How The Nation Views The Public Schools.* Princeton, N.J.: Gallup International, 1969, p. 2.

GAMSON, WILLIAM A. *Power and Discontent.* Homewood, Ill.: The Dorsey Press, 1968.

GITTELL, MARILYN. *Educating an Urban Population.* Beverly Hills, Calif.: Sage Press, 1967.

————, and HOLLANDER, T. EDWARD. *Six Urban School Districts.* New York: Praeger, 1968.

GOLDHAMMER, KEITH. "Community Power Structure and School Board Membership," *American School Board Journal*, 130 (1955a), pp. 23–25.

————. "How Do School Boards Determine Policy?" *School Executive*, 74 (1955b), pp. 84–85.

————. *The School Board.* New York: The Center for Applied Research in Education, 1964.

————, and FARNER, FRANK. *The Jackson County Story.* Eugene, Oregon: The University of Oregon, Center for the Advanced Study of Educational Administration, 1964.

————; SUTTLE, JOHN E.; ALDRIDGE, WILLIAM D.; and BECKER, GERALD. *Issues and Problems in Contemporary Educational Administration.* Eugene, Oregon: Center for the Advanced Study of Educational Administration, 1967.

GOODLAD, JOHN I., and KLEIN, M. FRANCES. *Behind the Classroom Door.* Belmont, Calif.: Wadsworth, 1970.

GRIEDER, CALVIN; PIERCE, TRUMAN; and ROSENSTENGEL, WILLIAM EVERETT. *Public School Administration*, 2nd edition. New York: Ronald Press, 1961.

GRIFFITHS, DANIEL E. *Human Relations in School Administration.* New York: Appleton-Century-Crofts, 1956.

GROSS, NEAL. *Who Runs Our Schools?* New York: John Wiley & Sons, 1958.

————; MASON, WARD H.; and McEACHERN, ALEXANDER W. *Explorations in Role Analysis: Studies of the School Superintendency Role.* New York: John Wiley & Sons, 1958.

HELMER, OLAF. "The Delphi Technique and Educational Innovation," in Hirsch, Werner Z. et al., eds., *Inventing Education for the Future.* San Francisco: Chandler Publishing, 1967.

HESS, ROBERT D., and KIRST, MICHAEL. "Political Orientation and Behavior Patterns: Linkages Between Teachers and Children," *Education and Urban Society*, III (1971), pp. 453–477.

HINES, C. "A Study of School Board Administrative Relationships: The Development of the Eugene, Oregon Superintendency, 1891–1944." *American School Board Journal*, 1951, pp. 122(2), 19–21; pp. 122(3), 28–29; pp. 122(4), 17–19.

HOFSTADTER, RICHARD. *The Age of Reform; From Bryan to F.D.R.* New York: Knopf, 1955.

HOMANS, GEORGE C. *Social Behavior: Its Elementary Forms.* New York: Harcourt, Brace & World, 1961.

IANNACCONE, LAURENCE. *Politics in Education.* New York: The Center for Applied Research in Education, 1967.

————. "School Board Conflict is Inevitable," *American School Board Journal,* 154 (1967), pp. 5–9.

ILLITCH, IVAN. *Deschooling Society.* New York: Harper & Row, 1970.

JAMES, H. HENRY. "School Board Conflict is Inevitable," *American School Board Journal,* 154 (1967), pp. 5–9.

JAMES, H. THOMAS; KELLEY, JAMES; and GANS, WALTER. *Determinants of Educational Expenditures in Large Cities.* Stanford, Calif.: Stanford University School of Education, 1966, pp. 55–80.

JENCKS, CHRISTOPHER. *Education Vouches.* Cambridge: Center for the Study of Public Policy, 1970.

JENNINGS, KENT M., and ZEIGLER, HARMON. "The Politics of Teacher-Administrator Relations," *Education and Social Science,* Vol. 1. Great Britain: Pergamon Press, 1969a, pp. 73–82.

————, and ZEIGLER, HARMON. *The Governing of School Districts.* Ann Arbor, Mich.: Institute for Social Research, University of Michigan Press, 1969b, p. 4.

————, and ZEIGLER, HARMON. "Political Expressivism Among High School Teachers," in Sigel, Roberta S., ed., *Learning About Politics.* New York: Random House, 1970, pp. 434–453.

————, and ZEIGLER, HARMON. "Response Styles and Politics: The Case of the School Boards," *Midwest Journal of Political Science,* XV (1971), pp. 290–321.

————, and ZEIGLER, HARMON. "Avenues to the School Board and Political Competition," paper read at the American Educational Research Association, Chicago, Ill., 1972b.

————, and ZEIGLER, HARMON. "Interest Representation in School Governance," in Hahn, Harlan, ed., *People and Politics in Urban Society.* Beverly Hills, Calif.: Sage Publications, 1972a, chap. 8.

KERLINGER, FRED N. "The Mythology of Educational Research," *School and Society,* 93 (1965), pp. 222–225.

KERR, NORMAN D. "The School Board as an Agency of Legitimation," *Sociology of Education,* 38 (1964), pp. 45–55.

KEY, V. O., JR. *Public Opinion and American Democracy.* New York: Alfred A. Knopf, 1963.

KIMBROUGH, RALPH B. *Political Power and Educational Decision-Making.* Chicago: Rand-McNally, 1964.

KIRST, MICHAEL W., and MOSHER, EDITH K. "Politics of Education," *Review of Educational Research,* 39 (1969), pp. 623–640.

————, and WALKER, DECKER F. "An Analysis of Curriculum Policy-Making," *Review of Educational Research,* 41 (1971), pp. 479–509.

KOERNER, JAMES D. *Who Controls American Education? A Guide for Laymen.* Boston: Beacon, 1968.

LANE, ROBERT E., and SEARS, DAVID O. *Public Opinion.* Englewood Cliffs, N.J.: Prentice-Hall, 1964.

LAZARSFELD, PAUL F., and THIELENS, WAGNER, JR. *The Academic Mind; Social Scientists in a Time of Crisis.* Glencoe, Ill.: Free Press, 1958.

LIEBERMAN, MYRON, and MOSKOW, MICHAEL H. *Collective Negotiations for Teachers: An Approach to School Administration.* Chicago: Rand-McNally, 1966.

LIPHAM, JAMES M.; GREGG, RUSSELL T.; and ROSSMILLER, RICHARD A. "The School Board as an Agency for Resolving Conflict." Bethesda, Md.: Educational Resources Information Center, 1967.

———. "The School Board: Resolver of Conflict?" *Administrator's Notebook,* XVII (1969).

LIPSKY, MICHAEL. "Protest as a Political Resource," in Zisk, Betty H., ed., *American Political Interest Groups: Readings in Theory and Research.* Belmont, Calif.: Wadsworth, 1968.

LUTTBEG, NORMAN, and ZEIGLER, HARMON. "Attitude Consensus and Conflict in an Interest Group: An Assessment of Cohesion," *American Political Science Review,* LVIII (1966).

MARTIN, ROSCOE C. *Government and the Suburban School.* Syracuse, N.Y.: Syracuse University Press, 1962.

MASOTTI, LOUIS H. *Education and Politics in Suburbia: The New Trier Experience.* Cleveland, Ohio: Western Reserve University Press, 1967.

———. "Political Integration in Suburban Education Communities," in Scott Greer, et al., eds. *The New Urbanization.* New York: St. Martin's Press, 1968.

McCARTY, DONALD J. "School Board Membership: Why Do Citizens Serve?" *Administrator's Notebook,* 8 (1959), pp. 1–4.

———, and RAMSEY, CHARLES E. *The School Managers.* Westport, Conn.: Greenwood, 1971.

MINAR, DAVID W. "Community Characteristics, Conflict, and Power Structures," *The Politics of Education in the Local Community,* Cahill, Robert S., and Hencley, Stephen P., eds. Danville, Ill.: The Interstate Printers and Publishers, 1964, pp. 132–133.

———. *Educational Decision-Making in Suburban Communities.* U. S. Department of Health, Education and Welfare, Office of Education, Cooperative Research Project #2440. Evanston, Ill.: Northwestern University Press, 1966a.

———. "The Community Basis of Conflict in School System Politics," *American Sociological Review,* 31 (1966b), pp. 822–835.

———. "Community Politics and The School Board," *American School Board Journal* (1967), pp. 33–38.

NATIONAL EDUCATION ASSOCIATION. "Teacher Strikes and Work Stoppages," *Research Memo,* (1968), p. 1.

PEAK, G. WAYNE. "Policy Leadership in the Governance of Public School Systems." Eugene, Ore.: unpublished doctoral dissertation, Department of Political Science, University of Oregon, 1971.

PELLEGRIN, ROLAND J. "An Analysis of Sources and Processes of Innovation in

Education." Eugene, Oregon: Center for the Advanced Study of Educational Administration, University of Oregon, 1968.

ROGERS, DAVID. *110 Livingston Street; Politics and Bureaucracy in the New York City Schools.* New York: Random House, 1968.

ROSENTHAL, ALAN. *Pedagogues and Power.* Syracuse, N.Y.: Syracuse University Press, 1969.

SALISBURY, ROBERT H. "Schools and Politics in the Big Cities," *Harvard Educational Review*, XXXVII (1967), pp. 408–424.

————. "An Exchange Theory of Interest Groups," in Salisbury, Robert H., ed., *Interest Group Politics in America.* New York: Harper & Row, 1970.

SCRIBNER, J. D. "A Functional-Systems Framework for Analyzing School Board Action," *Educational Administration Quarterly*, 2 (1966), pp. 204–215.

SHARKANSKY, IRA, and HOFFERBERT, RICHARD I. "Dimensions of State Politics, Economics and Public Policy," *American Political Science Review*, 63 (1969), pp. 867–879.

SILBERMAN, CHARLES E. *Crisis in the Classroom.* New York: Random House, 1970.

SMOLEY, EUGENE R., JR. *Community Participation in Urban School Government.* Washington, D.C.: U. S. Office of Education, Cooperative Research Project #S-029, 1965.

SNOW, REUBEN JOSEPH. "Local Experts: Their Roles as Conflict Managers in Municipal and Educational Government." Evanston, Ill.: doctoral dissertation, Northwestern University Press, 1966.

STELZER, LEIGH. "The Receptivity of School Board Members: A Study of Reform and Representation," unpublished doctoral dissertation, University of Michigan, 1971, chap. 2.

STROUFE, GERALD. *Political Systems Analysis in Educational Administration: Can the Emperor be Clothed?* Paper presented at the American Educational Research Association, Los Angeles, Calif., February 1969.

SUMMERFIELD, HARRY L. "Cuing and the Open System of Educational Politics," *Education and Urban Society*, III (1971), pp. 425–439.

TOFFLER, ALVIN. *Future Shock.* New York: Bantam, 1971.

TYLER, RALPH W. "The Field of Educational Research," in *The Training and Nurture of Educational Researchers*, Guba, Egon C., and Elam, Stanley, eds., Bloomington, Ind.: Phi Delta Kappa, 1965, chap. 1.

UNITED STATES BUREAU OF THE CENSUS, Vol. 1, 1967, pp. 1–8; Vol. 6, 1968, p. 3.

VIDICH, ARTHUR J., and BENSMAN, JOSEPH. *Small Town in Mass Society.* Garden City, N.Y.: Doubleday-Anchor, 1960.

WALDEN, JOHN C. "School Board Cleavage and Superintendent Turnover," *Administrator's Notebook*, 1967.

WALDMAN, SIDNEY R. *Foundation of Political Action: An Exchange Theory of Politics.* Boston: Little Brown, 1972.

WALKER, WILLIAM G. *Centralization and Decentralization: An International Viewpoint on an American Dilemma.* Eugene, Oregon: Center for the Advanced Study of Educational Administration, University of Oregon, 1972.

WILSON, JAMES Q. "The Strategy of Protest: Problems of Negro Civic Action," *Journal of Conflict Resolution*, 3 (1961), pp. 291–303.

WIRT, FREDERICK M., and KIRST, MICHAEL W. *The Political Web of American Schools*. Boston: Little, Brown, 1972.

ZALD, MEYER. "The Power and Functions of Boards of Directors: A Theorectical Synthesis," *American Journal of Sociology*, 75 (1969), pp. 97–111.

ZEIGLER, HARMON. *The Political Life of American Teachers*. Englewood Cliffs, N.J.: Prentice-Hall, 1967.

———. "Teacher Militancy: An Analysis of the Strike-Prone Teacher," in Bruno, James E., ed., *Emerging Issues in Education*. Lexington, Mass.: D. C. Heath, 1972, pp. 103–122.

———, and BAER, MICHAEL. *Lobbying: Interaction and Influence in American State Legislatures*. Belmont, Calif.: Wadsworth, 1969.

———, and BOSS, MICHAEL O. "Racial Problems and Policy-Making in the American Public Schools," Sociology of Education, 1974.

———, and DYE, THOMAS R. *The Irony of Democracy*. Belmont, Calif.: Wadsworth, 1970, 2nd edition, 1972.

———, and JENNINGS, KENT with PEAK, G. WAYNE. *Governing American Schools*. North Scituate, Mass.: Duxbury, 1974.

———, and PEAK, G. WAYNE. "The Political Functions of the Educational System." Sociology of Education, 1970.

The Presidency, Congress, And National Policy-Making

JOHN F. MANLEY*

In the late 1960s, a variety of pressures increased the traditional concern of political scientists with the analysis of public policy. Who gets (or fails to get) what, when, and how had been a popular definition of politics for many years. But in the 1950s and later, the dominant concerns of many political scientists seemed only remotely related to public policy. Some of the best behavioral research was done on voting behavior and public opinion, but, as V. O. Key argued (1961), the linkages between those who "count" politically and the counted had not been well forged; nor were the policy consequences of their interaction extensively researched.

As a partial reaction to the remoteness of some behavioral research to important policy questions, and as a partial response to cries for a more "relevant" political science, any number of authors in the past ten years have discovered policy-relevant aspects of their work. "Policy analysis" became a code word for relevant research as a segment of the discipline tried, in part, to meet the fuzzy challenges of the "post-behavioral movement." However unclear the dialectical process leading to changes in

* The literature on the Presidency, Congress, and national policy-making is too large to cover completely even in an extended review essay, and no pretense is made here to such coverage. Rather, the writings that are cited have been selected because, in the author's judgment, they represent the major work that is relevant to the policy-making themes developed in the essay. Fortunately, most of the major literature on the Presidency can be included in a relatively short essay, and the vast literature on Congress has been comprehensively reviewed by others. See for example, Robert L. Peabody, "Research on Congress: A Coming of Age," in Ralph K. Huitt and Robert L. Peabody, eds., *Congress: Two Decades of Analysis*. New York: Harper & Row, 1969, pp. 3–72.

A second major caveat on this essay is that little or no attention is paid to the inter-relationships between the political and economic systems, nor to the constraints imposed on national policy-making by the American belief system.

I am indebted to Heinz Eulau and Bruce Oppenheimer for their comments on this article.

political science, and however unclear the meaning of policy analysis, there was no doubt that the discipline of political science was undergoing great stress. This became manifest in 1969 when David Easton, as president of the American Political Science Association, urged his colleagues to "re-examine fearlessly the premises of our research and the purposes of our calling" (Easton, 1969, p. 1061).

One consequence of the internal turmoil may be to direct the attention of better trained, empirically oriented scholars to a new formulation of research questions, questions that bear explicitly on the outputs and outcomes of political decisions. On this assumption—or hope—it might be useful to assess some of the literature in the amorphous area of elite analysis to see where we stand in our understanding of elite policy-making, and where we might direct our attention in the future. Toward this objective, we will assess the literature on two institutions, the Presidency and Congress, which are, theoretically, at the apex of the elite policy-making structure of this country. The purpose of the exercise is to evaluate the state of knowledge about these policy-making institutions, and to suggest some ways in which future studies might enhance our knowledge of policy-making at the national level.

STUDIES OF THE PRESIDENCY

The outstanding characteristic of the general literature on the Presidency is that, with one or two notable exceptions, it reflects the worst of all possible worlds: it is neither empirically rich nor revealing about how the Presidency affects who gets what, when, and how in the United States.

One of the major concerns of writers on the Presidency is the relative power position of the President vis-à-vis other national policy-makers, most notably Congress. Harold Laski (1940), Pendleton Herring (1940), and Clinton Rossiter (1960), men who produced three general treatises on presidential power prior to Richard Neustadt's 1960 landmark study, all try to cope with presidential power at this level. The empirical foundation is so limited, however, that the result is a series of conflicting interpretations of presidential power with little or no basis for evaluating the conflicting schools of thought. One is left struggling with generalizations about the "decline of Congress" or the "aggrandizement of the Presidency," generalizations that are matched in their intrinsic interest only by the difficulty of demonstrating them one way or the other.

Laski's 1940 essay on the Presidency is traditional political science at its best, but its orientation is normative, not empirical. Like other British observers, Laski stresses the limitations on presidential power, and by and large deplores them. For Laski, the strength of private economic interests, the traditional American bias against strong governmental regulation of the private sector, the fear of concentrating too much power in one place, and the lack of strong party ties all shackle the President and make for incoherence, lack of responsibility, and avoidance of important issues. The President, he argues, is usually less than he might be because Congress is diminished if the executive assumes command, and Congress is less than it might be because it is organized to prevent the acceptance of "clear sailing directions" (Laski, 1940, p. 159). In this view the President is so weak that the American Legion is alleged to have had more success with Congress since World War I than the President. Only if the President is a supremely great man, like Lincoln, or operates in the midst of great disaster, like Wilson or FDR, is public opinion sufficiently aroused to suspend the normal assumptions of the American system. Realignment of the parties along basic social and economic cleavages, Laski continues, is both necessary and imminent; as this change occurs, the balance of power between the President and Congress will shift in favor of the former.

Laski's blending of description and prescription is quite in keeping with traditional writings on American government. Some writers, like Woodrow Wilson (1885), examine the workings of Congress and the Presidency and deplore the imbalance in favor of the legislature, while others (Black, 1919) see the growth of presidential power as destructive of liberty. Still others, like Herring (1940) and Rossiter (1960), warn against drastic alterations in the existing system.

Writing at the same time as Laski, Pendleton Herring, in his characteristic way, avoided romantic idealizations of the presidential office and focused more on analyzing the way in which the government functions instead of propounding a substitute for it. His account is remarkably similar to Laski's. The United States government operates within a continental framework that makes control over diverse interests difficult. Sectional interests are so strong in times of peace that the "administration often does little more than keep order in the bread line that reaches into the Treasury" (Herring, 1940, p. 22). The President has no instrument capable of reaching down into local constituencies and controlling local party organizations. Hence his power in Congress is weak. Yet, for all this, Herring pronounces the system fundamentally sound.

Grand syntheses of the kind attempted by Laski and, to a lesser degree by Herring, have an ethereal quality to them partly because they were attempted before the necessary detailed empirical work on the Presidency was done. Hyman's study (1954) shows the same tendency, although he generally shies away from developing any general themes about the Presidency. Before Neustadt, general interpretations of the Presidency rarely got more analytically specific than a rudimentary categorization of the presidential job in terms of diverse roles. Milton (1944) detected a number of roles played by different Presidents (People's Leader, Commander-in-Chief, Trustee of All the People, Spokesman of the People, World Strategist, Chief of State, Chief of Government, Chief of Foreign Relations, Chief of Party, Chief Morale Officer), and Rossiter later compiled a very similar list (Chief Diplomat, Chief Legislator, Voice of the People, Manager of Prosperity, Protector of the Peace, Chief of State, Chief Executive, Commander-in-Chief, Chief of Party). Milton's study has the virtue of recognizing that certain roles are emphasized by certain Presidents and other roles not at all, but his and Rossiter's major contribution lies in directing the attention of scholars to the necessity of splitting the Presidency into more manageable analytical units before making generalizations about the office. The cliché about the Presidency being what a particular occupant decides to make of it contains enough of the truth to warn against easy generalizations. Indeed, the ways of being President have varied so much that highly qualified and strictly limited generalizations may be the ultimate statements that one can make about the office.

Rossiter and Milton, although they have a somewhat clearer analytical focus than other students of the Presidency, both struggle with the grand problem of presidential power. They reach the same conclusion: presidential power has ebbed and flowed, but in general the impressive fact is its expansion. "The outstanding feature of American constitutional development," according to Rossiter, "has been the growth of the power and prestige of the Presidency" (Rossiter, 1960, p. 83). Yet, at the same time, he asserts that the Presidency is by no means *too* powerful. The President is, rather, a "kind of magnificent lion who can roam widely and do great deeds so long as he does not try to break loose from his broad reservation" (p. 73). And what are the boundaries of presidential power? Rossiter, in one of his most perceptive passages, answers that they are set not by one or two limiting forces but by a number of restraints, all of which constitute an interlocking *system* of control: Congress, Court, administration, parties, states, economy, and the people (p. 72). Against this array of restraints the President can roam far and wide but never go on a rampage that destroys the check-and-balance system so skillfully engineered by the makers of the Constitution. It is true, nonetheless, says Rossiter, that the Presidency has outstripped Congress (and the Court) in the race for power and prestige.

The presidential literature is rich in the area of executive-legislative relations (MacLean, 1955; Dexter, 1967; Holtzman, 1970; Koenig, 1965; Egger and Harris, 1963; Polsby, 1971; Binkley, 1962; de Grazia, 1965). There is no universal consensus on the balance of power between the two institutions; nor, given the nature of the question, is this surprising. Walter Lippmann (1956) sees grave danger in the enfeeblement of the executive, and Binkley sounds the same theme (Binkley, 1955). De Grazia (1965) argues the counter case. Virtually every author concedes great autonomy and power to Congress, particularly as measured against other national legislatures, but few authors specify the sources of conflict and cooperation better than Polsby (1971). Different time perspectives arising from the fixed term of the President and the open-ended nature of the congressional career, the necessity for Presidents to woo their opponents on some issues while trying to retain the loyalty of their friends, and the value to congressmen of postponing clear-cut commitments all make for tension between the branches. On the other hand, the limited ideological character of American political parties, the "honeymoon" period following the election of a President, the special character of foreign policy, and the impulse toward cooperation under crisis conditions make for harmony.

All of the studies mentioned above make important contributions to our understanding of national politics, and one need not disparage any of them in noting that we are still far away from a set of generalizations that explain how policy is originated and determined at the national level. To make some progress along these lines would seem to require at least four things: (1) an appreciation for the fact that institutional roles and functions are likely to vary across different issue areas as well as over time; (2) the specification of the variables and conditions that affect the performance of Congress and the Presidency; (3) the creation of some analytic categories or concepts that will permit one to make comparative statements about a large number of individual policy cases; and (4) an extensive examination of a number of different policy decisions (including decisions *not* to take action) in order to determine the patterns (if any) of executive-legislative interactions. Despite the "tallness" of such an order, some progress has been made and, if current trends are any guide to the future, greater advancements should be forthcoming.

In this connection, the most systematic and policy-relevant work yet done on executive-legislative relations is Lawrence Chamberlain's masterful 1946 study. Through detailed case studies of ninety pieces of major legislation in the 1880–1940 period, he assembled the best body of evidence to date on the policy-making role of Congress and the Presidency in a number of issue areas: business legislation, the tariff, labor legislation, national defense, agriculture, credit legislation, banking and currency, immigration, conservation, and railroad legislation. With these data he is able to make generalizations about the influence of Congress and the Presidency—plus interest groups—on the content of the legislation, and the results tend *not* to support the conventional wisdom about the paramountcy of the President in the legislative process. Forty percent of the laws were chiefly the product of Congress, 30 percent fall into a joint presidential-congressional category, just under 10 percent were primarily shaped by interest groups, and only about 20 percent can be credited to the President. Moreover, he argues, in many cases of presidential preponderance the issues and proposals were first raised in Congress, and the legislature may therefore be in on the initiation of policy even though subsequent presidential support is essential to enactment.

Chamberlain also sheds light on two additional questions: changes over time in the role of Congress and the Presidency, and variations across subject matter. Looking at the 1932–1940 period, for example, he detects some increase in presidential influence compared with earlier years, but even here the role of Congress is substantial. When one looks at policy arenas, the President is dominant in national defense and business regulation. Congress dominates most of the other categories, and interest groups dominate one area, the tariff. The President and Congress or, more exactly, administrative agencies and Congress, dominate natural resources legislation.

Chamberlain's findings are less important in the context of this essay than his method. That there are several problems with his approach goes without saying. Interestingly enough, he is aware of most of the difficulties: assigning predominant influence (or even defining the term "influence") is a risky business when one is dealing with interrelated and complex processes; subjective judgment plays a major part in the analysis; not all major fields are covered (social, relief, tax, and government reorganization legislation are among the fields omitted); and the springs of legislation run deep. Yet, despite all the difficulties, a large-scale assault along lines suggested by Chamberlain might yield data that will fill in many of the gaps between the real world of national policy-making and the rarefied generalizations that constitute conventional wisdom. On this score, too, Chamberlain offers sound advice: given the tendency of the press to magnify every action of the President, appearances are often misleading.

Chamberlain's research lead has not been widely followed, but the independent role of Congress in certain policy-making areas has cast doubt on the accuracy of the "decline of Congress" theme (Manley, 1970). Moe and Teel's (1970) replication of Chamberlain's study in twelve policy areas for 1940–1967 concludes that Chamberlain's generalizations about the important policy-making role played by Congress are basically correct for this period as well as for 1880–1940. Amlund (1965) reaches similar conclusions, although the evidence he presents is not extensive.

To make sense out of policy-making roles one must, of course, distinguish between domestic policy and foreign and defense policy. Most writers would agree that Congress has slipped less in the domestic realm. Dahl, writing in 1950, finds that Congress rarely provides the initiative in foreign policy, and Robinson (1967), on the basis of twenty-two major decisions since the 1930s, assigns predominant influence to Congress in only six. Wildavsky (1969a) goes so far as to contend that the Presidency is so much stronger in defense and foreign policy that there are, in effect, "two presidencies," one for domestic and one for international affairs. The role of Congress in defense policy-making varies (Kolodziej, 1966), but Wildavsky's argument captures the essential drift of most of the research in this area.

Congress is sometimes charged with giving too much attention to parochial issues in defense and too little attention to major policy issues. Samuel P. Huntington's research, however, refutes this claim. "The separation of powers demands that Congress become involved in administrative detail in the budget process as in other areas. In practice, moreover, Congress also gives considered and effective attention to the major issues of military policy involved in the budget" (Huntington, 1959, pp. 408–409). Huntington also notes several cases since World War II in which Congress and the President disagreed and the legislature took an independent course. Generally, however, the two branches of government agree on defense policy and the cases of conflict are few.

In the *Common Defense* (1961), however, Huntington distinguishes between "structural issues" (e.g., military organization, pay, and training) and "strategic programs" (e.g., size and composition of the armed forces). He concludes that in the 1945–1960 period Congress played an important role in structural decisions but lost power to the Presidency (or, more precisely, to the executive branch) in strategic matters. Huntington seems to have exercised his right to change his mind; in any case, his later emphasis on declining congressional influence finds wide support in the literature.

It is important to note here that a revisionist argument is emerging in the area of foreign and defense policy-making. Congress has been shown to have important influence on such policies as the Development Loan Fund and the International Development Association, even though congresssional initiative is doubtful (Baldwin, 1966). Moreover, when the Department of Defense budget is broken down into its component parts, it appears that, although Congress makes minor changes in the areas of personnel and organization and management, it has a significant programmatic effect on procurement, research, development, testing, and evaluation (Kanter, 1972). As the Vietnam War grew increasingly unpopular, doubts were raised about congresssional passivity in international affairs, and Congress, or at least the Senate, began reclaiming some of its suspended prerogatives (Manley, 1971). In April 1972, the Senate, by a vote of 68–16, passed the so-called war powers bills intended to correct the deficiencies in the policy-making process made manifest by the Vietnam War and to assure congressional involvement in the early stages of future international armed conflicts. These developments cast some doubt on the accuracy of established generalizations about defense and foreign policy-making and raise new questions for future research in this area. Carl Vinson's boast when he was chairman of the House Armed Services Committee that he preferred to run the Pentagon from his position on Capitol Hill rather than as Secretary of Defense might have been an extreme claim, but so, too, might some of the claims about congressional impotence in this field. (For some leading studies of these issues see Dawson, 1962; Dexter, 1969a; Carroll, 1966; Stephens, 1971; Smith and Cotter, 1960.)

DECISION-MAKING IN THE INSTITUTIONALIZED PRESIDENCY

Midway through his book on the American Presidency, Clinton Rossiter quotes a famous statement by Harry S. Truman that the essence of presidential power is the power to persuade. Rossiter comments that an "entirely new theory of the Presidency can be spun out of that folksy statement" (1960, p. 154). Richard Neustadt (1960) acted on the same thought and wrote a classic study of presidential power as persuasion.

Other writers before Neustadt wrote perceptively about the Presidency—particularly Schlesinger (1957, 1959, 1960)—but it was left to Neustadt to develop a theory about presidential power. Some critical work has been done on Neustadt's theory (Sperlich, 1969; Polsby, 1971) but, as Polsby notes, the most ambitious analytical study of the Presidency has curiously not stimulated a critical dialogue.

Neustadt, as we saw above, is not unique in his stress on the limited power of the Presidency. But his work is unique in the way in which it conceptualizes and explains presidential power. As seen from the White House, presidential power is the power to persuade other important policy-makers that their self-interest requires them to act in accord with the President's wishes. The President persuades others through bargaining; only under rare circumstances can he issue self-executing commands. What determines the effectiveness of the President as a bargainer? Neustadt cites three major factors: (1) the bargaining advantages that are inherent in the office (formal powers, authority, status—"vantage points"); (2) professional reputation, i.e., the judgments by others regarding the President's ability and will to use his advantages; and (3) public prestige, i.e., the anticipation by Washingtonians of how outsiders will react to their reactions to presidential initiatives. Of the three, popular prestige acts more as condition than direct cause of presidential power. Of the presidential analysts surveyed, Neustadt places public opinion lowest in the hierarchy of factors affecting presidential power.

Neustadt's perspective on the Presidency, his effort to isolate the factors that account for presidential power, and his case studies of presidential decisions make his book the most theoretically interesting study of the Presidency ever done. Yet in a sense *Presidential Power* has been treated by scholars as an overly definitive statement of the nature and limitations of the Chief Executive's power. No systematic research of the quality of Neustadt's account has been conducted on the range of variables that condition or determine the *variable* nature of presidential power. It appears as if scholars have been content to point to Neustadt's account as not only the best but the last word on the subject. Yet, as everyone knows, some Presidents exercize much more power than others. They may all face similar challenges to their leadership, and the components of presidential power examined by Neustadt may be the most significant ones to consider, but presidential power varies enormously from one incumbent to another. Hence it would seem mandatory that some attention be paid to the factors that explain variability and change in presidential power if a fully developed theory of presidential power is to be attained. Neustadt's theory should, in short, be treated as problematical rather than gospel if studies of the Presidency are to be advanced beyond 1960.

This essay is not the place to test Neustadt's theory, but it is appropriate to ask some preliminary questions about its general adequacy as a guide to presidential power. On an impressionistic level one might ask if the theory exaggerates the dependency of the President on squaring his interests with the self-interest of other Washington policy-makers. The egoism of policy-makers and their promotion of self-interest are hardly strangers to anyone who has ever given so much as a glance at Washington decision-makers, but surely this factor is more salient for some policy-makers than for others. Not every presidential relationship is a bargaining relationship and, although the President may be limited in the number of commands that he can make stick, no other individual or office has as many potent resources of influence as the President. Whether he makes use of them is up to him, but they are there to be used. Even a "weak" President like Eisenhower could, as Neustadt shows, turn tables in his second term, *once he had decided to do so*. A President subject to effective checks in one domain may be relatively unfettered in another domain. Comparing the President to other policy-makers, no other individual in Washington has as many "significant others" looking for ways to do his bidding and ingratiate themselves with him. "Bargaining" seems a rather inapposite term for describing these relationships. That some parts of some or all of these relationships may involve bargaining is indisputable; but to cut most of them down to bargaining is a bit Procrustean, pending the results of research. If the most inept bargainer in the country were elected to the Presidency, he would still be able to exert decisive influence over a great range of policies. By the same token, one had in Lyndon Johnson a President not noticeably deficient as a bargainer but whose decision in one crucial policy area, Vietnam, was governed less by the constraints of bargaining than by substantive appraisal of the situation (neither of which guarantees sound judgment). The policy-making process in the White House may be viewed as a mixture of bargaining, substantive evaluation, and judgment, as John F. Kennedy learned with the Bay of Pigs and his successor learned in Vietnam. At the close of his book Neustadt expresses a judgment that may be even more profound than his celebrated view of persuasion and bargaining: we may have to pick effective Presidents from among experienced politicians of extraordinary temperament, an even smaller class than the wise and prudent athletes nominated by Woodrow Wilson in emphasizing the burdens of the job.

POWER AS POSITION

Bargaining is, of course, a way of exercising political power, not the antithesis of power. The major source of presidential bargaining power is the fact that the President occupies more strategic locations in the policy-making process than anyone else. Nowhere are the scope and limitations of presidential power seen more clearly than in the budgetary process.

In theory, the budget that the President sends to Congress every year is "his" budget; in fact, there are tight limitations on the degree of flexibility the President has in any given year to change things around. He must perforce operate at the margins of the budget. Yet the fact that the limitations are tight and the changes in any given year relatively small should not obscure the fact that sizable changes may accumulate over a few years; nor should the restraints obscure the fact that statistically marginal changes may sometimes be quite major in their impact on programs.

In his study of the 1971 budget, Schultze (1970) shows budget outlays for national defense in the fiscal year 1965 of $49.9 billion, and $81.4 billion for FY 1969; income maintenance programs in FY 1965 called for $34.2 billion, compared to $56.8 billion in FY 1969; education, health, and manpower more than doubled, from $4.1 billion in FY 1965 to $10.3 billion in FY 1969; housing went from $1.5 billion to $3.3 billion to $6.8 billion in FY 1971. Other programs declined, and some remained fairly stable, but the President may, if he desires, be in on most if not all of these changes and, within limits, he can significantly redirect federal spending. Looking at the total change in outlays contemplated by the FY 1971 budget, one gets a picture of modest change: a $2.9 billion increase. But the $2.9 billion is the net result of $14.4 billion in increases and $11.5 billion in decreases. How much of this $25.9 billion is open to presidential influence?

In FY 1971 the President exerted greater control over budget decreases than increases. Most of the $11.5 billion reduction was under his control whereas $9.8 billion of the $14.4 billion in increases was relatively "uncontrollable," i.e., the result of social security benefit increases in prior years, normal growth in the number of beneficiaries, federal pay raises, and the like. These uncontrollable increases left $4.6 billion representing specific decisions and priority judgments, Schultze observes. Though a comparatively small amount, it is nonetheless significant that most of the $4.6 billion was allocated for rural housing, pollution control, transportation, welfare assistance, and revenue sharing—not for education, health, or a myriad of other programs that could have been chosen.

Presidential relations with his major formal tool of budget control, the Budget Bureau, were set by the Bureau's unique capacity to meet certain presidential needs. As long as control over agency spending, administrative management, and legislative clearance were dominant concerns of the President, the Bureau thrived (Schick, 1970). But budgeting declined as a tool of presidential power as new instruments were developed to service programmatic needs. "In fact," Schick writes, "the budget process tends to operate as a constraint on presidential power rather than as an opportunity for the development and assertion of presidential policies and priorities" (p. 521). The more the President took the lead in policy development, the more White House Staff and special task forces displaced the Budget Bureau as the President's main policy advisors. The process culminated in the establishment of the Domestic Council in 1970 as the main permanent institutional source of policy development, with the Office of Management and Budget responsible for effective implementation of policy. How tightly this distinction holds up in the future remains to be seen, but it appears that the policy needs of the Presidency, in domestic affairs as well as in foreign, require the institutionalized Presidency to become increasingly the institutionalized White House. And with this development the Budget Bureau, like the State Department and other institutions, declined in importance.

PLANNING, PROGRAMMING, BUDGETING

No President, even if he were so inclined, can give detailed attention to a $300 billion plus budget. For the great bulk of executive branch operations, for which the President is ostensibly Chief Executive officer, a wise President can hope for nothing better than that these operations are conducted routinely, with a minimum of political embarrassment. The more the Agriculture Department, the Commerce Department, Labor, Post Office, and Treasury run themselves, the better. Bureaucratic routines conserve the President's time, freeing him to do other things and focus his attention on the frontiers of policy-making, the areas in which he will make his mark. And as long as this remains true, the incremental nature of federal policy-making, described so well by Wildavsky (1964), will remain undisturbed. So, too, will the role of the Cabinet (Fenno, 1959), most of whose members are more temporary custodians of the bureaucratic machine and paid political lieutenants of the President than policy-making executives. Robert McNamara is the exception to the rule.

But McNamara is an important exception. His exploits in the Department of Defense (DOD) became a model for other Cabinet officers and stimulated a movement that seriously threatened long-standing practices in the executive branch. Following McNamara's success at DOD, Lyndon Johnson decreed in 1965 that henceforth the old incremental and piecemeal policy-making process should give way to a new system, more rational in method and more comprehensive in scope. Planning, Programming, and Budgeting (PPB) became the watchword for executive branch decision-making, and its major thrust was to shift control over policy from the depths of the bureaucracy to the top, thereby facilitating control by the President and his allies.

As an innovation that deliberately disrupts much traditional decision-making, PPB provoked great discusssion inside and outside government. Lindblom's classic analysis of rational-comprehensive versus incremental decision-making (1959; 1965; Braybrooke and Lindblom, 1963) was found accurate for the budgetary process studied by Wildavsky (1964), and it is a plausible descriptive theory for other policy areas as well. Indeed, the proponents of PPB sell it as a partial solution to the tendencies Lindblom finds inherent in the process of decision-making.

Some of the loftier hopes for PPB have been effectively challenged (Huitt, 1968; Wildavsky, 1966), and the barriers to PPB in certain policy areas have been strongly expressed (Schlesinger, 1971; Schelling, 1971). Yet the problem for the President remains: "Under incremental rules," Schick writes, "the spending base—what agencies were authorized to do and spend last year—escapes rigorous presidential or Budget Bureau scrutiny, with the consequence that the President is locked into the spending commitments made in the past, and he possesses effective control over only a small fraction of the budget" (Schick, 1970, p. 524). PPB seeks to replace the "pernicious practice of incremental budgeting" with a procedure that identifies the goals and objectives of government programs, analyzes the output of programs in terms of goals, measures program costs against benefits, and plans for the long haul as well as the short (Schultze, 1968). It also seeks, implicitly, the transfer of political power from those favored by the incremental system of muddling through to those equipped to handle modern planning techniques, i.e., the natural allies, in most cases, of the President. For the President, PPB promises to complement the newly established White House machinery for developing policy, with a set of tools for exposing great portions of the budget to his influence.

Lindblom's theory is obviously applicable to a broad range of governmental decision-making. Yet government also makes numerous decisions that cannot accurately be described as incremental. New programs and/or dramatic changes in old programs are enacted on *some* basis, and given the inapplicability of incrementalism to these programs, it is hard to gainsay the merits of PPB. Once established, these new programs may be conducted along incremental lines or along PPB lines, but from the perspective of the President and his men PPB has great attraction.

PPB may also, upon closer inspection, hold some dangers for the Presidency. Several years ago Neustadt (1965) warned that competition from the bureaucracy might seriously threaten control of policy-making by the elected officials of government. The bureaucracy, in his view, is already a strong competitor against the Presidency and Congress. It is possible that a new class of professional PPB enthusiasts, armed with new analytical techniques, might make themselves a distinct force to be reckoned with in national policy-making. This has, to some degree, already occurred, although from the point of view of the President and his bureaucratic allies the effects generally have been benign. But if policy is to be subjected to cost-benefit tests, if it is to be evaluated strictly according to its utility in bringing about results, the half life of existing policy might be considerably shorter than political needs might require. Under these conditions, the tension between "PPB policy" and "incremental policy" might give Neustadt's warning added force. All things considered, this seems a distant prospect, but among other deficiencies in our understanding of national policy-making is a marked incapacity to project the future.

The institutionalized Presidency, which now includes over 2,000 staff assistants, has been the subject of numerous studies, many of the best of which have been collected together in readers (Wildavsky, 1969a; Cronin and Greenberg, 1969). Cronin's research (1970) on the attitudes of White House staff toward the executive departments has documented the difficulties facing the President in extending his influence over the bureaucracy. Participant observer accounts help reduce the huge office of the Presidency to manageable proportions (Sorensen, 1963, 1965;

Schlesinger, 1965) as do presidential memoirs (Johnson, 1972; Eisen-hower, 1963; Truman, 1955, 1956), the host of case studies of individual decisions (Robinson, 1967; George, Hall, and Simons, 1971; Snyder and Paige, 1958; Art, 1968), and studies of presidential staff (Koenig, 1960; Anderson, 1968). Studies of the institutionalized presidency in action and in recollection are valuable in getting some sense of the role and potential of the Presidency in policy-making, but they usually shed light indirectly and incompletely on what went on in the President's mind as he faced choices, and how the complex mix of situational and psycho-logical variables inclined him in one direction more than another. For this kind of data one must focus on the President as a person, a person who is, indeed, enmeshed in an intricate and demanding set of relation-ships but one who is also capable of making the machinery work for him. Whether and how he makes it work for him is, fundamentally, up to him.

PRESIDENTS AS INDIVIDUALS

Presidential biographies are helpful in dealing with these questions (Burns, 1956, 1970; Freidel, 1956; Pringle, 1931, 1939) but far more use-full are explicitly psychological studies. The George's study of *Woodrow Wilson and Colonel House* (1956) is a case in point. Hargrove's (1966) brief examination of the "political personality" of Theodore Roosevelt, Woodrow Wilson, FDR, William Howard Taft, Herbert Hoover, and Eisenhower attempts to analyze Presidents in terms of four personality variables: needs, mental traits, values, and ego. Each President is exam-ined from a similar conceptual vantage point, but how powerful this perspective is in explicating presidential behavior remains an open question.

James David Barber's (1972) analysis of Presidents is the most ambi-tious study to date of presidential personality and its relationship to presi-dential performance. Barber's research raises policy questions of the most basic kind. Why did Woodrow Wilson wage the fight for the League of Nations as he did? Why did Herbert Hoover and Lyndon Johnson persist in untenable policies long after many people recognized the need for change? What accounts for the policy choices of FDR and Harry Truman, and the lethargic leadership style of Dwight Eisenhower? And, perhaps most intriguing of all, can one predict the policy position of Presidents by knowing the psychological predispositions that are set early in the President's career and carried into the White House?

Barber attempts to demonstrate the impact of psychological factors on presidential decisions by examining *character*, defined as the way the President orients himself toward life, not for the moment, but enduringly; *style*, his habitual way of performing his political roles in three settings (rhetoric, personal relations, orientation toward work); and *worldview*, his primary political beliefs, particularly his conception of social causality, human nature, and the central moral conflicts of his time. By asking questions about the amount of energy a President invests in the job, and the way he feels about what he does (does he have fun in the job?), Barber classifies Presidents as either active or passive in the performance of the job, and positive or negative toward this activity. Thus Presidents, depending on character, style, and worldview, may be classified as active-positive (FDR), active-negative (Lyndon Johnson, Nixon), passive-positive (Taft), or passive-negative (Eisenhower). Most important of all, these central tendencies help account for presidential power and policy and serve as a basis for predicting presidential behavior.

The active-negative Presidents are particularly fascinating because they are potentially the most dangerous: their personal tragedy may plunge the nation into massive social tragedy. If one could spot them, one would defeat them (assuming a better alternative). Woodrow Wilson, Herbert Hoover, and Lyndon Johnson are the prime examples, with the book still open on another active-negative type, Richard Nixon.

Barber argues that Wilson, Hoover, and Johnson all suffered low self-esteem as children; as a result, they developed consciences that required rigid self-control and superior achievement. When they became President, these basic orientations led them to adhere rigidly to disastrous policies. Thus Wilson persisted in waging the fight for the League of Nations in a way that ensured its defeat, and he, not Henry Cabot Lodge, doomed the League. Hoover persisted on a steady course in the face of massive evidence that his anti-Depression policies were not working. And Lyndon Johnson persisted with the Vietnam War long after others, both inside and outside government, concluded that the war was far too costly. All three Presidents, as a result of their psychological dispositions, caused untold misery by their blind commitment to futile policies.

What can one say of this theory? It is surely true that Presidents, being human, both think and feel. It is also true that all three of these men became deeply and personally involved in the issues—so involved that their emotions might have clouded their judgment. The League, the Depression, and the Vietnam War were passionate issues. But how can one *show* a connection between the character of these men and their policy commitments? Everything that Barber says about the active-negative character—his concern with self, power, virtue, the all-or-nothing quality, the denial of self-gratification, the fight to control aggression, the temptation to fight or quit, the view of the world as dangerous, the perception of others as either weak or grasping, the need for approval, the tendency to personalize battles, and the feeling of destiny—may fit Wilson, Hoover, and Johnson perfectly. But how can it be demonstrated that on these particular issues, these particular characteristics were centrally important—compared to other variables—in shaping the policy?

Consider the League of Nations. Wilson confronted the hostile Senate Foreign Relations Committee and its adroit chairman. The balance in the Senate was exceedingly close. Wilson should have been more agreeable to "reservations" in order to win over a swing group of wavering Senators, according to Barber. But who is to say whether his adamant stand was provoked by long-standing character traits or a cold, hard judgment that the price for the League was too dear? Feeling as he did about the League, and feeling as he did about Henry Cabot Lodge, Wilson decided to resist compromising U.S. membership in the League by taking the issue to the country. This strategy, given Wilson's rhetorical talents, might be read as a perfectly rational move—going to a strength, not a weakness. The Republicans held a majority of seats in the Senate and it is problematical how many reservations would have been necessary for a two-thirds majority. In any case, Wilson decided on an alternative course—one which, in hindsight, proved ineffective. His miscalculation was costly, but was it the act of an active-negative man governed by affective forces rather than by deliberation? Barber cites a great deal of evidence that it was, but his argument requires a fair-sized leap of faith.

Similar reservations could be applied to any and all of the Presidents studied by Barber. In addition, the evidence upon which various Presidents are grouped into the categories is spotty. The case for Wilson rests on firmer foundations than that for Hoover or Johnson, and not enough allowance is made for the fact that common tendencies, depending on the circumstances, might weigh more heavily for some Presidents than for others.

It is a bit disingenuous to raise psychological variables to such eminence in the face of the obvious fact that the man and the situation intermingle in producing the result.

The Presidency is a unique office with vast supporting facilities designed to provide "rational" analysis of problems. That the perceptual filter of the President shapes the way in which he responds to this apparatus goes without saying; but so does the observation that presidential decisions are shaped by a multitude of factors, one of the most important of which is the institutionalized nature of the office. Neither Hoover nor Johnson were unique in the judgments they reached about the problems they faced, and the research for understanding these judgments may have to be extended far beyond the psychological makeup of the man.

Barber's study of presidential character is the most noteworthy work on the Presidency since Neustadt. In introducing psychological variables he stresses factors that had been slighted in studies of presidential decision-making; in linking these variables to basic policy questions he helps set future research on the right track. How important childhood experiences and the maturation process are to presidential policy-decision remains in doubt; but Barber forces one to wonder, and wonderment may be the beginning of creative breakthroughs.

CONGRESS AND NATIONAL POLICY-MAKING

It is easier to bemoan the shortcomings of the political science literature on the Presidency than that on the Congress. In the face of doubts about the relative importance of the two institutions in policy-making, the 1960s saw a remarkable expansion in our knowledge of Congress. Research on Congress was so intense that by the end of the decade scholars outside the group of congressional specialists (and some inside) began wondering if we did not know enough about Congress relative to other important questions. A serious attempt was made to abolish the APSA Congressional Fellowship Program which had done much to stimulate the take-off. To many observers this seemed an effort to punish a field for success, not failure, and it was resoundingly defeated by the APSA membership. In a curious sense, the attack paid tribute to the labors of those who found Congress eminently worth understanding—a tribute, it should be said, that most of these scholars felt they could do without.

The problem with the literature on Congress, if abundance in these matters can accurately be labeled a "problem," is that highly specialized studies which are enormously valuable at one stage of research must be synthesized somehow into coherent wholes. Case studies of one congressional committee or policy area are fine, but comparative studies are better if one wants to generalize about the subject. Case studies of one committee chairman or one set of party leaders are fine also, but comparative studies of sets of leaders are better. If the congressional literature has a major fault, it is that too much of it is case-study oriented and not enough of it is concerned with making generalizations about numerous cases. It takes a lot of exploratory research before one is in the position of making such happy complaints about any field in the social sciences; happily, enough of the ground on Capitol Hill has been cleared for more ambitious scholars to test their ability to make sense out of large portions of congressional policy-making.

It should be noted at the outset that if one's primary concern is with understanding public policy, then Congress may not be the best place to start. This is true not only because Congress is relatively unimportant in some policy areas (Dexter, 1969a), but because, as Bauer argues, there may be too much "noise" in the congressional system to permit effective analyses (Bauer, 1968). In the case of foreign aid, for example, Congress does exert leverage, but its role is shaped by so many complex variables (institutional context, other issues, information from AID, etc.) that in Bauer's view, it is difficult to tell what data should be collected. Regarding public opinion, Bauer contends that this has been so well covered that it does not seem worthwhile to gather new information. This leaves the executive branch as the starting point of research.

The problem Bauer raises is fundamental: the complexity of the policy-making process must be reduced before much analytical progress can be made. But this does not necessarily require a choice about which institutions should be studied. Complexity may also be reduced by subdividing the policy-making process into analytical categories and making the institutional focus dependent upon the relevant categories. Policy-making is a complex process in which different institutions perform specialized tasks. Thus the choice of which institution to study may rest on which task commands the greater analytical interest, not on which institution seems "quiet" enough to study.

In looking at the policy-making process in functional terms there are a variety of analytical schemes to choose from. Lindblom (1968) identifies nine tasks that might usefully be employed in future research: initiating, vetoing, coordinating, planning, establishing general constraints on the alternatives to be considered, widening the range of choice, stimulating new policy ambitions, adjudicating conflicting intentions, and controlling through the purse strings. Lasswell (1956) earlier identified seven variables that have guided some research: intelligence or gathering of information, recommendation, prescription, invocation, application, appraisal, and termination. One can expand and contract these categories in a variety of ways. The point is that the policy-making process may be broken down into its components and policy-making elites may be viewed according to the distinctive tasks that they perform in the process.

Two recent efforts to do this are David Price's study (1972) of the legislative roles of three Senate committees, and James Sundquist's impressive study (1968) of policy-making in the 1953-1968 period. Both warrant more than passing notice.

Price identifies six policy-making tasks that help him explore who does what in policy-making:

1. Formulation
2. Instigation and Publication
3. Information-gathering
4. Interest aggregation
5. Mobilization
6. Modification

He correctly notes that this scheme differs considerably from Lasswell's rather bloodless portrayal of decision-making, and that it allows one to avoid vapid debates over general policy-making. The focus is, rather, on the variable participation in policy-making of the major individuals and institutions, a focus that permits him to fix responsibility for thirteen major pieces of legislation much more precisely than Chamberlain, Robinson, or any number of other authors have done before. Price's results for the thirteen cases lead to the following generalizations about the functions performed by different institutions:

Function	Institution
1. Formulation	Shared: executive-legislative
2. Instigation and Publication	Shared: executive-legislative
3. Interest aggregation	Shared: executive-legislative
4. Mobilization	Shared: executive-legislative
5. Information-gathering	Executive
6. Modification	Congress (committees)

Price's results strongly confirm many common generalizations about the policy-making process under liberal Democratic Presidents and a

Democratic Congress. Four of the six functions are widely shared by
Congress and the executive branch, the executive tends to dominate the
gathering of information, and congressional committees are significant
modifiers. His findings also confirm some important qualifications on these
generalizations, e.g., that although Congress and the executive are both
engaged in interest aggregation, the executive tends to represent national
interest groups and Congress tends toward more segmental concerns
(Manley, 1970). Although the findings are not startling, and the balance
of functions under different historical and political conditions remains
an open question, Price shows, as Bauer, Pool, and Dexter before him
(1963), that a case study approach to policy-making can have great theoretical interest. His results support the view that, in Heclo's words, there
"appears to be nothing about the case study technique which is inherently nontheoretical or unscientific; the problem lies in assuming that
theoretical contributions will emerge automatically from narrative"
(Heclo, 1972, p. 93).

Sundquist's analysis (1968) of policy-making in six major policy areas
(unemployment, poverty, education, civil rights, health care, the environment) is less explicit in its analytical framework than Price's study
but, if anything, it has wider theoretical interest. At the general level of
executive-legislative relations he shows how, during the 1950s, a large
portion of the policy agenda of the 1960s was born in Congress, nurtured
during the Eisenhower Presidency, absorbed as part of John Kennedy's
platform in 1960, and enacted during the Kennedy-Johnson years. The
role of Congress was central to all of the policies debated in this period
and, when the Democratic Administration failed to take the lead, as in
the case of air and water pollution, Congress was quite capable of taking
the initiative.

More important than which branch seized the initiative, however,
is Sundquist's argument that regardless of where the source of policy
lies, the proponents of action (and, implicitly, the opponents) form a
single system: activist politicians looking for public support and interest
groups looking for political support form policy sub-systems and jointly
engage in the activities necessary to make new public policy. In the
Eisenhower years the story was largely one of frustration for Democratic
activists. But with the defeat of Nixon in 1960 the chances of enacting
the Democratic party platform obviously improved; following Kennedy's
death and with the 1964 election the platform became reality. For Sundquist, the policy process is the result of activist legislators, interest
groups, bureaucrats, and Presidents, all operating within the electoral
system which, ultimately, determines the success or failure of the elites.

Elections and voters, in this view, count heavily in policy-making, an argument that in the context of the oft-repeated attacks on nonprogrammatic parties and ignorant voters comes as a refreshing, if arguable, revisionist interpretation of the national policy-making process.

It is not accidental that in analyzing policy-making during the 1950s Sundquist gives more attention to the Senate than the House. Activist members of the House might have been intent on policy change, but the Senate, as the more liberal of the two (Froman, 1963), gave its activists wider scope. Members of the House had neither the visibility nor the internal organization to push new policies the way their Senate counterparts could. Thus Sundquist indirectly makes a major comparison between the policy-making roles of the two institutions, a comparison that promises to lead to new ways of thinking about the House and Senate.

THE SENATE

Nelson Polsby (1970) detects the same characteristic of the Senate as Sundquist, but Polsby seizes on it to develop an original theory about the general role of the Senate in policy-making. Polsby rejects the view that new policy proposals are generally initiated in presidential messages, arguing instead that innovations can be traced to two sources: (1) generally acknowledged problems that produce demands for governmental action; and (2) long-range processes by which innovative policies are incubated pending the development of a more favorable political climate. The Senate, more so than the House, is a crucial incubator for new policy. "What is needed in the Senate," Polsby concludes, "is as little structure as possible; its organizational flexibility enables it to incubate policy innovation, to advocate, to respond, to launch its great debates, in short, to pursue the continuous renovation of American public policy through the hidden self-promotion of its members" (Polsby, 1970, pp. 489–490).

Senators have long been pictured as verbose, free-wheeling individualists who are more interested in news coverage than substantive policy problems. Polsby, by accentuating this aspect of the Senate, calls attention to the centrality of debate and publicity in the policy-making process. What others take as picturesque about the Senate, he takes as central to policy-making, and as a result the Senate emerges in fresh garb: a crucial nerve end of the polity.

Some Senate observers will no doubt read Polsby as making a virtue out of a vice, but his theory of the Senate and policy initiation raises important questions for students of Congress. Among the most important are: (1) What facilitates or retards the capacity of the Senate to raise new policy issues to the point of resolution? (2) How does the incubation function of the Senate relate to its other functions as a legislative institution? (3) If the key function of the Senate is as an "echo chamber" or "publicity machine," and increasingly as a reserve for presidential timber, what are the functions of the House, and how do these functions mesh with the Senate?

Articulation and resolution of new policy issues

Liberal activists are the main engine of change in Congress. In articulating new proposals, the formal and informal rules of the Senate work to the activists' advantage but, if the popular view of the Senate as dominated by a "Club" or "Establishment" is correct, the informal distribution of power frustrates their policy objectives (White, 1957; Clark, 1963; 1964). In point of fact, the club-view of the Senate is open to serious question as a description of the contemporary Senate, and there is even doubt as to its accuracy for the period in which it was developed (post-World War II). Not too long after he published *Congress: The Sapless Branch*, Senator Joseph Clark declared that democracy had come to the Senate and, as a result of a series of elections beginning in 1958, it was no longer true that the conservative Establishment dominated the institution (*Congressional Record*, September 13, 1965, p. 23495).

Whether or not a power elite runs the Senate on most important policy matters is a small-scale version of the pluralist-elite controversy in community studies. It is hardly surprising, therefore, that Polsby, who scores high on imaginative critiques of conventional wisdom, should extend his critique of the power elite school in local politics to the congressional field (Polsby, 1971).

According to Polsby, the criteria used by White to define membership in the Club are vague, internally inconsistent, and violated by any number of "Senate types." Unusual tolerance for the quirks of others, exclusive devotion to a career in the Senate, a disinclination toward congressional reform, a certain type of personality—none of these clearly distinguish members of the Club from nonmembers. There are in the Senate some members who can be described as mavericks, i.e., men who do not abide by the norms as rigidly as some of their peers, but Polsby argues the existence of mavericks does not demonstrate the existence of a Club. Mavericks, as Huitt shows (1961a), are sometimes very influential Senators; moreover, if the existence of mavericks were support for the Club theory, it would have to be shown that many nonmaverick Senators were relatively powerless, a task that has not yet been accomplished. It may be noted that a middle position in this debate has been argued by Ripley (1969a). In his view, the elite theory is accurate for much of the post-1945 Senate, but the Club's institutional control has sharply declined as positions of power have been dispersed throughout both parties in the Senate. Unfortunately, most of Ripley's data pertain to geographic and ideological distributions on committees, and these data do not allow a direct test of the Club thesis. Hence his contribution to the debate is more in the realm of a suggested compromise than empirical demonstration of a solution to the problem.

In our view, the tangle over the existence or nonexistence of the Club is worth serious consideration because if the theory is proved it explains a good deal, though not all, of the policy decisions of the Senate. The more true the theory the more the liberal activists are confined to incubating, as opposed to enacting, policy innovation. Incubation remains an important part of policy-making, of course, but incubators do not insure that frail youngsters get a strong start in life; sometimes they are merely way-stations on the route to more difficult struggles; sometimes the patient expires.

White's theory of the inner Club is so nebulous that it defies systematic treatment, but Clark's theory is substantially more precise. The Establishment, according to Clark, is a bipartisan minority of conservative Senators who, by virtue of their seniority, control the most important committees, determine choice committee assignments, and, with exceptions, select the official Senate leaders. It is held together by a general consensus on five policy issues: (1) white supremacy; (2) devotion to property rights over human rights; (3) support of the military establishment; (4) belligerence in foreign affairs; and (5) a determination to prevent congressional reform. Clark supports his attack on the Establishment with data on committee assignments for Senators who favored and opposed changing the filibuster rule, the overrepresentation of southern Democrats on major committees, and with an examination of votes on a number of domestic and international issues. Thus he is able to identify empirically the boundaries of the Establishment and to discuss its strengths and weaknesses. (Clark also extends his argument to the House, although with considerably less force.)

Senator Clark, while he represented Pennsylvania in the Senate, was the archtypical liberal activist who chafed under Eisenhower's relaxed leadership and whose vexation was heightened by the congressional reception accorded John Kennedy's legislative proposals. He is a perfect example of the legislator-as-incubator discussed by Polsby and, in slightly different terms, by Sundquist (who once served as Clark's legislative assistant). How apt was (and is) Clark's description of Senate decision-making?

The essence of Clark's argument states that the policy decisions of the Senate, on a large and significant number of issues, are set by what other writers call the Conservative Coalition: conservative Democrats, mainly, although not exclusively, from the South, and conservative Republicans, mainly, although not exclusively, from the Midwest. Clark acknowledges that the Coalition does not govern all major decisions and that, when it appears, it does not always win. He acknowledges furthermore that the grip of the Coalition on the machinery of Senate power has changed and weakened over time. And he acknowledges that the Coalition allows for a good deal of doctrinal divergence from members who, by some criteria, can accurately be described as Establishment types. With all of these caveats it is difficult to reject the Establishment (Conservative Coalition) theory by pointing to the fact that power is widely dispersed among individual Senators, as does Polsby (1971), or to the fact that the position of the Southern Democrats on strategically important committees is waning, as does Ripley (1969a), or to the large number of Senators who have access to the decisions of such a key committee as Appropriations, as does Fenno (1966).

The advantage of the Establishment view of the Senate over the "pluralist" view is that it stresses a fact of congressional life that is crucial to policy-making: both parties have conservative and liberal wings. Many policy decisions are determined by coalitions of like-minded members who join forces in committee and on the floor to settle issues in accordance with their policy preferences. What Clark and other liberal activists attacked as the Establishment is the Conservative Coalition, an informal but nonetheless potent force established late in the 1930s (Patterson, 1967; Burns, 1963) and the major hurdle for liberal activists ever since. Power positions may be highly dispersed in the Senate but on certain committees, such as Armed Services and the Finance Committee, the Coalition continues to hold sway. And on the Senate floor it is this combination of Republicans and southern Democrats that still defeats the proposals of Senators like Clark (Price, 1963). In 1971, for example, the Conservative Coalition appeared on 120 Senate roll calls, winning 86 percent of them. Both figures were eleven-year highs according to *Congressional Quarterly* (*CQ Weekly Report,* January 15, 1972, pp. 74–80). Among the issues won by the Coalition were a modification in the filibuster rule, an amendment dealing with school desegregation, government guarantee of a $250 million loan to the Lockheed Corporation, defeat of the Cooper-Church amendment limiting the expenditure of funds in Vietnam to withdrawal or protection of withdrawing U.S. troops, and the nomination of William H. Rehnquist to the Supreme Court. The Coalition also lost a few important votes, but its batting average is sufficiently impressive to recommend a coalition perspective to future students of the Senate. The key to much of the policy-making in the Senate, as well as in the House, is found in coalition politics. Senator Clark, in pronouncing the demise of the Establishment, expressed the weakening of Senators whom he found particularly obnoxious; he need not be read as declaring an end to the power of the Conservative Coalition.

The Conservative Coalition may keep new policy proposals in the Senate incubator for several years, and it may deter radical initiatives from being initiated at all. But there is another—and related—aspect of the Senate that likewise affects the articulation and resolution of new policy: the informal norms or folkways of Senate life.

Senate behavior, according to Matthews (1960), is regulated by certain unwritten rules of the game: new Senators are expected to serve a proper apprenticeship, Senators should work hard at their legislative duties, they should specialize in a few issue areas and gain expertise, conflict should be tempered by courtesy towards one's antagonists, reciprocity should be followed in bargaining with other Senators, and Senators should feel proud of the great institution to which they have been elected. These norms make life in the Senate more pleasant, and they also shape legislative effectiveness. Matthews shows that, in the 83rd and 84th Congresses, Senators who talked less on the floor and who tended to specialize got more of their bills and resolutions through the chamber; hence they were more "effective" than their verbose and thinly spread colleagues.

If Matthews is right, there are powerful norms surrounding the manner in which policy is nurtured and enacted. Those Senators who are likely to score high on Polsby's index of policy innovation are precisely the ones who are less likely to abide by the norms and, at least in the short run, to be consigned to relatively ineffective status as lawmakers.

Unfortunately, little empirical work has been done on Matthews's hypotheses. The Senate is not a lawmaking factory in which the hands are paid on a piecemeal basis. Bill-passing is a collective endeavor in which key actors may not even introduce the original bill (Huitt, 1961b).

And it is certainly true that the innovator who is ahead of his time has a vital role to play in the policy-making process.

The most significant follow-up work that has been done to date on Matthews's work is Pettit's 1969 study in the mid-1960s. Pettit constructed indices of organizational power, reputation for ability and influence, and reputation for relevant expertise. In correlating these indices with others, he comes up with several interesting findings:

(1) There is a very small relationship (especially among Democrats) between seniority and reputation for relevant expertise, but there is a strong relationship between organizational power base and seniority.

(2) It is the relatively less powerful Democratic Senators who are most likely to support a Democratic President, uphold the party position, and vote liberal. But the opposite is true of Republicans.

(3) Ascribed members of the "inner club" are high on organizational power resources, and on reputation for legislative ability and influence. "Outsiders" score high in reputation for relevant expertise. (Regrettably, Pettit does not report how many of the forty-eight usable questionnaires from Senate administrative assistants indicated a belief in the inner club thesis, an omission that places the persuasiveness of his findings in doubt.)

(4) The low correlation between organizational power base and the other two power indices indicates, as Polsby argues, that "power" is considerably dispersed in the Senate.

(5) Power resides at the ideological center of the Senate, and, therefore, policy is most likely to be moderate in nature.

Pettit is dealing with potential and ascribed power, not actual power, and, therefore, his findings bear only indirectly on Matthews's effectiveness measure. Still, the results tend to confirm Polsby's view of the Senate and to cast doubt on the importance of abidance by the folkways to gaining influence in the Senate.

The Senate of the 1970s is not the exact same institution Matthews studied in the 1950s. Senators today are less apt to shun the public glare while they learn the ropes as apprentices to senior colleagues. The old system of Lyndon Johnson and Richard Russell is long gone; in its stead is the more loosely conducted leadership of Mike Mansfield and a bevy of Senators who would very much like to leave the greatest deliberative body on earth for an office down the street. Writing in 1960, Matthews detected the emergence of changes that have now become reality; in all, the Senate is now a more hospitable place for issue-oriented, publicity-seeking Senators than before. And, with this change, the Senate activists are better able to raise, if not resolve, new public policy issues. The grip of the Conservative Coalition on the Senate has by no means been broken, but new ventilation ducts have been added. This remodelling is worth noting even though it is more prelude to significant policy change than guarantee.

Incubation-plus: the functions of the Senate in the policy process

Incubation, however distinctive of the Senate, is not the only function performed by the Senate. In the course of incubation, Senators perform a number of associated functions: they represent interests that would benefit from new policy, they help mobilize interest-group support, they gather information and seek, through bargaining, the resolution of enough conflict to bring new policy to fruition, and they hope, often in vain, that through these efforts changes in public policy will be legitimized (and their own careers furthered). These functions are, of course, also performed in the House; policy allies from both chambers, in fact, perform them jointly.

Reciting a list of functions performed in the policy-making process is not difficult. As we saw above, Price (1972) employs six functions in a useful manner. Davidson, Kovenock, and O'Leary (1966) identify six functions too, and Jewell and Patterson (1966) emphasize two functions, management of conflict and integration of the polity.

From the galleries, the Senate resembles nothing more than a genteel, rather regal, if stuffy, private club; the House nothing more than a noisy locker room. With only one hundred members, the Senate is a more individualistic, personal institution with more flexible rules, more prestige, and a more even, less hierarchical distribution of power (Froman, 1967, p. 7). Both institutions are organized into committees and subcommittees, but Senate committees tend to be less autonomous than their House counterparts, less preoccupied with success on the floor, less knowledgeable on substantive matters, less strongly led, and more individualistic in decision-making (Fenno, 1973). Under these conditions, individual party leaders in the Senate have to compete on more or less even terms with their peers. An exceptional leader, like Lyndon Johnson, may piece together enough sources of influence to place himself at the center of

Senate decision-making across a large range of issues, but the modal pattern is likely to be decentralized (Huitt, 1961c; Evans and Novak, 1966).

If anything is clear about the Senate legislative process it is the hazardous nature of making broad functional generalizations. To posit, for example, that the legislative process promotes the integration of the polity seriously strains what we know about Senate decision-making. Some decisions promote integration, others not. A case could be made that few decisions *settle* conflicts; rather, decisions mark pauses in social conflict, allowing the major contestants to test the results and, more often than not, to make plans for overturning the transitory consensus embodied in law. That there is a momentary pause in the conflict process may be construed as promoting integration, but since most policies are a compromise with which few of the contestants are perfectly happy the results of the legislatve process are as likely to breed new demands as contentment with the status quo. Thus the process goes on, with old policies generating and sometimes intensifying future conflicts rather than preventing them.

Some committees of the Senate seem to specialize less in conflict resolution than conflict intensification. Highly partisan demands are reflected in the Senate Labor and Public Welfare Committee, for example, and the same is true of the House Education and Labor Committee. These committees are partisan battlegrounds whose distinctive characteristic is the prosecution of partisan conflict, not consensus seeking or integration building.

A great deal more research needs to be done on Senate decision-making before some of the generalizations about the process can be accepted. Some committees have been studied: Appropriations (Horn, 1970); Foreign Relations (Farnsworth, 1961); Banking and Currency (Bibby, 1966); Finance, Labor and Public Welfare, and Commerce (Price, 1972); Policy Committees (Bone, 1956). Fenno (1973) offers some suggestive leads in his analysis of Appropriations, Finance, Foreign Relations, Interior, Labor and Public Welfare, and Post Office. But the results so far show more dissimilarities than a firm base for generalizations, and a host of questions remain relatively unexplored. Many studies, furthermore, fail to relate the process of decision-making to the resulting policies. We know that Senators engage in the standard forms of bargaining (compromise, splitting the difference, making side payments, bluffing, logrolling), but whether different forms of bargaining are associated with different policy arenas, how the bargaining situation affects the substance of policy, and how Senators make their exchange calculations remain fairly open questions. Until these questions are explored, we will be confined to making such interesting but somewhat trivial statements as "Senators make their decisions through bargaining." Such common statements about the Senate may reveal quite a bit about what happens there, but what they hide is vital.

THE HOUSE OF REPRESENTATIVES

Just as it is easier to bemoan the literature on the Presidency compared to that on Congress, so too is it easier to bemoan the literature on the Senate compared to that on the House. As a result of the "discovery" of the House of Representatives in the early 1960s, the House is today probably the best-covered and best-understood institution in Washington. Insatiable scholarly appetites are, by definition, never satisfied. But ignorance is relative, and the gaps in the literature on the House look small compared to those on other parts of the policy-making system.

It would be foolhardy to attempt to do justice to the rich literature on the House in less than a separate and lengthy essay on that institution. Barring this, one is left with the problem of making some sense out of a multitude of highly specialized studies. Specifically, how well can we answer the question of how the House generally makes its policy determinations? Is it possible to generalize about the nature of House policy decisions in terms of their general direction—liberal, conservative, or some mixture? Is there a way of looking at the House as a policy-making institution that suggests a theory that explains large segments of House behavior?

The policy problem of the House

The representative character of the House may serve as a starting point for theorizing about the kind of decision-making found there. The decision-making processes of the House are, first of all, time-consuming. Second, these processes are more often than not marked by compromise and logrolling. Third, new policy proposals are likely to lie in House incubators (or pigeon-holes) longer than in the Senate. Fourth, if policy outputs can be placed on a liberal-conservative continuum, then House outputs generally tend to lean in the conservative direction compared to those of the Senate. Fifth, when all is said and done, there are few unequivocal winners and losers in the House struggle. All of these characteristics of House decision-making—slowness, compromise and logrolling, procrastination, conservatism, and ambiguity—flow from the representative nature of the House.

Major policy conflicts, to start with the obvious, pose multidimensional problems to decision-makers. Air pollution, for example, is now widely recognized as a dire problem. Yet how policy-makers cope with the problem is complicated by the intricate technical nature of the issue, the lack of technical expertise on the part of most legislative decision-makers, and by the complicated political nature of the issue, an area in which congressmen have greater expertise. An added factor that complicates policy-making is that the air pollution problem, as is true of many problems, cannot be separated from a number of other issues: the competing value of economic development, other problems judged equally or more severe, limited resources with which to attack pollution, encroachments on the freedom of the economic sector, and so on. Representatives of all sides of the multiple issues hiding behind one policy problem are found in Congress. Policy problems are, in short, multi-dimensional, and so, too, are the settlements.

If air pollution were the only, or the foremost, problem with which Congress had to cope, the job would be considerably easier than it is. Many important conflicts never become salient in Congress, but a lot of them do. Thus Congress has a multiplicity of multidimensional conflicts to handle. Conflicts between grape pickers and grape owners; conflicts between labor and management; between hawks and doves; between conservationists and economic developers; between blacks and whites; between proponents of bussing and their opponents; between internationalists and isolationists; between Arizona and California over water; between advocates of massive aid to education and those who fear government control of the schools; between tax reformers and tax avoiders— all of these, and a great many more, are on the congressional docket.

The abundance of conflicts and problems means that congressmen must choose which conflicts they will pay attention to (Bauer, Pool and Dexter, 1963, also, Dexter 1969b). This comes down to 435 members of the House making choices about the conflicts that most concern them, and to a notable lack of consensus on the rank ordering of important conflicts. For a member of Congress to pursue the conflicts that most concern him involves necessarily dealing with members who have somewhat different priorities (and some who care less about issues than personal advancement). Multiple, many-sided conflicts are inevitably packed together in the House, and one of the most difficult tasks of leadership is to unpack them. Under the circumstances, it is hardly surprising that House decisions are made by compromise and logrolling, that the process takes time, that some settlements are never reached, and that those that are reached are often unsatisfactory to those outside Congress who have a clearer view of the nation's needs. The congressman's view is, perforce, clouded by his colleagues, many of whom, to intensely issue-oriented members, seem remarkably indifferent to the perils of inaction.

If the above is a reasonably accurate view of the general policy problem facing the House, one might well wonder how the 435 Representatives ever eke out a strong enough consensus to pass legislation. One way this is done, of course, is by compromising issues so that all or nearly all of the conflict is drained from them, and the formal vote is less a cause for grave concern to congressmen than a relief. But despite sometimes heroic efforts, not every issue can be diluted this way. Why some conflicts can and others cannot be compromised away is an interesting and largely unresearched question, but the fact is that the House relies on a number of mechanisms besides compromise and logroll in arriving at its decisions. The oft-criticized political parties and the seniority system are two such mechanisms, and the committee system is a third.

Political parties

Political parties serve two central functions in House policy-making: first, they serve as a basis for organizing leadership in the House; and, second, they serve to orient members on matters of public policy. Most writers agree that the parties perform the first function much more easily than the second.

At the start of every new Congress the majority and minority parties reach a peak of solidarity seldom equalled as the session unfolds. Decisions on who will man the formal positions of power come easier in the House than decisions on how these positions are to be used in implementing policy. Party is one factor in policy-making, but it is often in competition and at odds with the judgments of individual Representatives, the position of important interest groups, constituency preferences, state delegations, local party considerations, committee allegiances, personal relationships that evolve in the legislature, and, in some cases, common perverseness. Despite the competing influences on congressional voting, many studies of roll-call voting in the House have shown that, compared to other variables, party is a very strong indicator of congressional voting (Truman, 1959; Turner, 1951; MacRae, 1958; Froman, 1963). Party cohesion in voting does vary by issue area and over time (Rieselbach,

1966; Grassmuck, 1951; Clausen and Cheney, 1970; Lerche, 1964; Turner and Schneier, 1970), but party differences remain high on such basic issues as organized labor, business regulation, and the role of the federal government. And if one probes behind the roll-call votes one finds considerable "party feeling," even among those members who deviate from the party majority (Ripley, 1967).

The most persistent and significant breakdown in party voting in the House, as in the Senate, occurs when a majority of southern Democrats and Republicans oppose a majority of northern Democrats (Manley, 1970; Key, 1949; Shannon, 1968; Donovan, 1970). In 1971, to take the same year used for the Senate, Congressional Quarterly's study showed that the Conservative Coalition appeared on 99 House roll calls, winning 79 per cent of them. Both figures were eleven-year highs. The House Coalition decided such major policy issues as the extension of the military draft, school bussing, withdrawal of U.S. forces from Vietnam, and the Lockheed loan. The Coalition lost votes on the SST, a child development program, and permitting prayers in the public schools.

The coalitional nature of the House Democratic party places a high premium on the legislative skill of the formal party leadership. If the Speaker, Majority Leader, and their allies are to exercise central control over the policy decisions of the House, they must extend their influence to the major factions of the party. Conservative Democrats, mainly from the South, and liberal Democrats, mainly from large urban areas, constitute the two largest blocs. The Democratic Study Group (DSG), the major organization of liberal Democrats in the House since the late 1950s, is on many policy issues the mirror image of the conservative Democrats and a crucial source of votes for the party leaders (Kofmehl, 1964; Ferber, 1971; Mann, Miller and Stephens, 1971). On other issues, the DSG causes headaches for the leadership by its active promotion of liberal causes that threaten the coalitional ties uniting the party. Party leaders, caught in the middle of the party struggle, wage the battle gingerly; denied the necessary tools to unite the party, they spend their time searching for the position that will unite the largest number of their Democratic brethren, a task that inevitably means the disaffection of intense minorities on both ends of the policy spectrum. Neither the Democratic party leadership nor the Republican leadership dictates party policy; they discover it through negotiations (Ripley, 1969b; Jones, 1968, 1970), just as they negotiate with their colleagues to get the job in the first place (Peabody, 1967; Polsby, 1969).

Seniority

Given the makeup of the parties sketched above, any decision rule that significantly affects the distribution of power is likely to be severely attacked by those who feel that they are deprived of their just deserts in the legislative process. That such is the case with the seniority system is understandable, as is the failure of the disadvantaged minority to overturn the system.

The seniority system, whereby committee chairmanships fall automatically to the majority party member with the longest continuous service on the committee, has for many years been a favorite whipping boy of congressional reformers, most of whom are policy liberals. Committee chairmanships enhance the power of those interests represented by the chairman and, on the most important congressional committees, those interests have been more conservative than liberal. Hence the logical conclusion by liberals that if they can alter the rule of seniority, they can alter the nature of policy in their direction.

The relationship between seniority and policy-making has been the subject of a great deal of scholarly attention. The "causes" of the seniority system have been analyzed (Polsby, Gallaher, and Rundquist, 1969), various charges against the system have been dissected (Goodwin, 1959), the rise of northern Democratic and decline of southern Democratic safe seats has been detected (Wolfinger and Heifetz, 1965), and a book on the subject concludes that the seniority system does not so much bias the legislature toward conservatism as reinforce preexisting conservative tendencies and delay liberal changes (Hinckley, 1971).

Liberal reformers are unlikely to have their unhappiness with seniority assuaged by statistics showing that their conservative opponents have little more than their fair share of committee chairmanships. And for a very good reason: the problem with seniority is not one of fair shares but that certain crucial committees are chaired by members who are out of step with the national, and more liberal, wing of the party. In the 92nd Congress (1971–1972), for example, southern and, in the main, conservative Democrats chaired all four top House committees: Ways and Means, Rules, Appropriations, and Armed Services.

As long as the seniority system places these committee chairmanships in conservative hands, it makes sense for liberals to seek changes in the system—if they have the votes to elect liberal chairmen under a new system.

The great unknown about the seniority system is how much it affects the policy outputs of the House, and how much those outputs would be changed if the system were changed. Liberals do have effective policy control of some committees (Education and Labor, Judiciary) and, if Wolfinger and Heifetz are correct, the relative position of liberals is bound to improve as they gain seniority. In 1971, moreover, major changes in the system were enacted. House Democrats adopted rules stating that the Committee on Committees need not follow seniority in composing committee lists, nominations to committees may be challenged in the party Caucus if ten members so desire, and, to free subcommittee chairmanships, no member may chair more than one subcommittee. House Republicans adopted procedures for a secret vote on all ranking member nominations of their Committee on Committees. A liberal effort to remove the chairman of the District of Columbia Committee was made in the Democratic caucus, but failed 96–126. These changes in the seniority system have not by any means realigned the balance of power in the House: witness the high batting average of the Conservative Coalition in 1971, and the 126 votes in favor of the District Committee chairman. The seniority system could be completely removed overnight, and it is doubtful that House liberals, barring a sizable increase in their ranks, would be able to enact a full liberal program. Their problems far transcend the seniority system, though reforms of that system would remove an important irritant.

The committee system

The seniority system is important because it determines leadership positions on committees, those "little legislatures" where, especially in the House, the great bulk of policy is made. The policy functions of the House are performed in committees and, in the great majority of cases, accepted by the parent chamber. Such facts have not escaped scholarly attention, though a great deal of time elapsed between Woodrow Wilson's *Congressional Government* (1885) and the upsurge of research on committees in the 1960s.

Students of congressional committees have analyzed committees from a wide variety of perspectives. Committees have been studied in the context of policy arenas (Carroll, 1966; Price, 1962; Munger and Fenno, 1962). General treatises have been attempted (Goodwin, 1970). Individual committees have been exhaustively studied (Robinson, 1963; Fenno, 1966; Manley, 1970; Jones, 1961). And Fenno (1973) has subjected six House committees to detailed and insightful comparative analysis (Appropriations, Ways and Means, Education and Labor, Interior, Post Office, and Foreign Affairs).

Lacking in the wealth of committee studies is a perspective that will accommodate comparative analyses of committees and also highlight the policy-relevant aspects of committee decision-making. Two approaches will be discussed here: Fenno's attempt to link the internal processes of committees with committee outputs, and a somewhat different approach that focuses on the policy coalitions that determine committee decision-making. The two approaches, as we shall see, are by no means unrelated and, indeed, are more complementary than opposed.

Fenno's approach to comparative committee analysis

In Fenno's scheme, six major variables serve as the common foci for studying congressional committees. *Member goals,* he argues, help explain how committee members organize internal committee operations. *Environmental constraints,* defined as the expectations of influential external groups, also affect the way committee members conduct business. To achieve individual goals and to satisfy key environmental expectations, committee members develop sets of *strategic premises,* operationalized as *decision rules,* that govern the way they behave as committee members, and from these decision rules flow committee policy *decisions.* Thus the scheme consists of the following:

Independent Variables	Intervening Variables	Dependent Variables
Member goals Environmental constraints	Strategic premises (decision rules)	Decision-making processes Decisions

In the course of his study, Fenno defines these variables more precisely. Regarding member goals, he compares general committee orientations toward three objectives: reelection, influence within the House, and good public policy. Environmental constraints are seen as stemming from four sources: other members of the House, the executive branch, interest groups, and party leaders. Strategic premises are defined to mean underlying agreements on the general policy purposes of the committees, and how the committees should go about realizing these objectives. The decision-making processes found in the six committees are linked and compared in terms of the extent and type of partisanship found in the committees, the nature of participation and specialization in decision-making, and the patterns of leadership that characterize the committees.

Finally, he attempts to show not only how the six committees vary with respect to all these factors, but how these variables help explain committee decisions.

Fenno's approach to the study of comparative committees is at least as broad and comprehensive as his classic study of the House Appropriations Committee. He raises and answers more questions about committees than any of his predecessors. Few scholars have shown as much patience or stamina in exposing the internal process as Fenno.

It in no way detracts from Fenno's work to recognize that, if understanding public policy is the objective, a somewhat narrower focus might also serve well in comparing committees and their decisions. In developing such a focus one may start with the well-documented findings about the parties as essentially coalitions of diverse interests. Roll-call studies of congressional voting, and particularly the work of David Mayhew (1966), are important here. From the leads suggested in these studies, one might ask questions about the modal patterns of party and coalitional line-ups in the committees. Are the parties united in the committees, as they are in the great majority of decisions reached by the Appropriations Committee, or are the parties basically split on policy issues, as they are in the House Education and Labor Committee? To what extent are committee decisions reflective (or determinative) of the Conservative Coalition found in general House voting patterns? A great deal of decision-making in the Appropriations, Rules, Ways and Means, Armed Services, and other committees would seeem to be explicable in coalitional terms. The grip of conservatives on committees varies from committee to committee, from issue to issue, and from time to time. But comprehensive studies of committee coalition-making would appear to be an economical entry-point for future studies of House policy-making, an entry-point which, furthermore, is amenable to the bargaining models of decision-making developed outside the congressional literature. In constructing a coalitional view of committee decision-making, and in thinking about the House in terms of coalition theory, there is no better place to start than those elements of Fenno's work that describe the variable coalition processes that underlie the decisions of different committees. In this sense, what is suggested here is less an alternative to Fenno's schema than a logical development of one of its most promising parts. Some work along these lines has been done on the House Ways and Means Committee (Manley, 1970), but a comprehensive coalition-based study of congressional policy-making has yet to appear.

CONCLUSION: TOWARD UNDERSTANDING
NATIONAL POLICY-MAKING

The literature on national policy-making by the Presidency and Congress has been subdivided into various parts because that is the way students of policy-making do their studies, and because it is impossible to talk about everything at once. In reality, of course, policy-making is a good deal messier than separate studies might reveal. A mind-boggling array of factors shape national policy and, if most of the major variables have been identified, our understanding of how they interact in the policy process is still in a primitive state. To analyze policy-making systems one must at some point close them off, despite the nagging realization that the actual systems remain defiantly open as their inhabitants go about deciding who gets what, when, and how.

An appreciation for what students of policy-making are up against may be gained by contemplating the best and most comprehensive study of policy in the last decade: Bauer, Pool, and Dexter's study of foreign trade (1963). This work is impressive for its use of communications theory, but even more impressive is its scope. Bauer, Pool, and Dexter work all the way around and through the policy process involving trade: they cover Congress, the executive branch, interest groups, local constituencies and businessmen, and the history of the issue area. Their book is an example of the best kind of policy analysis on a broadly defined, open system; students of other policies would do well to emulate it.

However, it took three senior authors ten years to complete the project. Hence the moral that research on open, complex systems is easier to endorse as a model for the future than to bring off, even if one decides to operate in only a single policy area. The policy process in trade is not identical to that in many other areas, and, if Lowi (1964) is right, there may be a number of different issue areas, each with its own distinctive combination of political forces and patterns. If so, the need for broad policy studies in other areas on the model of the Bauer, Pool, and Dexter study is obvious. Until such studies are completed, the generalizations drawn from the trade study remain questionable for other issues. This in no way lessens the utility of these generalizations as guides for future research, but it is not a bad measure of how far the literature is from comprehensive generalizations about policy-making at the national level.

The difficulties facing studies of open systems are severe, but scholars are becoming increasingly aware of the need to subject whole policy systems or subsystems to intensive examination. More precisely, it is increasingly clear that what happens in Washington, D.C. cannot be understood by narrowly focusing on one part of the machinery at a time, nor by leaping to grandiose generalizations that may be tempting intellectually but have little foundation in fact. We have known for some time that policy is made by subgovernments (Cater, 1965; Freeman, 1965), or in "whirlpools" of affected interests (Griffith, 1961), but studies of these subsystems remain all too rare (Eidenberg and Morey, 1969; Wolman, 1971).

There remains one final issue that should be raised in an essay on national policy-making: the extent to which elite policy-makers are responsive to the demands and interests of those in whose name they make decisions.

One approach to the study of the linkages between elites and nonelites in policy-making is to measure the fit between the voting behavior of congressmen and the attitudes of their constituents. Such an effort is important from the point of view of empirical democratic theory, and it is important also because of the normative questions involved in the responsiveness or lack of responsiveness of American political institutions. At the perceptual level, 28 percent of the members of the House view themselves as independent trustees vis-à-vis their constituents, only 23 percent see their role as delegates from their constituency, and 46 percent express both orientations simultaneously (Davidson, 1969, p. 117). How do these findings square with the behavior of Representatives on the major issues that they have to decide?

The best study of this question to date is by Miller and Stokes (1963). Based on data from a 1958 survey in a sample of congressional districts, interviews with Representatives, and an examination of roll-call voting in three issue areas, Miller and Stokes show that policy agreement between district and Representative is moderate and variable across policy areas. The correlation is high in the area of civil rights, but relatively weak in the areas of social welfare and foreign affairs. Most important of all, not more than a "chemical trace" was found in the constituency of detailed information about the policy stands of congressmen. Less than 20 percent of the constituents had read or heard something about the candidates, and well over half said they had read or heard nothing about the candidates. Party identification, not issue orientation, is the primary basis of voting in congressional elections.

The Miller-Stokes study is noteworthy because it points researchers in a lightly traveled direction: the relationship between elite policy-makers and their non-Washington clienteles. Students of Congress often seem preoccupied with the internal operations of the legislature and, in light of the Miller-Stokes findings, such a preoccupation seems warranted. The case for looking at what happens inside Washington institutions is strengthened by other findings as well: that just over half of the nation's adults are able to name their congressman, and that only 21 percent know how he voted on any major bill (Gallup Opinion Index, October, 1970, pp. 6–14).

Yet there is a danger in becoming preoccupied with the institutions in Washington. Such a preoccupation may close the policy-making system off too tightly from the people whose lives are affected by the system's decisions. It may be that a more precise definition of how these institutions relate to people outside Washington will lead to research that will show more complicated linkages among the various levels in the system than have heretofore been uncovered. Research on elite subconstituencies within congressional districts, for example, may show that congressional decision-making is heavily influenced by those who do know their congressmen, do communicate with them, and are, therefore, relevant participants in the policy-making process. Or it may show that congressmen are as free of constraints from these sources as they appear to be to Bauer, Pool, and Dexter. The point is that the permeability of Congress and the Presidency has received less attention than their insularity from non-Washington clienteles, and the imbalance needs correction before answers to some of the most profound questions of empirical and normative democratic theory can be made. One could do worse in closing an essay on policy-making than calling attention to the opening reference to V. O. Key: linkages between elites and mass remain central topics for future research.

BIBLIOGRAPHY

AMLUND, CURTIS A. "Executive-Legislative Imbalance: Truman to Kennedy?" *Western Political Quarterly*, 18 (1965), pp. 640–645.

ANDERSON, PATRICK. *The Presidents' Men*. Garden City, N.Y.: Doubleday, 1968.

ART, ROBERT J. *The TFX Decision*. Boston: Little, Brown, 1968.

BALDWIN, DAVID A. "Congressional Initiative in Foreign Policy," *Journal of Politics*, 28 (1966), pp. 754–773.

BARBER, JAMES DAVID. *Presidential Character*. Englewood Cliffs, N.Y.: Prentice-Hall, 1972.

BAUER, RAYMOND A.; POOL, ITHIEL DE SOLA; and DEXTER, LEWIS A. *American Business and Public Policy*. New York: Atherton, 1963.

BAUER, RAYMOND A. "The Study of Policy Formation: An Introduction," in Bauer, Raymond A., and Gergen, Kenneth H., eds., *The Study of Policy Formation*. New York: Free Press, 1968, pp. 1–26.

BAUER, RAYMOND A., and GERGEN, KENNETH J., eds., *The Study of Policy Formation*. New York: Free Press, 1968.

BIBBY, JOHN F. "Committee Characteristics and Legislative Oversight of Administration," *Midwest Journal of Political Science*, 10 (1966).

BINKLEY, WILFRED E. "The Decline of the Executive," in MacLean, Joan C., ed. *President and Congress*. New York: H. W. Wilson, 1955, pp. 115–121.

———. *President and Congress*, 3rd rev. ed. New York: Random House, 1962.

BLACK, HENRY C. *The Relation of the Executive Power to Legislation*. Princeton, N.J.: Princeton University Press, 1919.

BONE, HUGH A. "An Introduction to the Senate Policy Committees," *American Political Science Review*, L (1956), pp. 339–359.

BRAYBROOKE, DAVID, and LINDBLOM, CHARLES E. *A Strategy of Decision*. New York: Free Press, 1963.

BURNS, JAMES MACGREGOR. *Roosevelt: The Lion and the Fox*. New York: Harcourt, Brace, 1956.

———. *The Deadlock of Democracy*. Englewood Cliffs, N.J.: Prentice-Hall, 1963.

———. *Roosevelt: The Soldier of Freedom*. New York: Harcourt, Brace, Jovanovich, 1970.

CARROLL, HOLBERT N. *The House of Representatives and Foreign Affairs*, rev. ed. Boston: Little, Brown, 1966.

CATER, DOUGLASS. *Power in Washington*. New York: Random House, 1965.

CHAMBERLAIN, LAWRENCE H. *The President, Congress and Legislation*. New York: Columbia University Press, 1946.

CLARK, JOSEPH S. *Congress: The Sapless Branch*. New York: Harper & Row, 1964.

———. *The Senate Establishment*. New York: Hill & Wang, 1963.

CLAUSEN, AAGE R., and CHENEY, RICHARD B. "A Comparative Analysis of Senate-House Voting on Economic and Welfare Policy, 1953–1964," *American Political Science Review*, LXIV (1970), pp. 138–152.

CRONIN, THOMAS E. " 'Everybody Believes in Democracy Until He Gets to the White House'—An Analysis of White-House-Departmental Relations," in *Law and Contemporary Problems*, XXXV (1970), pp. 573–625.

CRONIN, THOMAS E., and GREENBERG, SANFORD D., eds. *The Presidential Advisory System*. New York: Harper & Row, 1969.

DAHL, ROBERT A. *Congress and Foreign Policy*. New York: Harcourt, Brace, 1950.

DAVIDSON, ROGER H.; KOVENOCK, DAVID M.; and O'LEARY, MICHAEL K. *Congress in Crisis*. Belmont, Calif.: Wadsworth, 1966.

DAVIDSON, ROGER H. *The Role of the Congressman*. New York: Pegasus, 1969.

DAWSON, RAYMOND H. "Congressional Innovation and Intervention in Defense Policy: Legislative Authorization of Weapons Systems," *American Political Science Review*, LVI (1962), pp. 42–57.

DE GRAZIA, ALFRED. *Republic in Crisis*. New York: Federal Legal Publication, 1965.

DEXTER, LEWIS A. " 'Check and Balance' Today: What Does It Mean for Congress and Congressmen?" in De Grazia, Alfred, ed. *Congress: The First Branch of Government*. Garden City, N.Y.: Doubleday, 1967, pp. 80–110.

———. "Congressmen and the Making of Military Policy," in Peabody, Robert L., and Polsby, Nelson W., eds. *New Perspectives on the House of Representatives*, 2nd ed. Chicago: Rand McNally, 1969a, pp. 175–194.

———. *The Sociology and Politics of Congress*. Chicago: Rand McNally, 1969b.

DONOVAN, JOHN C. *The Policy Makers*. New York: Pegasus, 1970.

EASTON, DAVID. "The New Revolution in Political Science," *American Political Science Review*, LXIII (1969), pp. 1051–1961.

EGGER, ROWLAND, and HARRIS, JOSEPH P. *The President and Congress*. New York: McGraw-Hill, 1963.

EIDENBERG, EUGENE, and MOREY, ROY D. *An Act of Congress*. New York: W. W. Norton, 1969.

EISENHOWER, DWIGHT D. *Mandate for Change*. New York: Doubleday, 1963.

EVANS, ROWLAND, and NOVAK, ROBERT. *Lyndon B. Johnson*. New York: New American Library, 1966.

FARNSWORTH, DAVID N. *The Senate Committee on Foreign Relations*. Urbana, Ill.: University of Illinois Press, 1961.

FENNO, RICHARD F., JR. *The President's Cabinet*. Cambridge: Harvard University Press, 1959.

———. *The Power of the Purse*. Boston: Little, Brown, 1966.

———. *Congressmen in Committees*. Boston: Little, Brown, 1973.

FERBER, MARK F. "The Formation of the Democratic Study Group," in *Congressional Behavior*, Nelson W. Polsby, ed. New York: Random House, 1971, pp. 249–269.

FREEMAN, J. LEIPER. *The Political Process*, rev. ed. New York: Random House, 1965.

FREIDEL, FRANK. *Franklin D. Roosevelt*. Boston: Little, Brown, 1956.

FROMAN, LEWIS A., JR. *Congressmen and Their Constituencies*. Chicago: Rand McNally, 1963.

————. *The Congressional Process*. Boston: Little, Brown, 1967.

GEORGE, ALEXANDER L., and GEORGE, JULIETTE L. *Woodrow Wilson and Colonel House*. New York: John Day, 1956.

————; HALL, DAVID K.; and SIMONS, WILLIAM E. *The Limits of Coercive Diplomacy*. Boston: Little, Brown, 1971.

GOODWIN, GEORGE T. "The Seniority System in Congress," *American Political Science Review*, LIII (1959), pp. 412–436.

————. *The Little Legislatures*. Boston: University of Massachusetts Press, 1970.

GRASSMUCK, GEORGE L. *Sectional Biases in Congress on Foreign Policy*. Baltimore, Md.: Johns Hopkins Press, 1951.

GRIFFITH, ERNEST S. *Congress: Its Contemporary Role*, 3rd ed. New York: New York University Press, 1961.

HARGROVE, ERWIN C. *Presidential Leadership*. New York: Macmillan, 1966.

HECLO, H. HUGO. "Review Article: Policy Analysis," *British Journal of Political Science*, 2 (1972), pp. 83–108.

HERRING, PENDLETON. *Presidential Leadership*. New York: Farrar & Rinehart, 1940.

HINCKLEY, BARBARA. *The Seniority System in Congress*. Bloomington: Indiana University Press, 1971.

HOLTZMAN, ABRAHAM. *Legislative Liaison*. Chicago: Rand McNally, 1970.

HORN, STEPHEN. *Unused Power*. Washington: The Brookings Institution, 1970.

HUITT, RALPH K. "The Outsider in the Senate: An Alternative Role," *American Political Science Review*, LVC (1961a), pp. 566–575.

————. Review of Donald R. Matthews, *U. S. Senators and Their World*, in *American Political Science Review*, LV (1961b), pp. 401–402.

————. "Democratic Party Leadership in the Senate," *American Political Science Review*, LV (1961c), pp. 333–345.

————. "Political Feasibility," in Ranney, Austin, ed., *Political Science and Public Policy*. Chicago: Markham, 1968, pp. 263–276.

HUNTINGTON, SAMUEL P. *The Soldier and the State*. Cambridge: Harvard University Press, 1959.

————. *The Common Defense*. New York: Columbia University Press, 1961.

HYMAN, SIDNEY. *The American President*. New York: Harper, 1954.

JEWELL, MALCOLM E., and PATTERSON, SAMUEL C. *The Legislative Process in the United States*. New York: Random House, 1966.

JOHNSON, LYNDON B. *The Vantage Point*. New York: Holt, Rinehart & Winston, 1972.

JONES, CHARLES O. "Representation in Congress: The Case of the House Agriculture Committee," *American Political Science Review*, LV (1961), pp. 358–367.

————. "The Minority Party and Policy-Making in the House of Representatives," *American Political Science Review*, LXII (1968), pp. 481–493.

————. *The Minority Party in Congress*. Boston: Little, Brown, 1970.

270 POLITICAL SCIENCE ANNUAL

Kanter, Arnold. "Congress and the Defense Budget: 1960–1970," *American Political Science Review*, LXVI (1972), pp. 129–143.

Key, V. O. *Southern Politics*. New York: Random House, 1949.

———. *Public Opinion and American Democracy*. New York: Knopf, 1961.

Koenig, Louis W. *The Invisible Presidency*. New York: Rinehart, 1960.

———. *Congress and the President*. Chicago: Scott, Foresman, 1965.

Kofmehl, Kenneth. "The Institutionalization of a Voting Bloc," *Western Political Quarterly*, XVII (1964), pp. 256–272.

Kolodziej, Edward A. *The Uncommon Defense and Congress, 1945–1963*. Columbus, Ohio: Ohio State University Press, 1966.

Laski, Harold J. *The American Presidency*. New York: Harper, 1940.

Lasswell, Harold D. *The Decision Process*. College Park, Md.: University of Maryland, 1956.

Lerche, Charles O. *The Uncertain South*. Chicago: Quadrangle Books, 1964.

Lindblom, Charles E. "The Science of 'Muddling Through,' " *Public Administration Review*, 29 (1959), pp. 79–88.

———. *The Intelligence of Democracy*. New York: Free Press, 1965.

———. *The Policy-Making Process*. Englewood Cliffs, N.J.: Prentice-Hall, 1968.

Lippmann, Walter. *The Public Philosophy*. New York: New American Library, 1956.

Lowi, Theodore J. "American Business, Public Policy, Case Studies and Political Theory," *World Politics*, XVI (1964).

MacLean, Joan C., ed. *President and Congress*. New York: H. W. Wilson, 1955.

MacRae, Duncan, Jr. *Dimensions of Congressional Voting*. Berkeley, Calif.: University of California Press, 1958.

Manley, John F. *The Politics of Finance*. Boston: Little, Brown, 1970

———. "The Rise of Congress in Foreign Policy-Making," *Annals*, 397 (1971), pp. 60–70.

Mann, Thomas E.; Miller, Arthur H.; and Stevens, Arthur G., Jr. "Mobilization of Liberal Strength in the House, 1955–1970." Chicago: paper delivered at the 1971 Annual Meeting of the American Political Science Association.

Matthews, Donald R. *U. S. Senators and Their World*. Chapel Hill, N.C.: University of North Carolina Press, 1960.

Mayhew, David. *Party Loyalty Among Congressmen*. Cambridge: Harvard University Press, 1966.

Miller, Warren E., and Stokes, Donald E. "Constituency Influence in Congress," *American Political Science Review*, LVII (1963), pp. 45–57.

Milton, George F. *The Use of Presidential Power: 1789–1943*. Boston: Little, Brown, 1944.

Moe, Ronald C., and Teel, Steven C. "Congress as Policy-Maker: A Necessary Reappraisal," *Political Science Quarterly*, LXXXV (1970), pp. 443–470.

Munger, Frank J., and Fenno, Richard F., Jr. *National Politics and Federal Aid to Education*. Syracuse, N.Y.: Syracuse University Press, 1962.

Neustadt, Richard E. *Presidential Power*. New York: John Wiley, 1960.

———. "Politicians and Bureaucrats," in Truman, David B., ed., *The Congress and America's Future*. Englewood Cliffs, N.J.: Prentice-Hall, 1965, pp. 102–120.

PATTERSON, JAMES T. *Congressional Conservation and the New Deal.* Lexington: University of Kentucky, 1967.

PEABODY, ROBERT L. "The Enlarged Rules Committee," in Peabody, Robert L., and Polsby, Nelson W., eds., *New Perspectives on the House of Representatives.* Chicago: Rand McNally, 1963, pp. 129–164.

———. "Party Leadership Change in the United States House of Representatives," *American Political Science Review,* LXI (1967), pp. 675–693.

PETTIT, LAWRENCE K. "Influence Potential in the United States Senate," in Pettit, Lawrence K., and Keynes, Edward, eds., *The Legislative Process in the U. S. Senate.* Chicago: Rand McNally, 1969, pp. 227–244.

POLSBY, NELSON W. "Two Strategies of Influence: Choosing a Majority Leader, 1962," in Polsby, Nelson W., and Peabody, Robert L., eds., *New Perspectives on the House of Representatives,* 2nd ed. Chicago: Rand McNally, 1969, pp. 325–358.

———; GALLAHER, MIRIAM; and RUNDQUIST, BARRY SPENCER. "The Growth of the Seniority System in the U. S. House of Representatives," *American Political Science Review,* LXIII (1969), pp. 787–807.

———. "Strengthening Congress in National Policy-Making," *The Yale Review,* LIX (1970), pp. 481-497.

———. *Congress and the Presidency,* 2nd ed. Englewood Cliffs, N.J.: Prentice-Hall, 1971.

PRICE, DAVID. *Who Makes the Laws?* Cambridge, Mass.: Schenkman, 1972.

PRICE, H. DOUGLAS. "Race, Religion, and the Rules Committee," in Westin, Alan F., ed., *The Uses of Power.* New York: Harcourt, Brace & World, 1962, pp. 1–72.

———. "Are Southern Democrats Different?" in Polsby, Nelson W.; Dentler, Robert A.; and Smith, Paul A., eds., *Politics and Social Life.* Boston: Houghton Mifflin, 1963, pp. 740–756.

PRINGLE, HENRY F. *Theodore Roosevelt.* New York: Harcourt, Brace & World, 1931.

———. *The Life and Times of William Howard Taft.* New York: Farrar & Rinehart, 1939.

RIESELBACH, LEROY. *The Roots of Isolationism.* Indianapolis: Bobbs-Merrill, 1966.

RIPLEY, RANDALL B. *Party Leaders in the House of Representatives.* Washington: Brookings Institution, 1967.

———. *Power in the Senate.* New York: St. Martin's Press, 1969a.

———. *Majority Party Leadership in Congress.* Boston: Little, Brown, 1969b.

ROBINSON, JAMES A. *The House Rules Committee.* Indianapolis: Bobbs-Merrill, 1963.

———. *Congress and Foreign Policy-Making,* rev. ed. Homewood, Ill.: Dorsey, 1967.

ROSSITER, CLINTON. *The American Presidency,* 2nd ed. New York: Harcourt, Brace & World, 1960. First published 1956.

SCHELLING, THOMAS. "PPB and the Complexities of Foreign Affairs," in Westin, Alan F., ed., *Information Technology in a Democracy.* Cambridge: Harvard University Press, 1971, pp. 383–394.

SCHICK, ALLEN. "The Budget Bureau That Was: Thoughts on the Rise, Decline, and Future of a Presidential Agency," in *Law and Contemporary Problems*, XXXV (1970), pp. 519–539.

SCHLESINGER, ARTHUR M., JR. *The Crisis of the Old Order.* Boston: Houghton Mifflin, 1957.

———. *The Coming of the New Deal.* Boston: Houghton Mifflin, 1959.

———. *The Politics of Upheaval.* Boston: Houghton Mifflin, 1960.

———. *A Thousand Days.* Boston: Houghton Mifflin, 1965.

SCHLESINGER, JAMES. "Two-and-a-Half Cheers for Systems Analysis," in Westin, Alan F., ed., *Information Technology in a Democracy.* Cambridge: Harvard University Press, 1971, pp. 395–408.

SCHULTZE, CHARLES L. *The Politics and Economics of Public Spending.* Washington: The Brookings Institution, 1968.

———. (with Hamilton, Edward K. and Schick, Allen). *Setting National Priorities: The 1971 Budget.* Washington: The Brookings Institution, 1970.

SHANNON, W. WAYNE. *Party, Constituency and Congressional Voting.* Baton Rouge, La.: Louisiana State University Press, 1968.

SMITH, J. MALCOLM, and COTTER, CORNELIUS P. *Powers of the President During Crises.* Washington: Public Affairs Press, 1960.

SNYDER, RICHARD C., and PAIGE, GLENN D. "The United States Decision to Resist Aggression in Korea: The Application of an Analytical Scheme," *Administrative Science Quarterly*, III (1958), pp. 341–378.

SORENSEN, THEODORE C. *Decision-Making in the White House.* New York: Columbia University Press, 1963.

———. *Kennedy.* New York: Harper & Row, 1965.

SPERLICH, PETER W. "Bargaining and Overload: An Essay on *Presidential Power*," in Wildavsky, Aaron, ed., *The Presidency.* Boston: Little, Brown, 1969, pp. 168–192.

STEPHENS, HERBERT W. "The Role of the Legislative Committees in the Appropriations Process: A Study Focused on the Armed Services Committees," *Western Political Quarterly*, 24 (1971), pp. 146–162.

SUNDQUIST, JAMES L. *Politics and Policy.* Washington: The Brookings Institution, 1968.

TRUMAN, DAVID B. *The Congressional Party.* New York: John Wiley, 1959.

TRUMAN, HARRY S. *Year of Decisions.* Garden City, N.Y.: Doubleday, 1955.

———. *Years of Trial and Hope.* Garden City, N.Y.: Doubleday, 1956.

TURNER, JULIUS. *Party and Constituency.* Baltimore, Md.: Johns Hopkins Press, 1951.

———. *Party and Constituency.* Baltimore, Md.: Johns Hopkins Press, 1951. Revised by Schneier, Edward V., Jr., 1970.

WHITE, WILLIAM S. *Citadel.* New York: Harper, 1957.

WILDAVSKY, AARON. *The Politics of the Budgetary Process.* Boston: Little, Brown, 1964.

———. "The Political Economy of Efficiency: Cost-Benefit Analysis, Systems Analysis, and Program Budgeting," *Public Administration Review*, XXVI (1966), pp. 292–310.

———. "The Two Presidencies," in Wildavsky, Aaron, ed., *The Presidency.* Boston: Little, Brown, 1969a, pp. 230–243.

————, ed. *The Presidency.* Boston: Little, Brown, 1969b.

WILSON, WOODROW. *Congressional Government.* Cleveland, Ohio: World Publishing Co., 1956. First published 1885.

WOLFINGER, RAYMOND E., and HEIFETZ, JOAN. "Safe Seats, Seniority, and Power in Congress," *American Political Science Review,* LIX (1965), pp. 337–349.

WOLMAN, HAROLD. *Politics of Federal Housing.* New York: Dodd, Mead, 1971.

Index

Abbott, Max G., 217
Accrediting associations and agencies, 210
Actions, 11–13
Admissable agenda, 71
Agenda-building, 18
American Association of School Administrators, 210
American Federation of Teachers, 195, 197
American Political Science Association (APSA), 244
Aranson, Peter H., 48, 63, 64
Arrow, Kenneth J., 3, 4, 12, 13, 22–35, 58, 71–72, 74, 76
Arrow's Mathematical Politics, 3, 22–35
Ashby, Lloyd W., 207
Axelrod, Robert, 44, 63

Bachrach, Peter, 18, 68
Baratz, Morton, 18, 68
Barber, James David, 241–44
Bargaining, 168
  in Senate, 255–56
  power of President, 235–37
Barnard, Chester I., 158
Bauer, Raymond A., 245, 257, 264, 266
Becker, Robert A., 67
Becker, Theodore, 101
Benefit-cost analysis, 166–67
Bensman, Joseph, 181, 191, 209
Bidwell, Charles E., 209
Bill-passing, 252
Black, Duncan, 2, 39, 58, 61
Blau, Peter M., 158, 180
Boss, Michael O., 212–13
Boucher, W. I., 166
Brams, Steven J., 8, 11, 48, 69
Braybrooke, David, 239
Brody, Richard A., 65, 66
Brown case, 100

Buchanan, James M., 1–3, 5, 43, 66, 135, 137, 139, 148–51
Budget Bureau, 238
Budget control, 237–38
Bullock, Charles, 104
Bureau, 144–48
Bureaucracy and Representative Government, Niskanen, 142, 147
Burns, James M., 241, 251

Cain, Glen C., 115, 117
Callahan, Raymond E., 198, 199, 203
Campbell, Donald T., 115, 193
Carlson, Richard O., 188, 189, 199
Caroll, Holbert N., 234, 261
Chamberlain, Lawrence, 232–33
Charters, W. W., Jr., 206, 208
Cheney, Richard B., 259
Choice function, 72
Choice structure, 72
Choice-theoretic perspective, 4–8
Citizen evaluations, 50–53
Citizen participation, 53–55
City Politics and Public Policy, Wilson, 106
Clark, Burton R., 189
Clark, Joseph S., 249–51
Clarkson, Geoffrey P. E., 150
Coase, Ronald H., 150
Cobb, Roger W., 18, 68
Coleman, James S., 48, 64, 110, 141, 213
Coleman Report, 102
Coles, Robert, 114
Collective action. See Collective choice
Collective choice, theories of, 1–87
  Arrow's principles, 22–44
  choice-theoretic perspective, 4–8
  institutional complexities, 65–69
  nature of collective choice, 17–22
  rational behavior, 8–17
  recent advances, 70–76

Collective choice, theories of—Cont.
  spatial models, 44–65
  summary, 75–76
Collective decision-making. *See* Collective choice
Collectivity, 1–3
Committee on Governmental and Legal Processes, 106
Committee system (in House), 261–63
Common Defense, Huntington, 233
Community Action Programs (CAP), 113, 116
Conant, James, 215
Condition of latin squarelessness, 41
Congress: The Sapless Branch, Clark, 249
Congressional Fellowship Program, 244
Congressional Quarterly, 251, 259
Congressional Record, 249
Congress and national policymaking, 244–56
Connectivity (one of Arrow's axioms), 25, 31
Conservative Coalition, 251–52, 259
Consistent goal-seeking, 6
Constitution, 72
Constitution, and constraints, 149–50
Cooper-Church amendment, 252
Corwin, Ronald G., 189, 196
Costs of decision-making, 135–39
Cotter, Cornelius P., 234
CQ Weekly Report, 251
Crain, Robert L., 106, 183, 186, 187, 188, 189, 190, 212, 213, 217
Cronin, J. M., 185, 187
Cues (feedback) in exchanges with school boards, 193
Cunningham, Lavern L., 177
Curriculum policy, 210–11
Curry, Robert L., 10
Cybernetics, 2
Cyert, Richard M., 132, 157, 158, 160, 161, 164

Dahl, Robert A., 167, 195, 233
Davidson, Roger H., 254, 265
Davis, James W., Jr., 105
Davis, Otto A., 48, 49, 53, 61, 64, 162
Decision-making
  costs of, 135–39
  process of, 137
Decisive choice, 72
Degroot, Morris, 64

Delphi (technique), 218
Demand constraints, 144–49
Democratic Study Group (DSG), 259
Democratic theory, 137
Dempster, M. A. H., 162
Department of Defense (DOD), 234, 239
Development Loan Fund, 234
Devine, Eugene, 143
Dexter, Lewis A., 231, 234, 245, 247, 257, 264, 266
de Grazia, Alfred, 231
Doherty, Robert E., 196, 197
Dolbeare, Kenneth M., xi, 89–130
Domestic Council, 238
Downs, Anthony, 4, 45–49, 61, 146, 148, 152, 160, 161, 162, 169, 170, 179
Downsian spatial model, 45–49
Dummett, Michael, 40
Dye, Thomas R., 132, 217
Dykes, Archie R., 201, 204
Dynamics of Compliance: Supreme Court Decision-making From A New Perspective, The, Johnson, 100

Easton, David, 107, 118, 177, 214, 215, 217, 228
Economic Theory of Democracy, An, Downs, 45, 47
Education, and policy-making, 13, 177–219
  board-superintendent exchange, 198–213
  linkage between governing groups and public demands, 190–98
  market place: strategies of influence, 184–85
  policy actors, 179
  policy levels, 178–79
  power and exchange, 180–84
  recruitment of board members, 185–90
Educational goals, 218–19
Edwards, Ward, 9–10, 132
Eidenberg, Eugene, 265
Eisenhower, Dwight D., 236, 241, 242, 247
Elder, Charles D., 18, 68
Electoral choice, 44–65
Eliot, Thomas H., 177–78, 210, 214
Environmental constraints, 140–54
  demand, 144–49
  legal, 149–51

Environmental constraints—Cont.
  normative, 153–54
  physical, 141–42
  political, 151–53
  resource, 142–44
Environmental Protection Act, 115
Equilibrium and convergence in spatial models of electoral choice, 58–65
Establishment (in Senate), 250–52
Exchange theory in education, 180–84
Extension, 75

Farnsworth, David N., 255
Farquharson, Robin, 37, 40, 44, 67
Federal Bulldozer, The, Anderson, 105
Federal Clearinghouse, 111
Federal Evaluation Policy, Wholey, 111
Feldman, Julian, 132, 154, 159, 163
Fenno, Richard F., Jr., 239, 250, 254, 255, 261, 262, 263
"Field Experimentation in Socio-legal Research," Schwartz, 99–100
Fishburn, Peter C., 76
Forecasting the future, 165–67
French National Assembly of 1789, 44
Friedman, Milton, 8, 219
Frohlick, Norman, 66, 69
Froman, Lewis A., Jr., 168, 248, 254, 258
Fundamental policies, 118, 119

Galbraith, John Kenneth, 148
Gallup Opinion Index, 266
Game theory, 67, 166
Gamson, William, 180
General Impossibility Theorem, 42
George, Alexander L., 241
George, Juliette L., 241
Gittell, Marilyn, 182, 183, 213
Goals (as a restraint), 164–65
Goldberg, Arthur S., 13
Goldhammer, Keith, 187, 195, 208, 216
Goldrich, D., 179–80
Goodlad, John I., 218
Goodwin, George T., 260, 261
Greenberg, Jack, 103–4
Griffith, Ernest S., 265
Griffiths, Daniel E., 195
Gross, Neal, 192, 201, 203, 217
Grossman, Joel B., 103
Grossman, Mary H., 103

Hansson, Bengt, 72, 76
Harris, Joseph P., 231
Hayes, Edward C., 118
Heclo, H. Hugo, 110, 247
Heifetz, Joan, 260, 261
Herring, Pendleton, 228
Hess, Robert D., 183, 197
Hinckley, Barbara, 260
Hinich, Melvin J., 48, 49, 53, 59, 61, 64
Hirschman, Albert O., 167
Hofferbert, Richard I., 132, 217
Hofstadter, Richard, 203
Hollander, T. Edward, 182
Hollister, Robinson G., 115, 117
Holtzman, Abraham, 231
Homans, George C., 180
House Appropriations Committee, 260–63
House Armed Services Committee, 234, 260, 263
House Committee on Committees, 261
House District of Columbia Committee, 261
House Education and Labor Committee, 255, 261, 263
House Foreign Affairs Committee, 261
House Interior Committee, 261
House Post Office Committee, 261
House Rules Committee, 260, 263
House Ways and Means Committee, 260, 261, 263
House of Representatives and National policy-making, 256–66
Huitt, Ralph K., 239, 249, 252, 255
Huntington, Samuel P., 233, 234
Hyman, Sidney, 230

Iannaccone, Lawrence, 193, 208
Illitch, Ivan, 219
Impact, 93–97
Impact studies, 89
Impact of Supreme Court Decisions, The, Becker, ed., 101
"Impact of the Supreme Court, The," Shapiro, 101
Impact of the United States Supreme Court, The, Wasby, 101
Impossibility Theorem, 28, 31, 32, 33, 47
Independence of Irrelevant Alternatives (one of Arrow's conditions), 25, 26, 27, 31, 32
Independence of path, 74, 75

Individualism, 4–5
Institute for Research on Poverty (U. of Wisc.), 113
Institutional complexities, 65–69
Internal constraints, 154–69
International Development Association, 234
Investment, theory of, 132
Irrational behavior, 6

Jackson, John E., 65
Jacob, Herbert, 106, 114
James, H. Henry, 198, 199
James, H. Thomas, 217
Jeffrey, Richard, 8
Jencks, Christopher, 219
Jennings, M. Kent, xi, 177–219
Jewell, Malcolm E., 254
Johnson, Lyndon B., 165, 236, 239, 241, 242, 247, 253, 254
Johnson, Richard, 100
Jones, Charles O., 259, 261
Jones, Ernest M., 100

Kahn, Robert L., 133–34
Kanter, Arnold, 234
Kanter, Herschel E., 132, 154, 159, 163
Katz, Daniel, 133
Katz, Ellis, 99
Kaufman, Herbert, 109
Keech, William, 53
Kelley, E. W., 69
Kelley, James, 217
Kendall, Willmore, 27
Kennedy, John F., 236, 247
Kerr, Norman D., 200, 206, 207
Kessel, Hohn H., 66, 101
Key, V. O., Jr., 213, 227, 259, 266
Kimbrough, Ralph B., 181
Kirst, Michael, 183, 197, 210, 211, 214
Koenig, Louis W., 231, 241
Koerner, James K., 195, 211
Kofmehl, Kenneth, 259
Kramer, Gerald H., 44, 54, 64, 67
Kuh, Edwin, 166
Kuhn, Thomas S., 6

Lane, Robert E., 213, 214
Laplace's Law of Insufficient Reason, 36
Laski, Harold, 228, 229, 230
Lasswell, Harold D., 246
Laswellian definition of politics, 89

Law and Change in Modern America, Grossman and Grossman, 103
Law and Social Change: Civil Rights Laws and Their Consequences, Rodgers and Bullock, 104
Law and social change, 103–5
Law and Society Review, The, 100
Lawrence, Paul R., 135
League of Nations, 241, 242, 243
Ledyard, John O., 59, 64
Legal constraints, 149–51
Leiserson, Michael, 69
Lempert, Richard, 100
Levin, Martin, 110
Levine, James P., 100
Levitan, Sar, 115, 116
Lieberman, Myron, 196
Lindblom, Charles E., 160, 161, 162, 167, 239, 240, 245
Linear programming, 166
Lipham, James M., 202
Lippmann, Walter, 231
Lipsky, Michael, 184
Lodge, Henry Cabot, 242, 243
Logic of Collective Action, The, Olson, 69
Long, Norton, 118
Lorsch, Jay W., 135
Lowi, Theodore J., 264
Luce, Duncan R., 69

MacLean, Joan C., 231
MacRae, Duncan, Jr., 13, 258
Manley, John F., xi, 227–66
Mann, Thomas E., 259
Mansfield, Mike, 253
March, James G., 132, 156–61, 164, 169
Marmor, Theodore, 109
Marschak, Thomas, 149–50
Martin, Roscoe C., 180, 181, 182, 190
Mason, Ward H., 201, 203, 217
Masotti, Louis H., 185, 210
Matthews, Donald R., 118, 252, 253
Mayhew, David, 263
Maximizing behavior, 17
McCarty, Donald J., 202–3, 217
McClintock, Charles G., 10
McEachern, Alexander W., 201, 203, 217
McKelvey, Richard D., 48, 54
McNamara, Robert, 239
Meehan, Eugene J., 90
Merewitz, Leonard, 165, 167

Merton, Robert K., 158
Midwest Political Science Association, 111
Militancy of teachers, 195–96, 198
Miller, Arthur H., 99, 259
Miller, Warren E., 265, 266
Miller Analogies test, 189
Milner, Neal, 100
Milton, George F., 230
Minar, David W., 182–83, 185, 203, 210
Miranda case, 100
Monte Carlo method (of operations research), 166
Morey, Roy D., 265
Morgenstern, Oscar, 69
Mosher, Edith K., 214
Moskow, Michael H., 196
Muir, William K., Jr., 100
Murakami, Yasusuke, 33
Murphy, Walter F., 98, 99, 101, 102

Nagel, Stuart, 102
National Advisory Committee on Selective Service, 116
National Education Association, 195–98
Nationalization of curriculum, 211
National policy-making, 227–66
  Congress and policy, 244–48
    House of Representatives, 256–66
    Senate, 248–56
  Presidency and policy, 228–44
National Science Foundation, 211
Negro in the New Southern Politics, The, Matthews and Prothro, 118
Neumann, John von, 69
Neustadt, Richard, 228, 235, 236, 240
"New Revolution in Political Science, The," Easton, 107
Niemi, Richard G., 43
Niskanen, William A., Jr., 68, 135, 142–48, 150, 169–70
Nixon, Richard M., 242, 247
Nondictatorship (one of Arrow's conditions), 26–28
Nonperversive choice, 72
Normative constraints, 153–54
Novak, Robert, 255
Novick, David, 165
N-person games, theory of, 69
Numerical representation, 71

Oberer, Walter E., 196, 197
Occam's Razor, 9
Office of Economic Opportunity, 211
Office of Management and Budget, 238
"On the Need for 'Impact Analysis' of Supreme Court Decisions," Miller, 99
Operations research, 166
Oppenheimer, Joe D., 66, 69
Ordeshook, Peter C., 7–8, 23, 27, 48, 50, 53, 54, 59, 60, 61, 63, 64, 65, 70
Ordinal revolution, 9
Orfield, Gary, 105, 110
Organizational constraints and collective choice, 131–71
Organizational Stress, Kahn et al., 134
Ostrom, Elinor, 2
Ostrom, Vincent, 2
Outcomes, 9–11, 13

Page, Benjamin I., 65, 66
Panola County, 104
Pareto Principle (one of Arrow's conditions), 25, 26, 27, 30, 31
Parkinson, C. Northcote, 146
Parks, Robert P., 75, 76
Patric, Gordon, 99
Pattanaik, Prasanta K., 33
Patterson, James T., 251
Patterson, Samuel C., 254
Peabody, Robert L., 259
Peak, G. Wayne, xi, 177–219
Pellegrin, Roland J., 217
Persuasion, as a presidential power, 234–35
Pettit, Lawrence K., 253
Physical constraints, 141–42
Pierce, Lawrence C., xi–xii, 131–71
Pierce, Truman, 199
Pigou, A. C., 150, 151
Planning, Programming, and Budgeting (PPB), 239, 240
Plott, Charles R., 20, 27, 32, 64, 71–76
Policy, 90–93
"Policy analysis," 105–6, 227–28
Policy Analysis in Political Science, Sharkansky, 107
"Policy Evaluation and Recidivism," Levin, 110
Policy goals (evaluation), 108–12
Policy impact studies, 90–97

Policy-making tasks and functions, 246–47

Political analysis, theory of, 69

Political choice, 19

Political constraints, 151–53

Political decision-making, 167–68

Political parties, 258–59

Political Science and Public Policy, Ranney, 106

Political scientists, and evaluation, 108–12

Political Science Annual, IV, 69

Politics of Southern Equality: Law and Social Change, Wirt, 104–5

Polsby, Nelson W., 231, 235, 248, 249, 250, 251, 259, 260

Polyardy, 167–68

Pool, Ithiel de Sola, 247, 257, 264, 266

Posited preference, 7–8

Poverty Policy, Marmor, 109

Prayer in the Public Schools: Law and Attitude Change, Muir, 100

Preference distribution of the electorate, 55–58

Preference expression in institutions, 66

Preference relation, 9

Premises, 4

Presidency and national policy-making, 228–44

Presidential Power, Neustadt, 235

Price, David, 246–47, 250, 251, 254, 255, 261

Pringle, Henry F., 241

Problems and crises in school districts, 192–93

Program budgeting, 165

Programmed decision-making, 156–58

PTA, 192, 193, 194

Public choice, theory of, 135. *See also* Collective choice

Public Housing, Freedman, 105

Public policy, 89–130
  defined, 90–93
  policy impact studies, 90–97
    definition of public policy, 90–92
    impact, 93–95
    output policies, 92
    purposes of inquiry, 95–97
  problems and prospects, 118–23
    major problems, 119–20
    policy consequences research, 118

Public policy—Cont.
  problems and prospects—Cont.
    possible solutions, 120–22
    prospects, 122–23
  research, 97–118
    conceptual problems, 112–15
    evaluation, 108–12
    law and change, 103–5
    methodological problems, 110–17
    policy effects, 105–8
    studies of Supreme Court decisions, 97–102

"Public Policy Analysis and the Coming Struggle for the Soul of the Post-Behavioral Revolution," Dolbeare, 118

Puryear, Paul, 110

Quade, E. S., 166

Rabinowitz, George, 65

Rabushka, Alvin, 27

Race relations, 103–4

Racial issue in education, 212

Raiffa, Howard, 69

Ramsey, Charles E., 202–3, 217

Ranney, Austin, 106, 110

Rapoport, Anatol, 69

Rational behavior, 8–17

Rational individual behavior, 10

Rationality, 7, 72–75

Rawls, John A., 3, 18

Reconstruction of Southern Education: The Schools and the 1964 Civil Rights Act, The, Orfield, 105

Regulating the Poor, Piven and Cloward, 109

Rehnquist, William H., 252

Rein, Martin, 115

Relational logic, 8

Relationship of school board and superintendent, 198–213

Resource constraints, 142–44

Revealed preference, 7–8, 43

Richter, Marcel, 71, 72, 76

Riker, William H., 2, 7–8, 23, 27, 37, 48, 50, 54, 60, 61, 63, 64–65, 66, 69, 70

Ripley, Randall B., 250, 259

Risk, 13

Robinson, James A., 132, 233, 241, 261

Rodgers, Harrell, 101, 104

Rogers, David, 209
Role behavior in organizations, 133–34
Role theory, 217
Roosevelt, Franklin D., 241, 242
Roosevelt, Theodore, 241
Rosenstengel, William Everett, 199
Rosenthal, Alan, 195, 198
Rosenthal, Howard, 63, 65, 69
Rossiter, Clinton, 228, 230, 231, 234, 235
Rossmiller, Richard A., 202
Rothenberg, Jerome, 9, 33
Routines (decision rules), 161–62
Rundquist, Barry Spencer, 260
Rusk, Jerrold G., 65
Russell, Richard, 253

Salisbury, Robert H., 180, 183, 190, 205
Samuelson, Paul A., 3, 17, 27
Sargent, Thomas, 36, 37
Scarrow, Howard A., 110
Schattschneider, E. E., 18, 68
Schick, Allen, 159, 163, 238, 239
Schlesinger, Arthur M., Jr., 235, 239, 241
Schneier, Edward V., 259
Schoenberger, Robert A., 48
School boards, 178, 180, 184–88, 190, 191, 193, 198–213
School prayer decisions, 99–101
School principals, 178
School superintendents, 178, 180, 182–84, 188, 189, 192, 193, 198–213
Schultze, Charles L., 141, 142, 162, 163, 164, 237, 238, 239
Schwartz, Richard, 99–100
Scribner, J. D., 215
Search strategies in problem solving, 161–62
Sears, David O., 213, 214
Selective Service, 105
Sen, Amartya, 3, 7, 21, 28, 33, 34, 35, 36, 40, 41, 63, 65
Senate and national policy-making, 248–56
Senate Appropriations Committee, 255
Senate Banking and Currency Committee, 255
Senate Commerce Committee, 255
Senate Finance Committee, 255
Senate Foreign Relations Committee, 243, 255
Senate Labor and Public Welfare Committee, 255

Senate Policy Committees, 255
Seniority system in Congress, 260–61
"Sensitivity analysis," 37
Set theory, 8
Shannon, W. Wayne, 259
Shapiro, Martin, 101
Shapiro, Michael J., 13
Shapley, Lloyd, 67
Sharkansky, Ira, 106–7, 108, 132, 160, 161, 162, 163, 217
Shepsle, Kenneth A., xii, 1–87
Shubik, Martin, 64, 67
Silberman, Charles E., 219
Simon, Herbert A., 2, 132, 156–57, 158, 159, 160
Simons, William E., 241
Smithburg, Donald W., 158
Smoley, Eugene R., 191, 192
Snow, Reuben Joseph, 181
Snyder, Richard C., 241
Social choice. See Collective choice
Social Choice and Industrial Values, Arrow, 3, 39
Social decision function (SDF), 33, 34, 35
Social preference relation, 75
Social welfare function (SWF), 23, 28, 29, 33, 35, 39, 40, 41, 43
Society, 71
"Some New Concerns of Legal Process Research Within Political Science," Nagel, 102
Sorauf, Frank, 99
Sorenson, Theodore C., 240
Sosnick, Stephen H., 165, 167
Southern Regional Council, 104
Spatial models of social choice, 44–65
Sperlich, Peter W., 235
SSRC, 106, 110
State of Welfare, The, Steiner, 105
Steiner, Gilbert, 105
Stelzer, Leigh, 185
Stephens, Herbert W., 234
Stevens, Arthur G., Jr., 259
Stigler, George, 2, 70
Stokes, Donald E., 49, 265, 266
Stroufe, Gerald, 216
Struggle for a Negative Income Tax, The, Williams, 111
Study of Public Law, The, Murphy and Tanenhaus, 101
Stumpf, Harry P., 99

Suits, Daniel E., 166
Summerfield, Harry L., 193
Sundquist, James L., 246, 247, 248, 250
Sunshine, Norris S., 217
Supreme Court decisions, impact of, 97–102
Swanson, B. E., 179–80
Systems analysis, 166
Systems decision-making, 163–64
Systems theory, 215–16

Taft, William Howard, 241, 242
Taggart, Robert, 111, 115, 116
Tanenhaus, Joseph, 101, 102
Task-performance rules, 157
Taylor, Michael, 2
Teachers, 188–89, 195, 196, 197, 198
Teel, Steven C., 233
Terkel, Studs, 114
Thompson, James D., 135
Thompson, Victor A., 153, 158
Transivity (one of Arrow's axioms), 25, 31
Truman, David B., 258
Truman, Harry S, 234, 241
Tullock, Gordon, 1, 2, 3, 33, 36, 135, 137, 150, 151, 153, 169
Turner, Julius, 258
Turvey, R., 167

Uncertainty, 13, 15–17
U.S. Commission on Civil Rights, 104
U.S. Office of Economic Opportunity, 213
U.S. Office of Education, 211, 212
Universal Domain (one of Arrow's conditions), 25, 26
"Urban Crisis: Who Got What and Why? The," Piven, 109
Urban renewal, attacked, 105

Valuation function, 9
Vanecko, James J., 106
Vidich, Arthur J., 181, 191, 209
Vietnam War, 234, 236, 242, 252
Vinson, Carl, 234

Wade, Lawrence L., 10
Walden, John C., 208
Waldman, Sidney R., 180
Walker, Decker F., 210, 211
Walker, William G., 179
Ward, Benjamin, 38, 41
Weisberg, Herbert F., 43, 65
Weisbrod, Burton A., 153
Weiss, Robert S., 115
Welfare Economics and the Theory of the State, Baumol, 3
White, William S., 249
White Ethics and Black Power, Ellis, 114
Wicksell, Knut, 150, 151
Wildavsky, Aaron, 146, 151, 153, 162, 163, 165, 167, 233, 239, 240
Williams, Walter, 111, 117
Williamson, Oliver, 36, 37
Wilson, Charles Z., 169
Wilson, James G., 106, 184
Wilson, Robert B., 76
Wilson, Woodrow, 229, 237, 241, 242, 243
Wirt, Frederick, 104–5, 214, 215
Wisconsin Law Review, 100
Wolfinger, Raymond E., 260, 261
Wolman, Harold, 265
Woodrow Wilson and Colonel House, George and George, 241

Young, Oran B., 66, 69

Zald, Meyer, 180, 204
Zeckhauser, Richard, 69
Ziegler, Harmon, xii, 177–219